Committee of Inquiry into the United Kingdom Prison Services

REPORT

*Presented to Parliament by the Secretary of State for the Home Department,
the Secretary of State for Scotland
and the Secretary of State for Northern Ireland
by Command of Her Majesty
October 1979*

LONDON
HER MAJESTY'S STATIONERY OFFICE
£6

Cmnd. 7673

1,185,691

The estimated cost of the preparation of this report (including the expenses of the Committee) is £228,934 of which £23,100 represents the estimated cost of printing and publication.

ISBN 010 176730 7

REPORT OF THE INTERDEPARTMENTAL COMMITTEE OF INQUIRY INTO THE UNITED KINGDOM PRISON SERVICES

To The Right Honourable William Whitelaw, C.H., M.C., M.P., Her Majesty's Principal Secretary of State for the Home Department, The Right Honourable George Younger, T.D., M.P., Her Majesty's Principal Secretary of State for Scotland, and The Right Honourable Humphrey Atkins, M.P., Her Majesty's Principal Secretary of State for Northern Ireland.

SIRS,

On 17 November 1978 the then Home Secretary, in the names of all three Secretaries of State, announced that the Departmental Committee on the United Kingdom Prison Services would have the following terms of reference: —

"To inquire into the state of the prison services in the United Kingdom; and having regard to:

(a) the size and nature of the prison population, and the capacity of the prison services to accommodate it;

(b) the responsibilties of the prison services for the security, control and treatment of inmates;

(c) the need to recruit and retain a sufficient and suitable staff for the prison services;

(d) the need to secure the efficient use of manpower and financial resources in the prison services;

to examine and make recommendations upon

(i) the adequacy, availability, management and use of resources in the prison services;

(ii) conditions for staff in the prison services and their families;

(iii) the organisation and management of the prison services;

(iv) the structure of tne prison services, including complementing and grading;

(v) the remuneration and conditions of service of prison officers, governors and other grades working only in the prison services, including the claim put forward by the Prison Officers' Association for certain "continuous duty credit" payments and the date from which any such payments should be made;

(vi) allowances and other aspects of the conditions of service of other grades arising from special features of work in the prison services;

(vii) working arrangements in the prison services; including shift systems and standby and on call requirements;

(viii) the effectiveness of the industrial relations machinery, including departmental Whitley procedures, within the prison services.

We met, either as a full Committee or in sub-committees, on a total of 53 days, of which 27 days were devoted in whole or in part to taking oral evidence. In addition, we visited a large number of establishments, training schools and colleges, and headquarters and regional offices throughout the United Kingdom and in certain other European countries. We now have the honour to present our Report.

Throughout our deliberations and in the preparation of this Report we have received unstinting help from our Secretary and his assistants. R M Morris brought to his work for us a deep familiarity with the administration of the prison services and with the operation of the Home Office as a whole. To this was added a clear understanding of all the underlying issues which we have had to consider. His assistance in our task and with our drafting has been invaluable and we are very grateful. He was most ably supported by Alan Harding and Edna Wood of the Home Office and Alan Fraser of the Scottish Office, each of whom has provided administrative, secretarial and drafting assistance which has been as efficient as it was thorough. We record with thanks our debt to them all. We should also like to express our thanks to Julie Turnbull, Lorna Pettigrew and Ann Freeland, who throughout shouldered the substantial burden of typing and circulating papers with great efficiency.

LIST OF MEMBERS

The Honourable Mr Justice May (Chairman)

Mrs Doreen Bellerby JP

Michael Bett Esq

Leonard F Edmondson Esq

John A Gardiner Esq

Mrs Rachel E Gibbs JP

Nicholas J Hinton Esq

Sir Myles Humphreys JP

Sheriff C G B Nicholson

Sir John Nightingale CBE BEM QPM

CONTENTS

GLOSSARY

ACAS	—Advisory, Conciliation and Arbitration Service
ACPS	—Advisory Council on the Penal System
ADP	—average daily population
Administration Group	—the collective term for administrative, executive and clerical grades from Clerical Assistant to Assistant Secretary in the Home Civil Service
AG	—Assistant Governor
BAPG	—British Association of Prison Governors
CDC	—continuous duty credits
Central Departments	—the collective term for the Treasury and the Civil Service Department (but not including the Cabinet Office in the sense used here)
CNA	—certified normal accommodation e.g. as undersection 14 of the Prison Act 1972
CPSA	—Civil and Public Services Association
CSD	—Civil Service Department
DES	—Department of Education and Science
DHSS	—Department of Health and Social Security
DPMS	—Director of Prison Medical Services
EO	—Executive Officer
Estabs 3	—Division 3 of the Establishment Department of the Home Office
Expenditure Committee Report	—Report of the Education, Arts and Home Office Sub-Committee of the Expenditure Committee in Session 1977-8 "The Reduction of Pressure on the Prison System", July 1978
FDA	—Association of First Division Civil Servants ("First Division Association")
FGS	—Functional Group Working Scheme; one of two attendance systems in operation for prison officers in England and Wales
Governors' Branch	—Governors' Branch of the Society of Civil and Public Servants (SCPS)
HEO	—Higher Executive Officer

Home Departments	—the collective term for the Home Office, Scottish Home and Health Department and the Northern Ireland Office
ILA	—inconvenience of locality allowance
ILPAS	—Inner London Probation and After-Care Service
IPCS	—The Institution of Professional Civil Servants
LHG	—long hours gratuity
NACRO	—National Association for the Care and Resettlement of Offenders
NAPO	—National Association of Probation Officers
NDA	—night duty allowance
NEC	—National Executive Committee
NES	—New Earnings Survey
NHS	—National Health Service
NIO	—Northern Ireland Office
NIPSA	—Northern Ireland Public Service Alliance
OTS	—Officer Training School
Outstations	—collective term used for prison service establishments (including prisons, borstals, training schools, etc) and Regional Offices
Outstations Branch	—Prison Department Outstations Branch of the Society of Civil and Public Servants (SCPS)
PCSPS	—Principal Civil Service Pension Scheme
PEO	—Principal Establishment Officer
PES	—Public Expenditure Survey
PFO	—Principal Finance Officer
POA	—Prison Officers' Association
Prison officer	—prison officers of both sexes unless the context indicates otherwise
PRU	—Pay Research Unit
PSA	—Property Services Agency
PUS	—Permanent Under Secretary of State
PVQ	—pensionable value of quarters
RSU	—Regional Secure Unit
RUC	—Royal Ulster Constabulary

SCPS	—Society of Civil and Public Servants
SDA	—shift disturbance allowance
SEO	—Senior Executive Officer
SHHD	—Scottish Home and Health Department
SPOA	—Scottish Prison Officers' Association
Vee Scheme	—one of two attendance systems in operation for prison officers in England and Wales
Wynn-Parry Report	—"Report of the Committee on Remuneration and Conditions of Service of Certain Grades in the Prison Services" Cmnd 544, October 1958, Chairman the Hon Mr Justice Wynn-Parry
YOI	—Young Offenders' Institution (Scotland)

CHAPTER ONE

INTRODUCTION

1.1 This Inquiry was set up on 17 November 1978 after a long period of deteriorating industrial relations, especially in England and Wales. The apparent causes of the industrial action were diverse, although they had most recently in England and Wales concentrated on claims for what are known as continuous duty credits (CDC). Scotland, on the other hand, has been much freer from industrial action, although some occurred briefly after our appointment in relation to the use of special segregation cells in Inverness Prison. In Northern Ireland, there had been action over the daily emergency allowance rate and CDC. Although the foregoing were the most apparent causes of the industrial unrest immediately prior to our appointment, it soon became clear to us, as we shall explain throughout this report, that the real causes were much more fundamental and had their origins in, amongst other things, a general dissatisfaction with the way the prison services are organised and run, with the state of prison buildings, and with the conditions in which staff and inmates alike are required to live and work.

1.2 From the beginning the then Home Secretary, Mr Rees, stressed the urgency of our review and, indeed, expressed the hope that the Inquiry would report by the end of March 1979. In the event, because of the wide nature of our terms of reference, we had early to intimate to Mr Rees that it would not be practicable for us to complete our work by that date. As a result, he announced on 21 February (Official Report, Cols 182–3) that it was then our hope to report in the summer of 1979. In explaining the position to Parliament he said it would not be possible for the Inquiry to do full justice to the task it had undertaken within the original timescale "because of the number and complexity of the problems facing the prison services which have become apparent to the Committee during an intensive programme of visits to all types of prison establishments throughout the United Kingdom, and which have been extended and amplified by the large amount of evidence already submitted to the Committee".

1.3 The original expectation that we would report with such haste necessarily dominated the early weeks of our work and required us to invite people to submit evidence to us against very short and tight deadlines. In the end we have been able to work within a more reasonable timescale and we are satisfied that what follows does proper justice to that which we are required to investigate.

1.4 For somewhat different reasons we decided it would be inappropriate to issue any interim report. When the necessity for a longer investigation became clear we did very carefully consider the case for an interim report on CDC or pay. We were particularly influenced by the realisation that the prison service grades had been led to expect a quick report and that they should not be disappointed if it could be avoided. However, we concluded that an interim report would not be feasible because there was no acceptable way of separating CDC and pay issues from all the other issues before us.

Interpretation of terms of reference

1.5 Confronted with terms of reference that required us to deal at one end with constitutional issues relating to Ministerial responsibility for the management of establishments and, at the other, with very detailed matters over pay, allowances and conditions of service, we were obliged at the outset to consider very carefully how far we should pursue all the items before us. Although in all the circumstances it seemed inevitable to us that we should concentrate on the organisational, resources, pay and industrial relations issues, it was equally plain we could not ignore wider criminal justice matters, despite the fact that our terms of reference did not ask us to make recommendations upon them. This was because we could not, amongst other things, make credible and worthwhile recommendations about the resources required for the prison system without an adequately informed view on the size and nature of the future prison population, including the possibility of reducing it, for example either by removing certain categories of offender altogether or by means of likely changes in sentencing practice. By the same token, although we were not specifically asked to make recommendations about the larger philosophical and penological issues that arise from imprisonment, there could be no question of our ignoring them. Just as we had to form a view on the criminal justice context, so has it been imperative to get clear in our minds what prisons are to be for and how, as a result, they should be constituted. Hence, we have spent some time on the factors that influence the size of the penal population, and sought to spell out as explicitly as possible what we think modern penal objectives should be. In addition, we have included an historical review of the main relevant developments, not for mere antiquarian purposes, but to remind ourselves both of the timelessness of some penal problems, and of the fact that avoiding them does not contribute to their solution.

1.6 Although we have tried to look at things in the round, it is a matter of great regret to us that the pace at which we have been obliged to work has unavoidably led to a number of omissions. The most important of these have been some aspects of female prisons, the rate of whose growth in recent years has been a significant feature, especially in England and Wales. We at one time consoled ourselves that the Expenditure Committee would be undertaking at least a partial review of them, but the election of May 1979 brought that investigation to an end. We would have liked, too, more time to spend considering regime issues in greater detail than was possible.

1.7 We have also made the deliberate decision not to endeavour to offer cut and dried detailed recommendations in every case. This was because we recognise that no outside committee, however conscientiously it seeks to inform itself, can be omniscient. Further, in respect of many of the issues before us detailed recommendations were either impossible or undesirable since what was required was a commitment to negotiating new arrange-

2

ments rather than our carving them in tablets of stone. Accordingly, we have aimed generally at setting out the criteria that should govern organisation, resource allocation and so on, as opposed to prescribing the exact extent of change in every case. Nonetheless, we have not shrunk from detail where we have thought it necessary, helpful or appropriate, and where we can be confident that we have acquired sufficient knowledge to do so.

Method of work

1.8 Despite the fact that we had initially to work quickly, we avoided adopting a narrow view about what evidence we should solicit. We wrote direct to all the staff associations in England and Wales, Scotland and Northern Ireland, as well as to all Boards of Visitors or Visiting Committees, and to all penal establishments. In addition we approached all we thought likely to be interested, both persons and groups, including the main political parties. We consulted the judiciary and those academics who we thought might be able to assist us. We also attempted, with success, to approach representatives of inmates and ex-inmates. For the rest, there has been considerable publicity about our existence and it was reasonable to conclude that anyone interested in the matters before us had ample opportunity to contact us if they wished.

1.9 We are most grateful for the very considerable response that our invitations produced. The most numerous communications were from present and past members of the prison services themselves, sometimes from abroad: in all cases they gave the authentic flavour of grass roots views. A list of those organisations who submitted written observations is at Appendix 1. We regret that we had to press for evidence to be submitted quickly and we realise that the deadline we had to impose may have influenced some against offering considered views: this underlines the diligence and capacity of those who nonetheless did respond. Indeed, some of the non-official contributions were of a high order and did much to challenge conventional wisdom and stimulate our thinking. In addition the Home, Central and Lord Chancellor's Departments produced a wealth of mainly factual material both spontaneously and in reply to our many interrogatory memoranda. We understand that the official memoranda were sent to the staff associations as well as to ourselves, and we have therefore taken a lack of rejoinder from the associations as implying no strong dissent where we have not received representations to the contrary.

1.10 In the usual way, the evidence we have received is not being published with this report. On the other hand, we have throughout indicated to everyone submitting written evidence that we could have no objection to their publishing it themselves. The object was to stimulate public discussion and debate. Unfortunately, we cannot say that on this score the result was as fruitful as we had hoped. Public interest in penal matters seems to remain a fitful affair. We hope that our report will stimulate the kind of public debate we think desirable. Closed institutions above all require open, well-informed discussion.

3

1.11 Where we felt it would be helpful, we invited people to come to give oral evidence. A list of those who did so is at Appendix 2. In all cases we assured our oral witnesses that they should feel free to speak since we did not intend to publish the transcripts. For the same reason, therefore, we think it desirable that access to them should be protected under the normal rules governing access to official papers.

1.12 From the outset we set a target of meeting on at least three days a week. On that basis we embarked on a substantial visiting programme whose objective was to visit representative penal establishments in each of the three countries. Being obliged to look at all three countries was itself instructive since there are many illuminating differences between them. Altogether we visited 38 establishments, 29 in England and Wales, 6 in Scotland and 3 in Northern Ireland, as well as the four Regional Offices in England and Wales, the two Officer Training Schools and the Prison Service College there, and the Scottish Prison Service College. In addition we visited the Special Hospital at Broadmoor and the Metropolitan Police training school at Hendon. We also visited officials in headquarters divisions in England and Wales and met their Scottish and Northern Ireland counterparts. Finally, we visited two prisons in France, three in Denmark and two in Sweden, and met senior officials from the appropriate agencies. (A list of the establishments visited and notes on the visits to France and Scandinavia are at Appendices 3, 4 and 5 respectively.)

1.13 At each United Kingdom establishment we tried to see as much as we could of all the accommodation available to inmates and staff, to meet representatives of all the staff, to visit typical quarters and wherever practicable to meet the wives and families of prison staff. We were never under any illusion that even the very full day long visits we made were capable of doing entire justice to the complexity of the establishments. On the other hand, such an extensive programme did a great deal to enhance our personal knowledge of the prison services as well as to allow staff to put their points to us individually. We hope, too, that the visits gave us a more informed understanding of the very large quantities of written evidence that we received and enabled us to get the most out of the witnesses who came before us. We are grateful for the way in which we were received at all establishments. Staff seemed universally frank and forthcoming. As regards quarters, we are conscious of the intrusion into people's domestic privacy that our visits entailed, and we are all the more appreciative therefore of the kindness of those who received us.

1.14 The foreign visits were designed to allow us both to see how they manage similar problems abroad and, with that experience, to help place United Kingdom experience in perspective. That the visits contributed so much to our understanding is a tribute to the great help we were given wherever we went, and, again, the much appreciated candour which accompanied it. Where relevant we sought to tap experience abroad in other ways. For example, we were impressed by many of the points (to which we shall refer later) made by Dr Hans Tulkens, the head of the

4

Dutch prison administration in a paper he delivered in October 1978 to the annual general meeting of NACRO. We read of the recent experience of New South Wales in the report of the Nagle Royal Commission, and we looked into some recent experiences of the authorities in New York State and elsewhere in the USA with their labour laws. We also corresponded with the Canadian Correctional Investigator, an official who reports to the Federal Solicitor-General in respect of federal prisons.

1.15 Lastly, we endeavoured to read as widely as we could in the available time about penal policy and practice both in this country and abroad. This included examining the Parliamentary debates that occurred during our work. We have had before us the main international instruments, e.g. the Standard Minimum Rules for the Treatment of Prisoners and the European Convention on Human Rights. There is, of course, a large contemporary literature and the extent to which we have been influenced by it will be evident in the body of the report.

1.16 Of special value was the recent Expenditure Committee report published in July 1978. We were also able to see copies of the evidence taken by the Sub-Committee on women's prisons prior to the dissolution and the General Election in May 1979. In addition, our Chairman was able to have an informal exchange of views with the Sub-Committee Chairman, Miss Fookes MP, who was kind enough to pass on informally the benefit of the Sub-Committee's experience.

Nature of the report

1.17 Whilst there are no special features of the structure of the report to which we wish to draw attention, we do have some preliminary comments on its contents.

1.18 We are above all anxious that it and the recommendations it contains should be seen, and treated, as a whole. Just as we have already explained that we thought an interim report would be inappropriate because pay matters could not be separated from the rest, so we must emphasise that there is a very close interrelationship between *all* the things we were invited to examine. By implication, of course, this was the assumption behind our lengthy terms of reference. However, it is a fact that requires spelling out lest there be any danger of its being overlooked when attention fastens on particular points.

1.19 By the same token, our recommendations are to be seen as a package applying as appropriate to each and every part of the United Kingdom however much we have had to concentrate on England and Wales. Whereas we appreciate that implementation may not be instant for every recommendation, we do not think that in reason and in good faith it should be open to anyone to accept only those parts of immediate advantage to themselves and seek to set aside or refuse to co-operate on other parts.

1.20 Further, there is one other point we should record now lest what follows be got out of perspective. We were set up because things had gone wrong. We have inevitably concentrated on those things, often of course to the exclusion of other matters. We have tried to be as frank as were all those who gave evidence to us. We shall, therefore, from time to time say some hard things. We hope, however, that no-one will misunderstand our concern with things that have gone wrong as representing a belief that nothing is right.

1.21 On the contrary, although some of us were new to prisons, none of us has completed this task without having acquired a great and lasting regard for the dedication of all the staff in the prison services to their frequently very difficult and usually unsung tasks, carried out in most cases in very poor working conditions. As with so many essential but unavoidably secluded social services, the world takes little notice of them except when something goes wrong. Whilst we hope that some of our recommendations if implemented will cause the public to obtain a livelier understanding of the achievement of the prison services, we would like to stress emphatically that the United Kingdom is fortunate in the men and women it has secured to run its penal establishments, that they have been energetic and resourceful in responding to their tasks, and that they deserve continuing support in what they do. Above all, the staff in the establishments themselves seem determined to avoid being mere turnkeys or passive guardians: the best have created and wish to maintain a caring tradition, frequently carried out in the least encouraging environments. It may be a hackneyed observation to make but it remains true that a great deal of a society's character can be seen in the way it runs its prisons. No-one, therefore, can plead ignorance or deny the staff the thinking and inquiring support, as well as the resources, which they need. If we turn our backs on our prisons, we turn our backs on our society and our values.

CHAPTER TWO

BACKGROUND

Introduction

1. It became clear, early in our deliberations, that not only do many features of prison life today have roots that extend far back in time but that many of the current problems, also, are ones that have appeared in different guises (and sometimes even the same guise) over the years. And this is true not only of the major organisational and philosophical questions that face the system, but of the detailed issues, such as pay or conditions of service, that affect its day-to-day operation. It was thus incumbent upon us to pay due regard to the historical dimension in which the present system is set, and we have attempted, so far as time permitted, to familiarise ourselves with the main features of penal history in the three countries. As we have done so, it has been a salutary reminder that just as the problems have so frequently occurred before, so too the answers which we have attempted to formulate are frequently not (nor, it may be suggested, should they be) fundamentally new in every case. At the same time it has been clear to us that the prison system has not moved in any single and consistent direction during its history, but that its form and ethos have passed through a number of distinct and separate phases. Thus we have been reminded that it is possible to strike out into new and original paths, despite what has gone before, but that there is a continual need to beware, in doing so, of jeopardising the strengths and achievements of the past. As Noel McLachlan comments in reflecting upon the development of the system over the last century, penal reform has not always been synonymous with penal progress (ed. L Blom-Cooper, *Penal Reform and Penal Progress*, 1974).

2.2 In this chapter, therefore, we have attempted to summarise the history of the prison services, particularly the series of previous inquiries that have been held over the last 100 years, and to describe the current organisational setting in which prisons operate. A final section indicates the main legal changes affecting the role of imprisonment within the total criminal justice system that have taken place in recent years.

HISTORY

The prison system prior to 1877

2.3 The underlying theme of penal history in England in the 19th Century was that of the gradual extension by central government of its involvement in prison administration. It had only been with the development of transportation in the 18th Century that central government became involved at all in what had hitherto been a matter for purely local administration through the authority of the justices. When the American War of Independence ended the first phase of transportation in 1776, it was to the use of old ships (the "hulks"), converted for the purpose, that government first turned as an alternative solution to the containment of those more serious offenders who had nevertheless escaped the rigours of a capital sentence. It was in response, in turn, to the conditions which prevailed on the hulks that calls were heard for the building of a national penitentiary.

7

The latter was not to materialise until 1821, with the opening of Millbank Penitentiary, but when it did it marked the start of a permanent government share in penal administration. From then until 1877 there were essentially two prison services: the local service administered by the justices, and the national service consisting, initially, of Millbank and the hulks.

2.4 The central theme of government policy towards the prison system in the following years was the extension of influence over the local service, in the interests of both efficiency and uniformity of treatment. The Gaol Act 1835 provided, for the first time, for the appointment of an inspectorate, and although this had no enforcement authority, it did have considerable influence through the publication of its reports. The inspectorate was undoubtedly beneficial in its effects, gaining in authority by its independence of the system it was reviewing, but that very independence also led to occasional charges of irresponsibility. Subsequent legislation attempted to extend governmental influence over the design of new penal establishments. In 1850 central government formalised its control over those areas of the system for which it was responsible, with the establishment of the Convict Service. At its inception this included, *inter alia,* Millbank and Pentonville (which had been opened in 1842), two prisons for public works (Portland and Dartmoor), one prison for juveniles (Parkhurst), the hulks, and a number of cells for separate confinement rented in certain local prisons. The influence of central government was extended again, in regard to the local service, with the Act of 1865 which laid down the staffing complements for all establishments, and empowered the Secretary of State to withhold grant to local authorities and, *in extremis,* to close establishments.

The Prisons Act 1877 and its effects

2.5 The Act of 1877 was the logical extension of these developments, and one that was in step with the pattern of greater centralisation, in areas such as education and poor law administration, and with contemporary moves to reduce local rates. The Act transferred to the Secretary of State all the powers formerly vested in the justices in regard to penal adminis-tration, and created a new body, the Prison Commission, responsible for the organisation and detailed administration of the new service and for the appointment of subordinate officers. The inspectorate remained to assist but became for the first time (although appointed by the Home Secretary rather than by the Prison Commissioners) part of the system it was review-ing, rather than a body separate from it. A vestige of local control was retained in the power for justices to inspect establishments within their jurisdiction, and the creation of Visiting Committees of Justices at each establishment.

2.6 The Act was said by its supporters to have two objectives, economy in the use of resources and uniformity of treatment. The former appears to have been a decisive factor in the passing of the legislation, and the years that followed bore out the claim: 38 of the 113 establishments taken over when the Act came into force in April 1878 were immediately closed, and pride was taken, as time went on, in the savings produced. In 1883, for example, the Home Secretary pointed out to the Treasury, in arguing for

8

certain minor improvements in conditions for prison staff, that total expenditure on prison administration in 1882–83 had been only £404,135, compared with £474,703 in 1873–74. It is arguable, however, that the second of the objectives mentioned, the creation of uniformity, was the more important motive so far as the framers of the legislation were concerned, uniformity which was regarded as essential in order to enforce a system based on the principle of preventing contamination of one inmate by another. This went to the heart of one of the major debates of 19th Century penology which divided itself between those who believed in permitting association between inmates (albeit silently) and those who believed that any form of association would lead to informal contacts between inmates, the development of an inmate sub-culture and moral harm; this school of thought, which held sway within the Convict Service, therefore argued for a "separate" system of cellular isolation. Separation, however, was not only morally beneficial, by preventing contamination and providing an opportunity for reflection and self-examination, but greatly facilitated the task of security and control.

2.7 Although all English prisons were now centrally organised and under the executive control of one man, Sir Edmund Du Cane, the Convict and Local Prison Services were to remain separate for some considerable time. In 1898 the Prison Commissioners became, as their Chairman had always been, Directors of the Convict Prisons, but the bodies remained separate entities in law until well into the 20th Century. Separate salary scales existed for the two services until 1919. In other ways, however, Du Cane's early task was to bring local prisons as far as possible into line with the Convict Service. A pressing need was standardisation of methods of appointment and general conditions of service for the local prisons, particularly in the face of a wide variety of perks and other informal practices that had pertained in the local service. Another was the introduction into local prisons of the hierarchical (or, as it is sometimes called, "paramilitary") staffing structure which had been a part of the Convict Service since its inception. Into the local prisons, too, was brought the system of clerk and schoolmaster officers which had been introduced into the Convict Service from around 1870. Such a development was particularly needed in the local service because of the range of administrative and financial tasks, formerly dealt with by the local authorities, with which the prisons now found themselves faced, and because of Du Cane's determination to phase out the last vestige of inmate involvement in the running of prisons, the system of prisoner clerks. Some have seen the opening thus created for a separate administrative group within prison (although, at that stage, still confined to uniformed officers) as the first step along the path towards the introduction of a wide variety of specialist civilian staff, with important and wide-ranging implications for prison officers.

Prisons in Scotland

2.8 The history of Scottish prisons has some parallels with that in England. There, too, the responsibility for providing prisons had been a local one, vested in the burghs, and there was growing concern in the early 19th Century at the poor conditions and low standards of security and discipline that frequently existed. One of the inspectors appointed under the 1835 Act was assigned to Scotland and his reports confirmed the position. An Act of 1839, following on from his recommendations, vested the financing and administration of prisons in a series of County Boards (which, for the first time, made the counties as well as the burghs responsible for prisons) and created a General Board of Directors to exercise a general oversight, as well as to construct and run a new central prison at Perth. The General Board continued for only 20 years (to 1860) but achieved substantial improvements in terms of uniformity of treatment and the rationalisation of penal establishments (the total stock being reduced from 178 to 77).

2.9 After 1860 the element of central oversight passed to the Board of Managers of Perth prison, which acted as a central resource for longer term prisoners from the whole of Scotland (although those sentenced to penal servitude continued to be sent to England until the opening of Peterhead in 1888). A further 21 prisons had been closed by the time of the Prisons (Scotland) Act of 1877 which, on English lines, established a Scottish Prison Commission. This was to continue until 1928 when Scottish prisons became the direct responsibility of the Secretary of State for Scotland. By that stage only 12 establishments remained, reflecting a fall in average daily population from over 3,000 (of whom over 1,000 were women) in 1878 to about 1,700 (of whom less than 200 were women) in 1928.

Prisons in Ireland

2.10 The pattern repeats itself in Ireland. Here again, control was local until the 19th Century, the county and borough gaols being under the control of local Boards of Superintendence appointed by the Grand Juries and funded from monies levied by the Grand Juries and Town Councils. An element of central inspection was introduced into Irish prisons slightly earlier than in England and Scotland, however, by the Act of 1826 which empowered the Lord Lieutenant to appoint two Inspectors-General. As with the 1835 Inspectors, the influence here was through the publication of reports. The same Act also extended the involvement of the Lord Lieutenant in penal administration by providing for the designation of hulks or depots for those awaiting transportation. Central government involvement was taken a stage further in 1854 when the Treasury began contributing to the Boards of Superintendence the cost of maintaining certain categories of convicted offenders, and when the Lord Lieutenant was empowered, in an Act of that year, to appoint a Board of Directors responsible for the provision of convict prisons. Finally, as in the other countries, 1877 saw the centralisation of all prison administration in the General Prisons (Ireland) Act which established a General Prisons Board for Ireland. Under the Government of Ireland Act 1920, the administration of prisons in Northern Ireland was transferred to the Government of Northern Ireland; a General Prisons Board for Northern Ireland was established but was abolished under legislation in the following year, Northern Ireland prisons becoming the direct responsibility of the Ministry of Home Affairs. That situation continued until the start of Direct Rule in 1972.

2.11 Since the 1877 Act there has been a series of inquiries into the prison services and various aspects of their work. Reading through the papers connected with these inquiries and their respective reports, it is remarkable how frequently the questions with which they, and now our present Inquiry, have had to deal have been the same. In 1883, for example, a committee under the Earl of Rosebery was asked to examine questions of pay, leave, hours of duty and grading for English prison and Broadmoor staff. The committee was presented with (to us) familiar complaints that the central administration was more concerned with the conditions for inmates than for staff, and calls for parity of status with the police, better promotion prospects and improved standards of recruitment and training. The committee did not accept the arguments in regard to police parity, and nor did their successor, the De Ramsey Committee of 1891, who faced fresh pay demands, triggered in part by the Police Act of the previous year. Some of the other issues confronting this committee—calls for greater uniformity of conditions between the local and convict services and residual complaints by staff who claimed to have suffered from the changes of 1877—are less relevant to our present purposes; significant among the changes that were proposed, however, were that free accommodation should be provided for local prison staff, with a money allowance payable where this was not possible, and that overtime payments should be made where additional hours could not be compensated with a subsequent time-off in lieu.

2.12 Looking more broadly at the prison service than either of these inquiries, however, was the committee appointed in 1894 under the chairmanship of Herbert Gladstone, then Parliamentary Under Secretary at the Home Office. Its report, published the following year, represented a land mark in English penal history in that, for the first time in an official document, it placed the reform or rehabilitation of prisoners as a primary objective of the penal system, along with retribution and deterrence. The report paid due credit to the efficiency with which Du Cane had carried out the administrative reorganisation provided for by the 1877 Act, but was critical of the system's failure to pay due regard to "the moral as well as the legal responsibility of the prison authorities". The committee's concern to stimulate the reformatory element in regimes led them to insist upon due recognition of the individual needs of each inmate, a task in which prison warders could be trained to play some part and which depended, in turn, upon better systems of classification. Productive work would also contribute to rehabilitation; proposals included permitting a measure of associated labour, and the introduction of both increased central control of prison industries and of local "industrial managers" to relieve the governor of responsibilities in this regard. The committee took particular interest in the treatment of young offenders and proposed a system of government penal reformatories, with an indeterminate release date and subsequent licence system, which has parallels with the borstal system as eventually introduced. Other matters with which the report of the Gladstone Committee dealt were the problem and treatment of mentally disordered offenders—which it will be seen is still an issue over 80 years later—and the introduction of medical expertise onto the Prisons Board. In addition they recommended an extension of the probation period for warders and the institution of a training period for all ranks of prison staff, with at least two establishments operating as training schools. This the committee believed would lead to higher qualified staff for which increased levels of remuneration would be necessary. The committee also attempted to gauge the extent to which staff resources were over-stretched, particularly as a result of the escort requirements of the courts—problems which we in our turn have also had to consider. Like us, the Gladstone Committee found this question a difficult one, but they concluded that staff had then reached the limit of hours that could be expected of them: they recommended increased staff reserves and an allowance for sleeping in.

2.13 Although the Gladstone Committee were not precise about a prisons inspectorate, they did consider in some detail the work of the Visiting Committees—later to become the Boards of Visitors. They regretted that neither the clear intentions of the 1877 Act, nor subsequent efforts by the Home Secretary, had succeeded in persuading Visiting Committees that, although deprived of a financial role, they still had and should exercise a significant local influence. To reassert that influence the committee proposed extensive powers for the Visiting Committees, including determination of the nature of prison labour, the making of regulations on visits and the nominations of chaplains. Each Committee moreover, was to meet monthly and to report to the Secretary of State after each meeting on the state of the institution including the prison industries, the suitability of newly-engaged staff, applications for the post of warder and any inmates wrongly classified.

2.14 Common though it is for the report of the Gladstone Committee to be regarded as representing a new, important and liberal trend in English penal policy, at least one authority sees it as the source of many of the problems which have affected the prison system and its staff ever since. Dr J E Thomas in *The English Prison Officer since 1850* (1972) suggests that the formulation of two primary tasks for the prison service, namely deterrence and reformation, created a fundamental and confusing dichotomy of purpose for prison officers. As the rehabilitative task increased in importance as the years went by, it is argued, so the uncertainty of discipline staff whether their function was really central to the objectives of the establishment also increased. At the same time the move towards increased association between inmates, which the committee's recommendations on prison work had initiated, made their task of controlling prisoners in their charge all the more difficult. Questions of the primary objectives of imprisonment have continued, to the present day, to affect the prison service and those who work in it, and are issues to which we return later in our report.

Developments up to 1914

2.15 No sudden change of direction took place within prisons as a result of the report of the Gladstone Committee, although the Prisons Act 1898 contained a number of provisions related either to its recommendations or to its underlying approach. One of the most far-reaching of the Act's provisions, however, was one that had not occurred to the Gladstone Committee, namely that giving power to the Secretary of State to make rules under the Act for the regulation of prisons—a power which meant that many subsequent developments in English prisons during the 20th Century could take place without further recourse to legislation. By one of the ironies of history, it was as the result of the phasing out of the unproductive treadmills, following the Gladstone recommendation, that many establishments were deprived of the pumping apparatus needed to run their previous system of cellular sanitation.

2.16 Other developments in the period up to the First World War included a drastic reduction in the period of separate cellular confinement; the emergence and refinement of the borstal system; the formal addition of probation to the other sentencing options of the courts; the establishment of juvenile courts; the introduction of a separate sentence of preventive detention for habitual offenders; and further steps, in the Criminal Justice Act 1914, to reduce the numbers of fine defaulters committed to prison. Attempts were also made to humanise specific aspects of prison regime, with regard to letters, visits and educational opportunities, and there were moves to extend the privilege of talking to some inmates in local prisons— although the latter concession was one about which the Commissioners were to remain sceptical and which was to be resisted by some of their staff. What occurred during these years was that as the controls which had underpinned the old system, separation and silence, were gradually eroded, other forms of control, seeking prisoner conformity through systems of remission and other privileges, were gradually extended. These developments, however important each of them was in itself, were nevertheless insufficient to effect the radical transformation of the English prison system along the rehabilitative path that the Gladstone Committee had envisaged. This had to wait for the changed climate and personalities of the inter-war years.

Staff representation

2.17 As we have said, the developments in the early years of this century posed to discipline staff in prisons a potential source of confusion about their role and tended to alienate them from what was slowly emerging as the new objective for imprisonment. These feelings, where they existed, were to be exacerbated as time went on by the development of the treatment role of assistant governors, first introduced into the system by the institution of borstal housemasters. Prison officers, however, were developing a collective outlook of their own. Meetings within establishments to "discuss among themselves questions relating to their duties and position in the prison service" were permitted under a Standing Order of 1906, but it was the founding of the *Prison Officers' Magazine* in 1910 that marked the real start of a corporate consciousness within the service. The National Union of Police and Prison Officers (NUPPO) was formed in 1913 and a Prison Officers' Federation, two years later; the latter was associated with the *Magazine,* and among its stated aims was the abolition of direct entry into the governor grades. The Federation amalgamated with NUPPO in 1918, after the latter had supposedly established the right to strike. Publication of the *Magazine* was suspended. Thus prison officers became involved in the debacle of the police strike of August 1919, called by NUPPO in response to the Police Act of that year which removed from the police the right to join a union. All who participated were dismissed, including some 68 officers from Wormwood Scrubs and six from Birmingham; the failure of successive governments to reinstate them was to be a source of great bitterness, and contributed at the time to the alienation of prison officers from the labour movement. The consultative body set up by government in the wake of this, the Prison Officers' Representative Board (the equivalent of the Police Federation, established at the same time), was seen by some within the service as the tool of management, and the *Magazine* was restarted in 1920 under the editorship of E R Ramsay who used it as the mouthpiece of staff discontent. The main themes of editorial policy during those years were hostility to direct entry to governor grades, criticism of the "autocrats and parasites" who were running the prison service, and disdain for the concern of both outside bodies (like the Howard League, which had now replaced the earlier Howard Association) and of those running the system, with inmates' rights (a particular target being the supposed anxiety which governors showed in the face of inmate petitions). It was not until 1938 that the Prison Officers' Association (POA) replaced the Prison Officers' Representative Board (PORB) for negotiating purposes, and took over the *Magazine* as its official organ.

The Stanhope Committee, 1923

2.18 After the First World War the next inquiry into the pay and conditions of prison officers was in 1923. Again the latter sought parity with the police. Although there had been no increases in pay for the majority of prison staff between 1878 and 1914 (apart from lodging allowances introduced in 1891) they had not, in fact, done badly in comparison with the police in the years up to the War. The inflation of the War years was the occasion of a series of bonus payments, from 1917, for all civil servants, from which prison officers benefited. There were also substantive pay awards for police and prison officers in both 1918 and 1919. What triggered further claims from the prison service soon after was the substantial increase in police pay, recommended by the Desborough Committee of 1919, in the aftermath of the police strike. The Prison Commissioners had already publicly supported the claim for parity, but once again a Committee of Inquiry, headed this time by Earl Stanhope, rejected it—on the grounds that the tasks and responsibilities of prison staff were less than those of the police and that actual incidence of serious injury was markedly lower. Further, having found that pay and working hours within the prison service had improved more than the average outside, they did not recommend any extensive pay increases.

2.19 The committee's attitude to the governor grades, however, was altogether different. The members were clearly much influenced by the Commissioners' views on the changing role and situation of prison governors: they now worked a full day instead of three or four hours as in earlier years; they no longer had service pensions to augment their income and without private means they were unable to maintain the social status "necessary for keeping in touch with persons of standing in the locality in order to secure the voluntary help required by modern reformative influences . . .". The committee proposed substantially increased pay scales and made a number of recommendations about the governor establishment and their promotion structure. They also recommended increases for chaplains and medical officers: the latter were then as now posing a recruitment problem as their salaries, even after an increase in 1919, still compared unfavourably with those in other public institutions and outside practice.

2.20 Subordinate officers in Scotland received treatment similar to that of their English counterparts, but the Scottish governors did rather less well in recognition of the fact that they were generally in charge of rather smaller establishments and enjoyed, it was said, rather less individual responsibility (although they were responsible, unlike English governors, for finding prison work). A special allowance was, however, recommended for the governor of Barlinnie in recognition of the particular demands of his post. The Broadmoor attendants were to continue being paid on prison officer scales but with an additional weekly allowance of 2/6 in recognition of the peculiar demands of their job and its dangers.

The inter-war years

2.21 One of the chief interests of the Stanhope Committee is the light it sheds on the extent to which assumptions about reformist objectives had already gained a considerable hold over the system—even if, as seems clear from the internal papers, some remained privately doubtful about the public optimism which they felt obliged to adopt. It was that optimism, however, which was to set the tone of the succeeding decades, a period which is particularly identified with the name of one man, Alexander Paterson. Paterson as a Commissioner but never Chairman of the Prison Commission, became associated, both inside and outside the service, with the search for a constructive approach to the treatment of offenders. That approach was exemplified most in regard to the borstal service which Paterson sought to model as closely as possible upon the public school model and ethos; in the 1930s this was taken a stage further with the development of open borstals. Developments in the name of reformative and progressive treatment also took place on the adult side with the extension of facilities—cinema, earning schemes, ending of separate confinement etc—and in the opening of the first adult open prison in 1936. In a variety of ways in the inter-war period, Britain became the centre of the prison reform movement. One sign of the strength which this tradition had gained was that it survived the wave of unrest, at Dartmoor and elsewhere, that affected English prisons in 1932. The Du Parcq Inquiry into the Dartmoor mutiny specifically dismissed the idea that it was 'humane treatment' that had led to the trouble, but it was only with considerable difficulty that the then Chairman of the Prison Commission persuaded the Home Secretary not to accede to the critics of penal reform (Harold Scott: *Your Obedient Servant*, 1959). One reason why he was able to do so was that the stability of crime and prison population levels during this period led to a lack of overt public concern over law and order issues. This is reflected in the absence of any marked reaction to growing numbers of escapes (an indifference which appeared to be largely shared by the Prison Commissioners, much to the resentment of basic grade staff). An underlying feature of the period, in retrospect, was the failure, amidst the perennial debate about staff shortages, to recognise the effects on prison staff of the new phase into which the service had moved, and the fact that the new approach was far more demanding of staff resources, even for basic security and control, than the highly restricted separate and silent system that it had replaced.

The post-war era

2.22 The Second World War interrupted the reformist tradition and by 1945 the setting had become more difficult: staff numbers had been reduced, new types of offender had begun to appear in prison and a steady (and, as it proved, continuing) upward push in the size of the prison population had appeared towards the end of the War. Paterson himself died in 1947. Yet although the Criminal Justice Act 1948 (a revised and embellished version of the Bill dropped in 1938) could be seen, in its introduction of detention centres, as in some senses the forerunner of a sterner element in penal policy, its main thrust was firmly in the liberalising tradition. The old concepts of hard labour and penal servitude were finally abolished, together with most of the remaining civil disabilities that had reinforced the stigma of imprisonment. The Criminal Justice (Scotland) Act 1949 contained somewhat similar provisions. Other developments over the following decades included the introduction into prisons of welfare officers, psychiatrists and psychologists; the so-called 'Norwich' system which sought to involve officers in welfare work, and which extended dining in association and workshop hours; the hostel scheme which enabled longer-term prisoners to work for outside employers towards the end of their sentence; and the introduction of home leave. Developments of a similar nature in Scotland included home leave and the training for freedom scheme. The first Scottish open prison, Penninghame, was opened in 1953. These years saw the full flowering of belief in the possibility of reforming offenders, the clearest statement of which was enshrined in the English Prison Rules 1964 in terms of enabling inmates "to lead a good and useful life". Such developments were not accomplished without both satisfaction on the part of prison officers at their greater involvement in the welfare task, and, at the same time, concern at the threat which these trends posed to security and control and the growing tendency to give new tasks to specialists imported for the purpose.

2.23 There were, however, other, more pressing, reasons for staff discontent in the decade following the War, over the establishment of appropriate levels of remuneration. The Stanhope Committee had not closed the debate about comparability with the police, nor were prison officers yet satisfied that their growing involvement in reform was adequately recognised in their rates of pay. A dispute over pay went to arbitration in 1938 and there was to be further recourse to arbitration in 1950, 1952, 1954, 1956, 1957 and

1959. The main arguments which were raised during these disputes included changes in outside levels of remuneration as demonstrated by published indices; the need to boost poor recruitment (in terms of both quantity and quality), and to reduce high wastage; the cost of living; police pay increases (both those of a regular nature and those resulting from special reviews, such as the Eve Report of 1951); and awards made to other civil servants or grades at broadly comparable pay levels. It was against this background that the Wynn-Parry Committee was appointed in October 1957 to enquire into the remuneration and conditions of service of both officer and governor grades in the English and Scottish services.

The Wynn-Parry Committee, 1958

2.24 This committee submitted its report to the Home Secretary on 11 August 1958. It began by describing the advances which had taken place in the involvement of prison officers in rehabilitation since the time of the Stanhope Committee (a contrast which, from the concern with rehabilitation shown at the time of the earlier inquiry, may have been overstated) and then enunciated the principle that the Prison Service was *sui generis* inside the civil service, as well as in comparison with activities outside. The first issue to which the committee turned their attention was the proposal for a unified entry system, the POA having claimed that there were sufficient suitable officers to fill the governor grades, but calling also for increased age and entry qualifications for officer recruits. This claim the committee rejected on the grounds that the poor showing of officers on the staff courses (run to select internal candidates for the governor grades) showed that the time was not yet ripe to abandon the open competition. General problems of undermanning suggested, moreover, that it would be inappropriate at that stage to embark on the major raising of entry standards the POA had suggested.

2.25 The committee turned next to conditions of service. The POA had complained to them of the slowness of promotion for basic grade officers, but as the committee saw little alternative in a service where there was a lot of routine work to be done, they could offer little in the way of a palliative. They were not convinced, for example, that there was sufficient work at that grade to justify the introduction of a rank between the basic grade and principal officer, but they did suggest that a "vocational examination" should be taken after 10 years' service, passing which should qualify for payment at the minimum of the principal officer scale. The committee favoured the resolve of both the POA and the Prison Commission to abolish all regular overtime, calculating that a thousand additional staff would eventually be necessary to eliminate the so-called "Morrison hour" (the war time device of an hour a day, built-in overtime) and to get all establishments onto the three-shift system in which no regular overtime was required. They were aware, however, that their recommendation that conditioned hours should be worked over an 11-day fortnight would, for the time being, increase overtime, and for that reason declined to go all the way with the POA claim for a 10-day fortnight. Claims that the conditioned fortnight should be made inclusive of meals were rejected.

2.26 The committee then dealt with various other points in regard to prison officers. The committee held that it was wrong in principle for supervisory grades to draw overtime pay, and proposed that overtime should accordingly be withdrawn from chief officers, with an appropriate compensation in basic pay. Living and working conditions, inside establishments and in quarters, were described as Dickensian, but the committee made no specific recommendation on these issues except that a joint Official/Staff Side committee should review the whole area. On the question of allowances, however, the committee made a number of recommendations. For present purposes it is necessary to refer only to the inconvenience of locality allowance (ILA): after an arbitration in 1945 these were paid at 27 establishments. The Wynn-Parry Committee doubted whether, had ILAs not already existed, it would have been necessary to invent them, but they declined to recommend any change. (The Stanhope Committee, according to the later comments of its secretary, had been similarly unimpressed by the arguments for them.)

2.27 With regard to the governors, the Wynn-Parry report ruled against their bid for the so-called two-for-one pension arrangement, paid to officers to enable earlier retirement on full pension, on the grounds that governors did not experience the strain for which the improved entitlement was paid. The committee was sympathetic about the mobility of governors and made some minor proposals in regard to the resettlement grants payable following moves. The Scottish governors, they urged, should be paid equally with their English counterparts.

2.28 It was on the issue of pay, however, that the Committee made its most significant contribution. Given the fact that the prison service was *sui generis*, what they did, they claimed, was to consider the degrees of responsibility, the growing emphasis on rehabilitation and the conditions of service of each grade; to compare this with what they knew of outside employments; and on that basis to pick what appeared to be a fair rate for the job, as at 1 July 1958. Specifically, they kept the entry point for basic grade officers virtually unchanged, but pushed up the scales, following probation, so that at the maximum they rose by nearly 11 per cent; they raised the principal officers' maximum by nearly 30 per cent, because they believed the grade had been undervalued, and they kept chief officers at their existing differential, once the compensation for the loss of overtime had been taken into account. The need to preserve internal relativities meant that these increases had a consequential effect on the rest of the scales; at the top, Directors in the Prison Commission were to be paid at a rate slightly above Assistant Secretaries in the Civil Service.

2.29 The committee also felt that it would have been desirable to link the pay of all grades to the same index for the purpose of future movements in pay; this they found impossible in practice and thus stressed that the links which they did suggest were only guides, although continuing regard should be paid to the maintenance of internal differentials. As Directors and Assistant Commissioners were doing essentially administrative work, they should be linked broadly to the administrative class of the civil service. For the same reason, governors should be linked generally to the executive class. As there were no comparable duties in the case of prison officers, the majority of the committee recommended that the link should be to movements in similar pay ranges in the Civil Service. In a minority report, however, Dr Mary Cairns said that as prison officers were *sui generis*, this ruled out any attempt to establish a civil service link and that any future movement in pay for the officer grades should therefore be considered on its own merits. In submitting the report, Mr Justice Wynn-Parry commented that Dr Cairns's views would mean the continuation of the series of arbitrations, to end which had been the intention of constituting the committee in the first place.

2.30 The Departments did not find it immediately easy to turn the pay proposals into a workable formula (largely because there was no guarantee that the various grades in the comparable pay range would all move at the same rate). Eventually it was agreed to divide prison officers' pay into three bands, and to compare each separately with corresponding civil service pay bands. On this basis settlements have since been reached with effect from 1 December 1958 and thereafter from 1 January 1964, 1968, 1971, 1973 and 1975. Thereafter the Civil Service Pay Agreement was suspended under government incomes policies and consequently the 1975 agreement was the last occasion upon which the Wynn-Parry recommendations were applied until the recent civil service pay settlement was agreed during the life of our present Committee with effect from 1 April 1979. Over the years since 1958 changes in the civil service grades whose pay has to be compared with prison officers' pay have been negotiated and agreed with the POA from time to time.

The Mountbatten Report, 1966

2.31 We must finally refer to one other prison inquiry. This was the one conducted by Lord Mountbatten and three assessors in 1966. His committee was set up by the then Home Secretary following a series of spectacular prison escapes in 1964 and 1965, culminating in that of the spy George Blake in October 1966. Their task was to examine the escapes which had taken place and to make recommendations for the improvement of prison security. Mountbatten's major recommendations were, first, for the introduction of a system of categorisation of inmates, ranging from those requiring the highest possible degree of security, whose escape would pose a major threat to the safety of the public or the security of the realm, down to those in the fourth category who could reasonably be entrusted to serve their sentences in open conditions. Mountbatten next proposed that men in the top security category (A) should be housed together in a new purpose-built top-security prison, to which he gave the name 'Vectis', rather than in the maximum security blocks which had already been established at certain existing prisons. He also believed that the pressures on prison staff had noticeably increased in recent years, and that staff increases were needed to compensate; he gave the gradual disappearance of landing officers in the large 19th Century prisons as an example of a particular area where staff shortages were affecting basic security precautions. For the sake of morale,

19

but also, it was claimed, because an intermediate supervisory level was needed, he recommended the introduction of a senior officer rank (which had been considered but rejected by Wynn-Parry). Other recommendations on staff included one that there should be more emphasis on security in training courses, that in each closed establishment there should be a security officer reporting directly to the governor, and that the job of night patrols should be taken over by prison officers.

2.32 With regard to organisational structures, Mountbatten criticised what he detected as a degree of isolation of governors from headquarters, the remedy for which he saw in the introduction of a regional structure and a more involved and supportive inspectorial function (to assist in which the Assistant Directors should have junior members of the governor grades to act as staff officers). The service needed a professional head who would be a recognisable figure, both within the service and outside it, but Mountbatten recognised that the field demands of such a job were incompatible with the office responsibilities (including the provision of advice to Ministers) which were also essential. He therefore recommended that the job should be split, with the headship, so far as the field was concerned, going to an Inspector General who on the first occasion might have to come from outside the service. Mountbatten then turned to the physical conditions necessary to prevent escape and outlined a number of physical devices which establishments might adopt (secure walls, detection devices etc). A separate prison dog service was also proposed. Equally important, in his view, was the prevention of communications with the outside world. Recommendations under this head included moving all pre-release hostels to outside the prison walls, and being prepared to tape-record the visit conversations of high-security inmates and to install microphones in the visiting rooms of all other closed establishments. For high-security inmates, he proposed the transcription of incoming and outgoing mail, in case coding devices had been used. Finally, as a means of improving morale within penal establishments and discouraging incentives to escape, the report directed attention towards the provision either of integral sanitation or of electric unlocking devices, and the introduction of regular home visits throughout sentence for all but the most serious offenders.

2.33 The immediacy with which the Mountbatten Inquiry was established and its principal recommendations about security (although not those for the increased surveillance of letters and visits) were implemented, are in marked contrast to the more relaxed response of the 1930s. This time the liberal ethic was less able to ride out the storm of public disquiet over major lapses in what were, on any reckoning, major objectives of the penal system. It is hard to evaluate just how much of a change in ethos the Mountbatten Report did initiate, but there is certainly a widespread belief that it ushered in an era in which concern with security became, and has remained, central to large parts of the system. In terms of practical results, a four-fold categorisation system, the senior officer rank and the post of Inspector General were introduced (although the functions of the latter continued as envisaged by Mountbatten only during the tenure of the original incumbent).

Most significantly, however, what was not done was to implement his proposal for a single maximum-security establishment. Instead, the issue was remitted to a sub-committee of the Advisory Council on the Penal System (ACPS) under Professor Leon Radzinowicz, which reported in 1968. This came out firmly against the idea of concentrating high-risk prisoners on a number of grounds—that it would be difficult to provide adequate work and recreational facilities in an establishment catering for the relatively few inmates so categorised, that there would be no alternative establishment to which to transfer unsettled or unsettling inmates and that the chances of creating a tolerable and constructive regime in an establishment known to all involved as the end of the road, would be minimal. Instead, it was decided to disperse the Category A population amongst a number of training prisons designated for the purpose, whose security had been appropriately up-graded; the idea was that relaxed regimes should be established within secure perimeter walls for all within such establishments, high-risk inmates being treated virtually the same as everyone else in the establishment. The history of the seven "dispersal" prisons that now cater for this class of inmate within the system has not generally been a happy one, and controversy has since raged over whether it is the dispersal policy itself which has led to inmate unrest, or factors connected more generally with the growth in the proportion of difficult offenders within the system; similarly it is alleged that the dispersal system entails the devotion of excessive amounts of security to categories of inmate who do not require it. To these issues, as to so many others that have arisen in the history of the prison service, we return in the course of this Report.

The abolition of the Prison Commission

2.34 The English Prison Commission which had been brought into existence by the Act of 1877, consisted by 1946 of a chairman and deputy chairman, both of whom were Commisioners, and a system of six directorates (Prison Administration, Industries, Works, Medical Services and Education and Welfare). After 1948 the Chairman, with the grade of Assistant Under Secretary of State, reported directly to the Home Secretary through the Permanent Under-Secretary of State at the Home Office instead of, as before, through the Criminal Division of the Home Office. The Scottish Prison Commission had been abolished in 1928, being replaced by a Prisons Department under the Secretary of State's control; and in 1938, in the Criminal Justice Bill of that year, it was proposed to deal similarly with the Prison Commission in England. The Bill was abandoned on the outbreak of war; the proposal was reintroduced in the Bill of a decade later, but was withdrawn by the Home Secretary in the face of opposition during the committee stage. The bid to abolish the Commission succeeded at its third attempt in the Criminal Justice Act 1961. A range of arguments was deployed on behalf of the change (it needed to be, since the opposition inside and outside Parliament was considerable): that a Commission was an inappropriate body for the complexity of tasks now to be performed; that the Commission had become rigid, inward-looking and over-centralised; that a co-ordinated approach was needed to the treatment of offenders; that it was wrong for the Home Secretary's responsibility in this area to be on any different basis from his other responsibilities; that amalgamation with the Home Office would provide a larger pool of staff on which to draw, and better job opportunities for staff; that it would be more efficient and economical for the establishment, finance and other specialist services of the two bodies to be combined; and that the Scottish precedent had been fully successful. Against abolition it was asserted that links with the Home Office were already close enough, that the enlightened work of the Commission would be hampered by Home Office control, and that the Prison Service would find itself in a position of lower priority in the wider fields of Home Office responsibility. The order giving effect to the dissolution of the Commission was laid in February 1963 and went to a vote, successfully but after some opposition, the following month.

CURRENT ORGANISATION

England and Wales

2.35 Since 1963 the prison service in England and Wales has been administered by the Prison Department of the Home Office. All prison department staff are Home Office staff and the Home Secretary, assisted by one of his junior ministers, has direct executive responsibility for all aspects of prison department work. The position in each of the three countries of the United Kingdom is now the same; ministerial responsibility for all aspects of criminal justice and the general maintenance of law and order apart from the appointment of the judges and some aspects of the provision and manning of the courts, now rests, respectively, with the Secretary of State for the Home Department, the Secretary of State for Scotland and the Secretary of State for Northern Ireland. The head of the Prison Service in England, the Director General, is one of the Home Office's Deputy Under-Secretaries of State, reporting to the Permanent Under-Secretary of State, who is accounting officer for the Home Office as a whole. The Director-General also has responsibility for the operation of the parole scheme, and the Probation and After-Care Department, otherwise the responsibility of another deputy secretary, reports to him on this aspect of its work. An important feature of the 1963 amalgamation was the decision to place Prison Department establishments and financial matters under, respectively, the Principal Establishment Officer (PEO) and the Principal Finance Officer (PFO) of the Home Office. Thus, it is the PEO and not the Director-General, who is responsible for all recruitment, manning, posting, conditions of service and similar personnel matters affecting all members of the Prison Department, although he acts, in regard to prison service grades, in co-operation with one of the divisions of the Prison Department itself. (The division of the Home Office Establishment Department responsible for prison service non-industrial staff is Establishment Division 3.) Similarly, the Finance Department of the Home Office is responsible for the management of the Prison Vote.

2.36 A Management Review Team was set up in 1967 with the broad aim of improving the general managerial efficiency of the prison service; of speeding up the development of regions and the devolution of work from headquarters; of providing a resource for longer term planning and development; of integrating prison experience into the Department and of

22

separating inspectorial functions from executive responsibility. As a result of that review, an integrated structure was introduced in 1968 which enabled governors to hold headquarters posts. The Inspectorate was introduced in 1969, and in the following year the headquarters organisation was reorganised and a regional structure introduced. The current organisational structure of the prison service is thus as described in the following paragraphs.

2.37 The prison service is run by a Prisons Board (the lineal descendant of the Board of Prison Commissioners, whose continuing existence was pledged to Parliament during the debate on the dissolution of the Commission) which is collectively responsible for the formulation of major policy and the general management of the prison service. It consists of the following members:

The Controller of Personnel and Services, who is responsible for prison service staffing requirements and training; prison industries, supplies and transport; and the prison building programme. His controllerate incorporates the Directorate of Industries and Farms, Supply and Transport Branch, and the Chief Architect's Branch and the Directorate of Works.

The Controller of Operational Administration, who is responsible for operational and administrative matters in the adult prison and young offenders systems.

The Controller of Planning and Development, who is responsible for medium and long-term planning and development (i.e. with prison building only to the conclusion of any relevant public inquiries), the Directorate of Psychological Services and the Chaplain General's Branch.

The Director of Prison Medical Services, who is responsible for the organisation of all medical services and all other matters relating to the health of inmates.

The Chief Inspector of the Prison Service, who is responsible for inspecting and reporting on the efficiency of regions and establishments.

The Controllers and the Director of Prison Medical Services hold the rank of Assistant Under Secretary of State; the Chief Inspector holds a rank equivalent to one between Assistant Under Secretary of State and Assistant Secretary.

2.38 The English prison service is divided into four regions covering the North, Midlands, South West and South East of England, and run respectively from Manchester, Birmingham, Bristol and Tolworth in Surrey. All establishments are in one or other of the regions but the degree of regional responsibility for them varies according to the type of establishment (for example, headquarters retain a high degree of day-to-day responsibility for establishments for women and girls, and close oversight of prisoners in security Category A and prisoners serving life sentences). Each region is under the control of a Regional Director with the rank of Assistant Controller (the equivalent of an Assistant Secretary in the Administration Group of the Civil Service) who is a former governor and who operates in a direct operational relationship with the governors in his region. Each region has an administrative deputy regional director (a Principal), a deputy regional director responsible for young offenders and one or two other deputy regional directors responsible for adult prisoners; all of these, with the exception of the first, are Governors II on secondment from the field. There are regional industrial managers and supervisors of works, and the various other specialist functions—chaplaincy, medical, psychological, educational, vocational training and physical education are also represented in the regional office, being responsible to the Regional Director for the general management and operational aspects of their specialities, while remaining accountable to their professional heads at headquarters. In the Circular Instruction on regions, the objectives of the regional organisation were said to be to establish an intermediate tier of support and control more intimately linked with establishments than headquarters could provide, and to delegate to the regions as much operational and administrative responsibility as was practicable. How much of this aim and these objectives have been realised in practice will be discussed in due course.

Scotland

2.39 The Headquarters of the Scottish prison system is the Prisons Division of the Scottish Home and Health Department (SHHD) in the Scottish Office, which reports to Ministers through the Secretary of the Scottish Home and Health Department, who is the accounting officer for the Prisons (Scotland) Vote. The head of the Prisons Division is the Director of Prisons for Scotland. Under him there are three Controllers, responsible respectively for Administration, Operations, and Personnel and Services. The Controller of Operations is now always an ex-governor who has the rank of Assistant Controller: the other Controllers are civil servants with the rank of Assistant Secretary. Different from the situation in England and Wales, the Scottish Prisons Division itself deals directly with establishment and personnel matters, though it maintains close links with the Central Services Department of the Scottish Office.

2.40 Attached to the Prisons Division are an Inspector (Governor I) and an Assistant Inspector (Governor III) of Prisons. Their main function is to inspect all penal establishments periodically, but they may also be asked from time to time to investigate and report on particular incidents or situations. The Prisons Division can also call upon a wide range of professional services available within other parts of the Scottish Office, in regard, for example, to building, medical, educational and social work matters. Because of the relatively small size of the prisons system in Scotland, there is no regional organisation as there is in England and Wales.

Northern Ireland

2.41 Executive responsibility for the provision and administration of prisons within the Province has rested on the Secretary of State for Northern Ireland since the start of Direct Rule on the 30 March 1972. He is assisted

24

by a junior Minister in discharging this responsibility. The day-to-day management and organisation of the penal system is carried out by the Prisons Administration section of the Northern Ireland Office (NIO) in Belfast. This is headed by a Deputy Secretary, a rank corresponding to Assistant Under Secretary of State in the United Kingdom civil service, who reports to the Permanent Secretary, Northern Ireland Civil Service Group, who holds a rank just below that of Deputy Under Secretary of State in the United Kingdom. This last officer in his turn reports to the Permanent Secretary to the Northern Ireland Office, who is the accounting officer for the Department as a whole.

2.42 The Prisons Administration in Northern Ireland comprises three divisions. The first, under an Assistant Secretary, is responsible for prison administration, general policy and casework. The second, under an Assistant Controller, is concerned with prison staffing, operations and security. The third, headed by a Governor I, concerns itself principally with prison industries, education, and vocational training on the one hand and new minor works and supplies services on the other. The prison staffing responsibilities of the second of these divisions relate only to the prison governor and prison officer grades. Similar questions affecting general service or other departmental grades employed in prisons are the responsibility of the Establishment Division of the Northern Ireland Office.

2.43 Major policy questions are considered at the meetings of the Prison Management Committee, which generally meets about once a month, under the Permanent Secretary, Northern Ireland Civil Service Group. It includes the Deputy Secretary in charge of the prisons administration and the heads of the three divisions reporting to him, and also the Deputy Secretary in the Northern Ireland Office with responsibility for penal planning and courts administration. The Assistant Secretary with responsibility for penal planning, the Controller of Prison Industries and Supplies, the Finance Officer of the Northern Ireland Office in Belfast and the Information Officer with responsibility for prison matters complete the membership of this committee.

2.44 There is no specific headquarters Inspectorate in the Province, but inspections are carried out from time to time on behalf of the Northern Ireland Office by the Prison Department of the Home Office in London. In addition the Assistant Controller and a Governor II at the Prisons Administration headquarters visit the five Northern Ireland establishments regularly. Again because of the relatively small size of the system, there is no regional organisation in Northern Ireland.

CRIMINAL JUSTICE DEVELOPMENTS

England and Wales

2.45 Chapter 3 indicates in detail how the English prison population, which remained strikingly stable between the Wars, began a dramatic and sustained rise from around 1940. Part of the response was a new building programme, but this could only ever be part of the story, and there emerged during the 1960s a parallel determination to find means of reducing the prison population. This was not wholly on the grounds of expediency, for there had grown up a clear belief that whatever the benefits of imprisonment, it also carried the risk of substantial damage if applied for too long or unnecessarily. Imprisonment, it was recognised, had a potentially damaging effect upon the future work prospects and family life of inmates, 'labelled' them as deviant in a way likely to reinforce future deviant behaviour, and was costly to society both in regard to the inmate himself and his family. The Criminal Justice Act 1967 marked the recognition of this principle by the introduction of parole, underlying which was the assumption that for certain longer-term prisoners there came a point in sentence where the benefits of imprisonment had been fully secured and where it was right to allow supervised freedom before the harmful effects began to assert themselves. A Parole Board for Scotland was introduced at the same time. The Act also introduced powers to suspend a sentence of imprisonment, on the assumption that the threat of a sentence would be as effective in securing future compliant behaviour as actually sending the offender to prison, and without any of the costs and damage involved.

2.46 A further example of the concern to respond to criminality, whenever possible, by measures short of the full rigours of the criminal law, was to be found, two years later, in the Children and Young Persons Act 1969 whose objective was to provide a flexible treatment system, preferably in the community, based upon the needs of the child. Under the Act (whose provisions did not take effect immediately, and some of which have never been implemented), the responsibility for the treatment of juvenile delinquents passed from the Home Office to the Department of Health and Social Security (DHHS), approved schools becoming local authority community homes; the intention was that there should eventually be no prosecution of children under 14 and that all proceedings against them should be civil and not criminal in nature. The following year witnessed a further stage in thinking about the treatment of young offenders with the publication of an ACPS report on detention centres, the thrust of which was that the existing detention centre order for young men should be retained, pending the outcome of a wider review of the treatment of young offenders, but that detention centres should take on a more positive training and educational role. A previous ACPS report in 1968 had recommended the abolition of detention centre training for girls, a proposal which had led to the closure of the only existing centre. The promised general review of the treatment of young adult offenders, to which the ACPS had looked forward in 1970, was published in 1974 and recommended that the present categories of young prisoner, borstal trainee and detention centre trainee should all be subject to a generic sentence of custody and control. That basic principle was preserved in the Green Paper, *Youth Custody and Supervision,* which was published in December 1978, although other elements in the proposals of the ACPS were not reiterated; the new Government has not yet indicated firm intentions in this area.

2.47 The courts' sentencing powers in regard to adult offenders were developed further in the Criminal Justice Act 1972 which gave effect to two further ACPS reports, *Reparation by the Offender* and *Non-Custodial and Semi-Custodial Penalties,* which had appeared in 1970. Among the new sentencing powers conferred on the courts were powers to order an offender to pay compensation for loss or injury caused, to confiscate property used in the course of a crime, to make criminal bankruptcy orders and to defer the passing of sentence to give offenders the opportunity, for example, to demonstrate their determination to take advantage of improved personal circumstances (marriage, a new job etc). Courts were given more discretion in the use of suspended sentences and were enabled to order supervision during suspension; further restrictions were placed on the power to imprison for the first time any persons who were not legally represented. Other provisions empowered courts to order attendance at day training centres (where social skills training of various sorts would be provided), gave the police power to take a drunken offender to a treatment centre and, most significantly of all, introduced community service. The latter, which was first introduced on an experimental basis but which has gradually been extended to cover the whole country, is the most major new sentencing option with which the courts have been provided in recent years; although it is difficult to estimate the extent to which those receiving community service orders would otherwise have gone to prison (and thus the effect of community service on the size of the prison population), estimates made during the first 18 months of its operation suggested that between 45 and 50 per cent of those so sentenced would otherwise have gone to prison.

2.48 In 1974 the report of the Working Party on Bail Procedures in Magistrates' Courts recommended a presumption in favour of the grant of bail. This presumption was made statutory in the Bail Act 1976 which, it was hoped, would affect the size of the remand population. The most recent English legislation relevant to our present purposes was the Criminal Law Act 1977. In addition to its major changes (in regard to conspiracy, the law on entry into property and the distribution of business between the Crown Court and magistrates' courts) and a variety of other provisions, this increased certain maximum fines and created order-making powers for future increases, while providing for the imprisonment of defaulters only in cases of wilful refusal or culpable neglect. Powers of partial suspension of sentence were introduced—not yet activated—and magistrates' courts were empowered to order that those remanded in custody might be brought up for subsequent remands before a court nearer to the prison where they are held. Some of the Act's provisions apply to Scotland.

Scotland

2.49 General developments in Scotland, with the exception of parole, have followed a rather different course, although the underlying approach of encouraging alternatives to imprisonment has been the same. Scottish courts have no powers to suspend sentences, in whole or in part, or to order reparation by offenders or attendance at day training centres. Powers to defer sentence, however, have existed under the common law in Scotland for a very long time, and were confirmed by statute in 1963 (the provision has subsequently been repeated in the consolidated Criminal Procedure

(Scotland) Act 1975). A presumption in favour of bail exists in Scottish law but legislation currently before the House will end the monetary element in bail in the majority of cases.

2.50 A major Scottish development of recent years was the Social Work (Scotland) Act 1968 which ended the separate existence of the probation service in Scotland and vested the probation function in the social services. Also resulting from the Act was the system of Children's Hearings, the philosophy of which was that children should be dealt with according to their needs rather than in respect of any offences they had committed, and that courts were not appropriate for such an approach. The Hearings have taken over most of the responsibility for dealing with children under 16 (and in some cases up to 18) who commit offences or who are in need of compulsory measures of care. Decisions of the Hearings may include supervision or various forms of residential order. Community service was introduced experimentally in Scotland in 1977, and is now being extended under the Community Service by Offenders (Scotland) Act 1978.

Northern Ireland

2.51 The Northern Ireland position is different again. There is no parole system in the Province, but there is instead a system of half remission, with liability to be ordered to serve the balance of the sentence, in addition to any fresh sentence, upon a further conviction of an imprisonable offence. These arrangements were introduced under the Treatment of Offenders (Northern Ireland) Order 1976, which also provided for the introduction of Community Service in Northern Ireland (in the event it was not possible to implement this particular provision until 1979). Powers exist for the suspension and deferment of sentences, but there are no detention centres or day training centres for offenders under 21, and no provisions for ordering reparation by offenders. Under provisions of the Treatment of Offenders Act (Northern Ireland) 1968, introduced in June 1979, courts in Northern Ireland may not sentence offenders under 21 to imprisonment other than for a period of three years or more. Offenders for whom less than three years is considered appropriate must be sentenced to borstal training or be ordered to be detained in a young offenders centre.

CHAPTER THREE

THE PRISON POPULATIONS

3.1 This chapter describes the UK's current penal populations, explains their recent and likely future trends, seeks to put them in their international context, and with particular reference to England and Wales examines ways in which the populations may be reduced.

Current populations

3.2 The various inmate populations at 30 June/1 July 1979 for England and Wales, Scotland, and Northern Ireland respectively were as follows:

England and Wales

MALES	CNA	Population
Remand Centres	1,881	2,237
Local Prisons	11,691	17,023
Closed Training Prisons	11,849	11,440
Open Prisons	3,508	3,128
Closed Borstals	3,860	3,508
Open Borstals	1,873	1,509
Senior Detention Centres	1,306	1,355
Junior Detention Centres	657	685
MALE TOTALS	**36,625**	**40,885**

FEMALES	CNA	Population
Closed Prisons and Remand Centres	685	887
Open Prisons	366	390
Closed Borstals	165	117
Open Borstal	40	40
FEMALE TOTALS	**1,256**	**1,434**
GRAND TOTALS	**37,881**	**42,319**

Scotland

MALES	Design Capacity	Population
Prisons	3,296	2,985
Open Prison	68	32
Young Offenders' Institutions ...	679	591
Borstals	639	446
Detention Centre	180	104
Remand Institution	197	281
MALE TOTALS	**5,059**	**4,439**

Prison	...	...	...	124	117
Young Offenders' Institution		...	42	11
Borstal	...	...	...	53	44

FEMALE TOTALS	219	172

GRAND TOTALS	5,278	4,611

(The population figures for Scotland are artificially depressed by the effects of industrial action in the Scottish courts during the winter 1978/9.)

Northern Ireland

MALES	CNA		Population
	Cells	Huts	
Cellular Prisons	1,600	—	1,756
Compound Prison	—	1,040	776
Open Borstal	80 (Dormitory)		93
Closed Borstal	54	—	75

FEMALES			
Cellular Prison	110	—	86

GRAND TOTALS	1,844	1,040	2,786

3.3 Apart from absolute differences of scale and the need to allow for seasonal distortions, the figures illustrate relative differences in capacity between the three systems. In England and Wales the average population is about 12 per cent greater than the CNA, in Scotland about 1 per cent, and in Northern Ireland about 10·5 per cent. A further measure of capacity is the level of cell-sharing. Over the last 10 years, this has in England and Wales been as follows:

Highest Totals	Two in a cell	Three in a cell	Total
1969	2,886	7,653	10,539
1970	4,886	9,288	14,174
1971	6,212	8,238	14,450
1972	7,128	6,609	13,737
1973	8,388	4,221	12,609
1974	10,024	4,122	14,146
1975	10,342	5,298	15,640
1976	10,726	5,709	16,435
1977	11,040	4,950	15,990
1978	11,016	5,082	16,098

As might be expected this problem is not so serious in Scotland where the figures for the last 3 years are:

Highest Totals	Two in a cell	Three in a cell	Total
1976	1,084	763	1,847
1977	912	319	1,231
1978	1,268	217	1,485

Cell-sharing in Northern Ireland has had an entirely different history from Great Britain. In 1978 the highest number required to share cells was 904, 66 three to a cell, and 838 two to a cell. Dealing in round figures, this means nearly 40 per cent of the population in England and Wales currently shared cells, nearly 30 per cent in Scotland, and over 20 per cent in Northern Ireland. These figures do not, of course, reflect absolute demands: they are in part the result of operational decisions about how the populations should be allocated to the available accommodation. How and why this is done is something with which we shall deal later when looking at the use of accommodation.

Modern Developments

(a) England and Wales

3.4 Figure 3.1 shows how the average daily population in England and Wales has changed over the last 100 years. It reflects since 1945 the post war rise in crime.

3.5 Figure 3.2 shows how the main components of the average daily prison population have changed since 1947. The average daily population has increased by nearly 2½ times. The number of remand prisoners has increased more than fourfold: this is partly the result of increases in reception but also partly due to the increased average time these prisoners are held on remand. There are now 2,000 young offenders in detention centres. A summary of the relevant figures is as follows:

	1947	1957	1967	1977	1978
Remand prisoners	1,211	1,783	3,066	5,281	5,631
Sentenced prisoners:					
Imprisonment	12,264	16,423	23,827	28,075	27,979
Borstal Training	3,163	3,409	6,055	5,798	5,692
Detention Centre	—	234	1,608	1,786	1,890
Civil prisoners	429	753	453	630	604
TOTAL	17,067	22,602	35,009	41,570	41,796

31

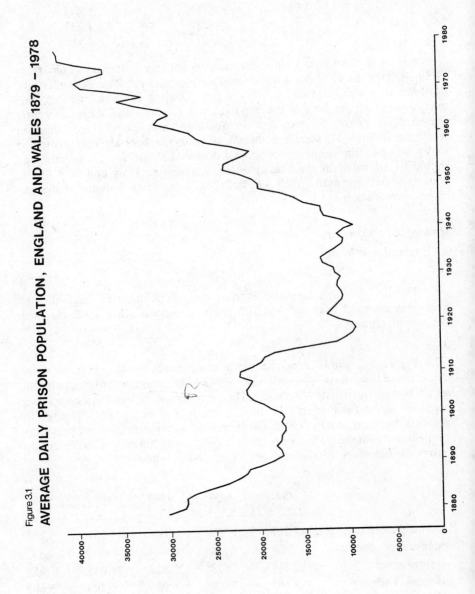

Figure 3.1
AVERAGE DAILY PRISON POPULATION, ENGLAND AND WALES 1879 – 1978

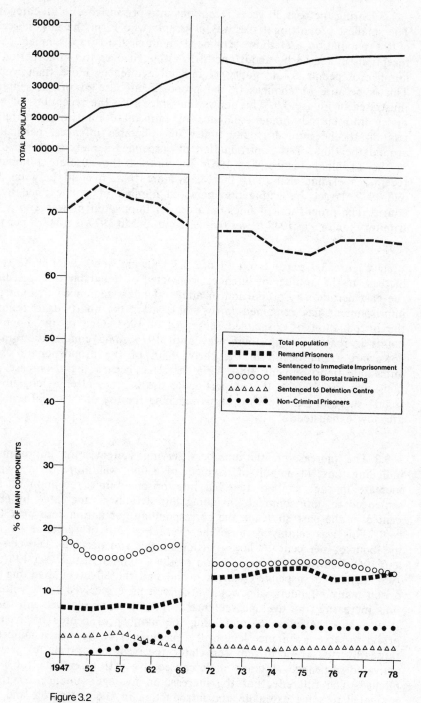

Figure 3.2

CHANGES IN AVERAGE DAILY PRISON POPULATION SINCE 1947 ENGLAND AND WALES

33

3.6 During the past 30 years receptions into prisons rose in all categories. The smallest proportional rise was of people who form the largest section of the population, i.e. those sentenced to immediate imprisonment. Such receptions increased by about one-fifth, although over the same period the number of people found guilty of indictable offences more than trebled. This is because of changes in the proportionate use of prison sentences illustrated in Figure 3.3. This shows that since 1955 the receptions of adult males into custody under sentence of immediate imprisonment fell in relation to the number found guilty of indictable offences, particularly around the time of the introduction of suspended sentences provided for in the Criminal Justice Act 1967. In contrast the absolute number of receptions of fine defaulters increased more than fivefold between 1947 and 1977, largely reflecting the increased number of people fined by the courts. The proportion of fines enforced by imprisonment was also a contributory factor: in 1947 it was 0·6 per cent, and in 1977 it was 0·9 per cent.

3.7 Figure 3.4 expands on Figure 3.3 showing how, despite the steady increase in the number of offenders convicted of indictable offences during the past decade, the proportion of adult offenders sentenced to immediate imprisonment has remained fairly stable after the sharp drop following the introduction of suspended sentences in 1968. One of the important points is that although there was until 1974 some continuation in the downward trend begun in the early 1950s of the proportionate use of immediate imprisonment, since 1975 there has been a slight increase. This fact—and the drop in the proportionate use of fines after a long upward trend—suggests that trends towards reducing the use of custodial sentences are now exhausted.

3.8 The increase in the numbers serving sentences of imprisonment, including those in default of payment of a fine, was more rapid than the increase in the numbers received into prison. While reception of those sentenced to imprisonment, including fine defaulters, increased by 60 per cent over the past 30 years, the corresponding population rose by 130 per cent. This was mainly because the average length of sentence increased by about 60 per cent. A large portion of this rise occurred between 1967 and 1968 following the introduction of the Criminal Justice Act 1967. The Act introduced suspended sentences and had the effect of diverting from prison many offenders who would otherwise have received short sentences, thus increasing the average sentence length of those received into prison. It also had the effect of increasing the number of people received into prison to serve a sentence length of a medium term, because a minority of those diverted from prison were later received into prison to serve an activated suspended sentence made consecutive with a sentence for a fresh offence. The full effect of the increase in average sentence length was mitigated to some extent by the introduction in 1968 of parole and other changes which meant that remission could be earned on the whole term of the sentence including time served on remand in custody before conviction.

34

Figure 3.3

RECEPTIONS INTO CUSTODY PER 1000 FOUND GUILTY OF INDICTABLE OFFENCES—MALES 1955–78 ENGLAND AND WALES

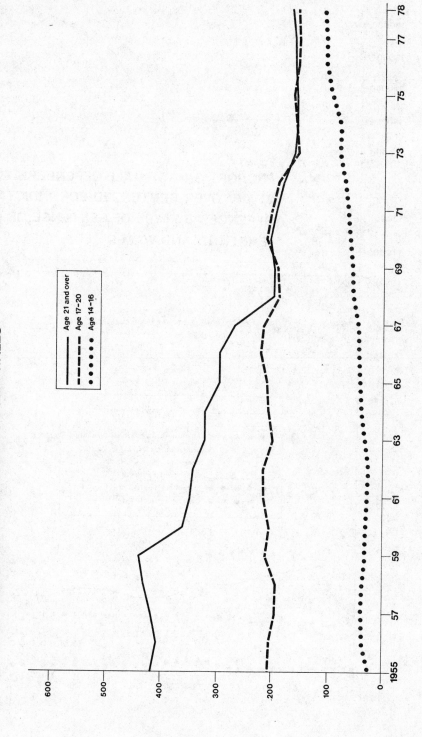

Age 21 and over
Age 17–20
Age 14–16

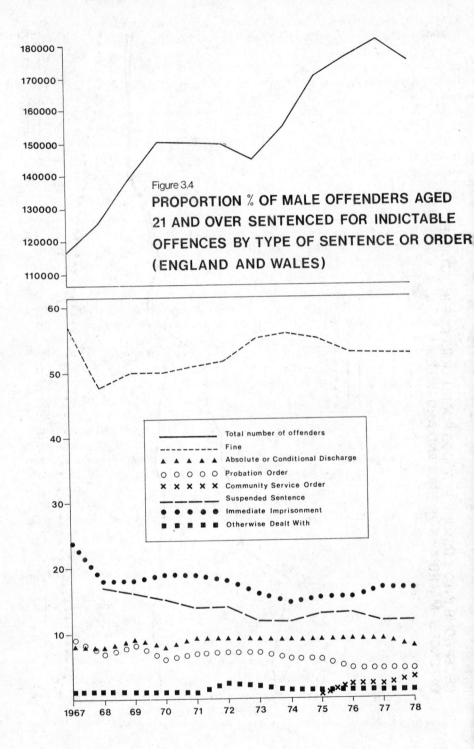

Figure 3.4

PROPORTION % OF MALE OFFENDERS AGED 21 AND OVER SENTENCED FOR INDICTABLE OFFENCES BY TYPE OF SENTENCE OR ORDER (ENGLAND AND WALES)

Total number of offenders
Fine
▲ ▲ ▲ ▲ ▲ Absolute or Conditional Discharge
○ ○ ○ ○ ○ Probation Order
✕ ✕ ✕ ✕ ✕ Community Service Order
Suspended Sentence
● ● ● ● ● Immediate Imprisonment
■ ■ ■ ■ ■ Otherwise Dealt With

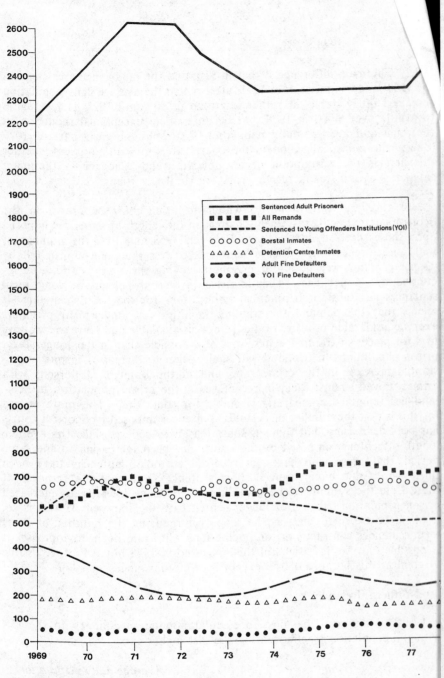

Figure 3.5

AVERAGE DAILY POPULATION – SCOTLAND – 1969-1978

3.9 The largest proportionate increase in the numbers received into custody over the period was in the number of young people received under sentence of borstal training or detention in a detention centre. The table on page 38 shows that they increased tenfold from 1902 in 1947 to 19,037 in 1978. This expansion was associated with the introduction of the detention centre system in 1952. Receptions into detention centres rose during the period as accommodation became available and this sentence was imposed in 1977 in over 7 per cent of all cases where a male juvenile was found guilty of an indictable offence. The table also shows that these changes happened in both the 14–16 and the 17–20 age groups. Nevertheless there was at the same time an increase over the period as a whole in the number of receptions of young people sentenced to imprisonment.

3.10 In contrast to the position with adults sentenced to imprisonment, the population of young people in borstals and detention centres has risen more slowly than the numbers received into custody. In the case of the borstals this occurred because the average training time was reduced—from about 20 months in 1947 to nine months in 1977. In the detention centres the population and receptions expanded together during the late 1950s and early 1960s when there was a rapid expansion in the number of places available. But on two occasions the pressure was reduced by increases in the remission granted to those in detention centres. In 1968 remission was increased from one-sixth to one-third to be the same as remission granted to prisoners; and in 1975, by which time the expansion in the demand for places in junior detention centres had outstripped the accommodation available, remission was increased in the junior centres from one-third to one-half. This mean that, with the same number of places, junior centres could take more receptions over a period, and the courts have taken full advantage of this. In part this rise in the numbers of receptions of young offenders into borstals and detention centres was due to the increasing number of offenders coming before the courts, but in the case of those aged 14–16 since the second half of the 1960s the courts have also been using custodial sentences for an increasing proportion of those sentenced as can be seen in Figure 3.3.

(b) Scotland

3.11 As the table below shows, the broad pattern of development during this century was generally similar to that in England and Wales:

Year						Average daily population
1910	...	...	...	...	...	2,777
1914	...	...	...	...	...	2,694
1921	...	...	...	...	...	1,874
1925	...	...	...	...	...	1,891
1930	...	...	...	...	...	1,670
1935	...	...	...	...	...	1,851
1938	...	...	...	...	...	1,543
1945	...	...	...	...	...	1,955
1952	...	...	...	...	...	2,089
1957	...	...	...	...	...	2,169

RECEPTIONS UNDER SENTENCE OF YOUNG PERSONS: BY AGE GROUP, 1947–78, ENGLAND AND WALES

Age	Type of sentence	1947	1952	1957	1962	1967	1972	1973	1974	1975	1976	1977	1978
14–16	Imprisonment	33	4	9	1	15	22	50	25	42	57	68	78
	Borstal training	286	186	179	402	587	1,117	1,208	1,300	1,583	1,748	1,782	1,741
	Detention centre	—	75	540	634	1,317	2,513	3,062	3,689	4,378	4,890	5,228	5,528
17–20	Imprisonment	2,879	1,366	1,534	2,911	3,668	3,519	3,676	4,344	5,469	6,201	7,120	7,929
	Borstal training	1,616	2,091	2,284	3,456	4,573	5,374	4,846	5,155	6,092	5,848	5,468	5,658
	Detention centre	—	—	553	2,969	5,903	6,694	5,048	5,462	5,825	5,554	5,635	6,110

1962	...	...	...	...	...	3,238
1967	...	...	...	...	...	4,238
1972	...	...	...	...	...	5,220
1977	...	...	...	...	...	4,871
1978	...	...	...	...	...	5,032

3.12 The main difference is that in Scotland the major increases came in the 1960s, reaching a peak in 1971, after which the average daily population remained fairly stable, at rather less than 5,000, until 1977. It rose again to a little over 5,000 in 1978, but because of an exceptional reduction in reception and average daily population figures in the early part of 1979 (due to the industrial action in the courts) it is difficult to assess whether this heralds the resumption of an upward trend. Changes in the main categories of inmates in recent years are shown in Figure 3.5.

3.13 The important trend to which attention must be drawn in the Scottish context concerns recent changes in the length of sentences imposed upon those received into custody. Between 1968 and 1977 the number of male direct receptions to serve sentences of less than one month fell by 23 per cent and receptions of prisoners serving three years and over increased by 46 per cent. This increase in the proportion of long term sentences has substantial practical implications for the Scottish system. It means that the demand for training facilities for longer-term prisoners exerts considerable pressure on the resources available and there are waiting lists for places in training wings. It is also possible that in the longer term prison populations in Scotland will again begin to increase. Despite a substantial increase in the crime rate, and in the number of persons with crimes proved against them in recent years, the prison population in Scotland has remained comparatively stable for some time. The main reason for this is that the number of custodial sentences imposed by Scottish courts has been decreasing, but there is some reason to believe, since the average length of sentence imposed by the courts has been increasing in the same period, that those who have not received custodial sentences have been those who would have received short sentences, and that the removal of these from the system has been masking a tendency towards an increased prison population because of longer sentences being imposed. If this is so, it might be expected that, as the scope for reducing the number of short term sentences contracts, prison populations will again begin to increase. It is possible that the first signs of this appeared in 1978 but it is not possible to confirm this because of the exceptional circumstances in 1979.

(c) Northern Ireland

3.14 This has seen the most spectacular population changes in the UK with the population trebling during the last eight years.

Year						Average daily population
1965	...	...	...	...	...	403
1966	...	...	...	...	...	433
1967	...	...	...	...	...	552

1968	...	...	...	...	...	614
1969	...	...	...	...	...	617
1970	...	...	...	...	...	816
1971	...	...	...	...	...	1,001
1972	...	...	...	...	...	1,498
1973	...	...	...	...	...	1,980
1974	...	...	...	...	...	2,517
1975	...	...	...	...	...	2,687
1976	...	...	...	...	...	2,530
1977	...	...	...	...	...	2,566
1978	...	...	...	...	...	2,947

Taking 1969 as the last "normal" year, the pattern as well as the volume of inmates has changed completely. Whereas in 1969 68 per cent of inmates committed to prison had sentences of less than six months, in 1978 the proportion was about 35 per cent. Similarly, at the other end of the scale, whereas in 1969 only 1 per cent received determinate sentences of more than four years, in 1978 the proportion was over 20 per cent. The different lengths of sentence reflected different kinds of crimes. Whereas in 1969 only 20 per cent of those committed had been found guilty of serious offences (e.g. violence, explosives and firearms offences, robbery and malicious damage), the corresponding proportion in 1978 was about 45 per cent. The largest proportionate increase of all, however, has occurred in the remand population which has grown almost twenty-fold between 1969 and 1978. On the other hand, whereas all remand populations in UK prisons have increased, there are special features in the case of Northern Ireland by virtue of legislation requiring the mandatory reception into custody of people charged with a specified but wide range of offences. Finally, the Northern Ireland system has the unique feature of a declining number of residual "special category" prisoners, i.e. inmates sentenced before March 1976 and who claimed political motivation for their criminal activities.

Some qualitative considerations

3.15 Any discussion, however detailed, of the numbers involved does not by itself indicate what changes, if any, have occurred in the *nature* of the inmate populations. Although this is difficult ground, we attempt to summarise the salient features.

3.16 The most marked changes have occurred, of course, in Northern Ireland. The prison service there has had to cope not only with the most rapid expansion but also with the most changed population. The nature of the change may be inferred fairly directly from the increase in the numbers of those convicted of the more serious crimes.

3.17 The nature of the changes in Great Britain, however, are less obvious. The first general point is that, following the decline in the proportionate use of imprisonment, the penal population is in some senses more especially selected. As a result it tends to consist more of habitual criminals, each with a number of previous convictions, than of first time offenders. On the other hand, this greater criminal sophistication of some —which has also put the borstal system under strain—has exposed the so-called "inadequacy" of other groups (e.g. homeless men with drink problems) and encouraged the wish that they should be dealt with outside the prison system. Peculiar to England and Wales have been the special difficulties over mentally disordered offenders (considered also in paragraphs 3.35–3.44 below) who are in prisons because appropriate places cannot be found for them in psychiatric hospitals. Their presence in identifiable numbers, often in the crowded local prisons, is said to have an effect disproportionate to their numbers, and this we accept. But it is the "hardening" of the population that is thought to be the main feature in recent years. As the Expenditure Commitee put it:

> "This decrease in the proportion of offenders sentenced to imprisonment seems to have occurred because the courts disposed of a wider range of non-custodial sentences and were increasingly willing to use them. The effect of this, together with the introduction of parole, has been to 'cream off' into non-custodial sentences the 'best risks' and to concentrate in the prisons an increasingly difficult, intractable and longer term group of offenders."

(Report, paragraph 19)

Not surprisingly, these changes have been most marked in the dispersal prisons which have had to absorb the worst offenders and these have included increasing numbers of terrorists. In his report on the Hull riot the Chief Inspector wrote:

> "The last five years, specifically, have seen in dispersal prisons the *withdrawal* of the prison officer from a central role involving both custody and treatment to the more peripheral role of observer. This has to a large extent been forced on him by the increasingly sophisticated nature of the prisoner population and some politicisation of crime."

(Report, paragraph 256)

3.18 In addition to the growth in numbers, therefore, there have been other important changes which have had long-term influences on how custodial and other tasks are discharged. In some areas it is possible that the qualitative changes have been more significant than the quantitative ones. Whereas resources deployed by the state can provide an answer to mere quantitative changes, qualitative ones require the deployment from the staff of inner psychological resources. These resources cannot be created by the state, although the state can do much to nourish a climate in which the staff can respond.

Population Forecasts

(a) England and Wales

3.19 All forecasting must involve some uncertainty and, however sophisticated it may be, it would be unwise to rely too much on what the forecasts show. Figure 3.6 combines quinquennium forecasts up to 1982, made in the late summer of 1978 by the Home Office Statistical Department, with longer range forecasts up to 1987, showing the actual figures for 1973–7 for comparison. As the Home Office has pointed out to us, even the short-term forecasts are not precise and have a margin of error which increases the further ahead the forecast is being made. Indeed, such considerations have led the Home Office to confine itself to publishing five year forecasts only and not making—including initially also to us—the 10 year forecasts available publicly.

3.20 The annual forecasts are made separately for each individual category of prisoner: for each such category separate estimates are made of the likely number of receptions and then of changes in the length of time that these prisoners will spend in custody, to arrive at forecasts of the prison population. In recent years there have been marked differences in the growth in the number of receptions and thus of the prison population in different categories. Forecasts of all categories assume a continuation of the increasing trend in the numbers appearing before the courts, although in the case of 14–16 year old males an adjustment has been made for the projected fall in the total population of this age group. In the remand category the projections have assumed that the number of people remanded in custody will in future not match the projected increase in the total number of people prosecuted, because the Bail Act is expected to reduce the number of people remanded in custody. The extent to which such expectations will be met, if at all, must be uncertain. Nonetheless, an arbitrary decision was made to forecast a steady number of receptions of remand prisoners throughout the forecast period. On the other hand, the average time spent in custody on remand was assumed to continue to increase. Thus the remand population was forecast to rise.

3.21 In so far as the forecast of the male inmate population is concerned, a distinction has been made between those aged 17 and over and those aged 14–16. In the former case it is expected that the increase in the number of people found guilty will not be matched by a corresponding increase in custodial disposals; in the latter case it is assumed that the tendency of the courts to use custodial disposals for an increasing proportion of those they find guilty will continue. Nevertheless, this trend has been assumed to continue at a slower rate than in recent years because it was thought likely that the courts would continue to make proportionately smaller use of custodial sentences for juveniles than for adults. No changes have been made to take account of the recommendation in the Report of the Advisory Council on the Penal System, *Young Adult Offenders,* that some kind of generic sentence should be introduced for young people in custody.

3.22 The population of female prisoners is expected to rise faster than that of other categories mainly because of a forecast increase in the actual number of women and girls sentenced to custody. For many years the courts used custodial sentences for women with decreasing frequency but since 1973 the proportion of women sentenced to custody has been stable

43

and the increasing numbers appearing before the courts have caused the population to rise.

3.23 For the reasons we have already mentioned we can understand the difficulties that there are in making forecasts for more than five years ahead. Nevertheless, we think that these should be continued because without them adequately informed long-term planning is impossible. In addition we think there is a case for publishing them with the short-term forecasts. Although we appreciate the public is sometimes prone to regard forecasting wrongly as predictive and blame Departments when what is forecast does not materialise, exposing planning problems as frankly as possible would seem to be an essential part of the open-ness to which we refer elsewhere.

(b) Scotland

3.24 Population forecasts for Scotland made on the same basis as those for England and Wales are shown in Figure 3.7. There are no particular features to which we should draw attention beyond those mentioned generally in the discussion above about the Scottish population.

(c) Northern Ireland

3.25 Forecasts at 30 September in each of the years including 1983 are shown in Figure 3.8. The projections are based on the assumption that current trends in receptions and sentencing patterns will continue over the next five years.

Some international comparisons

3.26 In the UK there are now about 50,000 people contained each day in penal establishments. Although it is difficult to make detailed international comparisons, the available information suggests that the UK prison population is proportionately high compared with other European countries but somewhat lower than in the USA. The reasons for the differences between countries we have found difficult to discover. The population in at least one country (France) is climbing steeply at present but no-one can really say why, and there are also, of course, widespread differences in sentencing behaviour and remand practices. In Europe the UK has a greater proportion of sentenced prisoners but a smaller proportion of remand ones. In the end, most of the differences between countries, although they can be substantial, seem to be differences of degree rather than of kind.

3.27 To this there appear to be only two exceptions: Sweden and the Netherlands. Both countries have developed sentencing practices wholly different from our own and which result in much less resort to prison not only absolutely, but also in the imposition of shorter sentences when imprisonment is used at all. Although it may be possible to discount the Swedish experience to some extent, because of its much smaller population and far less urban character, the Dutch experience cannot be explained so easily. The Netherlands, with a population a little over one-quarter of

3.9 The largest proportionate increase in the numbers received into custody over the period was in the number of young people received under sentence of borstal training or detention in a detention centre. The table on page 38 shows that they increased tenfold from 1902 in 1947 to 19,037 in 1978. This expansion was associated with the introduction of the detention centre system in 1952. Receptions into detention centres rose during the period as accommodation became available and this sentence was imposed in 1977 in over 7 per cent of all cases where a male juvenile was found guilty of an indictable offence. The table also shows that these changes happened in both the 14–16 and the 17–20 age groups. Nevertheless there was at the same time an increase over the period as a whole in the number of receptions of young people sentenced to imprisonment.

3.10 In contrast to the position with adults sentenced to imprisonment, the population of young people in borstals and detention centres has risen more slowly than the numbers received into custody. In the case of the borstals this occurred because the average training time was reduced—from about 20 months in 1947 to nine months in 1977. In the detention centres the population and receptions expanded together during the late 1950s and early 1960s when there was a rapid expansion in the number of places available. But on two occasions the pressure was reduced by increases in the remission granted to those in detention centres. In 1968 remission was increased from one-sixth to one-third to be the same as remission granted to prisoners; and in 1975, by which time the expansion in the demand for places in junior detention centres had outstripped the accommodation available, remission was increased in the junior centres from one-third to one-half. This mean that, with the same number of places, junior centres could take more receptions over a period, and the courts have taken full advantage of this. In part this rise in the numbers of receptions of young offenders into borstals and detention centres was due to the increasing number of offenders coming before the courts, but in the case of those aged 14–16 since the second half of the 1960s the courts have also been using custodial sentences for an increasing proportion of those sentenced as can be seen in Figure 3.3.

(b) Scotland

3.11 As the table below shows, the broad pattern of development during this century was generally similar to that in England and Wales:

Year					Average daily population
1910	...	...	...	...	...	2,777
1914	...	...	...	...	...	2,694
1921	...	...	...	...	...	1,874
1925	...	...	...	...	...	1,891
1930	...	...	...	...	...	1,670
1935	...	...	...	...	...	1,851
1938	...	...	...	...	...	1,543
1945	...	...	...	...	...	1,955
1952	...	...	...	...	...	2,089
1957	...	...	...	...	...	2,169

RECEPTIONS UNDER SENTENCE OF YOUNG PERSONS: BY AGE GROUP, 1947–78, ENGLAND AND WALES

Age	Type of sentence	1947	1952	1957	1962	1967	1972	1973	1974	1975	1976	1977	1978
14–16	Imprisonment	33	4	9	1	15	22	50	25	42	57	68	78
	Borstal training	286	186	179	402	587	1,117	1,208	1,300	1,583	1,748	1,782	1,741
	Detention centre	—	75	540	634	1,317	2,513	3,062	3,689	4,378	4,890	5,228	5,528
17–20	Imprisonment	2,879	1,366	1,534	2,911	3,668	3,519	3,676	4,344	5,469	6,201	7,120	7,929
	Borstal training	1,616	2,091	2,284	3,456	4,573	5,374	4,846	5,155	6,092	5,848	5,468	5,658
	Detention centre	—	—	553	2,969	5,903	6,694	5,048	5,462	5,825	5,554	5,635	6,110

1962	...	...	...	...	...	3,238
1967	...	...	...	...	...	4,238
1972	...	...	...	...	...	5,220
1977	...	...	...	...	...	4,871
1978	...	...	...	...	...	5,032

3.12 The main difference is that in Scotland the major increases came in the 1960s, reaching a peak in 1971, after which the average daily population remained fairly stable, at rather less than 5,000, until 1977. It rose again to a little over 5,000 in 1978, but because of an exceptional reduction in reception and average daily population figures in the early part of 1979 (due to the industrial action in the courts) it is difficult to assess whether this heralds the resumption of an upward trend. Changes in the main categories of inmates in recent years are shown in Figure 3.5.

3.13 The important trend to which attention must be drawn in the Scottish context concerns recent changes in the length of sentences imposed upon those received into custody. Between 1968 and 1977 the number of male direct receptions to serve sentences of less than one month fell by 23 per cent and receptions of prisoners serving three years and over increased by 46 per cent. This increase in the proportion of long term sentences has substantial practical implications for the Scottish system. It means that the demand for training facilities for longer-term prisoners exerts considerable pressure on the resources available and there are waiting lists for places in training wings. It is also possible that in the longer term prison populations in Scotland will again begin to increase. Despite a substantial increase in the crime rate, and in the number of persons with crimes proved against them in recent years, the prison population in Scotland has remained comparatively stable for some time. The main reason for this is that the number of custodial sentences imposed by Scottish courts has been decreasing, but there is some reason to believe, since the average length of sentence imposed by the courts has been increasing in the same period, that those who have not received custodial sentences have been those who would have received short sentences, and that the removal of these from the system has been masking a tendency towards an increased prison population because of longer sentences being imposed. If this is so, it might be expected that, as the scope for reducing the number of short term sentences contracts, prison populations will again begin to increase. It is possible that the first signs of this appeared in 1978 but it is not possible to confirm this because of the exceptional circumstances in 1979.

(c) Northern Ireland

3.14 This has seen the most spectacular population changes in the UK with the population trebling during the last eight years.

Year						Average daily population
1965	...	...	...	...	...	403
1966	...	...	...	...	...	433
1967	...	...	...	...	...	552

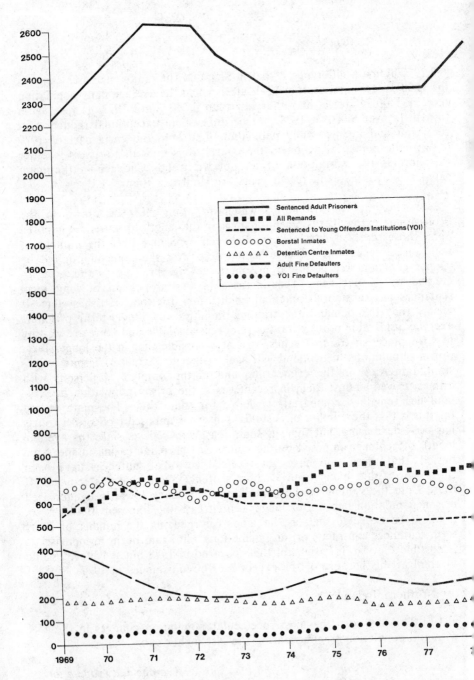

Figure 3.5
AVERAGE DAILY POPULATION-SCOTLAND-1969-1978

40

1968	...	...	...	...	...	614
1969	...	...	...	...	...	617
1970	...	...	...	...	...	816
1971	...	...	...	...	...	1,001
1972	...	...	...	...	...	1,498
1973	...	...	...	...	...	1,980
1974	...	...	...	...	...	2,517
1975	...	...	...	...	...	2,687
1976	...	...	...	...	...	2,530
1977	...	...	...	...	...	2,566
1978	...	...	...	...	...	2,947

Taking 1969 as the last "normal" year, the pattern as well as the volume of inmates has changed completely. Whereas in 1969 68 per cent of inmates committed to prison had sentences of less than six months, in 1978 the proportion was about 35 per cent. Similarly, at the other end of the scale, whereas in 1969 only 1 per cent received determinate sentences of more than four years, in 1978 the proportion was over 20 per cent. The different lengths of sentence reflected different kinds of crimes. Whereas in 1969 only 20 per cent of those committed had been found guilty of serious offences (e.g. violence, explosives and firearms offences, robbery and malicious damage), the corresponding proportion in 1978 was about 45 per cent. The largest proportionate increase of all, however, has occurred in the remand population which has grown almost twenty-fold between 1969 and 1978. On the other hand, whereas all remand populations in UK prisons have increased, there are special features in the case of Northern Ireland by virtue of legislation requiring the mandatory reception into custody of people charged with a specified but wide range of offences. Finally, the Northern Ireland system has the unique feature of a declining number of residual "special category" prisoners, i.e. inmates sentenced before March 1976 and who claimed political motivation for their criminal activities.

Some qualitative considerations

3.15 Any discussion, however detailed, of the numbers involved does not by itself indicate what changes, if any, have occurred in the *nature* of the inmate populations. Although this is difficult ground, we attempt to summarise the salient features.

3.16 The most marked changes have occurred, of course, in Northern Ireland. The prison service there has had to cope not only with the most rapid expansion but also with the most changed population. The nature of the change may be inferred fairly directly from the increase in the numbers of those convicted of the more serious crimes.

3.17 The nature of the changes in Great Britain, however, are less obvious. The first general point is that, following the decline in the proportionate use of imprisonment, the penal population is in some senses more especially selected. As a result it tends to consist more of habitual criminals, each with a number of previous convictions, than of first time

41

offenders. On the other hand, this greater criminal sophistication of some
—which has also put the borstal system under strain—has exposed the
so-called "inadequacy" of other groups (e.g. homeless men with drink
problems) and encouraged the wish that they should be dealt with outside
the prison system. Peculiar to England and Wales have been the special
difficulties over mentally disordered offenders (considered also in paragraphs
3.35–3.44 below) who are in prisons because appropriate places cannot be
found for them in psychiatric hospitals. Their presence in identifiable
numbers, often in the crowded local prisons, is said to have an effect
disproportionate to their numbers, and this we accept. But it is the "hardening" of the population that is thought to be the main feature in recent years.
As the Expenditure Commitee put it:

> "This decrease in the proportion of offenders sentenced to imprison-
> ment seems to have occurred because the courts disposed of a wider
> range of non-custodial sentences and were increasingly willing to use
> them. The effect of this, together with the introduction of parole, has
> been to 'cream off' into non-custodial sentences the 'best risks' and
> to concentrate in the prisons an increasingly difficult, intractable and
> longer term group of offenders."
>
> (Report, paragraph 19)

Not surprisingly, these changes have been most marked in the dispersal
prisons which have had to absorb the worst offenders and these have
included increasing numbers of terrorists. In his report on the Hull riot
the Chief Inspector wrote:

> "The last five years, specifically, have seen in dispersal prisons the
> *withdrawal* of the prison officer from a central role involving both
> custody and treatment to the more peripheral role of observer. This
> has to a large extent been forced on him by the increasingly sophisti-
> cated nature of the prisoner population and some politicisation of
> crime."
>
> (Report, paragraph 256)

3.18 In addition to the growth in numbers, therefore, there have been
other important changes which have had long-term influences on how
custodial and other tasks are discharged. In some areas it is possible that
the qualitative changes have been more significant than the quantitative
ones. Whereas resources deployed by the state can provide an answer to
mere quantitative changes, qualitative ones require the deployment from
the staff of inner psychological resources. These resources cannot be
created by the state, although the state can do much to nourish a climate
in which the staff can respond.

Population Forecasts

(a) England and Wales

3.19 All forecasting must involve some uncertainty and, however
sophisticated it may be, it would be unwise to rely too much on what the

forecasts show. Figure 3.6 combines quinquennium forecasts up to 1982, made in the late summer of 1978 by the Home Office Statistical Department, with longer range forecasts up to 1987, showing the actual figures for 1973–7 for comparison. As the Home Office has pointed out to us, even the short-term forecasts are not precise and have a margin of error which increases the further ahead the forecast is being made. Indeed, such considerations have led the Home Office to confine itself to publishing five year forecasts only and not making—including initially also to us— the 10 year forecasts available publicly.

3.20 The annual forecasts are made separately for each individual category of prisoner: for each such category separate estimates are made of the likely number of receptions and then of changes in the length of time that these prisoners will spend in custody, to arrive at forecasts of the prison population. In recent years there have been marked differences in the growth in the number of receptions and thus of the prison population in different categories. Forecasts of all categories assume a continuation of the increasing trend in the numbers appearing before the courts, although in the case of 14–16 year old males an adjustment has been made for the projected fall in the total population of this age group. In the remand category the projections have assumed that the number of people remanded in custody will in future not match the projected increase in the total number of people prosecuted, because the Bail Act is expected to reduce the number of people remanded in custody. The extent to which such expectations will be met, if at all, must be uncertain. Nonetheless, an arbitrary decision was made to forecast a steady number of receptions of remand prisoners throughout the forecast period. On the other hand, the average time spent in custody on remand was assumed to continue to increase. Thus the remand population was forecast to rise.

3.21 In so far as the forecast of the male inmate population is concerned, a distinction has been made between those aged 17 and over and those aged 14–16. In the former case it is expected that the increase in the number of people found guilty will not be matched by a corresponding increase in custodial disposals; in the latter case it is assumed that the tendency of the courts to use custodial disposals for an increasing proportion of those they find guilty will continue. Nevertheless, this trend has been assumed to continue at a slower rate than in recent years because it was thought likely that the courts would continue to make proportionately smaller use of custodial sentences for juveniles than for adults. No changes have been made to take account of the recommendation in the Report of the Advisory Council on the Penal System, *Young Adult Offenders,* that some kind of generic sentence should be introduced for young people in custody.

3.22 The population of female prisoners is expected to rise faster than that of other categories mainly because of a forecast increase in the actual number of women and girls sentenced to custody. For many years the courts used custodial sentences for women with decreasing frequency but since 1973 the proportion of women sentenced to custody has been stable

43

and the increasing numbers appearing before the courts have caused the population to rise.

3.23 For the reasons we have already mentioned we can understand the difficulties that there are in making forecasts for more than five years ahead. Nevertheless, we think that these should be continued because without them adequately informed long-term planning is impossible. In addition we think there is a case for publishing them with the short-term forecasts. Although we appreciate the public is sometimes prone to regard forecasting wrongly as predictive and blame Departments when what is forecast does not materialise, exposing planning problems as frankly as possible would seem to be an essential part of the open-ness to which we refer elsewhere.

(b) Scotland

3.24 Population forecasts for Scotland made on the same basis as those for England and Wales are shown in Figure 3.7. There are no particular features to which we should draw attention beyond those mentioned generally in the discussion above about the Scottish population.

(c) Northern Ireland

3.25 Forecasts at 30 September in each of the years including 1983 are shown in Figure 3.8. The projections are based on the assumption that current trends in receptions and sentencing patterns will continue over the next five years.

Some international comparisons

3.26 In the UK there are now about 50,000 people contained each day in penal establishments. Although it is difficult to make detailed international comparisons, the available information suggests that the UK prison population is proportionately high compared with other European countries but somewhat lower than in the USA. The reasons for the differences between countries we have found difficult to discover. The population in at least one country (France) is climbing steeply at present but no-one can really say why, and there are also, of course, widespread differences in sentencing behaviour and remand practices. In Europe the UK has a greater proportion of sentenced prisoners but a smaller proportion of remand ones. In the end, most of the differences between countries, although they can be substantial, seem to be differences of degree rather than of kind.

3.27 To this there appear to be only two exceptions: Sweden and the Netherlands. Both countries have developed sentencing practices wholly different from our own and which result in much less resort to prison not only absolutely, but also in the imposition of shorter sentences when imprisonment is used at all. Although it may be possible to discount the Swedish experience to some extent, because of its much smaller population and far less urban character, the Dutch experience cannot be explained so easily. The Netherlands, with a population a little over one-quarter of

44

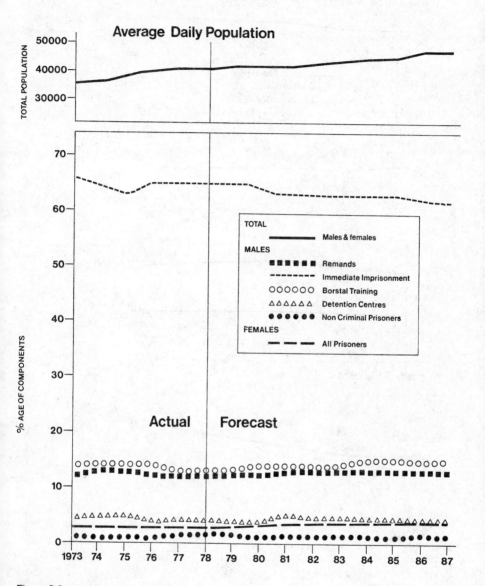

Figure 3.6
ACTUAL AND FORECAST AVERAGE DAILY POPULATIONS ENGLAND AND WALES 1973-1987

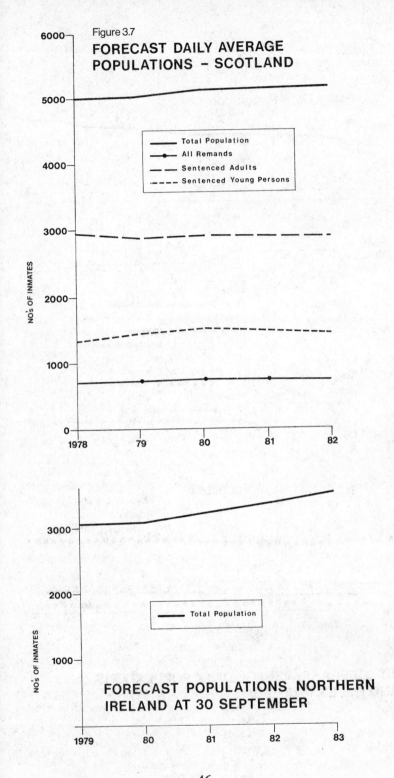

Figure 3.7
FORECAST DAILY AVERAGE
POPULATIONS – SCOTLAND

Total Population
All Remands
Sentenced Adults
Sentenced Young Persons

NOs OF INMATES

6000
5000
4000
3000
2000
1000
0

1978   79   80   81   82

FORECAST POPULATIONS NORTHERN
IRELAND AT 30 SEPTEMBER

Total Population

NOs OF INMATES

3000
2000
1000

1979   80   81   82   83

46

that of the UK, shares many of its densely urban characteristics. In addition it has seen almost identical increases in reported crime to comparable proportionate levels. However the Dutch prison population is only about 3,200 compared with well over 40,000 in England and Wales. In other words, although the general population of England and Wales is less than 4 times the other, the prison population is more than 12 times higher.

3.28 The reason for the difference lies in distinct prosecution and sentencing practices. For example, as the head of the Dutch prison administration, Dr Hans Tulkens, recently pointed out (*Some developments in penal policy and practice in Holland,* NACRO 1979) whilst between 1964 and 1975 reported crime in both countries roughly trebled, the number of custodial sentences increased by 218 per cent in England and Wales but by only 50 per cent in the Netherlands. In the latter country in 1975 almost half the charges were not proceeded with by the public prosecutor and over the years there has been a marked decline not only in the number of prison sentences but also in their length. Such changes have been facilitated by the closely integrated nature of the national prosecution arrangements. The prosecutors are independent officials amounting to about 200 in all, spread over 19 district courts and 5 courts of appeal. They are empowered not to prosecute unless they deem it to be in the public interest and they influence sentencing directly by arguing for particular disposals in court. Curiously, the Netherlands has not we understand developed many alternatives to custody. Amongst other things this is thought to be because the use made of the right not to proceed with cases has in many instances been where the defendants have not been the sort of people for whom a wider range of non-custodial disposals would be appropriate. The relatively undeveloped nature of probation service resources has probably been another reason.

3.29 So far as we are aware, the Dutch practice and experience is unique. Dr Tulkens attributed it to the fact that the penal policy makers in his country had acted upon their growing doubts about the purpose and effect of imprisonment, fed by the evidence of the research to which we shall refer in the next chapter of this report. In their turn, the Dutch prosecutors had felt encouraged and supported by the realisation that there had been substantial social improvements in the Netherlands since the war. In addition, it was easier in a country with as small a general population to obtain wide agreement with the prosecutors' doubts and to the consequent results.

3.30 The advantages of the Dutch practice, not least on cost grounds, are undeniable. However, we think that it is necessary to know much more before one can make a secure judgment upon it. It is possible that the kind of criminality involved is less serious or otherwise different. Further, a great deal depends on the decisions of professional officials before cases reach the courts, whereas in England and Wales the criminal justice system leaves such decisions much more to the courts themselves. Perhaps, nevertheless, these are all matters into which the Royal Commission on Criminal Procedure may wish to look. In any event they prompt reflection about UK sentencing policies and practices, to which we now turn.

3.31 Whilst the prison population has been rising for some time, it would be wrong automatically to assume that it will continue to do so. The extent of criminal behaviour can change. The extent of the reliance by the courts on imprisonment as a sanction against criminal behaviour can also change. However, except for occasional reductions, as in 1973 and 1978, there has been a steady and apparently inexorable upward trend both in the number of crimes reported to the police and in the number coming before the courts. We have neither received nor are we aware of any evidence that these trends are likely to be reversed.

3.32 It follows that the evidence we have considered about the possibility of reducing the prison population has related, first, to redirecting from prison categories of inmate who, it is argued, might be better dealt with elsewhere; secondly, to developing existing or fresh non-custodial alternatives; thirdly, to resorting to various means of direct executive intervention to reduce the penal population; and fourthly, to the prospects for changing sentencing and remanding practices. Because the most acute problems arise in England and Wales, we concentrate on conditions there but we will refer where necessary to any particular features relating to the rest of the United Kingdom.

3.33 We have not overlooked the fact that important cost considerations are involved and we therefore return to some of the issues below when we discuss resources in Chapter 6. Building new prison places (let alone keeping people in prison) is expensive. For example, the unit cost per place in category B and category C prisons is about £40,000 and £20,000 respectively as compared with about £43,000 for a special hospital place but only £23,000 for a purpose-built detoxification centre place and much less (about £7,000 and £4,000 respectively) for converted places in probation hostels and hostels for alcoholics. Keeping the prison population down, therefore, could result in real savings.

Redirection

3.34 The categories of inmate to be considered under this head are mentally disordered offenders, maintenance and fine defaulters, people convicted of offences of drunkenness, and what are sometimes described as inadequate petty offenders, that is people who, although they have committed crimes, are not violent or individually a substantial threat to society.

3.35 There has allegedly been a growing number of mentally disordered offenders in prison. By "mentally disordered" we mean those groups susceptible to treatment, i.e. within the categories of mental illness, subnormality etc of a nature or degree warranting detention in hospitals for medical treatment. This is peculiarly a problem in England and Wales: Scotland and Ireland do not have the same difficulties; in the former country the figures we have seen show that there are more hospital places available than are actually needed. Even though in England and Wales the difficulties do not principally relate to transfers from prisons to hospitals under s.72 of the Mental Health Act 1959, there were on 31 May 1979, 22 cases awaiting transfer, nine of them for more than three months, and one for more than 12 months (Official Report, Commons, 12 June 1979, Cols 169-170).

3.36 The general argument is that, because changes in methods of treatment in mental hospitals have greatly reduced their original need to have secure wards, these hospitals have over the years for various reasons become increasingly reluctant to take mentally disordered offenders. They have gradually abandoned, as it were, their asylum role. This has had the effect that prisons have had to become the institutions of last resort, because the courts have had no alternative but to send offenders who need psychiatric treatment to prison, either because psychiatric hospitals cannot take them or only with a degree of security which the courts feel offers insufficient protection to the public. Further, the prisons are not only generally overcrowded as it is, but they also lack the nursing and other facilities necessary for dealing with such people whose management makes demands on scarce resources out of proportion to their numbers. Their presence also adds to the control problem in prisons and can be as inconvenient and disturbing to inmates as to staff.

3.37 Many examples of this have been brought to our attention by members of the prison medical service, staff generally and Boards of Visitors. In one instance a Board of Visitors told us how on a visit an inmate had been demonstrating the most bizarre behaviour. What is more, this was not the only case of severe mental disturbance observed during that particular visit and the Board commented:

"The effects of this kind of abnormal behaviour by prisoners on a staff not specifically trained in the nursing and care of mentally ill persons are very serious indeed. The officers feel impotent and one can readily understand their viewpoint when faced with this problem as an addition to their prison officers' duties which at best are onerous in a disciplinary section of the prison."

We have also had drawn to our attention the problems encountered by the Parole Board in dealing with offenders who were sent to prison only because no suitable psychiatric place was available, who should not be in prison but whom it is impossible to discharge because there is no suitable alternative place to which they can be sent. Nevertheless, when their sentence expires they have to be discharged irrespective of their condition.

3.38 No-one has sought to argue that this category should in fact be in prison, but there has been some uncertainty both about their numbers and also the urgency with which their problem should be considered. Indeed, some members of the prison medical service are so sceptical of anything ever being done that they feel the Home Office should make the best of a bad job and accept them as a permanent part of the prison population. Whilst we understand why some of these doctors may hold that view, we reject it entirely. Our reasons are effectively summarised by what the Director of Prison Medical Services himself said to us:

"A penal system, any penal system, is an official mechanism designed to inflict deprivation on those who break the law. Just as important as the unpleasantness is the fact that they are, and have to be, highly organised institutions. They contain a lot of people in a small space against their will. There therefore has to be a rigid daily timetable of movement: unlocking, collecting food, exercise, and so on. The mentally disordered cannot cope with this routine or with prison discipline. As prisons are at the moment, a therapeutic environment can be provided for only a tiny minority of inmates."

3.39 We have been unable precisely to establish the numbers involved. The Prison Department estimated in 1976 (Report, Cmnd 6877, paragraph 257) that there were then "some hundreds of offenders who were in need of and capable of gaining benefit from, psychiatric hospital care, management and treatment in psychiatric hospital." Quite how many hundreds is, however, a matter of dispute and a research project is being set up to identify the number and characteristics of the group. On 31 December 1978 there were said by the prison medical service to be 519 such persons, of whom 389 were sentenced (Official Report, Commons, 12 June 1979, Cols. 162–168).

3.40 We were assured there are no differences between the Departments about the right policy. As the Butler Committee on Abnormal Offenders first recommended in July 1974 in their Interim Report (Cmnd 5698), it is that there should be Regional Secure Units (RSUs) established in each of the 14 health service areas in England and Wales capable of accommodating, amongst others, the disordered offenders now in prison. The DHSS told us that present plans are to provide 1,000 places in RSUs in a programme they expect to be completed by 1985. Meanwhile a very few regional authorities have set up interim secure units. Provision is being made in a number of ways, for instance by using or converting existing sites as well as by developing fresh ones. Although we were aware that there had been some suggestions to that effect, it is not apparently the case that sums earmarked for this programme have been diverted irregularly elsewhere, since it was money which was available anyway for general use. The DHSS told us that many problems had been encountered in getting the programme off the ground, e.g. in securing planning agreements and the right staff.

3.41 The Health Department also stressed that RSUs were not to be seen in isolation, just as the more innovative provisions of the Mental Health Act 1959 had not been intended to lead to the abolition of a proper reserve of secure accommodation in ordinary psychiatric hospitals. On the contrary, the DHSS reported to us with approval current moves within the Royal College of Psychiatrists to inform that profession about the problem of caring for the more unrewarding and difficult psychiatric patient. Even relatively small shifts in professional behaviour in psychiatric hospitals (e.g. by taking in one or two more of such patients) would, it was contended, have a considerable impact on a problem which, though important, was relatively small in relation to NHS problems as a whole.

3.42 This last point clearly appeared to us to be an important element in DHSS thinking. As one DHSS witness put it: "The problem of people who are both offenders and ill is that they are a very small group of people compared with the number of people who are either in the prisons or in the health service and, wherever you put them, they are a minority group, and it is very difficult to see how these big services can adjust to look after this minority group without altering the whole structure for what is a very small number of people." This seems to us to put more weight on the convenience of not disturbing the structure of the NHS than ensuring that it carries out its functions effectively. A similar attitude was apparent in their explanation of how it had been difficult to allocate NHS funds to this group: ". . . our priority system, which has a tremendous amount of local participation, means that people would rather spend money on people who are known to be ill than on people who are felt to be offenders and who may be ill as well." To us it seems that something more than bureaucratic convenience and local preferences are at stake. Further, bearing in mind especially the way in which the situation has been handled in Scotland, the differences in England and Wales are all the more difficult to defend.

3.43 Whilst we appreciate there are difficulties now in providing additional places in England and Wales, achievement has fallen so far short of the government's original decision on the Butler Committee recommendations that we are, frankly, more than sceptical that a programme which has achieved so little by 1979 will be completed by 1985. It is impossible to avoid agreeing with the Report of the Expenditure Committee that the NHS in England and Wales has failed to measure up to its responsibilities towards mentally disordered offenders, bearing in mind that no-one contests the undesirability and the injustice of allocating them to penal regimes. Unlike the Expenditure Committee, however, we do not consider that part of the solution is for the Prison Department to expand its psychiatric services (Report, paragraph 77 (i)–(iv)). We think the best way to achieve change is for the DHSS to press regional health authorities as a matter of priority to bring to fruition plans already made and to continue to press them until success crowns their efforts after so many years.

3.44 Finally, when RSUs are established we think that two dangers must be avoided: first, filling their places by transferring to them from psychiatric hospitals those of their patients who are merely troublesome and unrewarding; and secondly, a hardening of attitude in the psychiatric hospitals to the extent that they will take in even fewer disordered offenders than now. In our view the Butler Interim Report rightly emphasised the need to avoid the fragmentation of services for the mentally abnormal offender (Cmnd 5698, paragraph 9) and we think that view should prevail.

3.45 The other groups may for our limited purposes be more briefly covered. There seems no lack of agreement in principle that imprisonment

should be only a last resort for drunkenness, and that, in so far as petty crime is associated with alcoholism, then it is the alcoholism that should be treated preventatively as much as the crime punished. In the same way most of the evidence we received was that imprisonment should be avoided so far as possible for the enforcement of both maintenance orders and fines. We agree that what reasonably can be done should be done to keep both these categories out of prison and that the steps taken under the Criminal Justice (Scotland) Act 1963, the Criminal Justice Act 1967 and the Criminal Law Act 1977 were in the right direction. Whilst we feel that imprisonment has to continue to be available in all these cases as a last resort, and we have to recognise that there are limits as to what may be achieved (e.g. for alcoholics where not all want to receive or complete treatment), no-one could conceivably be satisfied with recent progress over alcoholism. The case of detoxification centres is especially relevant. Following the Habitual Drunkenness Offender Report 1970 and the Criminal Justice Act 1972 only two centres have been set up in England and Wales. We are in no doubt that the ultimate availability of imprisonment should not be permitted by itself to encourage any slackening of effort to provide treatment for alcoholics, or to increase the efficiency of maintenance and fine enforcement short of resort to that final sanction. To accept the continuing need for imprisonment should not imply reliance upon it, or a complacent disregard for developing alternative disposals. As to alcoholism, greater determination seems vital. In addition we think that voluntary endeavour could play a substantial part in this area, provided that grants from government to start and maintain such schemes were made available. We recommend that the DHSS should do so: relatively speaking the sums needed would not be large.

3.46 The phrases "inadequate petty offenders" or "social inadequates" are commonly used as descriptions for groups of men found primarily in local prisons who are felt neither to deserve nor to require the expense of imprisonment. Whilst they may have substantial criminal records, most are for relatively trivial offences and the offenders cannot be said to constitute a danger to the public even though they may well be a substantial nuisance. On examination, however, the groups involved appear to be not only less homogeneous than a good deal of earlier discussion may have tended to suggest, but also more intractable to deal with.

3.47 Recent research has suggested that these groups are not necessarily as prone to alcoholism or to mental illness as was at one time thought. Their main shared objective characteristic is difficulty over accommodation. Describing them as *inadequate* petty offenders or *social inadequates* tends to involve, however accidentally, an overtone of moral judgment on idiosyncrasies of personality and orientation rather than to draw attention to gaps in social welfare or the provision of housing. A more neutral and useful description would be "persistent petty offenders". In addition, whereas much discussion so far has been preoccupied with keeping people out of prison, there is a better case for concentrating on keeping them out of the criminal justice system altogether. This, it has been pointed out, requires an appreciation of police behaviour and the availability of alterna-

52

tive facilities, as well as a knowledge of how in given areas the courts tend to deal with this type of defendant.

3.48 Once this category of offender can be more precisely defined, so more accurately can its size be determined. At present the latter is uncertain. For example, the Expenditure Committee (Report, paragraph 112) quoted estimates which varied btween 1,700 and 10,000 in prisons in England and Wales. Also uncertain is the best way of dealing with the problems the groups present. There appear to be real dilemmas. At present police practice seems generally directed at minimising arrests of vagrants and drunks unless their behaviour offers some kind of threat either to the public or to the alleged offenders themselves. Increasing sheltered accommodation of one kind or another might on the other hand—as apparently in the case of the Leeds detoxification centre—only encourage greater police involvement without decreasing the involvement of the criminal justice system as a whole. Thus, the total effect may not lessen that system's present tendency to take on inappropriate welfare roles. It cannot automatically be assumed either that those who have adopted vagrant ways will accept accommodation even when found for them, any more than it can be assumed that all heavy drinkers will volunteer for treatment. Above all, no-one seems to have found satisfactory ways of redirecting these offenders away from the criminal justice system without recourse to alternative resources. As in so many other cases, therefore, prisons pay the penalty for being the resources that are available as opposed to the one that is appropriate in the particular case.

3.49 Our conclusion is that, although there are still gaps in society's understanding of their problems, nothing shakes the fundamental point that wherever possible petty offenders should not be sent to prison. We were therefore interested to learn amongst others of the creative and useful work being undertaken at Pentonville prison and in West Yorkshire by the local probation and after-care service. We have no easy solutions of our own to offer except to recommend that all the relevant services—and this includes the DHSS, local authorities and voluntary agencies as well as the prison, police and probation services—should be encouraged to develop solutions to the many different kinds of problems petty persistent offenders present. To some extent other measures which we discuss in this part of the report will be relevant. We do not consider, however, that any particular one has a unique contribution to make. We also think that sentencers should be told as much as possible about the findings of the relevant research and practical experiment so that their decisions may be the more informed. On the other hand, the difficulties that sentencers face should not be under-estimated when they are confronted with people whose way of life and rootless existence makes them unsuitable for the usual range of structured non-custodial disposals, even where they are available.

Developing non-custodial alternatives

3.50 By these we mean the range of disposals available to the courts which are devised to allow the courts to deal with offenders outside prison from the outset. The disposals include probation (and all its modern variants, e.g., day training centres), community service orders, and forms of suspended sentence.

3.51 Probation orders have been declining for some years. Although the precise reasons are not clear they are probably because of the changing attitude to "treatment", the devotion of probation resources to fresh tasks and the successive invention of other non-custodial disposals like the suspended sentence and the community service order. It is possible too that the courts, seeing that the probation service had so much to do in other directions reacted in time by employing less and less a disposal likely to receive less and less real attention from the probation service, or in Scotland the Social Work Services. Whether this progressive displacement can be reversed seems open to doubt and, like the Expenditure Committee, we are not too hopeful. We understand, too, that there are no largescale resources available for such a shift back to the probation order, even though useful local changes could no doubt be made.

3.52 As regards the offshoots of probation orders, what little we have been able to learn of day training centres suggests that they have in principle much to commend them, but that they are also highly selective of their clientele, expensive and probably no more effective in their outcomes than any other disposals. In England and Wales probation hostels, expanded since 1972 for adults as well as persons under 21, have made a useful contribution. We were told at the end of 1978 there were 58 hostels with 966 adult places and 12 with 249 for offenders under 21. An expansion so far as resources allow would seem desirable but, again, they seem expensive facilities and they are difficult to establish in the face of resistance from the local community.

3.53 Community service, however, has been the great current success story, growing from nothing in 1972 to over 12,000 orders a year in England and Wales now. Its actual diversionary effect is difficult to estimate but research early in its operation suggested that but for it 50 per cent of those who were made subject to a community service order would otherwise have received custodial sentences. The Expenditure Committee was keen to see it expanded to include fines and maintenance defaulters as well as a greater range of offenders (Recommendations 11 and 46), although that would raise some important questions of principle and practice. For example, community service lacks an obvious rationale for maintenance defaulters where the prime object is to persuade people to pay up rather than purge their offence by exhibiting socially useful attitudes in one context which they have failed to display in another. Similarly, the scope for further growth will probably be limited by diminishing returns if there is attempted expansion into increasingly marginal and less co-operative groups.

3.54 Although the power to suspend sentences (broadly, up to a maximum of two years) has been available since 1967, the power partially to suspend sentences under section 47 of the Criminal Law Act 1977 remains inactivated. We understand this is because of experience of the original power to suspend the whole sentence after 1967. Whilst its introduction then had the immediate effect of reducing the prison population the effect was short-lived because it was followed by a sharp increase as suspended sentences were activated, often with a consecutive sentence for the new offence. From early days it was also apparent that many suspended sentences were being passed where the courts would otherwise have imposed a fine or a probation order instead of a prison sentence. The decrease in the use of immediate prison sentences was much more than offset by the subsequent activation of suspended sentences. Even now, despite a decline in the use of both, if suspended sentences are aggregated with immediate prison sentences, the proportionate use of imprisonment is higher than in the years immediately preceding the introduction of the power to suspend.

3.55 In the face of this experience, there is bound to be caution about the case either for activating section 47 or any variants of expanding suspension, e.g. making section 47 available below the Crown Court, or increasing the ambit of full suspension. The aim of partial suspension in theory is that the initial taste of imprisonment will act as a deterrent thereafter, in effect doing at the sentencing stage what the parole boards try to do later. The difficulty is that the judiciary might, on the lines of what happened originally with suspended sentences, impose the immediate sentence of imprisonment they would have imposed anyway and add a suspended portion to that. Over time, the result would be to increase rather than diminish the prison populations.

Executive intervention

3.56 Under this head we propose to review the ways in which the government of the day may itself directly reduce the population, i.e. by a general once and for all amnesty (e.g. in respect of sentences below a certain maximum of, say, two years where the offences must *ipso facto* be less serious); by an increase in remission from, say, the present one-third to one-half either in respect of all sentences (which is the practice already in junior detention centres in England and Wales) or in respect of sentences up to some stipulated maximum, say three or four years; by a conditional release scheme similar to that operated in Northern Ireland where there is no parole as such but where a defendant conditionally released after serving one-half of his sentence is liable to serve the balance up to the whole of it if there is a conviction for a subsequent offence during that period; or by some system of flexible remission, perhaps on a sliding scale, which varied according to the absolute size of the population and was responsive therefore to overcrowding. Straightforward changes in remission could be accomplished by alterations to the Prison Rules: all the rest would need legislation.

3.57 Of course there are objections to and practical difficulties in all such schemes of intervention. There might be strong public objections to some, however carefully they were drafted to exclude dangerous or serious offenders, and however carefully the schemes were explained. All the changes would involve fresh and direct executive interference, sometimes to an unpredictable (and unprecedented) extent, in judicial discretion. The case for making changes in Scotland is not strong based on the degree of overcrowding there, but it would be forced in any event to fall into line with England and Wales. The morale of law enforcement agencies outside the prison services, especially the police, could be adversely affected.

3.58 Nor should the practical problems be underestimated. An amnesty would have only a once for all effect: if no other long term changes ensued, the prisons would simply fill up again to the same levels. After an initial reduction in the prison population any increase to half remission would have a lesser continuing effect. If introduced for only part of the population, it would induce a sense of injustice amongst the rest, e.g. if the maximum sentence to benefit was two years, then someone sentenced to two years one month would be obliged to serve four months and 20 days longer in prison than someone sentenced to only one month less. Whilst no doubt the parole boards could mitigate such inequities, especially amongst co-defendants, a two-tier system of remission such as this would have all sorts of problems. Of all the possibilities a more sophisticated version of the conditional release scheme operated in Northern Ireland seems on the evidence before us to possess the least disadvantages: for instance, the courts would no doubt have to be given power to stipulate that it should not apply in respect of those on whom long sentences are passed principally for the protection of the public. If introduced, it would mean that parole would have to be abolished. However, it may be noted that the present parole scheme can only do anything for those sentenced to 18 months or more. Schemes of flexible remission would require relatively elaborate arithmetic to ensure that inmates could reliably expect at least a particular maximum sentence and that the changes were not stepped so steeply that very different sentence lengths resulted in identical amounts of time served. In addition, of all the possibilities, it is schemes of flexible remission which are the most nakedly linked to prison population levels and, accordingly, the least reflective of what it was the court on individual merits thought appropriate. Such objections might be reduced, however, by devices like putting to Parliament in annual debate the decision on the appropriate remission rate for a 12 month period.

3.59 Subject to what we have already said about a conditional release scheme, there is one further area that should not be ignored, viz increasing parole. This could be done in two ways: giving parole more generously than at present to those eligible; and increasing eligibility by reducing the parole threshold, at present as we have said a sentence of at least 18 months. The first could be done without fresh legislation but the second could not.

3.60 As to greater generosity, in 1978, 59 per cent of all eligible prisoners were given some parole in England and Wales. (The Scottish rate is about half that for England and Wales.) The growth of parole since 1967 has been a substantial achievement and without the "failure" rate exceeding 10 per cent on average of parolees. Only as little ago as 1974 the proportion in England and Wales paroled was 35 per cent. The increase since has occurred following the more liberal criteria introduced by the then Home

56

Secretary in 1975. It is possible there is room for even more granting of parole, but it must be doubtful whether there is much when it would seem reasonable to assume that the overwhelming majority of the "good risks" are already identified under the present criteria.

3.61 The difficulty of reducing the parole threshold itself is that the more thorough the reduction, the slenderer would be the basis upon which parole decisions are made. At present parole is granted, amongst other things, as a result of reports made by practised observers on the conduct of inmates during their sentences. Although the paroling process takes about four months, it means that even for the shortest sentences there should still have been a reasonable period in which to observe behaviour and put the offender fairly and reliably in his social context. Dropping the threshold only so far as to 12 month sentences and retaining a one-third (or creating even a one-half) parole eligibility date would not only greatly increase the number of cases to be considered (and therefore the cost of the scheme) but also would inevitably rob the internal review process of any validity and in practice require decisions to be taken on such social inquiry and other information available to the courts in the first place. In as much as even present parole arrangements are criticised for the propensity to re-sentence offenders, then such criticisms would have more force since the parole system would be in little different position from the courts who had originally passed sentence. In other words, parole would at such levels cease to have any independent rationale and its credibility (let alone acceptability) would disappear. Worse, the credibility of what the paroling system continued to do at the upper sentence levels might suffer too.

3.62 In our opinion, whilst it would be wrong for any of these various kinds of change to be ruled out, none is free from difficulty and most would tend so to alter the balance within the criminal justice system that it would be difficult to be confident about their outcomes. Nonetheless there seems to be no overwhelming objection in principle to any of them and it is possible circumstances may justify resort to them.

Changing sentencing and remand practices

3.63 As we point out in Chapter 4 the climate of opinion about the efficacy of imprisonment as a "treatment" has been changing for some years. It has also been changing in respect of imprisonment's effectiveness as a general deterrent. The relevant facts and arguments are set out in the Interim Report, *The Length of Prison Sentences,* of the ACPS in May 1977. Invited to review the maximum penalties available to the courts, in its Interim Report the Advisory Council concluded:

"In considering the influence the system of maximum penalties has or has not had on the behaviour of the courts, we have inevitably had to study current sentencing practice. In the course of that study we have come unanimously to the conclusion that a large number of sentences of imprisonment passed by the courts, especially in the short and medium term band of sentences, are longer than they need be, in the interests either of society or of the offender".

(Paragraph 3)

3.64 We have neither received nor have our inquiries disclosed any evidence that conflicts with this view. We are unanimous and emphatic in endorsing it. Whatever qualifications must be made about how these things are done abroad, it remains the case that Dutch and Scandinavian experience demonstrates that civilised society can coexist with significantly lower sentencing tariffs. Whilst we are as concerned as anyone about giving full weight to the demands of retributive and deterrent justice as well as the need at the very least to keep some kinds of offenders out of circulation for substantial periods, the fact that other advanced societies have achieved an imprisoning balance qualitatively different from ours cannot be set aside. It strongly reinforces, of course, one of the Interim Report's concluding reflections:

> "In our view, a sound penal philosophy must place a greater reliance upon data about the effectiveness of our penal system and move away from tradition and emotional reactions to crime and punishment."
>
> (Paragraph 20)

The later press reaction to the Advisory Council's main report, *A Review of Maximum Penalties,* published in 1978, demonstrated how sound was the point about emotional reactions.

3.65 It is not our business to comment on specific recommendations of the Advisory Council. However, we must be concerned with their tendency and effect. We hope very much they will be acted upon by the courts now so far as possible and, ultimately, by Parliament. In the long run they represent amongst present available means the best prospect for reducing the prison population. In the short run, however, their impact can be but gradual. Nevertheless, they could certainly give relief, but it will not be immediate relief or come, when it comes, all at once.

3.66 Remand practices are in a different category. We have already drawn attention to the fact that, apart from the detention centre population, the rate of increase in remand prisoners since the war was the highest for all groups of prisoners in England and Wales. It must also be a matter of continuing concern that as many as 44 per cent of those remanded in custody do not receive an immediate sentence of imprisonment and, further, that remand periods in England and Wales are frequently excessively long and have generally been increasing. The Bail Act 1976 reinforced changes in bail procedures implemented following a Home Office circular in 1975, and the Criminal Law Act 1977 sought to reduce Crown Court delays in a number of ways. Whilst the effect of the earliest of these measures was to reduce to 17 per cent the percentage of those committed for trial who were remanded in custody, we have been surprised to see that figure reached 19 per cent in 1978. We hope this does not represent a new trend and that no effort will be spared to minimise custodial remand in future.

3.67 The development of bail hostels has been important because they provide an opportunity to release on bail, on condition of residence in a hostel, people who would otherwise have been remanded in custody because they have no fixed address. There were in England and Wales 286 available places at the end of 1978, with 78 others in the pipeline and plans for more.

They seem admirable and we support their reasonable extension. As to the rest, the need remains even greater than it did prior to 1972 of doing everything possible to bring defendants remanded in custody to trial as soon as possible.

3.68 In passing it is worthy of note that in Scotland the law has since the nineteenth century provided that all accused must be brought to trial within 110 days of a custodial remand provided the whole period has been spent in custody and that, although it is possible more custodial remand proportionately is used, it is on average shorter. We have considered whether there might not be a place in England and Wales for a similar provision. However, it has been pointed out to us that a mere statutory requirement without the simultaneous provision of court and judicial resources to respond to it would achieve nothing. We were reminded, too, that emergency legislation was introduced in Scotland to suspend the requirement because of industrial action by court staff.

Conclusions

3.69 Although everyone who comes to it for the first time may think so, in fact none of this ground is new. Redirection is in principle desirable, especially for mentally disordered offenders, but will not be productive of much relief to present population levels either by itself or in respect of other groups. New non-custodial disposals are highly desirable, but only where they can be calculated not ultimately to make the problems for prisons worse. Executive intervention is available, but chiefly perhaps to cope with a condition of actual as opposed to imminent crisis. The result of changed sentencing practice can only be realised over a long period and without predictable population effects. The scope for less remand in custody may, at least for the moment, be exhausted. For the purposes of this Inquiry, therefore, none of these means offers substantial relief and we are obliged to conclude the population forecasts offered by the Home Departments are well-founded. On the other hand, they cannot be exact and, such seems to us to be the penal momentum at present, that we feel they are more likely to underestimate than exaggerate current trends.

3.70 At this point we think that we should make some additional general points. Whilst we have not overlooked the possibility of creating fresh alternatives to imprisonment, it seems very likely that over-hopeful—sometimes merely fashionable—expectations of non-custodial disposals have persistently been used to defend the allocation of inadequate resources to the prison services in Great Britain, and particularly in England and Wales. (It may have been significant, for example, that in our view the Treasury evidence tended to exaggerate this point.) Indeed, it seems sometimes assumed that "alternatives" automatically mean alternatives to imprisonment when they may mean nothing more than replacing existing non-custodial sentences.

3.71 There seem to be two ways of looking at what has happened here. On the one hand, there has been a natural reluctance to invest in penal institutions and a preference for developing more attractive, community based alternatives in partnership with the burgeoning social work professions. On the other hand, this has, relatively, diverted resources away from penal establishments and the staff trying to run them. There can, of course, be no criticism of that *per se,* but it cannot simultaneously be used as a justification for starving prisons of the resources they need, unless individually or collectively genuine alternatives to imprisonment can demonstrably produce actual and substantial reductions of a lasting kind in the prison population. Finally, some observers have pointed out that as a society we should be cautious about the long run effects of placing more mechanisms of social control in the community in the guise of alternatives to custody. The result in the end may be only to increase rather than decrease the number of people drawn into the criminal justice system, and generally to augment the apparatus of state intervention.

3.72 However, although we have throughout this chapter tried to be realistic, we do not intend in any way to appear despairing. For this reason and in the light of our other findings elsewhere in this report we think that all available and any future devised methods to reduce the populations should receive urgent examination and, wherever possible, action. At the very least the combined effects of the measures we have described above should be to help check the increasing penal populations, and in the long run some could do more. We are fully aware that the success of policies here will have implications for the allocation of resources to the prison services, and we take account of that fact in Chapter 6. The point remains, however, that the existence of these possibilities, and the hope they must carry for individuals who without them could expect to be in prison, cannot absolve society from the duty of continuing to support for the foreseeable future a substantial penal population.

CHAPTER 4

OBJECTIVES AND REGIMES

4.1 At a very early stage in our deliberations it became clear that we could not do justice to a substantial part of our terms of reference without first considering, and reaching conclusions upon, the purpose of imprisonment.

4.2 Clearly its first objective must be the secure custody of the prisoners, whether convicted or on remand. Society expects that any person committed to prison by the courts will be kept there by the prison service using whatever degree of security is necessary for that particular inmate. This objective is becoming increasingly important in the light of the growing numbers of terrorists, dangerous murderers and other sophisticated, violent and professional criminals on whom the courts pass long sentences for at least the principle purpose of protecting society from their further depredations for a substantial time. But these represent only a small proportion of the prison population: in June 1978 76 per cent of it was serving terms of 18 months or less and 95 per cent terms of four years or less. For the great majority of the prison population, therefore, and indeed for those serving long sentences as well, is mere containment or custody the only objective? We cannot accept that this is so. But if it is not, to what other objectives should those who manage and staff our prisons aspire in carrying out their respective tasks?

4.3 A great deal of the evidence we received maintained that at the present time these objectives were unclear or confused or both, and that this had brought about or contributed not only to a lack of incisive and purposeful leadership but also to indecision, frustration and the consequent lowering of morale throughout the prison service. Whilst we are not satisfied that this is the cause of all the ills which presently afflict the service, we think that confusion about objectives has been a significant cause of the present malaise. Further, it is also clear from this and other evidence given to us that informed opinion about the purpose and expectations of imprisonment has been undergoing significant changes in recent years. Finally, people generally do have very different expectations of what imprisonment can achieve. Despite the great variety in the inmate population, its differing character and its various needs, the world outside expects prisons in varying degrees to contain, punish, deter and rehabilitate, although not necessarily in that order, or in all cases. To achieve each of these requirements and expectations simultaneously is not possible, and we are satisfied that no short statement of objectives is feasible.

BACKGROUND

4.4 Despite its ancient roots, modern imprisonment in Britain arrived only with industrial society itself. When it became no longer possible or acceptable to exile offenders altogether from the rapidly rising urban populations by transporting them, alternatives had to be found. The same reasoning which had led to the workhouse and the mental asylum produced institutions for criminals also. In effect exile was continued but the new penal colonies were to be within and not outside the society against whom the inmates had offended.

4.5 This new institutional involvement of the state required a new public ethic. At first it was concerned with imposing deterrent, retributive justice on offenders, whilst being prepared to hold out the hope of a staged return to society when this had been earned. In their attempt to achieve this our Victorian predecessors employed a great deal of their engineering and organising skills. No more than now, however, was there agreement on aims. On the contrary, different people stressed different elements at different times.

4.6 In a famous passage in its report, the Gladstone Committee in 1895 sought to knit the two objectives together: "We start from the principle that prison treatment should have as its primary and concurrent objects deterrence and reformation." This was adopted as official policy and the base from which any subsequent discussion or action in penal practice should start.

4.7 Post-Gladstone developments, however, were slow, the most important changes in the period up to the First World War being, as Chapter 2 has shown, in respect of young offenders in the borstal system. The rather different climate in the period between the Wars, when further developments occurred in regard to adult as well as young offenders, took place, significantly, against the background of a remarkably stable prison population in which there was little anxiety about rising crime. The apparent success of borstal training, together with a number of other factors, sustained the reformist tradition in the less favourable environment which followed the Second World War, and encouraged the important innovations in adult prisons that we have described in Chapter 2. Despite Paterson's paradox about trying to train men for freedom in conditions of captivity, the belief appeared firmly established that "treatment" capable of changing men for the better was possible in penal institutions.

4.8 The clearest declaration of this view is the one endorsed for England and Wales by Parliament in Rule 1 of The Prison Rules 1964 (1964 S.I. No. 388):

"The purpose of the training and treatment of convicted prisoners shall be to encourage and assist them to lead a good and useful life".

This was not, however, the first time this wording had been used. A virtually identical Rule had existed less prominently since 1949, just as the Scottish equivalent of Rule 1 is to be found in Rule 5 of The Prison (Scotland) Rules 1952 (1952 S.I. No. 565). (There is no equivalent in the Northern Ireland Rules.) All the 1964 Rules did was to put the treatment objective officially at the head of the list and thus give it special force.

4.9 The concepts implicit in Rule 1 still remain the formal ideology and there can be no doubt that they have had beneficial effects for inmates. Real attempts have been made to enrich penal regimes, although less successfully in local prisons; industry has been improved; education, vocational training and welfare have all been greatly expanded. These changes have not only required prison staff of all grades from governors down to approach their traditional tasks differently, they have also involved the introduction into prisons and into the prison service itself of specialists of many callings.

4.10 However, confidence in the treatment model, as it is usually called, has now been waning throughout the Western world for some years. The drive behind the original borstal ideas has fallen away and there is now no belief that longer sentences may be justified because they make actual reformative treatment more possible. There are several causes for this.

4.11 First, there has been the cumulative impact of the work of social scientists in the United Kingdom, Europe and North America. They have demonstrated how closed "total" institutions function and how the environment which they provide limits their reformative capacity. In addition, intensive research has so far failed to demonstrate that any particular penal regime is superior to another, or has any general success from the rehabilitative point of view. The current (1978) edition of *The Sentence of the Court,* the official manual for sentences published by the Home Office, puts it—"there is no evidence that the prison system does or can exert such a positive reformative influence as to justify the imposition of a longer custodial sentence than would otherwise be appropriate to the offence, or the imposition of a custodial sentence where other sentencing objectives do not require custody". Or as the ACPS report *Young Adult Offenders* expressed it in 1974—"It is thought unsound to consider a propensity to commit offences as a kind of sickness which, on the medical analogy, can be rectified by relatively brief treatment in an institution from which the offender will emerge cured."

4.12 However, we think it wise to bear in mind what social scientists have *not* proved. They have not shown that penal establishments can have no reformative effect, nor that individual members of the staff can exert no influence for good. Nor have they proved that inmates are invariably incapable of responding to whatever is provided.

4.13 A further main cause of the loss of faith in treatment has stemmed paradoxically from the fact that the courts have been enabled and encouraged by Parliament in a series of statutes to make use of a number of new non-custodial types of sentence. The result has been that the courts are now encouraged to regard prison as the last resort, as the place where people should go only when there is no other course to take with them. Thus for many years, although the number of people coming before the courts consistently increased, the proportion sentenced to imprisonment until recently declined. By the same token, however, these changes have reinforced a view of imprisonment which stresses its purely custodial nature.

4.14 A third important feature has been significant changes in direction in the management of prisons themselves, related to some extent to the changes in sentencing practice we have just mentioned. The "treatment" model emphasised the improvement of the institutional environment for inmates. On the other hand, the Mountbatten Inquiry of 1966 and the various prison disorders of the 1970s (including the escape of Thomas William Hughes) were public reminders that the age-old functions of security and control cannot be ignored, and that they remain the first duty of the staff. Accordingly, a substantial upgrading of physical security has taken place in closed prisons and the entire dispersal prison system has come into being. This has been responsible for a large part of capital expenditure in recent years and has required a good deal of adjustment by the staff, not only as they undertake fresh duties as dog-handlers or in emergency control rooms, but also seek to maintain security. A number of witnesses argued that the emphasis on security was greatly overdone and that, far more frequently than was necessary, the whole population of a prison had to endure a degree of security necessary for only a small minority. On the other hand, others have pointed to the impact of terrorist prisoners on security problems and have argued that recent years have seen a harder, more sophisticated criminal entering prison, coincident with greater success in keeping the less serious offenders out of prison altogether. As we have said, long sentences have been passed on this type of criminal principally to protect society from them and for this reason security must be increasingly strict wherever such men or women are contained.

4.15 As confidence in the treatment model has waned in this way no alternative philosophy commanding wide public support has taken its place. Members of the prison service of all grades from governor downwards, responsible for locking up their inmates and for providing regimes for them, have in consequence tended to lose faith in any positive justification for the inherently unpleasant tasks which are their job. Further, the wide intellectual debate which, as we have indicated, has beeen undermining the treatment model and simultaneously trying to provide a satisfactory alternative philosophy, has on occasions merely given fresh currency to the old ideas that imprisonment could be no more than punitive and deterrent.

4.16 In addition, in so far as there has been fresh thinking on this subject, it has tended to concentrate on a prisoner's rights rather than his needs. In what has been described as the "justice" model it is argued to be axiomatic that a person sentenced to imprisonment should surrender only those normal rights and freedoms as are necessarily and inevitably lost by virtue of the fact of that imprisonment. In so far as there is any rehabilitative content in such a model, it is contended that an offender can only be taught to respect the rights of society if it is demonstrated to him, whilst in prison, that his own rights are being respected. In a period of increasing serious crime this argument, even if soundly based, has not been attractive to the public at large, still less to prison officers who so often feel that more is always being done for inmates than for themselves.

4.17 The typical argument for the justice model, voiced in its most developed form principally amongst academic lawyers, is that since the subjective aims of treatment have been discredited, then one must look to an objective approach to the problem. Just as the treatment model concentrated on the alleged needs of the inmate, so must the justice model concentrate on his deeds. Length of imprisonment and the regime in prison must not be influenced by considerations not based on the particular offence. It follows, it is said, that there should be no compulsory treatment and that the executive and gaolers should have no powers over the inmate which cannot be supervised by the courts.

4.18 The evidence we have received suggests that these views have resulted substantially from experience in the USA. Until recently State criminal codes permitted recourse to indeterminate sentences to a degree unknown in the United Kingdom, where the sole indeterminate sentences are life imprisonment and borstal training. Commonly, therefore, the decision in America when to release an inmate flowed not from the initial judicial determination but from a review process, usually undertaken by a parole board. In the course of time, however, this system was seen to have a number of defects: for instance the inmate and his family could not be certain when he would be released and the paroling procedure amounted in practice to a further trial without the normal protection afforded accused persons. Consequently great emphasis is now placed on ensuring that all stages of an inmate's treatment are governed by proper regard to "due process", a direct reference to a provision of the US Constitution and meaning in effect a decision of some tribunal after a hearing on the model of an ordinary trial. In Europe developments have been different partly because of the small place given to indeterminate sentences and to distinct traditions of inmates' grievance review, where the political remedy has been relied on more than the judicial one. Nevertheless, the European Convention on Human Rights, upon which prisoners and their representatives seek to rely more and more in prisons in the United Kingdom, is an amalgamation of judicial and political remedies to redress individual grievances.

4.19 Further, there is a danger, when describing the decline of the treatment model, of implying that it ever commanded universal acceptance in the first place. It did not. There have always been those who have argued that the twin Gladstonian objectives of deterrence and reform are incompatible. They impose an unreasonable strain on the staff, particularly the discipline staff, whose importance is too often ignored in inmate-centred approaches to imprisonment. Put most bluntly and extremely, it is contended that rehabilitation is and always has been a goal impossible of attainment and it is hypocrisy to claim otherwise.

4.20 Further, most of these arguments have taken place outside the political arena. There developments have been heavily influenced by growing anxiety over the continued increase in reported crime. At the most extreme this increase has even led to fears of incipient social breakdown. Law and order is a live political issue to which we think all recent governments have sought to respond. They have done so chiefly by increasing police manpower and equipment, stressing their preventive and deterrent roles. At the same time they have sought to reduce the proportionate resort of the courts to imprisonment. In this, however, their success has been masked: the effect of the relatively smaller proportion of offenders until recently sentenced to imprisonment has been overwhelmed by a combination of the absolute increase in the number of offenders brought before the courts and the increasing length of the sentences which the latter have been passing.

EVIDENCE RECEIVED

4.21 Most of the evidence we received on objectives was unsystematic and rarely precise. None of the staff associations, including the governors, attempted to redefine penal objectives. The BAPG said that there was confusion both within and outside the prison service and suggested that priorities should be clarified, but did not offer proposals of its own, affirming that Rule 1 was in general terms good enough and should be proclaimed as an objective, regardless of its feasibility. Some other witnesses said Rule 1 was imprecise but were unable or unprepared to say what exactly should be done. Others went further and contended that the sentiments implicit in Rule 1 had been shown to be unreal. One of the clearer statements of this character was:

> "If we are right in our regretful view that the reformative effect on prisoners in minimal, and the experience of most of the staff of prisons we visited appears to confirm this conclusion, then it must be accepted that at present the main practical value of prisons is to punish serious or repeated crimes, and where necessary to protect society from dangerous criminals".

4.22 It is possible that some witnesses hesitated to specify strictly penal objectives because they were much more concerned with getting criminal justice objectives and priorities right first. Our limited terms of reference may well have inhibited their preference for taking a wider view of the place of imprisonment both in the criminal justice system and in the context of delinquency as a whole.

4.23 One of the most thoughtful pieces of evidence we received on this as on a number of other subjects was from Dr King and Mr Rodney Morgan. They argued that, since the "treatment" model has been shown as invalid, the only proper replacement is a system devoted to secure and humane containment based on three principles, minimum use of custody, minimum use of security, and the "normalisation" of the prison. As they put it:

> "We take the view that precisely because humane containment may fail to fire the imagination so it may prevent the excesses of the past. The function of prison *is* a limited one and its use and administration should no longer be guided by claims which it cannot fulfil."

4.24 In general, we think that his kind of statement is representative of many informed observers' views at present. Whilst we feel it has much force, particularly in its impatience with wishful thinking, there is a great danger that it may throw out the good with the unattainable and we are sceptical about the extent to which it may justify, as is claimed, sweeping changes in the allocation of resources in penal establishments (see Chapter 6). Further, as one group of witnesses pointed out to us, "humane containment" suffers from the fatal defect that it is a means without an end. Our opinion is that it can only result in making prisons into human warehouses—for inmates and staff. It is not, therefore, a fit rule for hopeful life or responsible management.

THE FUTURE

4.25 We take it as axiomatic that imprisonment is bound to remain as the final sanction for imposing social discipline in our community under agreed rules of law. For the reasons which will appear hereafter, we are forced to the conclusion that it should be used as little as possible.

4.26 If Rule 1 is to continue to set out the objectives of the prison service, then we think it should be re-written and we suggest the following for contemporary purposes:

"The purpose of the detention of convicted prisoners shall be to keep them in custody which is both secure and yet positive, and to that end the behaviour of all the responsible authorities and staff towards them shall be such as to:

(a) create an environment which can assist them to respond and contribute to society as positively as possible;

(b) preserve and promote their self respect;

(c) minimise, to the degree of security necessary in each particular case, the harmful effects of their removal from normal life;

(d) prepare them for and assist them on discharge."

Suitable amendments should be made simultaneously to the Borstal and Detention Centre Rules. Although strictly Rule 1 does not apply to remand prisoners, we think the spirit of the suggested new Rule 1 should. If separate Rules are made for remand prisoners, then such Rules too should appropriately reflect the suggested new Rule 1.

4.27 We think that the rhetoric of "treatment and training" has had its day and should be replaced. On the other hand, we intend that the rhetoric alone should be changed and not all the admirable and constructive things that are done in its name.

4.28 Secondly, we hope that by suggesting this alteration to Rule 1 we make it clear that in our view mere "secure and humane containment" is not enough. Prison staff cannot be asked to operate in a moral vacuum and the absence of real objectives can in the end lead only to the routine brutalisation of all the participants. There may be ample room for argument about the extent to which imprisonment should be used, but there can be no neutrality about it once it is imposed. We think that there both can and should be purposive objectives in imprisonment, but we do not feel that realistically they can be set any higher than we have just suggested.

4.29 We now turn—concentrating principally on prison establishments—to consider briefly the nature of the regimes which we think should be established and operated to give life and effect to the new spirit embodied in the proposed new Rule 1 which we hope may help in part to rejuvenate and settle the prison service.

4.30 No prison routine is so sterile, degrading and harmful to the prisoner, and equally barren for the staff who have to operate it, than one in which the inmate is locked in his cell for a substantial part of the day and only released perhaps for the statutory one hour's exercise.

4.31 We think that a concerted effort should be made by both management and staff alike to ensure that as many inmates as possible are out of their cells and occupied for as much of a full working day as possible. This is not a new concept and is reflected both in Rule 72.3 of the European Standard Minimum Rules:—

"Sufficient work of a useful nature shall be provided to keep prisoners actively employed for a normal working day."

and in Rules 28(1) and 29(1) of the Prison Rules 1964: —

"A convicted prisoner shall be required to do useful work for not more than 10 hours a day, and arrangements should be made to allow prisoners to work, where possible, outside the cells and in association with one or another . . .

Every prisoner able to profit from the educational facilities provided at a prison shall be encouraged to do so."

For a number of reasons in recent years actual performance has fallen disappointingly short of these ideals. For example, the number of unemployed male inmates in England and Wales has steadily risen in recent years (Prison Statistics 1978, Cmnd 7626, Table 10.5).

4.32 The types of work which are to a greater or lesser extent potentially available for the employment of inmates within establishments are industrial, domestic and on the prison service's farms and gardens. Dealing with these in reverse order, in establishments possessing land where farms and gardens work is done, it has seemed to us on our visits and from the evidence we have received that for those inmates who are employed upon this work it provides full employment, the department is well organised, and we think reflects substantial credit upon all those who administer, manage and instruct from headquarters and throughout literally down to the field.

4.33 Domestic work has of course to be done in every establishment. There are many necessary cleaning, catering and other similar tasks upon which inmate labour has to be and is employed daily. As might be expected, however, this is by no means sufficient fully to occupy all the inmates in a given establishment, nor indeed does it keep those who are so employed busy for what might be called a full working day of even eight hours.

4.34 Industrial work has been intended to provide the major work activity in penal establishments. However, owing to a number of circumstances, amongst them the shortage of trained instructors, shortages of disciplinary staff where they are present in workshops, industrial action on the part of prison officers from time to time, overcrowded establishments so that such facilities as are available in them are nevertheless totally inadequate, the present situation in England and Wales is that, although workshops are generating output to the value of over £20 million a year, they are operating at less than half capacity. Space, plant and equipment, as well as industrial staff, are being seriously under-used, orders for work are being turned away or lost and a deficit of about £4 million is being incurred. The main reason—itself the result of the factors to which we have referred—is the low number of hours worked: against a target of a 40 hour week, the working week is on average little more than 20 hours and for many work-shops is far less than this. The position in Scotland and Northern Ireland is similar.

4.35 This is not a new phenomenon. It is sufficient for us to say that since industrial work was first generally introduced into penal establishments after the report of the Gladstone Committee in 1895, the reports of five subsequent committees have all commented on the under-use of the industrial facilities available. In the early stages the cause was an insufficient number of technical supervisors and instructors: later reports have all expressed the view that the prison service as a whole was still not paying enough attention to prison industries and that regimes laid down for establishments—the responsibility of governors—paid too little attention to the importance of using to the full the capacity available in the interests of both profitability and the well-being of the inmates themselves.

4.36 In England and Wales, the provision and use of educational facilities within establishments has been much more successful, much of the expansion occurring in recent years. As a result, relatively substantial educational and library facilities have been provided in most establishments. These have catered for academic courses in all subjects and of every standard, vocational training in many fields and courses to fit inmates for work at various trades in the construction industries. Recently increased attention has been paid to education and training in social skills but this has so far only been on a relatively small scale. We think that this can and should be enlarged substantially. Education has always been voluntary for inmates, except for those below school-leaving age. One further point, however, is important: most of the courses and classes are arranged to take place in the evenings to avoid interfering with work regimes which, as we have already mentioned, have however been sadly deficient.

4.37 In Scotland the picture is not quite so happy. The Report of the

Parole Board for Scotland for 1978 shows that there has been some advance there since the "Alexander Report" on adult education in 1975 but that in essence this has been insufficient. The report makes various recommendations in paragraph 9 of its chapter 3 which for our part we would support. Although we are aware of efforts to develop industrial and educational provision there, we have had insufficient evidence to entitle us to make any specific comment on the situation in Northern Ireland.

4.38 We are not satisfied that the present poor showing on the industrial work front is unavoidable. Our own observations and the evidence given to us lead us to think that headquarters, most governors and the majority of prison staff beneath them have adopted a fatalistic and defeatist attitude towards this aspect of prison regimes. We appreciate that national economic circumstances may make the task less than easy; nevertheless, given greater purpose shown by governors and reasonable co-operation from prison staff at every establishment, we have no doubt that a substantial number of the workshops now shut could be opened and the industrial work situation could be improved.

4.39 We think that the first target should be to keep every sentenced prisoner occupied for at least what would be a normal working day of eight hours. The activities which we think should be available in establishments are, first, work of every description. This will comprise the necessary cleaning, washing, catering and similar domestic tasks which have to be done in order to keep an organisation running smoothly and efficiently. They should also include all the work done in workshops and on the land which is presently controlled by the Directorate of Industries and Farms. We think too that the facilities for education in establishments should be developed so far as resources allow and that these could, subject to certain overriding considerations to which we refer below, be a full-time alternative to work. In addition, we see no reason of principle why the facilities should not be made available as appropriate to prison staff and their families. In the same way we see no reasons of principle against, and many positive and practical reasons in favour of, the use of inmate instructors where appropriately qualified in the development of such inmate "self-help" programmes as local ingenuity and resourcefulness can devise. By "education" we mean not only academic instruction, but also vocational training courses of all kinds, including the present construction industry training, physical and recreational activities, and in addition remedial classes in literacy and in numeracy, and those concerned to develop the inmate's social skills and social conscience.

4.40 We do not propose that education, in whatever aspect, shall in any way be seen as a "soft option". Rather, it should be an activity at which an inmate must work, must work hard and must work successfully within his capacity for so long during the working day as facilities permit. Over the age of 16, education should be voluntary but those who volunteer and ask for it should only be accepted if, either at the outset or after a probationary period, they show themselves capable of taking advantage of the facilities offered. Further, as is likely to be the case, if educational courses do not occupy the whole of the working day, and those taking them are not provided with what in another context would be described as "homework" to occupy them, then we would expect the inmates to be required to work at other activities for the remainder of the working day. It is not for us to lay down any specific timetable or curricula, but it might, for instance, be convenient for those taking advantage of the educational facilities to be responsible for cleaning, tidying and repairing the educational block in which they are being taught.

4.41   In so far as what we have described as remedial education is concerned, we think that this should be provided for those who ask for it and demonstrate the need for it, as well as those who, at the outset at the least, are assessed as needing it. Once again, we do not intend this to be thought of as an easy way out for those involved. By their very nature it is unlikely that those taking remedial education or classes designed to develop social skills or the like, will be doing so for the whole of the working day. For the rest, we think that the regimes should be designed as far as possible to ensure that when not in class they are working at whatever task may be thought to be most appropriate for them.

4.42 Precisely how these targets are to be achieved cannot be for us. We can only recommend the guidelines and it must thereafter be for the Home Departments, governors, and prison staff generally, in a spirit of purposive co-operation to work out the details. We appreciate that vital to the motivation of inmates is an appropriate system of paying them. Again, time has prevented our exploring this topic as much as we would have wished. The present weekly rates of pay vary generally between 80p and £3, depending on the type of work and how hard the inmate works. At Coldingley, where the regime is designed to be as like outside industry as possible, we were told that the maximum rate with overtime was £4·50 per week. Compared with wage levels in outside industry, these figures are of course very low. They are low, too, in comparison with some other prison systems abroad. However, absolute pay levels do not resolve all penal work problems. Whereas in one system we saw inmates could earn wages comparable to those outside, a very high proportion of inmates were unemployed. In another system, high wages had not solved problems of motivation or secured a 40 hour week.

4.43 The Home Office told us that their long-term aim is to move towards outside wage levels, but that the prospects are very remote. They argued that the level of earnings was inseparable from the fortunes of prison industries and the financial results of prison work generally. Cost was not, however, the only constraint: there would be formidable practical administrative problems deriving from social security considerations. If the Home Office were to pay an inmate any wage approaching that which he might obtain outside prison for the same work, then the DHSS would look to his earnings, in whole or in part, to offset any social security benefits they were paying to his family. This we accept as right, as well as the

71

further argument that until a prisoner's work is of such a value that will meet the aggregate cost of keeping his family in the outside world and himself in prison, as well as pocket money for him there, then any arbitrary sum that one does pay him for whatever work he does do is bound to be an artificial one. Nevertheless, on the evidence we have had we think that as soon as may be possible there is everything to be gained by increasing inmates' maximum earnings to motivate them to a degree not practicable at present levels. If this were done, then at least in the industrial work field we think that the additional expenditure would be wholly, or at least substantially, self-financing. Nevertheless, we also think that prisoners undertaking domestic work or some form of education should equally be able to earn larger sums and we recommend that the Home Departments should forthwith consider devising schemes or revising existing ones to this end, but which in all cases reward effort or results. At the same time we think that consideration should be given to extending the prison disciplinary offences of being idle, careless or negligent at work, or of refusing to work after being required to do so, in Rule 47(17) of the Prison Rules, to cover any activity upon which an inmate may be engaged as part of his regime in prison.

4.44 Finally, although remand prisoners cannot be compelled to work whilst they are detained in custody, we recommend that appropriate facilities for work and education should be made available to them as are made available to the convicted prisoners. Owing to the overcrowding in the local prisons this is now seldom possible. This is an added reason why this overcrowding should be alleviated as soon as possible and to this point also we return later in this report.

Positive custody

4.45 Although we hope what we have said so far in this chapter indicates the general direction in which we think penal establishments may best move, we wish to emphasise some more general themes. This is both to make them explicit and to stress how we intend what follows in this report to be read and interpreted in the light of them.

4.46 Above all, we repeat that in putting "treatment and training" and "humane containment" aside, the last thing we intend is to suggest nothing should take their place. On the contrary, we fully appreciate that every community, whatever its nature, requires a suitable ethic. As will have been seen from our suggested redraft of Rule 1 in paragraph 4.26 we think that what we envisage might be best described as "positive custody". That is, it has to be secure and it must carry out all the intentions of the courts and society, in that respect. On the other hand, penal establishments must also so far as possible be hopeful and purposive communities and not be allowed to degenerate into mere uncaring institutions dulled by their own unimaginative and unenterprising routines.

4.47 We feel fortified in recommending such an approach because the prison services in the United Kingdom have historically displayed by any account a remarkably flexible and compassionate response to their tasks and charges. We therefore have no doubt they are capable of rising, in so far as that is necessary, to what we intend.

4.48 We also think that they need support from an informed and interested public. We have therefore throughout the report repeatedly sought to consider how the public might best be involved. We consider that the management of penal establishments must be consistently characterised by an openness of approach and mind not only to all the staff but to all public requirements and proper inquiries, as well as to the interests of inmates. We appreciate this is easier to say than to describe in detail or to maintain in all respects. However, we think it should nonetheless be the governing principle. Over time we would expect this to help the services themselves to be more understood because they have explained and shared their problems more with the outside world. We anticipate, too, that it should bring about changes for inmates, for example, in dismantling supererogatory elements of control, such as some aspects of censorship. In the same way we would want to see the dominant attitude of everyone in the services to be one of active search for development and change, and concerned to enable these to happen. We hope that this report will provide the opportunity to release fresh energies and initiatives rather than to support constricted views and offer impediments to development.

See p 277

CHAPTER FIVE

ORGANISATION

5.1 This chapter reviews the evidence and contains our recommendations about the future organisation of the prison services. Their present structure and how this has developed in the past have been described in Chapter 2. This chapter will be chiefly concerned with the position in England and Wales.

5.2 The organisation of the Scottish prison service has been reviewed only recently: we have received no evidence suggesting a present need for further changes, nor have we ourselves observed any such need. Though here and in other chapters we shall refer to some special Scottish difficulties, they do not represent significant organisational problems.

5.3 In Northern Ireland, although there has been no recent review, there similarly seems to be no case for any substantial change. Indeed, in both Scotland and Northern Ireland they seem to have all the advantages of relatively small scale operations, exactly those denied to the prison service in England and Wales and the chief apparent source of its current—and recurrent—organisational problems.

5.4 Most of the direct comments we received on organisation in England and Wales were from members of the staff in the field, either individually (including in their official capacities) or from their staff associations. There are few informed outside observers and they tended to be sparing in their organisational observations. The more direct participants, on the other hand, were frequently forthright and trenchant. A good deal of frustration with headquarters was vented. Whilst we would not expect any headquarters of a large organisation to be universally popular we were sometime surprised at the strength of the feelings which were expressed. These were sometimes misplaced, for instance even headquarters could not be blamed for the effect of successive governments' pay and economic policies. On the other hand, we have to say that at the very least there seemed to have been a failure at the centre to carry the service along with it, and that the lack of clear, identifiable, effectively communicating leadership had played its part.

5.5 We now consider in turn each of the main components of the organisation in England and Wales and make our recommendations in each case.

Headquarters

5.6 Although by itself this is not the largest component, it is the one whose design raises some of the main issues about the prison service. These are what should be the service's future constitutional status and relationship, if any, with the Home Office; what functions should headquarters have; how should they be arranged and under whom.

5.7 On the cardinal issue of whether there should be continued Ministerial control there was no real disagreement. The general feeling was that a senior Cabinet Minister should remain accountable to Parliament for the running of the prison service. We have no doubt that this is right. The responsibility is so important, indeed unique, and of such particular public interest that it would not be practicable to separate Ministers from it altogether. For similar reasons we think the Minister must remain the Home Secretary because of his overall responsibilities for the criminal justice system.

5.8 There was less agreement on the form that Ministerial accountability should take. Amongst the staff it was common to find nostalgia for the Prison Commission abolished in 1963, including among people who had not been in the service at the time. This sprang from their criticism of what they contended was the excessive influence of the civil service and civil servants at headquarters in the Home Office. Apart from the delays in obtaining answers to inquiries, about which there was substantial complaint, a number of people felt that the headquarters departments of the prison service, being answerable to their political master, the Secretary of State, were influenced by political considerations to a greater extent than was necessary and this to the detriment of the service as a whole. It was suggested to us that if any difficult question arose, the line of least resistance was taken, to the media, to prisoners' complaints and to other agitators for changes within the system, as officials and Ministers kept too close an eye on the ballot box. Witnesses told us that although they did not dispute that concern should be felt and expressed for the condition of inmates within prisons, this concern at headquarters was not matched by equal concern for the staff who had the unpleasant task of looking after and containing those inmates. Headquarters contained, it was contended, no public relations branch of sufficient strength to hit back and to put the point of view of the prison service and its members when any criticism was made of them. Further, all the relevant casework was done by civil servants to whom expediency and precedent were thought to be paramount. It was argued that the organisation and ethos of a civil service department was inappropriate for the management of an operational organisation dealing 24 hours a day with the difficult human problems of both staff and inmates alike. Thus, the argument continued, the function of headquarters should in the circumstances be reduced largely to one of policy making only: operational organisation should be left to the regions. Prison officers in the field, it was said, find it frustrating and maddening to be told how to handle prisoners in a particular situation by someone who has never had that experience himself. Whether rightly or wrongly, and as many will no doubt contend is only to be expected as central government becomes increasingly complicated, the prison officer unlocking 40 criminals on a wing in an establishment two or three hundred miles from London saw the headquarters of his service as a faceless monolith caring not for human beings but merely for efficient administration.

5,9 We understand and sympathise with much of this feeling. We have made appropriate allowance for the probability that it was only those who wished to criticise adversely who troubled to write to us. Further, much of the criticism was what one would have expected of the headquarters of any large organisation. Nevertheless we cannot escape the conclusion that many of those employed in the service feel a deep sense of dissatisfaction with the organisation and management of it as a whole and that a gulf has grown up between the establishments in the field and the staff who work in them on the one hand and headquarters at the Home Office in London on the other. Making all allowances that we think it right to make, we cannot escape the conclusion that central administration ought to have shown itself more responsive to these growing feelings over the years, especially in the field of personnel management.

5.10 However, we do not think that there can now be any going back to 1963 or beyond. The Prison Commission was much less independent in fact than commonly now supposed. Nor was it the case that, with the possible exception of Du Cane, it had ever been headed by a prison service department professional, although its chairmen had tended to stay for reasonable, and sometimes long, periods. In its later years it had been finding it increasingly difficult to take on the fresh and larger tasks imposed upon it. No doubt its demise and the form that absorption into the Home Office took did change the service's sense of identity, but this did not necessarily by itself affect its efficiency. Above all, nothing is to be gained by fighting old battles, whether those of 1963 or those of more recent years. The problem before us and the service today is to find something appropriate and acceptable for today, not try to re-live the past.

General evidence

5.11 To go to the other extreme, the minimum change upon which everyone agreed did concern personnel administration. As we have explained, with the exception broadly of the manpower, training and career development work undertaken in P6, all personnel work in respect of staff grades peculiar to the prison service is located in Establishment Division 3 (Estabs 3) which is not part of the Prison Department. Estabs 3 reports to the Principal Establishment Officer (PEO) who is of equal rank to the Director-General, and himself reports to the Permanent Under Secretary (PUS). This arangement dates from the merger in 1963 and stemmed from the intention of integrating "staff" functions within the larger support resources of the Home Office. Accordingly, apart from Estabs 3, the Prison Department relies on Estabs 2 for various management services and Estabs 4 for the personnel management of the general civil service grades working both in headquarters and establishments.

5.12 It is now common ground that Estabs 3 at least should now become part of the Prison Department. The main reason for this is that the advantages of integrating these functions within the latter alongside P6 are greater than the advantages of preserving a supposed functional specialisation intact in a unified Establishment Department. The change should enable Estabs 3 to be closer and more responsive to the prison service grades and others. It should give the head of the service a clearer management responsibility and a direct personnel accountability. At a time when maintaining good industrial relations is a major preoccupation, then these considerations must prevail. We therefore have no hesitation in recommending the absorption of Estabs 3 within the Prison Department.

5.13 Looking more widely at the question of organisation, the weight of evidence from the staff associations showed a preference for greater Prison Department autonomy. The Governors thought that the administrative processes followed in the Home Office were singularly inappropriate for running an increasingly complex and sophisticated operational service such as the prisons:

> "Part of the difficulty lies in the attempt to use the same machinery for immediate operational matters that require speedy decision taking and execution, as for longer range planning and other administrative work."

5.14 What both they and the regional directors thought was required was a strengthened and reorganised planning department at headquarters, with far more decentralisation of immediate operational matters and decisions both to regions and also to the governors in their various establishments. There should be an independent Inspectorate reporting directly to the Home Secretary and whose reports should be published. Whilst some of them suggested that the Director General (DG) should be the person who had risen through the service, that is to say an ex-governor, others felt that this could only come at a later date: at present no governor had the administrative skills, in addition to his gubernatorial expertise, to enable him adequately to find his way around the corridors of power in Whitehall. We shall have more to say about this when we deal with the question of training in a later chapter. Nevertheless it was felt essential that whoever was appointed Director General should be directly responsible to the Secretary of State.

5.15 To the extent that the POA expressed any views on this subject, they were that on balance they favoured a recognisable and identifiable head of a service with a substantial degree of independence from what was described as the civil service bureaucracy. At present the Prison Department seemed to the Association to be a centralised edifice content to allow matters to develop in their own manner and at their own speed in the hope that problems would resolve themselves. The Association recognised that management of the prison service was complex and difficult to define: no doubt it was for this reason that although they felt that radical change was required they were unable to go further and identify the nature of that necessary change with any particularity. The furthest they felt able to go was to suggest that the first and most necessary corrective for the protracted decision-making that occurred throughout the service was for an unambiguous policy to be devised based on practical reality and the ability of the prison service to meet its obligations. This, it was said, ought to be taken in conjunction with recognised and sensible policy objectives. The Association then went on to say—"Decision-making and policy formulation within this framework should be maximised at the local level. This should involve adequate consultation not only with the representative unions but with the staff directly involved."

5.16 When the representatives of the Institution of Professional Civil Servants (IPCS) came to give oral evidence to the Committee, it became apparent that within the timescale which the Inquiry had sought originally to impose the Institution had been unable to give the amount of time and thought that they would have liked to any proposals for the reorganisation of the Prison Department as a whole. In essence they told us that something new was necessary but that what was in their original paper was merely a first attempt at a solution. They realised that they had probably not got it right and that the Committee and anyone else could no doubt show up its deficiencies with little difficulty. However, they went on to say that what they were really doing was in effect making an impassioned plea that something must be done about the top of what they described as "this confounded department". They too told us that they had seemed never to be able to get face to face with the representative of the department to whom they wished to speak: that they never knew who it was who was making, or failing to make, the decisions on the points which they were raising; and in any event that the time which was being taken to answer their inquiries was excessive. It was perfectly clear to us that, like so many others, they felt thoroughly frustrated.

5.17 At our invitation the Institution took further time to consider their recommendations about the organisational structure of the prison service and kindly submitted supplementary evidence in writing to us on this point. We should add that a number of witnesses took this course of action; it has proved extremely helpful to us; and we are most grateful for the additional time and trouble which witnesses have taken to give us the clearest exposition of their views. Effectively the IPCS in their further evidence contended that the prison service should become a separate government department with its own Principal Establishment Officer and Finance Officer, and its own Establishment and Finance Departments, responsible for all those matters within the prison service, enabled to negotiate independently and directly with the Treasury and the CSD on manpower, pay and staffing issues as, they said, other government departments now do. The Director General would be Chairman of the Prisons Board and would be the accounting officer for all expenditure on prisons, reporting direct to the Home Secretary in the same way as does the present Permanent Under Secretary of State at the Home Office. The Institution recognised that, although they wished to see the prison service as a separate department, it would still have to be answerable to Parliament through the Home Secretary, given that he is the Minister responsible for the various law and order agencies. In this connection, on questions of policy and resources which affected the criminal justice system as a whole, the Institution's proposals envisaged the Permanent Under Secretary at the Home Office sharing responsibility with the Director General of the prison service so that the right decisions could be made, taking all aspects of criminal policy, policing and prisons into account. We should just add that the Institution's proposals contemplated a Prisons Board of substantial size, containing representatives from the main functioanl areas, such as industries and farms, and psychological services as well as the policy areas, and also two or more representatives of the relevant staff associations. They seemed to us to be contemplating a Board of something of the order of 14 members.

5.18 The Outstations Branch of the SCPS said that the amalgamation of the Prison Commission with the Home Office in 1963 had been an ill-considered and ill-advised measure undertaken for political expediency. As the first step in a major re-organisation of the prison service now, which they considered to be necessary, they recommended the formation of a fully autonomous Prison Department responsible directly to the Home Secretary. Such a department should have complete responsibility for all aspects of its operation including finance and staffing matters. It was a major weakness of the present organisation that such a situation did not presently obtain, and a prime cause of the present industrial unrest. The autonomous Prison Department should be controlled by a Director General possessing an extensive prison service background. They did not look with favour upon the facility for interchange of Home Office staff between the Prison Department and other departments in the office. In their view it resulted in the loss of trained administrators from the prison service to other sectors of the Home Office and a move of untrained and inexperienced staff from other parts of the office into the prison service. The result was that in the headquarters of the Prison Department there was a substantial lack of the general knowledge of prison affairs that should be there.

5.19 The evidence from the London Branch of the SCPS was to the effect that the most important single cause of the widespread dissatisfaction and disaffection so obvious today in the prison service was the failure of government over many years to make even remotely adequate financial provisions for the service, on either capital or current account. The service was expected to perform its task of containment and treatment and yet to do so in conditions which were nothing short of a national disgrace and fell far below standards appropriate to the last quarter of the 20th century.

5.20 Differing from the evidence of the Outstations Branch of the same Society, the London Branch did not share the view that the Prison Department should be separated from the Home Office and made autonomous. The chief defect resulting from the abolition of the Prison Commission was the division of responsibilities between P6 Division and Establishment Division 3. The Prison Department formed part of the overall penal and law and order system in the country and accordingly should continue to be administered by the Home Office as are the other agencies in the system. They were against departmentalisation: they saw substantial advantages in remaining members of the Treasury grades and in the resulting possibility of interchange between the Prison Department and other sectors of the Home Office. Indeed they went further. They took substantial issue with the contention of the Governor's Branch of their same Society that the Director General of the prison service should be appointed from within the service. The training of governors and administrators was totally different. Each tended to achieve a high degree of professionalism in his own sphere. Nevertheless, whilst accepting the high degree of professionalism of a governor in one breath, the London Branch of the Society went on to comment in the next that the task was essentially a "fairly parochial one with no requirement to acquire a vision for the wider scene". Such a sentiment, with which we do not agree, no doubt nevertheless explains some of the relationships and attitudes we have discovered in the present organisation.

5.21 Amongst the academic criminologists, Members of Parliament and past Ministers and civil servants who also generously gave up a lot of their time to provide us with both written and oral evidence, there was unanimity that something needed doing about the organisation of the prison service. There was again, however, considerable difference of opinion about what really was required.

5.22 We understood one of these witnesses to recommend the separation of the operational side of the prison service from its general policy and planning function, as well as that function from all the other criminal justice agencies, and then to form from the operational side alone a prison administration as a body independent of and outside the Home Office—indeed very much like the old Prison Commission. In this witness's view there was nothing that could be criticised about the suggestion from the constitutional point of view: the only constitutional "necessity" was that it must always be possible for any individual prisoner to obtain access by way of petition to the Home Secretary. Administering prisons by an autonomous body separate from the Home Office in no way involved any denial of the right of a prisoner to petition the Secretary of State.

5.23 This witness also mentioned the general feeling to which we have frequently referred that the head of the new prison administration should be a member of the present prison service. However, in his view there was no one in that service at present sufficiently capable to do the job. Accordingly it would be necessary to appoint someone from outside both the prison and the civil services, and it was essential that he should be appointed for a minimum of five years. This appointee should not become involved in arguments about penal policy. His job would be to run an efficient prison administration, caring for prisoners in the ways in which in 1979 society thought that they should be cared for: his job was not to consider who should be sent to prison nor to think up alternatives to it as a sentence of the court.

5.24 Another of these witnesses, while accepting that there had to be Ministerial responsibility, in the sense of accountability, to Parliament for prisons, was of the view that no Home Secretary, with all the other matters that occupied his attention, had sufficient time to give to penal affairs. It followed that there should be a penal department in government with a Minister fully responsible for it, of which the prison service would be part. From the information which had been given, governors were most unhappy about the present situation and arrangements; as he said, they felt that there was a deplorable lack of leadership. The new prison service, under its new Minister, should be a professional body with a professional head.

5.25 Of the remaining witnesses within this group, one regretted the demise of the Prison Commission, but now that it was dead would not seek to resuscitate it. Another, whilst accepting that some alterations to the organisational structure had to be made, expressed himself as strongly against the Prison Commission both at the time that it was wound up and any re-creation of it now. It had, he thought, become very inward looking and not at all efficient.

5.26 The only worked up proposals we received on organisational change came from the Home Office. The proposals consisted of setting out the advantages and disadvantages of four options. The first and fourth need not detain us. The first did not do much more than incorporate Estabs 3 in the Prison Department, that is to say the minimum feasible adjustment, and improve the corporate planning capacity of the Board. The fourth would have gone even further than a resuscitated Prison Commission in its degree of complete separation from the Home Office, though the Home Secretary would remain answerable to Parliament for its work. We reject both these courses because the first does not go far enough and the last goes too far. What we think is required is an identifiable prisons administration with clear, integrated managerial responsibility and as fully a professional operational direction as circumstances allow.

5.27 It follows that we consider that for practical purposes the argument on organisational change centres on how best these objectives may be attained. In the Home Office evidence the range of options was set out in two options, described as models B1 and B2. Whilst we agree with the Home Office that these options do not exhaust the whole area of realistic possibility for change, nor that the correct final choice may not lie somewhere between the two, we now turn to consider them because they illuminate what the main organisational design problems are.

5.28 The main features of model B1 were that the Director General would become the accounting officer for all expenditure on prisons, reporting direct to the Home Secretary for the day to day operations and management of the prison service. The prison service would have its own separate Establishment Department, responsible not only for the grades peculiar to the prison service but also looking after the general service grades serving in establishments, thus giving them too the advantage of a clear integration in the prison service. The PEO would become PEO for both the Prison Department of the Home Office and also for all the other departments of the latter. As such he would report to the Director General in the former capacity and to the Permanent Under Secretary of State in the latter. It was proposed that the division of responsibilities between the two Establishment Departments should be arranged, so far as practicable, to recognise the unity and identity of purpose of staff of all grades serving in the prison service, but nevertheless preserving for those in the general service grades opportunities for interchange with other parts of the Home Office, particularly at senior level. There would remain a single Finance Department which would serve both the Prison Department and the other departments of the Home Office, but again the Principal Finance Officer (PFO) would, like his colleague the PEO, report to the Director General on financial matters affecting the Prison Department and to the Permanent Under Secretary of State on financial matters relating to other departments within the Home Office. The Prison Department would continue to share with other departments within the Home Office various other services, such as public relations, legal advice, statistics, pay, research and scientific advice.

5.29 Model B2 was an extension of B1. It contemplated the Prison Department having both its own PEO and its own PFO, with their separate Establishment and Finance Departments, and being responsible for all matters of staffing and finance in the prison service.

5.30 Questions of policy and resources affecting the criminal justice system as a whole would be for the PUS at the Home Office; the DG would be consulted, but he and his department would tend to become less closely involved in Home Office discussion of these matters. The Home Office would provide, on an agency basis, the normal common services.

5.31 We were told that B2, although remaining under the Home Secretary's direct control, would tend to cut off the prison service from the Home Office. We found and still find this difficult to accept. The principal disadvantage attributed by the Home Office to model B2 was that, if the Prison Department obtained its own PEO, then once a member of the civil service had been posted to the prison service stream, his career prospects would be blighted because it would be difficult, if not impossible, for him to be moved from that stream into one of the other streams within the Home Office, whose postings were dealt with by another PEO. Indeed the PUS told us that although at the start these disadvantages of model B2 would not be apparent, they tend to grow over the years and he for his part would be charry of placing a promising young recruit within the prison service stream in the fear that he would not be able to move him out of it later and put him in some other part of the Home Office in order to obtain further and more extensive experience. (Such a sense of diminished opportunity would be common to both junior and senior grades whether at headquarters or in outstations.) Further, we were told that, if model B2 were to be adopted, then the Home Secretary would need to be provided with some department within the Home Office itself to advise him about the validity of advice he received from the new Prison Department. We quote a passage from the oral evidence: —

"I think he (the Director General) would be discussing much more from outside than he does at present or he would under the B1 scheme. I fear that the consequences of that would be that the Home Office would feel obliged to develop its own capacity for developing a prison interest in these matters. Because the Prison Department became a separate organisation, the successive Home Secretaries would feel the need for some capacity within the Home Office of separate advice which would bring the interests of the prison service into balance, into perspective with the Home Secretary's other concerns. This is the fear that I have: that while I believe it could start as you suggest, over time we could develop a new limb, as it were, which would accentuate the tendency of the prison service to drift off."

5.32 Those of us who are less familiar with the workings of government departments than is the Permanent Under Secretary have had considerable difficulty in reconciling ourselves to these views. We can readily understand that if one part of a department of state is to some extent being separated from the rest of that department, then there will be a need simultaneously to ensure that suitable and sufficient means of communication and liaison are established so that the Minister can at all times be fully aware of what is happening and be in a position to take decisions based upon a sound, co-ordinated view of the affairs of his whole department. We do not think that the changes which we propose later in this chapter should or will have the effect of distancing the prison service in any way from the Home Office, but will merely enhance its status within it and increase its efficiency. If, however, they may have such effect, then we recommend that steps be taken to establish the necessary communication and liaison machinery which we have mentioned: as will be seen, we do hereafter make a specific recommendation in relation to co-ordination in the whole field of criminal justice policy. In these circumstances, if the passage from the evidence which we have quoted was intended to mean no more than we have considered above, then we need pursue this question no further.

5.33 On the other hand, the passage does appear to go further and suggest the necessity for the creation of a separate advisory body to advise the Home Secretary, if necessary in opposition to the Prison Department itself, on prison matters. If this was what was intended, then we feel bound to say that we cannot understand the need, far less the inevitability, of such a body. Under the arrangements which we subsequently recommend, the Home Secretary will have available to him, for advice on prison matters, both the Prison Department and HM Inspectorate of Prisons; for advice on other related matters, such as those concerned with criminal justice policy generally, he will have available to him the advice of the Permanent Under Secretary and those who are part of whatever communication and liaison arrangements are set up as we have mentioned. In these circumstances we can see no need for any further advisory body and we strongly express the hope that it will not be thought necessary to proliferate bureaucracies in this way.

Financial control and accounting

5.34 We must now say something about present accounting and financial control systems because they have been an important factor in our thinking about organisation. Any organisation as large as the Home Office Prison Department requires an effective, if not elaborate, system of financial control and budgeting. We cannot say that we have found that it possesses such a system. As we see it, all organisations of any sophistication should have a reliable view of comparative unit costs of their operation and be capable of developing financial controls which enhance efficiency and managerial performance.

5.35 At present the accounting system for the Prison Department, with one exception, is based wholly on the model of Parliamentary votes. The whole of the accounting for the Home Office, including the Prison Department, is done within the Home Office Finance Department. The system is such that, although it does discharge its accounting responsibilities to Parliament, it is not capable of delivering more than general and rudimentary information about operating costs. We were surprised to learn, for example, that the Home Office was unable to tell us how much each prison costs to run each year. Information is published in the annual report showing the cost of the main activities, but broken down into only four categories of institution, viz prisons and remand centres, borstal and young prisoner centres, detention centres, and female establishments. We were told that it was not possible to produce information establishment by establishment without mounting a special exercise.

5.36 The one exception to the system is the management accounts operated within the Directorate of Industries and Farms in relation to industries. In this case each industry in each establishment submits monthly accounts and these are used in the ordinary way as tools for management control in an environment simulating that of manufacturing industry. It is therefore possible from these accounts to monitor, for example, the level of resource utilisation, profitability and other significant trends.

5.37 We received evidence from SCPS (Outstations Branch) (i.e. largely Administration Officers in establishments) that there should be a system of local budgeting upon which national expenditure would ultimately be based. It was suggested that each financial year each establishment should prepare in advance an estimate of expenditure for all areas in which expenditure occurs. The estimate should be aimed to collate all expenditure needs of the establishment and should be done as one exercise, rather than separate estimates being prepared for some items at different times as is now the case. The estimate would be passed to regional offices who should be given as much discretion as possible to approve. This would replace a system where in large areas of current expenditure such as the acquisition of clothing, bedding and general equipment, stationery and salaries and travelling expenses establishments operated without regard to financial limits. The proponents of this change said: "We believe that the time is indeed right for an overall review of expenditure control strategy and that definite, and to some extent, sweeping changes can be introduced, with benefit".

5.38 Because there seemed much to commend such an approach, we put it to the Home Office. They were very reluctant to accept that such an approach had merit. They argued that such a sweeping change would require extra staff resources in each establishment and headquarters, without there being any guarantee at all that any financial savings that might ensue would justify the costs of introducing the new system. Above all, it had to be borne in mind that, even where individual establishment costs were identified, in a large proportion of cases there was not much a governor could do to change their incidence. This was because the most significant costs arose from circumstances outside managerial control, for instance staff pay and the supply costs of keeping establishments open and feeding the inmate population.

5.39 Whilst we understand the force of these arguments, we do not think that they rule out making any kind of change at all. We continue to feel that there must be advantage in making the managers of institutions effectively accountable for the money that they spend. If such steps are not taken, then the result remains that managers in control of quite substantial resources and having to make crucial decisions about their use (e.g. the deployment of officers) are fully protected in what they do and yet answerable to no-one. Whilst we do not believe for one moment that governors deliberately waste public resources or that there is a great deal of inefficiency, we cannot believe that the present situation is a healthy one. Although it is right that governors must be concerned with their caring responsibilities for inmates and staff, they must also be capable of having proper regard to the efficient and economic use of public resources. We do not accept that arguments against a wholesale change of accounting practices are arguments that may be used also against making any sort of change at all.

5.40 Further, it was only at a late stage in our deliberations that we learned that the CSD had also had these matters under examination in connection with a general survey of finance organisation in the Home Office. We have now seen the relevant chapter of the survey and note that it too adopts the same approach to Prison Department accounting practices as that to which we have just referred in paragraphs 5.38 and 5.39 above. We regret that the comments which the Home Office sent us on the CSD survey exhibited the same reluctance to accept that some of the latter's recommendations could be of value as they had shown when we raised this question with them initially. We recommend that steps should be taken at the earliest possible opportunity to develop selective accounting improvements within the Prison Department at the Home Office to increase the quality and detail of the financial information available to headquarters, as managers of the whole service, and to each governor, as manager of his or her establishment. We recommend that this should be one of the first tasks of the relevant division in the new Directorate of Finance and Administration to which we refer below and which will no doubt combine part of the existing P1 Division and a new prison service finance function. (We say more about the Directorate's relationship with the field below.) The Home Office did, however, tell us that they intend to implement the CSD survey's recommendation by the introduction of management accountancy expertise at headquarters. This we think essential. They are aware too of the need for adding in this area to the training of governors. This we think is also essential. The Home Office pointed out, however, that restraints on the growth of civil service manpower seemed likely to inhibit what they could do and there was doubt even whether likely reductions in civil service manpower would be allowed to leave the Prison Department headquarters unscathed. We appreciate, of course, these difficulties but we think that they could be overcome if, initially at least, improvements were selective. Further, we feel it probable that with modern technology a relatively very small investment at the prison service headquarters in modern accounting machinery could achieve the changes we would wish to see without any increase in civil service manpower. In any event we hope that the Government's understandable concern with civil service manpower as a whole,

85

and the cost of administration, will not preclude its allocating small extra resources when the outcome must be improved managerial performance as well as possible cost savings.

5.41 However, even considerations as important as this should be put in perspective. This organisation is not a commercial one: there are no financial profits to be obtained from imprisonment; and again we reiterate that society must realise that to keep and care for prisoners in custody in the conditions which they have the right to expect, and which we think that society should now afford them, may well appear to be expensive.

Objects of reorganisation

5.42 It is against this background and in the light of the views expressed to us by those working in all parts of the service, that we make our proposals for future organisation of the prison service in England and Wales. In doing so we have sought to achieve three things. First, to create a substantially greater degree of unity and identity than the service currently appears to feel. Members of the prison service, it seems to us, wish to be part of an organisation with which they can identify and which is more the master of its own affairs than it often seems to be at the moment. The structure which we recommend is, accordingly, one which, while keeping it within the Home Office, will give the prison service a greater corporate sense and enable those in charge to be more directly responsible for all aspects of its organisation than is currently the case. Secondly, we think that the Prison Department must have and be seen to have more standing within the Home Office. As we have said elsewhere in this report, once prisoners have been sentenced and committed to custody the tendency is for society then to forget about them, the establishments in which they are held and the staff who have to look after them. We think that this attitude may insidiously depreciate the standing of the Prison Department within the Home Office and it is only when things begin to go wrong that its affairs receive the degree of attention that they merit. Thirdly, we have sought to identify those areas of the administration and work of the prison service which should be the concern and responsibility of the most senior management and attempted to create an organisation structure which will enable this to be so.

5.43 We should also stress we have been particularly concerned that the organisation we propose should not affect the Home Secretary's ability to take a co-ordinated view of criminal justice policy. The need to consider together all aspects of society's response to crime and the treatment of offenders is as strong today as ever it was at the time of the dissolution of the Prison Commission in 1963 and to distance the Prison Department from the Home Office would run clear counter to policy planning needs. Decisions taken in regard to other parts of the system—for example, in regard to police manpower, the court building programme or the sentencing powers of the courts—may well significantly affect the demands placed upon prisons; at the same time, it would be quite wrong for the custodial treatment of offenders to be considered in isolation from non-custodial measures.

There is one last preliminary point. No organisation we recommend will, or indeed can, operate satisfactorily unless it has the full commitment and loyalty of all the participants at headquarters and in the field. On the other hand, we do not contemplate that any system we recommend should remain rigid and immutable as circumstances change. Changes may well have to be made in due course in order to facilitate or improve the operational efficiency of the service as a whole. For example, we recommend later substantial alterations to regions, including the withdrawal of specialists working there. We appreciate, however, that over the years the necessity for filling out the regions again could arise either with some of the specialists or in some other way we cannot now foresee, nor at which we propose to guess. In such circumstances the necessary organisation changes should be made, although for the reasons which we have already indicated we would advocate caution in making changes unless and until the necessity for them is patent.

Recommended structure

5.44 The affairs of Her Majesty's Prison Service in England and Wales should continue to be directed by a Prisons Board. This is not and will not be a true corporate body but the collective name for the group of men or women who we recommend shall be generally responsible for the affairs of the service.

5.45 We recommend the appointment of a *Chairman* of the Prisons Board, who would be the accounting officer for the prison service, with direct access to the Secretary of State. In our view, the size and importance of the prison service and the fact that its functions are unique makes it essential that its administrative head should have direct access to the Home Secretary. As to his civil service grading, we recommend that this should be that of a Second Permanent Secretary. As will be apparent from other parts of this report, over the next few years the administrative head of the prison service will have to demand, obtain and then account for the efficient and economic use of very substantial resources much greater than have been vouchsafed to the service by any government this century. Further, because after some hesitation we consider there should continue to be only one Principal Establishment Officer for the whole of the Home Office including the Prison Department, and that he will remain of Deputy Under Secretary of State rank, then there must on the Prisons Board itself be at least one member senior to that in rank. Finally, from whatever field the chairman is chosen we think that he should have the experience and be of the calibre of a Second Permanent Secretary.

5.46 The Chairman should either be a career civil servant with the experience and skills to fit him for such an important post, an ex-governor grade or someone from outside the civil service, but again with the high administrative qualities required, and also, in his case, with that knowledge and experience of the machnery of government as will enable him to fight for, obtain and administer the resources for the service which are vital. It is essential that the Chairman should remain in post for not less than at least five years, and preferably seven years. We contemplate him as the chief administrator of the service, working principally in London, though of course making such visits to regional offices and establishments as may be necessary to enable him properly and efficiently to discharge his responsibilities. Subject always to the requirement that the best available man should be appointed, in due time we hope that this post will be filled by someone who has had practical experience in governing an establishment: we are satisfied on the evidence given to us that no member of the governor grades has yet been able to acquire the necessary administrative experience. This underlines the point which we make elsewhere in this report that the training of governors must be fuller and longer than it presently is, and that in future selected members of the governor grades must spend substantially longer periods in regional offices and in headquarters in London to enable them to acquire the necessary administrative skills and experience.

5.47 We recommend that the Prisons Board should include a further six members, four of whom should originate either from the general civil service or the governor grades. The first should hold a rank between that of Deputy and Assistant Under Secretary of State, but the others be of the latter rank, with the following titles and responsibilities: —

(a) *Deputy Chairman and Director of Operations* He would ordinarily be that man whom on advice the Secretary of State considers to be the most suitable former member of the governor grades. He will be a man of personality, experience and enthusiasm and the chief operational executive on the Prisons Board. He should be regarded as the head of the operational service, and function, accordingly, as chairman of the senior appointments board. We do not think it is for us to stipulate any particular period for which he should hold the post, but his tenure should ensure as much continuity as possible in the leadership of the service. He should be responsible to the Chairman for all operational aspects of the service in the field and at headquarters. We would expect him to be out of London visiting regional offices and establishments for a proportion of his time. It will be him to whom press and television will look first for statements and explanations about anything and everything that may occur in the field in the prison service. It is not for us to recommend precisely how his divisions within the Prison Department should be constituted. However, we recommend that the casework at present dealt with both at headquarters in London and in the regions should all be dealt with at headquarters.

(b) *Director of Personnel* He would head a Prisons' Establishment Department responsible for all personnel matters throughout the prison service, including training, in respect of all the grades peculiar to the prison service. His department should incorporate not only the present Establishment Division 3 and P6 Division of the Prison Department but also have a shared responsibility for the management of those other grades working in the Prison Department and outstations who ordinarily fall to other present Establishment divisions. It would be to this Director in practice that all serving within the prison service would look for guidance on any personnel question. We would expect the active involvement of the Home Office PEO in prison service matters to be limited in practice to consultation with the Director of Personnel about the appointments of members of the general service grades to the more senior posts at headquarters. We feel that it is imperative, particularly as we have not recommended a separate PEO for each of the prison service and the rest of the Home Office respectively, that so far as practicable the unity and identity of purpose of staff in all grades serving in the prison service at headquarters or outstations should be recognised, but that there should nevertheless be preserved the opportunities for interchange of staff throughout the whole of the Home Office at all levels. It is particularly important that none of the Treasury grades should be given reason to think their careers will suffer during or because of service in the prison administration. We must stress, too, that we regard this Director's post as one of vital importance in the new structure. He will have to shoulder the main responsibility for creating and maintaining a new climate in industrial relations. He too must therefore cultivate an effective presence in the service and by visiting and all other available means become well known to staff everywhere.

(c) *Director of Regimes* He would report to the Chairman but necessarily work in close co-operation with the Deputy Chairman and his other colleagues. He would be responsible for devising, instituting and maintaining the work regimes and the educational and training programmes in establishments. We also attach great importance to this aspect of our recommendations and this Directorate will have a substantial part to play. As a general indication of the Directorate's scope, we would expect it to take over most of the functions exercised by P2 Division and the Directorate of Industries and Farms, and have oversight also of the work of the Chaplain General and the Prison psychological services. In so far as the Directorate of Works employs inmate labour, then that department should report to the Director of Regimes.

(d) *Director of Finance and Administration* He would report direct to the Chairman and be responsible for all future planning and all administration not the responsibility of the Director of Operations, or that of the other two Directors. He would be responsible for finance (including particularly the fresh initiatives we have mentioned previously in this chapter), and for detailed advice to the Chairman on the extent of the need for new prison places, of what type, and where the consequential necessary prisons should be built. Again as a general indication of scope we would expect him to take over most of the functions of P1 and P7 Divisions and also of the Chief Architect's Branch and Directorate of Works. We have also considered whether we should recommend that the Prison Department should have its own Principal Finance Officer. Earlier in this chapter we examined the need to introduce into the Prison Department new and improved systems of financial control and accounting leading to the creation of what we have described in paragraph 5.40 as "a new prison service finance function". Looking to that, and to the fact that our proposals will in any event lead to the Department's acquiring a greater corporate identity than it presently enjoys, we think it probable that the appointment of a separate PFO for the Prison Department will be found to be desirable. The new prison service should in any event have its own Finance Division or capability, where the PFO, if appointed, would be located, and this new financial centre will control all financial affairs. Its chief agents in the field will be the Administration Officers whose functional superior should in future be the Director of Finance and Administration. Whilst we do not consider this means any entirely novel responsibilities for Administration Officers, it will require a fresh impetus to their financial work and give them and their staff a new consequence beyond the substantial one their work already has.

(e) Finally, we recommend that the Prisons Board should also include a further two entirely independent non-executive members. These should be appointed by the Home Secretary on such terms and for such periods as he, the CSD and they agree. Their functions would be two-fold. First, to bring to the meetings and deliberations of the Board their own particular knowledge and expertise. Secondly, to represent on the Board the views of independent society as a whole, and thus contribute to the opening up to public knowledge of all aspects of prison administration as we have recommended at a number of places in this report. To enable them adequately to perform these functions we think that these non-executive members of the Board should be kept properly informed at regular intervals about the activities of the Board and of the Prison Department generally.

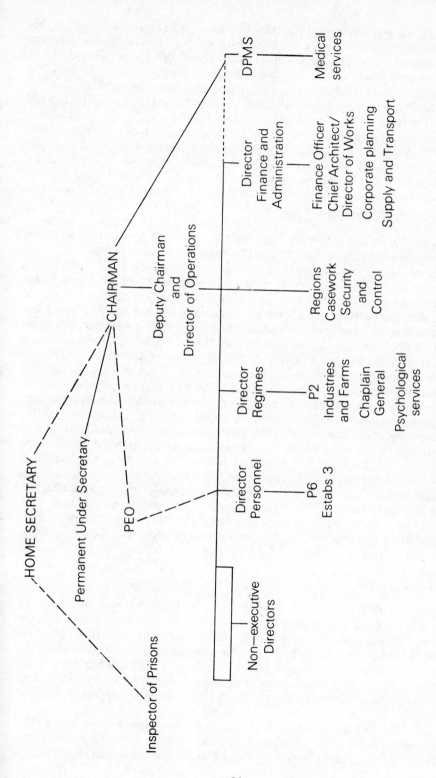

RECOMMENDED ORGANISATION STRUCTURE

HOME SECRETARY

Permanent Under Secretary

Inspector of Prisons

PEO

CHAIRMAN

Non—executive Directors

Director Personnel

P6
Estabs 3

Director Regimes

P2
Industries and Farms

Chaplain General

Psychological services

Deputy Chairman and Director of Operations

Regions
Casework
Security and Control

Director Finance and Administration

Finance Officer

Chief Architect/ Director of Works

Corporate planning

Supply and Transport

DPMS

Medical services

5.48 As will be seen from the above organisation chart, we do not recommend the retention of either the Director of Prison Medical Services (DPMS) or the Chief Inspector as members of the Prisons Board. As to the former, when he and his colleagues gave evidence to us, he took the view that whereas from time to time questions were discussed at meetings of the Prisons Board which affected his Department, more often they did not. He felt that his time could be better spent seeing to the work of this specialist department, rather than remaining a member of the Prisons Board. We agree with this view, particularly when, as will be seen, we shall recommend the withdrawal from regional offices of regional medical officers. We think that the management line of communication for the medical officers in establishments should be direct to the Medical Directorate in London and not via the region.

5.49 We should add that we received a certain amount of evidence contending that the Prison Medical Service should be incorporated in and become part of the National Health Service. To do this issue full justice would have needed not only more time than we have had but also substantially more evidence. Nevertheless we think that we are able to and should say that the material which we have received has not satisfied us of the desirability of transferring responsibility for the Prison Medical Service to the DHSS. That we do not recommend that the DPMS should remain a member of the Prisons Board is no reflection upon either him, his Department or its members. Rather it is a recognition of the fact that he and his colleagues have a very specialised job to do and require as much time as possible to do it. Whilst recommending that the DPMS should no longer be a member of the Prisons Board, we nevertheless couple this with a recommendation that if and when the Board has on its agenda at any of its meetings any issue which involves medical questions, they should automatically ask the DPMS to join them in order to give them the benefit of his skilled professional advice. Finally, in our view there are insufficient prison medical officers in the service. At the same time as giving effect to our recommendations about the physical conditions in which those now in the service do have to work, we hope that an urgent review will be initiated of what should be done to encourage more and better qualified doctors to join the Prison Medical Service.

INSPECTION

5.50 As to the future of the present Chief Inspector post, we now turn to deal with the question of inspection generally. We have found this the most difficult organisation issue. No-one could deny that there must be effective inspection or that it should in some sense be as "independent" as possible. However, the degree of practicable or useful independence is not something that may be taken for granted or requiring no further discussion. This is because independence raises in practice various constitutional issues.

5.51 Most of the evidence we received did not explore these issues. The governors stated only that there should be an independent inspector reporting to the Home Secretary direct and his reports should be published.

The regional directors took a similar line. Reports should be published and contribute to opening up the service generally. The inspector should be less concerned with detailed in-depth examinations of particular institutions than with general themes relating to the service as a whole.

5.52 Although no other staff groups had thought out positions even this far on inspection, we received a number of views from various outside observers. In general they favoured independent inspection. In some respects they went even further. One considered a totally independent inspector reporting to the Home Secretary direct would obviate the need for the prisons' ombudsman one or two witnesses had thought desirable.

5.53 Another thought such an inspector could deal with casework. He acknowledged, however, there would be some difficulty since the inspector would necessarily be at one remove from the administrative machine upon whom he would yet be dependent in practice for all information if some duplicating counter-bureaucracy were not to be set up.

5.54 The Home Office submitted a lengthy and detailed paper. Having first described the existing arrangements for inspection, it went on to discuss inspections generally, the nature of the various types of inspection, and the precise meaning of "independence" that could be said to arise in certain contexts.

5.55 A distinction was drawn between an "efficiency" audit on the one hand and a "propriety" audit on the other. The first was defined as concerned to examine the efficiency with which a unit or organisation was carrying out its responsibilities: the second with whether the establishment was paying due regard to established procedures and safeguards. We doubt whether in practice there is any real difference between these two types of inspection: any of the former must be concerned at least in part with matters considered by the latter and vice versa. Be that as it may, the Home Office argued that one would have to continue these types of inspections, whatever organisation be adopted, and that therefore we should recommend the retention of an Inspectorate for this purpose. Although it was unnecessary to inspect all aspects of a given establishment at the same time, a good case could nonetheless be made out for increasing the frequency of effective inspections of establishments from once every five to once every three years.

5.56 The third type of inspection considered by the relevant Home Office paper was that of inmate grievance procedures. Existing procedures comprising, for instance, the Boards of Visitors, the Parliamentary Commissioner for Administration (the Ombudsman), access to the Home Secretary by way of petition or through Members of Parliament, and so on were deemed sufficient. Whilst it was recognised that there had been a call in some quarters for the appointment of a "Prisons Ombudsman", if he were given the power, after the investigation of a grievance, to over-ride a decision reached by the Prisons Board, which in effect meant a decision of the Home Office Secretary if the Prison Department remained within the Home Office, then that would be difficult to reconcile constitutionally with the theory of Ministerial responsibility to Parliament. If a Prisons Ombudsman were not to have the power to over-ride a decision of the Prisons Board, then he would not be in a position to do anything more than the existing Parliamentary Commissioner for Administration.

5.57 We think that these points are sound. We note, however, that an official rather like a Prisons Ombudsman has been appointed in Canada reporting to the Solicitor General direct, and that there may be useful lessons to be learned from experience there although time has not allowed us to pursue the matter to a conclusion. We also understand that consideration is being given within the Home Office to the form which the review of grievance procedures recommended in the Expenditure Sub-Committee report might take. We certainly think there should be one. A number of important issues are involved. We have not, for example, been impressed by the length of time taken to answer petitions.

5.58 On independence the argument was twofold. First, for so long as the prison service remained the direct responsibility of a Minister answerable to Parliament, then the latter was the only body which had the authority to judge the quality or efficiency of the management of the prison service. In such circumstances, the argument proceeded "There is no basis for an efficiency audit to be conducted by a body established so as to be independent from Government". The argument is a nice one, but we think it is based upon the assumption that Parliament and government can be equated. In practice this may be so; in strict constitutional theory it is fallacious. In practice, provided a government can command a majority in Parliament, then it can defeat any motion critical of its handling of prison matters based upon any inspector's report, whether made outside the Home Office, for instance by a Prisons' Ombudsman, or inside the Home Office by the Chief Inspector. In this sense no inspection can be described as independent of government, although theoretically one can contemplate Parliament taking a different view of an inspection from government if the latter fails to obtain the necessary votes.

5.59 Secondly, and alternatively, if by "independent" in this context was merely meant independent of the prison service itself and those responsible for its operational management, and it was contemplated that reports should be made direct to the Home Secretary, these too would not be truly independent. This was because the recipient of the reports (the Minister), and his chief lieutenant (the Permanent Under Secretary of State) were themselves the very same people who were constitutionally responsible for that management of the prison service upon which the reports had been made. In these circumstances the apparent independence was again illusory. Further, if nevertheless that type of inspection were adopted, then there would have to be created within the Home Office some further department or facility outside the Prison Department to advise the Permanent Under Secretary of State whether the quasi-independent inspector's report should be accepted or not. This was because the prison service itself

94

could not proffer that advice upon an "independent" inspection, of itself. Accordingly, there was no case for an "independent" inspection, whether the prison service remained within or without government. The best course would be to retain the present system with a Chief Inspector on the Prisons Board to reinforce his substantial experience with appropriate status. It was accepted that whatever could be done to improve the efficiency and frequency of the reports of his department should be done.

5.60 As to publication, the Chief Inspector's reports, because they might well contain frank criticisms of personal performances which it would be better to keep within the sphere of management and not make available to a larger audience, should not be published. On the other hand it was accepted that there might be merit in the suggestion that the Chief Inspector should each year make a general report on various broad aspects of the prison service and its work. This could be incorporated in that year's Report on the work of the Prison Department and so give wide circulation to more general comments, good or bad.

5.61 Whilst we accept the validity of the Home Office argument and that it leads to the conclusions stated, we do not think that this is enough. We accept that in both theory and practice no inspection can be independent of Parliament, and thus generally in practice cannot be independent of government: we also accept that both in theory and practice no inspection carried out by a member of the Home Office can be independent of that government department nor thus of a prison service which also forms part of it. Nevertheless we have no doubt both that the prison service would benefit from and that public sentiment requires that as many aspects of government, which includes the prison service, should be opened up to as wide an audience as possible. We therefore think that there should be a system of inspection of the prison service which although not "independent" of it in either of the senses canvassed in the Home Office paper, should nevertheless be distanced from it as far as may be practicable.

5.62 In so far as the in depth inspections hitherto carried out by the Chief Inspector and his Department of particular establishments are concerned, we think that in future these should be carried out by the regional directors. This should be a part of their operational management duties and their reports should be to the Director of Operations. They should make these inspections, either of a whole establishment, or a particular part of it, as frequently as they think necessary and they should be given the resources to do so. We do, however, recommend that there should be constituted within the Home Office an independent department to be called the "Prisons Inspectorate", headed either by someone independent of the civil service entirely or by a senior ex-governor as the Home Secretary may decide, with the post of HM Chief Inspector of Prisons, holding the same rank between that of Deputy and Assistant Under Secretary of State as will be held by the Deputy Chairman and Director of Operations. This department should not be a big one, but it should contain people with relevant prison service experience as well as such others as the Home

Secretary thinks appropriate. HM Chief Inspector of Prisons and his staff should be available to make *ad hoc* inspections of any incidents which may occur at the request of the Home Secretary: they should be empowered to set out unannounced and make an inspection of a particular establishment or a particular part of an establishment as and when they think it necessary or desirable to do so: they should also make inspections of more general aspects of the work of the prison service—for instance, of accounting procedures, or into questions of quarters, or into particular aspects of security or control. We recommend that except where security considerations dictate otherwise the reports of HM Chief Inspector of Prisons should be published and laid before Parliament and that each year his Department should also make a general report on the whole prison service, in so far as they have seen it during the year, which should be included in that year's Report of the work of the Prison Department. We do not anticipate that the Prisons Inspectorate should deal with particular grievances, either of prison staff or of inmates, unless one or more of these suggest that an inspection of one or other of the types that we have described should be made. As we have already said, we think that casework relating to inmates should be done at headquarters in London. Individual grievances of prison staff should be dealt with promptly and sympathetically by governors in the first place, if possible, or alternatively by the Directorate of Personnel as swiftly as possible.

REGIONS

5.63 As explained in Chapter 2 the four present regions in England and Wales were set up in 1969–70 as the result of a management review. The main questions that faced us were what sort of future should the regions have and what should their relationship with headquarters be:

5.64 For their part the present regional directors all told us in effect that as regionalisation had developed, they were nevertheless unable to do effectively the job that they ought to be doing, that is to say the management and direction of operations within their regions. With their combined experience they felt that they should have substantially more authority to take operational decisions in the field and not be circumscribed by frequent circulars and instructions from headquarters. Although the latter contained some people with substantial experience as governors, a large number of the decisions seemed to be taken by those who had no operational experience at all. Once Estabs 3 had been brought within the Prison Department, the regional directors contended that they should be given authority to deal at least with some personnel matters: they said that their position as managers lacks credibility in the eyes of governors and prison officers when they themselves had so little authority to act positively, particularly in these areas of personnel management and industrial relations.

5.65 Although the regional directors were unanimous in their evidence that the regional structure as at present constituted did not work efficiently and needed alteration, they had different views about how this could best be achieved. One took the view that the regional organisations should be strengthened and enlarged on all fronts, effectively leaving headquarters with only a small policy, planning and general oversight function. The remaining three were of the opposite view. They contended that regional offices should shed most of their present functions other than that of operational management and administration, but that their authority in the field should be greatly enlarged, not only in what might generally be described as field work, but particularly in those matters to which we have already referred, namely personnel management and industrial relations.

5.66 Similarly, opposing views were expressed about where the increasing amount of casework should be dealt with. On the one hand it was suggested that more could and should be done in the regions: on the other, it was suggested that all casework should go back to headquarters, where in any event the answer would ultimately have to go.

5.67 If the view that the regions should concentrate more, and indeed almost exclusively, on operational field work should prevail, it followed that there would no longer be a need in the regional offices for a number of the specialists that there are at present. Those of the regional directors who advocated thinning regions down to an authoritative operational function felt that for this purpose it would be necessary to retain the regional catering officer, the regional education officer, the regional industrial officer and the regional psychologist. In the regional directors' opinion the other specialities could equally well report to superiors at headquarters. Another view was, however, expressed in relation particularly to the regional education officer and the regional chaplain, and this was that instead of having these posts in the regional offices a particular establishment would look to the local Canon or senior churchman in its area, or alternatively to the head of the local polytechnic, sixth form college or technical institute for advice on educational and vocational matters. The point was made that in this way, and perhaps in other disciplines, a start could be made in involving a given establishment in its local community and gaining the latter's interest in it.

5.68 When the governors came to give oral evidence to the Inquiry we had considerable discussion with them about the present regional system. The general view was that presently it falls between two stools and should go one way or the other. Either there should be substantially more regionalisation, taking operational matters away from headquarters; alternatively the regions should be trimmed, leaving them in essence merely as the operational spearhead of prison headquarters in London. One point which did trouble the governors was the increasing amount of casework which had to be dealt with, that is to say answers to petitions by inmates, applications to the European Commission, letters to Members of Parliament and the like. We thought that the governors were somewhat ambivalent about what should be done with this increasing casework, but in the end we think that they took the view that it would probably be better to have it all done at headquarters and not to attempt to split a part between the regions and part between headquarters as is done at present. The present system as laid down in the circular instruction cannot be faulted in theory: nevertheless

97

there are few petitions which do not need some interference between the region and headquarters. It would be much better if one organisation dealt with the casework entirely. It was quite clear that the governors did not think that the regional organisation was in fact presently playing a very large part in the system, although it was also apparent that they were not averse to having an experienced regional director within their area to whom they could go for advice and upon whose shoulder they could lean as the occasion might demand. In the governors' view the regional organisation as at present constituted certainly wasted resources but it was substantially better than having to deal with the headquarters direct.

5.69 Although the POA had nothing specifically to say about regions, the Outstations Branch of the SCPS had quite a lot. They wanted more autonomous regions. Headquarters should be confined to policy and legislative matters, leaving the executive functions of implementing that policy and the day to day control of establishments to regional offices. This should result in closer and more effective support for governors. There should be six not four regions with greater administrative support. Regional directors should be Assistant Under Secretaries of State supported by a Governor I and a Senior Principal.

5.70 Of the outside observers none was very enthusiastic about regionalisation, although for different reasons. Some doubted whether the regions performed any worthwhile function, particularly at the cost of having substantial specialist staff at each regional headquarters. Others took the view that decentralisation through the regional organisation was essential, but that, largely as the result of the economies that had been imposed upon the prison service and the regions over the past few years, the regions had no "teeth" and needed to be given substantially greater powers and resources than they presently had. Although there seemed general agreement that the amount of casework on prisoners' complaints and rights was bound to increase, there was no agreement whether this should all or only to a limited extent be done at regions, or whether, as the Secretary of State was bound ultimately to be involved, at least in name, it would be better to transfer all casework up to headquarters.

5.71 The Home Office evidence was that regionalisation had been long enough in operation to admit of a valid assessment of the work of regional offices and their value. The general conclusion was that, except in the specialist fields, the regions were under-resourced for the work they were theoretically required to undertake. In particular, although a substantial amount of casework had been devolved from headquarters to regions, the latter had not been given the necessary staff with which to do it. The result was that, despite a considerable investment in the regional organisation, headquarters had not been relieved of the routine work that tended to burden administrative divisions with casework and divert them from policy development. In turn the combination of the lack of sufficient resources and the burden of casework had together prevented the regions from devoting themselves to the supportive relationships with establishments that had characterised the former prison directorate. Similarly, the detailed surveillance of the operational work of establishments in the field had suffered and the role fallen largely to the present Inspectorate. All this had led to a strongly held view, especially amongst staff in the field, that regions should be considerably reinforced to enable them effectively to fulfil all these tasks and thus facilitate further transfer of authority from headquarters to regional level. This view, however, overlooked the problems of developing operational support and of transferring more casework, and ignored public expectations about consistency, and inescapable constraints on finance and manpower. Developing the regions further was likely to cause the rise of four considerable bureaucracies with the characteristics, already discernible in the existing regions, often attributed to headquarters. On one view too it could be argued the creation of regions had led to headquarters becoming more remote because they were interposed between it and establishments.

5.72 What was required was not to transfer any further areas of operational responsibility to regional offices, but to expand the latter's existing operational roles and so enlarge the field work which they were able to undertake. If regions were to be so redirected, then a number of the specialists presently there were either unnecessary, or alternatively would be able to do their jobs more effectively in headquarters. As was the present case, for instance, with the Directorate of Industries and Farms, a specialist transferred to London could there still be made responsible for a particular region, or part of a region, but from the centre do his work as effectively. There was no need for regional medical officers: medical officers in establishments could and should have a direct line through to the Medical Directorate in London. Similarly, the need for regional educational officers and chaplains was doubted. As to regional psychologists, their work monitoring such things as classification procedures, regimes and their results could better be undertaken in London, even though a particular psychologist's responsibility might relate only to a particular part of the country, or indeed to a particular group of establishments. On the other hand there seemed a stronger case, if not for retaining regional industrial managers, then at least for a regional officer in charge of works and regime matters.

5.73 We have considered all this evidence very carefully in conjunction with what we heard and saw on our visits. We think the effective choice lies between substantially reinforcing regions to undertake their present roles and freshly devolved work from headquarters; cutting them back to concentrate on operations, support, surveillance and other similar roles; or abolishing them altogether and withdrawing all the functions to headquarters.

5.74 We reject the last because, powerful though our reservations about regionalisation are, we acknowledge that any prison system as large as that of England and Wales requires some form of localised field administration. Abolishing regions, therefore, would only improverish the quality of the professional management of the service. In so far as support functions were carried out from headquarters—as we think would be necessary—then these would in fact call into existence the very nascent regional structure of the former directorates formalised by the regional outposing of 1969–70.

Developing regions further, on the other hand, could be done at the cost only of a substantial increase in staffing costs and a higher degree of bureaucratisation.

5.75 We have concluded and recommend that at least for the present the future of the regions lies principally in the field of operations together with the limited personnel role that at present goes with it. Regional directors must be considered to be active divisions under the Director of Operations. Rather than circumscribe the powers and duties of regional directors in this field, as we think has been the case in recent years, partly as policy and partly as the result of economic stringency, we think that they should be given the widest possible operational powers. They are all experienced ex-Governor Is and they must be allowed to use their knowledge and experience. The more that they can do in the field, the smaller need be the Director of Operations' department in London, and this is a trend which we would wish to encourage. Regional directors must be given adequate resources to do their jobs. They will be visiting establishments within their regions even more frequently than they are able to at present, with the assistance no doubt of a deputy regional director. They should be responsible, as we have already indicated, for carrying out the detailed management inspections heretofore carried out by the Chief Inspector. On all operational matters the regional director should report to the Director of Operations. They should continue to have power to transfer all but category A inmates amongst establishments within their region and, by agreement, between regions under any general instructions issued by the Director of Operations. The disposition of category A prisoners should remain a matter for the Director of Operations in consultation with the Chairman. In general, we consider all the regional specialists should be dispensed with or withdrawn to headquarters.

5.76 Whether there should remain the present four regions, or whether some degree of reorganisation is called for—say, by creating six smaller or three larger regions or turning Greater London into a region of its own—must we think be a matter for the new Deputy Chairman and Director of Operations, in the light of his operational experience.

OUTSTATIONS
5.77 This section is concerned with the organisation of all the various establishments in the field within the prison service—prisons themselves, borstal institutions and detention centres.

5.78 In their evidence the Governors' Branch recognised that in order to keep abreast of all the various aspects of their work today, they required substantially greater and deeper training than they presently received. This applied not merely on entry as an Assistant Governor II, but also throughout their service. They needed training, they told us, not merely on the professional side, but on the public relations side, on the management side, and on the administrative side. In particular, training and experience in industrial relations as they must now be handled in 1979 was essential in

100

so far as they were concerned. We agree and we return to this aspect elsewhere in this report.

5.79 Reflecting perhaps the present feelings of inadequacy of some governors in these fields, the Governors' Branch contended governing governors were not given the operational powers which they should have to enable them properly to run their establishments. They found that they had to refer to regional office or to headquarters matters which they ought to have the power to deal with themselves. To this contention, two of our informed independent witnesses replied that this has been a recurrent complaint from governors: in the majority of cases they do have the necessary power, but do not use it.

5.80 The Governors' Branch also contended that the governing governor of an establishment was unable to delegate sufficiently; he had to concern himself with the minutiae of the day to day operations within his establishment with little or no time for planning new regimes or initiating fresh developments in this or that field. The general rule is that the deputy governor of an establishment is two ranks below the governing governor. They suggested that the rule should be that the deputy governor should be only one rank below the governing governor and that it should be he who should act, as it were, as the adjutant responsible for the day to day running of the establishment, leaving the governing governor time to apply his mind to the wider considerations to which we have referred. They also made it clear that there were effectively no budgets for which they were responsible. Accounting was done centrally and the governors had very little idea, for instance, how much it cost per week to feed each inmate within their own institution. They did not have control over their own resources and were not able to govern their establishments as they wanted, but had to practise a somewhat dull uniformity imposed upon them from above.

5.81 The Outstations Branch expressed similar views in the course of their evidence. They, however, went further and argued, first, for the departmentalisation of all those of Executive Officer level and above who were carrying out administrative duties in outstations; and secondly, for the appointment at each establishment of an Administration Officer of equivalent rank to the deputy governor. They suggested that the latter should take all the day to day purely operational matters off the shoulders of the governing governor, whilst the equivalent Administration Officer should become responsible to the latter for all the other services and activities in establishments, including such matters as the discipline office, staff quarters, prison officers' detail and censorship of mail.

5.82 As we have said, we accept and will recommend substantially improved training for governors at all stages of their career. We have insufficient material to express any view upon the present adequacy or inadequacy of governors' powers. We do, however, recommend that if they do now lack necessary operational powers, not only should they be given them to the fullest extent possible but also they should be encouraged to use them. Regional directors should discourage governors from seeking their advice or consent on every occasion when a difficult decision has to be made. The prison service as a whole, through the Director of Operations and his regional directors, should not seek to achieve a dull uniformity amongst establishments with similar purposes. There is no reason, we think, why the regime in one prison of one type should be identical with the regime in another prison of the same type either within the same region or throughout the United Kingdom. We think that regional directors should encourage individualism and indeed experiment by experienced governors within their own establishments, subject always to the overall direction of the regional director and, if necessary, the Director of Operations. We also recommend that governors should be given as wide powers as possible to deal with those personnel and industrial relations problems which will arise in their particular establishment.

5.83 In so far as the other contentions of the Governors' and Outstations Branches to which we have referred are concerned, we think that there is a case, in the larger establishments, for a three-tier gubernatorial hierarchy. It is not for us to specify the particular establishments but we do recommend that discussions should start between the Home Office and the Governors' Branch to identify those large and complicated establishments, where the governing governor may have to be absent from his establishment relatively frequently, to which a deputy governor only one rank below that of the governing governor might be appointed to relieve the latter of some of the day to day operational and management duties. We envisage this deputy governor as additional to the complement of these large establishments as this is presently constituted but we would only expect such an appointment in a very limited proportion of the present establishments. Elsewhere governing governors must govern, which means being directly responsible for all that occurs within their establishments. In so far as Administration Officers are concerned, whilst everything we have seen and heard testified to the devotion which they and their staff bring to their tasks, we do not think that any sufficient case has been made out for any alteration to their status or position. Indeed, we feel that "departmentalisation" were it to be introduced as the Outstations Branch argued, might well redound to their detriment and reduce the opportunities for interchange with and promotion in other parts of the Home Office.

5.84 There is, however, one area where we think administration staff need much more support: Prison Department outstations seem woefully deficient of adequate office machinery. Time after time we visited pay sections where weekly pay was being done in the most laborious fashion possible, that is by hand. It is evident that such a system cannot long survive and is already seriously over-burdened. Attempts to persuade prison service grades to be paid monthly (with the usual financial inducements to open bank accounts) have apparently so far substantially failed. Whereas we appreciate management must be reluctant to resort to payment practices not popular with staff, when particular staff preferences result in tying down scarce staff resources in the way that they are at present, then we think that larger questions of public policy than staff convenience must arise. We feel, therefore, that the staff associations should endeavour to be more sympathetic to questions of operating convenience in future and that, if necessary, more determined steps should be taken to reduce the costs of pay administration, for instance including requiring all fresh entrants to accept monthly payment. Further, we would strongly recommend that up to date business machines (such as desk top calculators) should be allocated to penal establishments with the object not only of simplifying pay administration but also providing all the other local facilities of budgetary and stock control which are desirable.

Management Style

5.85 Structure is one thing, style is another. Style expresses the life of the organisation and gives it recognisable shape and content to the people who work in it. A revised organisation structure gives an opportunity for a revivified management style and we hope the opportunity will not be lost. This is because every organisation requires fresh impetus from time to time and in that respect the Prison Department is no worse and no better placed than any other organisation.

5.86 We have felt that present management attitudes seem somewhat defensive. Some critics would say this is because there is a lot to be defensive about. Whatever the truth of that, there is bound to be a stand-still both in the approach to and during an Inquiry such as ours, and the enforced condition of expectancy cramps fresh initiative. Further, if it is true that the Prison Department in England and Wales has been defensive, it is in good measure because it has been under attack and, as the saying has it, it is unfair to call an animal dangerous merely because, when attacked, it defends itself.

5.87 The attack has come from a number of directions. There has been the inexorable eating away of the physical fabric of establishments and the persistent pressure of increasing numbers on declining resources. There have been the psychological attacks of all those groups who, for one reason or another, do not wish the prisons administration well. There have also been novel problems arising from staff militancy.

5.88 The result has been that management has become preoccupied with fighting the daily tactical battle. We hope the general effect of what we recommend will lift some of that load and allow management to resume more creative roles. Of course, we do not imagine that we have found the solution to all the problems, and as we have said the prison services will have themselves to find some of the most important solutions to current problems. Some of our solutions cannot in any case be "final". For example, the absorption of the personnel function into the new Prison Department in England and Wales will not by itself solve all personnel problems at a stroke: the new Personnel Directorate will still have to decline requests for transfer and turn down many other applications. The point of the change is to make prisons management *generally* more responsive to, as well as responsible for, personnel matters.

5.89 What we would like to see is the unambiguous re-assertion of leadership from the centre both at headquarters and also by governors at establishments. This can be achieved in many ways and may be sustained by new blood at the top from time to time stressing new things. But finding and developing a positive style is an important priority. Having found it, then communicating it effectively is another. This means some fresh thinking and supplementing office notices and notices to staff with more attractive and discursive bulletins. We must say we have found it remarkable that, apart from the POA magazine, there is no publication that circulates throughout the service, and no management newsletter at all. The case for a house journal seems unassailable and one is long overdue. We think that it would also be an advantage if day to day press relations were brought more within the Prison Department itself.

5.90 As we have said in the introduction, the reasons for setting up the Inquiry in the first place have obliged us to pay more attention to what is wrong than to what is right. Accordingly, this is a place where we should also say that we have no doubt there is much energy and competence in prison service management. That energy and that competence will be so much more effective when allied to a more self-confident management style. New energies and new abilities will be released and used for the good of the service in consequence.

BOARDS OF VISITORS

5.91 We have not had time to examine all their duties or take evidence on them generally in a formal way. This is yet another case that illustrates how the speed with which we have been obliged to work has prevented our giving some subjects the attention their importance deserved. On the other hand, we were aware that their functions had been recently, albeit "unofficially" reviewed so that they have received their fair share of attention. At the same time, too, we have had a lot of contact with them. We spoke to representatives of the Boards during each visit to establishments, and we sought the written comments of them all on the matters before us. As to other evidence, staff associations hardly referred to them, although they seemed of interest to a number of outside observers.

5.92 We think the Boards are vital institutions which, although their work is little known and appreciated, are important parts of the prison system. Their chief role is to act as agents of local accountability and control over the good management of institutions. They should, therefore, be well informed and acute but friendly watchdogs of the public interest. Whilst formally their powers are limited to certain disciplinary and control functions, the potential for their activity is substantial, if not uniformly exploited by them. We think the recent growth in interest in their functions in England and Wales is entirely healthy, and we think the same appropriate elsewhere in the United Kingdom. Attempts to widen their background should obviously continue, and further development of their training and collective conscience would seem sensible.

5.93 In general the main question we thought it necessary to consider was whether the adjudicatory and inspectorial function of Boards should be separated. Separation was one of the recommendations of the independent committee under the chairmanship of Lord Jellicoe set up in respect of England and Wales by Justice, the Howard League and NACRO and whose report, *Boards of Visitors of Penal Institutions,* was published in 1975. We understand the Home Office consulted Boards about the Jellicoe Report. Although this revealed a wide measure of support for the "pastoral" recommendations, there was widespread opposition to separation. The Home Secretary in December 1976 commended a number of the recommendations to Boards, but declined to implement, amongst others, the one on separation.

5.94 There was disagreement amongst the outside observers about the Boards, a majority being in favour of separating the roles. One went further and suggested that, once the adjudicatory role had been taken away from Boards of Visitors and some other tribunal set up, there should be legal representation supported by legal aid for both prison officer and prisoner in any disciplinary proceedings before the tribunal. Whatever the complications and additional cost, sooner or later prisons had to be opened up to public knowledge and inspection. Another witness, although accepting that there was an apparent inconsistency between the two roles, was cautious about separating them. He was anxious about bringing those who would in truth be outsiders into prisons, and pointed out that Boards did, or at least should, know their prison and thus be in a better position to adjudicate fairly upon matters which come before them. Creating some form of external tribunal for adjudications on prisoners within prisons would make it very difficult to deny legal representation and thus legal aid. This was bound to involve additional expense and it had to be asked whether in the present economic circumstances such additional expenditure could be justified.

5.95 In their written evidence only one Board favoured separation. In our discussions with Boards, although none was in favour as a whole of separation, a few individual members were. They argued that the two functions clashed in principle and inmates would regard Boards as irretrievably management biased for so long as they had adjudicatory powers. If Boards lost those powers, then they could avoid becoming an inmate pressure group and losing staff support by taking a more positive interest in the staff, an area of Board activity some members thought much neglected.

5.96 We have taken the opportunity of studying the two recent judgments of the Court of Appeal and the Divisional Court (and particularly the second judgment in the latter of 15 June 1979) in the cases of *R. v The Board of Visitors of Hull Prison, (ex parte Cotterill and others)* and *R. v The Board of Visitors of Wandsworth Prison, (ex parte Rosa).* Apart from helping to clarify our thinking substantially, the effect of these judgments has been to define the position of Boards and lay down the standards that

105

are to apply to their conduct of adjudications. Henceforth adjudications will be liable to review in the Divisional Court by *certiorari*. This important change powerfully reinforces, of course, the recent Home Office advice to Boards on the conduct of adjudications and which stemmed from the Home Office Working Party on Adjudication Procedures that, like the Jellicoe Committee, reported in 1975.

5.97 We consulted some of HM Judges informally when the Divisional Court's second judgment was fresh in their minds. Most did not think separation was desirable, provided Board adjudications could be kept up to a proper standard by appropriate review. Resort to the full procedure of a criminal court was not justified on merits and could only increase costs. On the other hand, they were sympathetic to more cases being put out to the ordinary criminal courts where an offence against discipline was also an offence under the criminal law.

5.98 Although it was not addressed directly to these points, the Crown Office in Scotland (i.e the headquarters of the Procurator Fiscal Service) put an interesting paper to us illustrating the difficulty of ensuring a truly fair trial in the criminal courts in cases where inmates were accused of assaults on staff and where the case turned on the jury's assessment of the relative credibility of staff and inmate witnesses. Attention was also drawn to the fact that a trial might not take place for some months after the assault but the accused spend the intervening period in solitary confinement. Courts had in practice no deterrent sanction available in respect of life prisoners (having no remission to lose) or others where the inmate had established a record so bad that release on licence or on parole was so distant a prospect that his behaviour was not constrained by it.

5.99 This last point was only one of several practical points drawn to our attention as applying should the Board's adjudicatory function be given to a fresh tribunal. For example, that tribunal (in so far as it was not a criminal court) would need to be empowered to deal with disciplinary offences that were not at the same time criminal offences. In addition, though Boards deal with less than five per cent of all discipline offences in England and Wales, offences arise in all establishments, a number of which are fairly remote. Some way would have to be found of ensuring adequate, if only occasional, tribunal cover in each case and ensuring too that the members were familiar with local circumstances.

5.100 The Home Office in their evidence adhered to the decision of 1976. Guidance had been circulated to all Boards in 1977 on the procedure for conducting adjudications to ensure that the proceedings were fair to all concerned and the principles of natural justice observed. An adjudication was essentially a forum for dealing with internal disciplinary matters in which the adjudicating panel had an inquisitorial function as opposed to simply weighing the evidence advanced by both sides as in court proceedings. The recent court rulings did not alter that essential difference. It was claimed, too, that the most serious situations and those where there seemed to be a particular need for a less domestic and more formal investigation were referred to the police, e.g. serious criminal offences. The Jellicoe Committee itself had seemed to accept that the prison environment was special, and that the pressures of a closed society in which individuals could not escape from each other when proceedings were over meant that witnesses might be reluctant to come forward or tell all they knew. It did not seem that outsiders would be any more successful in avoiding such difficulties. There was no way of allowing appeals from Boards to the courts which did not increase delay and costs substantially as compared with current review arrangements.

5.101 These are serious issues. Boards may award 180 days loss of remission for the most serious offences and that is a substantial jurisdiction. We appreciate that remission is a privilege and not a right, but that distinction is in practice now a fine one.

5.102 The choice lies between two views. The one contends that since many, if not most, adjudications by Boards are on facts which do at the same time constitute offences against the criminal law triable in the ordinary criminal courts (e.g. assaults), the adjudications should also effectively be criminal trials, with all the safeguards for the accused that these involve. The second view is that adjudications are not, and should not be thought of as criminal trials: they are the proceedings of domestic tribunals to which the principles of natural justice, which really only means those of common fairness, apply; that to equate adjudications with trials would be to misrepresent their true nature; and that to provide legal representation and legal aid could only introduce unwarranted cost and delays where continuing uncertainty can quickly affect the mood of staff and inmates in volatile institutions.

5.103 On balance we do not think a sufficient case for change has been made out. We have come to the conclusion that, despite the apparent inconsistency between the two roles, we should recommend that these should continue as they are presently exercised. We think that the recent court decisions have substantially clarified the position and, in conjunction with the recent advice from the Home Office on the conduct of adjudications, will ensure that adjudications overall are properly and fairly carried out. The fact that judicial review is now available means Boards are subject to a discipline of public, judicial review more effective than that formerly undertaken by the Home Office.

5.104 We are conscious that concentrating on this one issue is in danger of appearing to put our views on Boards out of balance. In fact we consider their other functions of equal significance and susceptible of greater developments. For example, we would like to see the function of Boards extended in two particular areas. First, their statutory concern is at present solely for inmates. We think that they should have an obligation similarly to concern themselves with the welfare of prison staff and their families and to bring any question to the notice of the appropriate authority, be

107

he the governor, the medical officer, the regional director, or perhaps the Chairman. Secondly, members of Boards should consider the desirability of making themselves available at their establishments at specific and advertised times to talk to any member of staff or inmate who wishes to see them. Thirdly, we think that Boards should be encouraged, if not required, to do more than they do now to involve their prison and its community, staff and inmates, in the local community from which they as members of the relevant Board are drawn. We think that members of Boards of Visitors should consider themselves not merely as independent outsiders from the local community coming into a prison as overseers in the inmates' interests, but also as informed insiders with a duty to increase their local community's knowledge and understanding of what goes on in their prison, and to involve as many of the latter in its work as possible. In due time practically every prisoner has to re-enter the society from which he has for a period been forcibly separated. He will do so the more easily, and be the more likely to conform with its standards and requirements when he comes out if, whilst he is serving his sentence, that free society on the outside maintains a continuing and interested contact with him. In these respects we find ourselves entirely at one with the similar concern expressed by the Jellicoe and Expenditure Committees. How best such initiatives should be made and renewed is something that should remain the constant concern of individual Boards and the Home Departments at all times.

Visiting Committees in Scotland

5.105 With one or two relatively unimportant differences the functions of Visiting Committees in Scotland are the same as those of Boards of Visitors in England and Wales, and what we have just said about the latter accordingly applies equally to the former. There is however a difference in the constitution of the two bodies and, for reasons that will become apparent, this merits some comment. In Scotland the Visiting Committees for young offender and borstal establishments are appointed, as in England and Wales, by the Secretary of State, but those for adult establishments are appointed not by him but by local authorities. The authorities are those in the area where the establishment is located and additionally in the case of long-term establishments, those in the areas from which the majority of the inmates come. The reasons for this method of appointment are largely historical and need not concern us here. What is of more importance is that the appointing authorities are listed in a schedule to the Prison (Scotland) Rules 1952. Under the Local Government (Scotland) Act 1973, however, all of these local authorities were abolished but six years later there has still been no amending legislation to alter the schedule to the 1952 Rules. There were, of course, transitional provisions in the 1973 Act, but it must surely be a reflection of the importance attached to Visiting Committees in Scotland that it has taken so long to regularise their position.

5.106 This apparent lack of official interest in Visiting Committees also shows itself in other ways. We understand that, unlike their colleagues in England and Wales, members of Visiting Committees are offered no formal training and are given no official guidance on the nature of their duties or on how these duties, and in particular their adjudicatory functions, should be discharged. We have already made it clear that we consider that Boards of Visitors occupy an important role in the operation of the prison system: this must be equally so in the case of Visiting Committees, but can be so only if those concerned are properly trained, instructed and encouraged. We accordingly recommend that immediate steps should be taken, first to secure the necessary statutory authority to regularise the position of Visiting Committees for adult establishments, and, secondly, to secure that proper and adequate training, instruction and information are made available to the members of all Visiting Committees.

Boards of Visitors and Visiting Committees in Northern Ireland

5.107 Northern Ireland has a mixture of Boards and Committees depending on the nature of the establishment concerned. We are not aware of any difficulties concerning their appointment or training and would simply confirm that what we have said in relation to Boards in England and Wales applies equally to Boards and Committees in the Province.

CHAPTER 6

RESOURCES

6.1 The first of our terms of reference requires us to examine and make recommendations upon "the adequacy, availability, management and use of resources in the prison services" and it is to these matters that we turn in this chapter. We also deal with "conditions for staff in the prison services and their families", in so far as they are not dealt with elsewhere in the report. We have borne in mind throughout our deliberations that in making recommendations we are required to have regard to the considerations listed at (a)–(d) of our terms of reference. In this chapter, therefore, we assess the capacity of the current manpower and physical resources within the prison services, and the efficiency with which they are used; we look at how prisons have fared over the years in comparison with some other services; and we finally recommend what should be done.

MANPOWER
Background

6.2 The following tables show the growth of staff in post respectively in England and Wales, Scotland and Northern Ireland over the past 14 years:

NON-INDUSTRIAL STAFF IN POST IN PRISON DEPARTMENT ESTABLISHMENTS: ENGLAND AND WALES
(1965-1979)

Date	Prison officer class	Executive clerical + typing	Govs.	Other non-industrial staff					Total
				Med. offcs.	Psycho-logists	Civ. instr. offcs.	Nurses	Others	
	(1)	(2)	(3)	(4)	(5)	(6)	(7)	(8)	(9)
1 April									
1965	8,050	1,046	338	110½	27½	375	86	440	10,473
1966	8,314	1,184½	355	118	28½	400	87½	468½	10,956
1967	9,058	1,235	361	120	35½	402	98	494	11,803½
1968	9,778	1,382½	393	126½	39½	426	99	480	12,724½
1969	10,468	1,458	427	131½	45½	472½	115	526	13,643½
1970	11,155	1,485	454	136	56	498½	99½	524½	14,426½
1971	11,420½	1,621	478	146½	61	547½	111½	574	14,960
1972	12,568½	1,670½	499	119	65	635	114	555	16,226
1973	13,178	1,700½	501	127	70	692	125	574	16,967½
1974	13,133½	1,772	497	122	78	706	115½	591	17,017
1975	13,994	1,828½	487	124½	75	745	115½	626	17,995½
1976	14,829	1,882½	508	119	69	806	132	540	18,885½
1977	15,383½	1,978½	510	107	64	785	130½	647	19,605½
1978	15,663½	1,989½	507	92	67	859	144½	636½	19,979
1979	15,708	2,026½	518	94½	72	855	158	652½	20,084½

Note: Because of a change in the method of presentation, part-time staff employed for less than 10 hours a week are not included after 1971.

Part-time staff are shown as half.

NON-INDUSTRIAL STAFF IN POST IN PRISON SERVICE ESTABLISHMENTS: SCOTLAND (1965-1979)

Date	Prison Officer Class (1)	Govs. (2)	Civ. Instr. Offcs. (3)	Typists (4)	P & TO (5)	Med. Officers (6)	Nurses (7)	Others (8)	Total (9)
1 April									
1965	1,213	33	8	9	4	2	—	9	1,278
1966	1,296	36	9	10	5	2	—	10	1,368
1967	1,373	35	11	11	5	2	—	9	1,446
1968	1,483	40	13	14	5	2	1	10	1,568
1969	1,538	43	17	16	5	3	1	11	1,634
1970	1,638	52	23	17	5	3	1	11	1,750
1971	1,682	51	25	21	5	3	2	14	1,803
1972	1,883	52	28	27	5	3	2	17	2,017
1973	1,888	53	33	29	5	3	2	18	2,030
1974	1,803	62	38	31	6	3	2	20	1,965
1975	1,882	66	51	34	6	3	2	25	2,069
1976	2,062	70	62	37	6	2	2	26	2,267
1977	2,159	70	69	37	15	3	2	29	2,384
1978	2,114	74	79	35	13	3	2	28	2,448
1979	2,233	76	92	36	17	3	2	25	2,484

STAFF IN POST IN PRISON SERVICE ESTABLISHMENTS: NORTHERN IRELAND (1969-1979)

1 January	Prison Officer Class	Governor Grades	Clerks	All Others	Total
1969	238	8	14	32	292
1970	275	8	12	43	338
1971	317	8	12	40	377
1972	472	14(1)	21	48	555
1973	793(160)	17(3)	30(3)	45	885
1974	1,007(282)	24(5)	34(3)	59	1,124
1975	1,217(275)	28(2)	46(2)	90	1,381
1976	1,733(150)	30(3)	44	119	1,926
1977	1,817(99)	39(5)	58	144	2,058
1978	2,076(86)	36(2)	71	157	2,339
1979	2,210(68)	40	85	178	2,513

Figures in brackets represent officers on loan from Great Britain.

6.3 In a number of respects it could be argued that the prison services have shown a decline in productivity. For example, in England and Wales over the financial years 1 April 1965 to 31 March 1978 the total staff employed increased by 88 per cent (11,759–22,146) whereas the inmate population increased by 38 per cent (30,452–41,745). (The comparable figures for Scotland were a staff increase of 82 per cent (1,395–2,540) as against 50 per cent for inmates (3,400–5,087).) Thus in England and Wales the average staff/inmate ratio has risen from 1:2·6 in 1965 to 1:1·9 in 1978, the ratios being 1:3·8 and 1:2·7 if the uniformed officers only are considered. In addition throughout the period high levels of overtime were worked varying between 8·5 hours a week on average in 1966–7 to 12 hours now. (Overtime has a very special place in the prison services and we shall deal with it separately below.)

6.4 We have been told by the Home Departments that the explanation for this phenomenon in respect of the uniform grades (who in England and Wales increased by 94 per cent over 1965–1978) rests in a combination of the additional tasks undertaken and the effect of changes in conditions of service. The main impact arose from implementing the Mountbatten Report. This led to higher manning levels at dispersal prisons, improved security measures, increased supervision, and improved classification and allocation procedures all of which required more staff. Changes in conditions of service included the introduction of a five day 40 hour week for staff previously working a 12 day fortnight of 84 hours, and new standards of annual leave and training allowances. In addition, fresh demands generally have been placed on the prison services by the opening of new establishments, the reporting requirements of parole, and improving regimes and facilities for inmates. Broadly similar features have been responsible for similar developments in Scotland. A Home Office study in 1977 valued the prison officer staff costs of the changes as follows:

	Estimated number of officers
(i) Growth in commitments (notably increases in prison population, court commitments and the opening of new establishments)	3,100
(ii) Improvements in security following the Mountbatten Report on prison security	4,000
(iii) Improvements in the prison regime for inmates and arrangements for parole and allocation procedures ...	1,200
(iv) Improvements in conditions of service for prison staff	1,200
(v) Introduction of new staff attendance schemes ...	700
	10,200

6.5 The reasons for the increases in other non-industrial staff principally reflect fresh administrative burdens and, in the case of civilian instructors, in part a reflection of the decline in the recruitment of prison officers qualified for specialist instructor posts. Of the industrial staff increase, half

113

could be ascribed to general growth, especially in place-producing direct labour schemes, and the remainder to special efforts over the period to refurbish unsatisfactory premises, and the difficulty in recruiting trades officers.

Services to the courts

6.6 Escorting inmates to and from the courts and, in England and Wales, manning the docks consumes a large proportion of the manpower of the prison services. In addition, because the demands of the courts are unpredictable and must be given priority, two consequences flow: first, it is difficult to allocate manpower resources rationally or even with adequate warning—details for the day following are often not completed until the late afternoon; secondly, answering to the needs of the courts means that all other penal activities must take second place and this can lead to restriction of all out of cell activities, including of course industrial work and the profits generated thereby. It follows that, when considering efficiency, it has been necessary for us also to consider whether, and if so to what extent, prison officers should continue to be employed on these duties.

6.7 The extent to which the prison services provide services to the courts varies throughout the United Kingdom. In England and Wales the prison service escorts prisoners to magistrates courts except in London, escorts all inmates to Crown Courts and mans the docks there. Once the inmate arrives at a magistrates court, he becomes the responsibility of the police officers who also return him to the prison unless an arrangement has been made for the prison officers who brought him to await the conclusion of, say, a remand appearance. Transport arrangements vary. In London it is the police who convey inmates to magistrates courts, although in the case of the Crown Courts the Home Office use Metropolitan Police transport under contract with their civilian drivers but otherwise manned by prison officers. The cells at the Crown Courts are manned by prison officers who take custody of inmates from their colleagues who have undertaken the escort. Frequently two prison officers (or more if there is more than one defendant) sit in each dock with the defendant.

6.8 In Scotland the police staff the courts and provide escorts between prison and court for untried prisoners remanded in custody. Otherwise, the prison service provides escorts to and from court only where a prisoner who is already serving a sentence attends court for appeal proceedings, to answer further charges or as a witness; or where a prisoner convicted by a lower court is remanded to the High Court for sentence. In Northern Ireland arrangements are slightly different again. Universally the police escort remanded prisoners to the magistrates courts and all transport is a police responsibility. On the other hand, prison officers escort Awaiting Trial Prisoners at the City Commissions, the Quarterly Assize Courts, the Recorder's Court and the County Courts. Their tasks include escorting prisoners to and from the courts, manning the docks, supervising the holding cells, and taking into custody people surrendering to their bail. They are also responsible for the production of convicted prisoners already in custody who have to answer further charges in courts of summary jurisdiction.

6.9 The cost of these operations is substantial. In England and Wales it was estimated in 1976 that court and escort duties by staff from local prisons and remand centres took about two million prison officer man hours at an annual cost at 1976 prices of £6·8 million. The duties involve a lot of overtime because of the need to match court hours and because an establishment may be many miles away from the court it services. Of the two million man hours it was estimated that 806,000 (15,500 a week) represented the overtime being worked by local prison and remand centre staff on escort and court duties. If the costs of transport and officers' subsistence are added, then the estimated total cost for these establishments in 1976 was in the region of £9 million a year. Since that time the extent of the commitment has increased both by reason of a growth in the number of courts as well as a growth in the amount of court business, now increasing at the rate of 6 per cent a year. Still more courts are planned to reduce delays in criminal cases. More recent figures estimated that about 20,000 hours of overtime a week (or just over one million hours a year) were being worked by staff at local prisons and remand centres in England and Wales on court and escort duties, and put the annual cost at about £11 million.

6.10 We do not have any comparable estimates of the costs in Scotland. Proportionately the burden there is less because more is undertaken by the police. Nonetheless, the manpower burden is significant, particularly in certain under-21 establishments. In addition, since escort duties are not taken into account in normal complementing of establishments, they entail extensive overtime working.

6.11 In Northern Ireland it is also the case that services to the courts make heavy demands on manpower resources. It has been estimated that in 1978 court duties took 123,981 officer man hours. The total cost was about £264,000 when account was taken of overtime, subsistence and other allowances.

6.12 Because of the increase in criminal business before the courts, there seems no prospect of the amount of this work diminishing. We have nonetheless considered what room there might be for effecting economies. The main possibilities seem to lie in the creation of a separate escort service, and attempting to improve the efficiency of courts' administration in order to diminish the number of avoidable productions of inmates.

6.13 A separate escort service would have many attractions. It would remove the direct manpower burden on the prison services and allow them to operate more stable and uninterrupted regimes even in local prisons where workshop closures seem to be most frequent. The force could take a number of forms depending on the width of the responsibilities allocated to it. It could be answerable to the police, the Home Office or the Lord Chancellor's Department.

6.14 On the other hand, the formation of a separate force would not be free from difficulty. However constituted it would not of itself be more economical of manpower than present arrangements, so there would be no financial saving. On the contrary, it would almost certainly cost more. In addition, it would be likely to encounter the same recruiting difficulties as are experienced by the prison services and, from time to time, by the police themselves. Even where it did not, its success might be at the expense of the police and prison services. Further, there seem to be important security considerations. To some extent a separate force would make the maintenance of proper custody more difficult than it is at present with the employment of the two disciplined services. The escape of Thomas William Hughes in January 1977 was a reminder of the need to maintain security at all times and any step which was likely to make that more difficult by a further division of responsibilities could not be contemplated lightly. We conclude, therefore, that there is no sufficient case at present for the establishment of a separate force.

6.15 Appreciating the fact that escorts provide their members with relief from the bleak conditions of local prisons as well as opportunity for over-time earnings, we should not leave the matter without mentioning that we discussed escorting with the POA. They made it abundantly clear that they would resist any attempt to remove escorting duties from the prison service in England and Wales. Whilst we have not been swayed by such con-siderations, they are not irrelevant. We merely think that the other arguments on the merits are by themselves strong enough without the need to consider in this particular case the objections of the staff involved. It follows that we also think that, if the balance of the arguments on merits changes, then the prospect of making such a change should not be ruled out.

6.16 The other possible measures relating to efficiency of operation turn mainly on the fact, for example, that the prison service in England and Wales is providing services to courts whose administration is the responsi-bility of the Lord Chancellor's Department. We put to that Department various suggestions about improving efficiency e.g. reducing the need for production of sentenced prisoners to answer further charges which might have been dealt with at the original trial, better information about trial times to avoid otiose productions, and various steps designed to improve remand efficiency. It had also occurred to us, amongst other things, that the performance of the Lord Chancellor's Department might be improved if the cost of the services to the courts provided by the prison service were borne by the Department rather than the Home Office. We were concerned too about the number of prison officers employed manning docks in the Crown Courts and wondered whether the numbers could be reduced.

6.17 In correspondence the Lord Chancellor's Department maintained that, although they did not wish to rule out any feasible means of speeding up the administration of justice, they found their main difficulty was striving to keep abreast of the continuing increase in court business, especially the

50 per cent increase in the Crown Courts' work from 1972–1978. They were very conscious, amongst other things, that their attempts to meet that increasing burden, e.g. by increasing the number of courts, could only add to the burdens on the escorting services. They maintained also that removing the accounting responsibility to them would not have any real advantages. Divided control of a single work force would provoke difficulties and there would be no advantage in the Department having accounting responsibility without adequate control over the relevant part of the prison service's work. Even if it did have management control of escort duties, conflicts of interest would arise between the Department's requirements, which as paymasters they might seem able to press, and those of the prison service. Accordingly, they did not think that an agency arrangement would secure any stronger interest than the Department already had in getting the courts' work done efficiently and economically. As to dock manning in Crown Courts, the Department expressed concern about the present burdens on the prison service, and said discussions were in progress with the Home Office about the scope for reducing the workload.

6.18 We think that economies in the use of prison officers on escort duty and in manning the courts and docks can and should be achieved. First, the observation of some of us and the inquiries we have made lead us to the conclusion that a substantial reduction could be effected in the number of prison officers manning the docks in courts, particularly at large centres. For instance, there can be no need to have two officers for the whole day in or beneath a dock in which there is one, or even two defendants on trial for an offence or offences for which they were not remanded in custody and are most unlikely to receive an immediate custodial sentence, even if convicted. If even one of those two officers were at his establishment rather than at the court, this might well enable a workshop, closed through a shortage of discipline staff, to be open for that day and so provide work for anything up to 40 or 50 prisoners. Indeed, we doubt whether in some cases a dock needs to be manned by a prison officer at all. Only a small proportion of defendants in court provide a security risk and in most courts during a trial, and particularly where a defendant appears to plead guilty and be sentenced, there will be police officers and court staff who can provide such control, if any, as may be required. Secondly, and as we have already mentioned, our own observation and the evidence we received at both the remand centres and at local prisons that we visited was that it may well be late in an afternoon before the remand centre or prison knows which and how many inmates will be required at court the following day—which may well necessitate transport and escorting prison officers leaving the prison at an early hour to be at a distant court on time. No satisfactory detail for the officers at that centre or prison can be produced in such circumstances and thus no stable regimes for the inmates can be operated. Further, we are satisfied that the attraction of escort duties to prison officers, and of their consequent absence for the day from an overcrowded, battened-down establishment are such that there is no incentive for them to arrive at court with their charges only so long before the court sits as is reasonable, nor, more particularly, to leave the court with such inmates as have to be returned to prison as soon after the court rises as practicable.

6.19 The points we make in the previous paragraph may in isolation seem small but even if only one prison officer less a day were used on escort and court duties at only 50 court centres throughout England, let alone Scotland or Northern Ireland, the financial saving could not be less than £320,000 in a year, and perhaps an extra 1,000 inmates or more could be working each day rather than shut up in their cells.

6.20 Finally, whilst we have given full weight to the answers from the Lord Chancellor's Department to the suggestion that the Home Office should provide prison officer services to the courts on an agency basis, charging the cost to the Lord Chancellor's Department, we think that the likely advantages outweigh the disadvantages and we recommend that this change be made. In the first place, it would require the Home Office to prepare accurate accounts of the actual cost of providing the services, which should enable it to identify areas in which savings might be made. In the second, the new arrangement would lead the Lord Chancellor's Department also to look for savings and in doing so to examine carefully the demands made by it for the services provided by the Home Office to reduce these to their practicable minimum.

Overtime, complementing and attendance systems

6.21 Wherever the number of uniformed staff available is fewer than the number required to work the necessary duties within a 40 hour week, then, provided the tasks have been properly assessed, additional coverage can be obtained solely by resorting to overtime. In England and Wales there is even an overtime agreement under which uniformed grades may be required to work up to 10 hours overtime a week. In practice at present they work an average of 12 hours a week. Such a level means, of course, that some officers are working very substantial amounts of overtime—30 hours or more are not unknown. (The evidence from the earnings survey and the NES that we discuss in Chapter 8 shows the peculiar reliance of officers' average earnings on overtime and that there are very few other occupations where overtime is such an important component of earnings.) There are no overtime agreements in Scotland and Northern Ireland. In the former only about 6–8 hours overtime a week is worked, but in the latter the amount of overtime commonly exceeds that in England and Wales.

6.22 There can be no doubt that high levels of overtime can have a most deleterious effect, not only on individual officers and their families, but also on staff/management relationships generally. Just as management becomes accustomed to stretching manpower (much in the same way as prisons have been overcrowded to accommodate demand), so do staff become reliant on a standard of living dependent on a degree of overtime which, although part of their earnings, cannot be relied upon as a permanent part. It is even said that some officers, known as "overtime bandits", take maximum advantage of available duties and have not been above attempting so to manipulate affairs that it is possible to retain high levels of overtime. The POA have told us they accept that it must be for management and management alone to regulate overtime but in practice the resistance amongst their members to sudden changes in overtime levels is only understandable. At present overtime is controlled by a "budget of hours" which allocates a ceiling of working hours to each establishment. This system was introduced with effect from April 1976 with the then object of saving £2 million a year as a contribution to the cuts in government spending that financial year. For almost two years from July 1977 the POA adopted a policy of non-co-operation in the control of manpower resources. As a result it was necessary to suspend the monitoring system whereby establishments provided headquarters through regional directors with weekly returns. Monitoring was thus entirely dependent on deriving the information less speedily and more laboriously from monthly financial returns. To us this action seemed incompatible with an acceptance that overtime is to be regulated by management, and we find it was also an unnecessary impediment to the efficient allocation of public money.

6.23 We have been troubled about the extent to which the prison services are dependent on overtime working by uniformed grades. Whereas overtime cannot be regarded as an evil by itself, we cannot believe that the present levels are good either for the service or, just as important, the officers and their families.

6.24 Overtime has been presented to us in very different ways. Management argues that it would not be possible to keep prisons running without it, not only in local prisons which have to respond to the often unpredictable demands of the courts, but also in the training prisons where the daily routine is generally more stable. Officers have often argued to us that their overtime is necessary, as they see it, to enable them to earn a decent wage. Numbers in England and Wales seem to look on it as a right deriving from the overtime agreement, and resent the fact that it is not a dependable or constant part of their emoluments. The ordinary exercise of disciplinary procedures has been challenged in so far as suspension ordinarily means, of course, suspension on basic pay only without overtime earnings as well. Sometimes it almost appears as if there were some sort of collusion between local management and staff, at least to the extent that each group did not in the past look too closely into the motives of the other for co-operating with high overtime demands. It is possible, too, that the high rate of overtime in the last three or four years has been the way in which one part of the public service was informally able to circumvent restrictions on income which would otherwise have followed from incomes policy.

6.25 The extraordinary persistence of overtime even when strength has been increasing has naturally prompted us to inquire whether manpower is being allocated efficiently. Time has not allowed us to initiate any special exercises of our own and we have therefore had to concentrate on the nature of the complementing systems supplemented by what we have been able to observe on our visits.

6.26 We have to say straight away that we do not think that the situation in England and Wales is satisfactory. At no point, for example, have we been given figures which state unambiguously what total manning levels should be in order to eliminate dependence on overtime and what they in fact are, nor are such figures published in the Prison Department's annual reports. On visits it was frequently alleged that the figures in our brief did not correspond with local understanding. Over the entire area there appears to rest a pall of uncertainty, if not incomprehension. There are several reasons. We appreciate, for example, that where there is a substantial gap between needs and numbers, then the precise estimation of the former is largely academic. Many complements, too, are under review. We realise as well that it is necessary to distinguish between absolute maxima and the levels up to which it is permissible to recruit at any one time. Nonetheless, the general situation was one not prone to generate confidence that management at all levels was firmly in control. The fact that the personnel function is not under the Director General's responsibility no doubt plays its part, and the state of affairs in this case underlines the need for some of the organisational changes we recommend elsewhere.

6.27 In the ordinary civil service sense there is no system of staff inspection for prison service grades in England and Wales and those grades are the sole remaining significant area of the civil service to which staff inspection does not apply. That is, there is no regular programme of triennial review of complements by trained staff inspectors to investigate whether manpower is adequate grade by grade and the work itself both efficiently allocated to and efficiently undertaken by staff. Instead a local variant of complementing review has developed since the final introduction of five day week working in 1970 and in the face of continued increases in overtime spending. At that time a Manpower Control Project was set up with teams of governors and officer grades to make an assessment of the prison officer staffing needs of every establishment based on its commitments, objectives and tasks. In addition to providing advice to governors on the economic utilisation of manpower and supplying them with reliable information on the number of staff required, it was hoped that the project would lead to the tighter control and even reduction of overtime. By 1974 all establishments had been visited but it became apparent that the demands for staff perceived overall by the teams could neither be met within the approved manpower levels nor by recruitment, and although the reports were issued as management documents for governors' guidance, the recommended figures were not formally approved and issued. The teams, with the exception of a central team retained at headquarters, were in 1974 dispersed to the regions to work from there. Prompted apparently by the Central Departments, the Home Office put proposals last year to the relevant staff sides for improvements in staff inspection which would have had the effect of introducing regular triennial staff inspection for all grades. (It exists already for non-prison service grades.)

6.28 In our judgment new and improved arrangements should be got underway as soon as possible. They will require, of course, the co-operation of the staff and we hope that this will be forthcoming, particularly since they were unhelpful about budgetary control of hours worked, which was the system introduced in 1976 for controlling overtime and to which we referred in paragraph 6.22 above. This seems to be a sensible system and one that should continue operating as before following consultation with staff. On the other hand, we feel bound to observe that introducing the system in 1976, in effect to police a forced reduction of earnings, was hardly likely to give the scheme the best send-off, and the staff's resentment is all too easily understood. The damage done in the pursuit of annual savings of £2 million certainly exceeded in the long run the value of the savings and, although how cuts are done must be a matter for Ministers, we must draw attention to the potential diseconomies that are bound to arise from non-selective cuts applied to manpower intensive services.

6.29 We do not expect improved staff inspection to solve everything. On the contrary, its main product must be order and more equal distribution of the best manning practices. Neither do we think that it can produce uniformity. Penal establishments are all different and they do not correspond to the more settled clerical procedures of some of the standard civil service bureaucracies. No system of staff inspection can be useful that does not recognise the special features of prisons. Equally, none of those special features can justify the absence of informed, regular and expert review capable of assessing the validity of special claims, including the requirements of security and control. Even though it be true that the demands of security can never be precisely assessed and no governor or manager could wish to ride roughshod over staff apprehensions, it is another thing to regard "security" as justifying manning prodigality and waste. Our inquiries abroad showed that no manning levels were proof against claims that they were insufficient even where staff actually *exceeded* inmates. In the UK we would consider it beyond question that such levels of staffing are impossible and a more modest approach is unavoidable.

6.30 Finally, no discussion about complementing can ignore attendance systems, i.e. the agreed rules for rostering the duties of staff. Prisons pose special problems for economic rostering because they are seven day a week institutions where staff demands peak at varying times of the day and week In Scotland and Northern Ireland duties are arranged on three shift systems similar to the one used prior to the introduction of the five day week in England and Wales. They seem simple and relatively straightforward, features undoubtedly assisted in Scotland by the much lighter load of escort duties.

6.31 In England and Wales, however, two schemes of attendance are in operation—the Vee scheme and the Functional Group Scheme (FGS). The former was designed with the requirements of local prisons in mind, the latter for training prisons, and each produces on duty a different proportion of the staff at certain points of the day. As Chapter 9 on the CDC claims makes clear, the schemes are quite remarkably complex and difficult both to understand and operate. (Lord McCarthy remarked when arbitrating on a dispute in 1978, that the Vee Scheme Code was "an unsatisfactory and ambiguous guide".) It is not surprising therefore that the administration of the schemes not infrequently gives rise to dispute. Complexity has other important effects, too, because the construction of the daily detail takes on the air of a mystery understood only by the detailing officer and in circumstances which have made us wonder whether he is subject to effective supervision. Not only does it seem that governors have withdrawn from trying to manage the use of the most important and expensive resource at their disposal, but chief officers too. Although theoretically no detail officer can expand or alter the task lists which alone generate staff demands, it seems unlikely they are totally without discretion in practice.

6.32 There are, in addition, other arguments which seem to us to tell against perpetuating the two present systems. The Vee scheme, for example, was drawn up in 1967 when escort duties were in fact lighter than today. Not only were there fewer superior courts, but they sat for shorter periods. The staff requirement is no longer therefore predictably peaked during the year but at a similar high level throughout, with concomitant inroads on the viability of the internal regime of establishments.

6.33 Again, the natural anxiety of the staff to move to five day week working led a number of other than local prisons (in fact 23 training prisons and one borstal) to adopt the Vee scheme and yet retain it when the FGS came into operation notwithstanding it is a less economic way of meeting their regime requirements. Finally, and this underlines the crucial point that no system of attendance can be introduced or last without the fully consulted support of the staff, the POA themselves feel the time has come for change:

"The existence of two systems in the same service is unsatisfactory and divisive both in terms of staff morale and the treatment of inmates. For these reasons it is the policy of the Association that there should be a single attendance system, flexible enough to be adapted to differing penal regimes to replace both scheme Vee and FGS."

6.34 Having discussed these problems very fully with the POA and the Home Office, and made our own inquiries into shift working practice elsewhere in the public and private sectors, we have no doubt the POA are right to press for change and that they are right in arguing for it in the direction that they do. It is not our role to devise a fresh scheme because it seems to us a cardinal principle that one may be devised only as a result of negotiation between management and staff. The best thing we can do is set out the criteria of which we consider any final scheme should take account.

6.35 These criteria are:
(a) A single basic shift system, with scope for flexible application to local and changed circumstances subject to agreed principles.
(b) Maximum continuity of staff in inmate contact posts.
(c) Predictable cycled duties of reasonable incidence matched with the most economic deployment of staff.

(d) Maximum compatability with a purposive regime for inmates.

(e) Priority ranking of tasks so that an orderly withdrawal from activities may be made where necessary.

6.36 We do not consider negotiations on attendance systems should take place in a vacuum without reference to other matters. On the contrary, it would seem impracticable as well as undesirable to look for piecemeal change. We therefore expect change to occur as part of a thoroughgoing review of working methods including conditions of service. We do not underestimate the difficulties of setting a new balance of this order. From management it will require considerable flexibility and a genuine readiness to take account of the staff's wish to preserve a reasonable incidence of hours in the working week so that there should ordinarily be no avoidable inpairment of the quality of their private lives. The staff, on the other hand, will reciprocally need to contemplate and adopt changed working practices matched not only to their convenience but also to the need for efficiency and economy in the use of public funds. Finally, we do not anticipate that any perfect balance is possible. It follows there will have to be give and take on both sides. We return to some of these themes when discussing general resource recommendations at the end of this chapter.

The Condition of the Penal Estate

(a) England and Wales

6.37 At Appendix 6, List A, is a Home Office assessment of the accommodation in use at the end of 1978. Of the total CNA of 37,880, 20,872 places or 55 per cent were built before 1930, a number of them well before then. The appendix assesses the "physical condition" of 38 (33 per cent) establishments as "Good", 53 (46 per cent) as "Fair" and 24 (21 per cent) as "Poor". It should be pointed out that this assessment relates solely to the condition of the physical fabric and is not a judgment on the use to which it is put. For example, there can be no sense other than a physical one in which it could be appropriate to describe Birmingham prison as "Fair" and having potential for "Improvement". Even taking a solely physical view, it has seemed to us that the assessment's judgments have been heavily influenced by long and now ingrained habits of tolerating low physical standards. Regardless of these qualifications, on the other hand, it is plain that the assessment of future potential does not suggest that substantial redevelopment is by any means feasible even if the funds were available.

6.38 Although the antiquity of the penal estate is a byword, it would be wrong to get things out of proportion. It has been pointed out to us that many of the old prisons have undergone substantial modifications and have had various modern facilities added. The date of first occupation, therefore, can be no infallible guide to condition. In addition, concentrating on the number of old establishments should not allow the number of modern ones to be ignored. Thus, it must be borne in mind that 22 per cent of the places listed in the assessment relate to post-1930 buildings. This proportion could be raised by adding in some of the camps. In addition, rather than by

123

aggregating places around a 1930 fulcrum, they could be put in a different perspective by viewing the estate establishment by establishment in another timescale. Dr King and Mr Morgan, relying on the date of first penal use, estimated that of 125 separate functional units in use in 1977, 82 (61 per cent) had been purpose-built, or converted for prison use, since 1945. Of the remainder 46 (34 percent) were built before 1900, and 7 (5 per cent) were built or brought into use between 1901 and 1939. Further, they argued that the degree of antiquity should be seen beside the age of the public estate elsewhere (e.g. in schools and certain hospitals) which had not invariably fared better. This is an interesting perspective, but it is vitiated by the fact that date of first penal use is a poor guide to condition. For example, although all the service camps were occupied after the War, some were quite old when taken over and all were originally built with a short life expectancy. In other cases, occupied buildings (for example The Verne and Ashford remand centre taken over in 1949 and 1961 respectively) were already of some considerable age.

6.39 In practice, we feel that such different dating approaches are not competing but complementary ways of looking at the same data. More important than age itself is actual condition and this must apply regardless of what obtains in services outside prisons. Looking at the estate from that perspective we have no reason to doubt the broad assessment of the Home Office Directorate of Works. Apart from anything else, to do so would be to deny the evidence of our own eyes which suggests that the assessment is a restrained one.

6.40 At this point we should make it clear that we have approached the estate bearing two distinct viewpoints in mind, namely that of the inmates and that of the staff. Too often we feel outside observers have in practice concentrated on the inmates—in this as perhaps in many other matters—to the practical detriment of the staff whose tenure is invariably the longer. It is the staff who have to endure the effects of overcrowding over the years, who have to experience day in and day out the inadequacies of buildings erected over a century ago, and who must strive to keep operational in the kitchens, the workshops and the wings regimes which are sometimes in imminent danger of the same collapse that threatens the fabric in which they are contained.

6.41 To put it baldly and without equivocation but choosing our words carefully nonetheless, we think that the worst prisons are very bad indeed. Worst does not necessarily equate with Victorian: some of the converted camps are on their last legs, and some Victorian establishments (e.g. at Barlinnie, Belfast and Portland) are coping with reasonable success where they are blessed with more acreage and something has been done to update their facilities. Equally, some of the post 1945 prisons seem doomed to be pinchpenny slums. In the whole of England and Wales, however, there can be no doubt that the main problem is obsolescence. This is not surprising when it is borne in mind that no closed penal institution at all was built between 1918 and 1958, and very few between 1877 and 1918. At the bottom are most of the urban Victorian local prisons i.e. those that are responsible for remand and trial prisoners. Of the ones we have seen, Birmingham, Bristol, Brixton and Liverpool deserve special mention. However, we should stress the fact that we have singled them out does not mean we think things are satisfactory elsewhere. Both Wakefield and Parkhurst, for example, require a great deal of attention if they are not, literally, to fall down. Dartmoor, despite its listing as "Fair" and capable of improvement, is in fact in a special category of its own: what was permissible in a convict prison for the rigours of penal servitude on the reoccupied Napoleonic site of the 1850s, is nowadays simply against nature. Finally, in case the point gets missed, what we are saying amongst other things is that remand prisoners (i.e. those not convicted and less than half of whom eventually receive custodial sentences) suffer the worst accommodation when, arguably, they should have the best.

(b) *Scotland*

6.42 Appendix 6, List B, also lists the state of Scottish penal establishments in the same way as List A did for England and Wales. Again, out of a total CNA of 5,256, about the same proportion of places (55 per cent) are in pre 1930 premises. The establishments are assessed as 12 (50 per cent) "Good", nine (37 per cent) "Fair" and three (12 per cent) "Poor". These proportions suggest the Scottish estate is in better condition than that of England and Wales. Again, what we saw of it reinforces the paper assessment. That is, we think Scottish establishments have fared better than their counterparts in England and Wales. In general it seems to us that the Scottish system has enjoyed some benefits because of its relatively much smaller scale and the fact therefore that the investment of more modest sums of money could have a greater proportionate effect. In England and Wales, on the other hand, the task of modernising must have always seemed more daunting.

6.43 But there is at least one exception in Scotland. This is Peterhead prison which occupies still the kind of role in respect of difficult recidivist prisoners that Dartmoor, its structural counterpart in many ways, has largely lost. The fact that Peterhead was for so long going to be replaced by Shotts (see paras. 6.89–6.90 below) has undoubtedly been the cause of a degree of neglect which seems all the more remarkable when the problems faced daily by the staff are borne in mind. Whilst we have noted the announcement that £1 million is to be spent on improvements at the prison, we think that not only is that a relatively modest sum with which to remedy past neglect but that it is also insufficient to turn Peterhead into a satisfactory establishment. Although the total prison area is very large, the main prison is cramped and its facilities inadequate. The workshops are of very poor quality and may be reached only by a long, exposed march which adds to the staff's problems of control. We therefore recommend that consideration be given to substantial redevelopment on the ample site available, especially if the Shotts development is not persisted in for its original purpose.

125

(c) *Northern Ireland*

6.44 Again, the Northern Ireland experience has been so different from Great Britain's that there are few points of similarity. The sole Victorian (and pre-Victorian) establishments are Belfast and Armagh but their joint CNA of 610 represents only about 23 per cent of the total. Indeed, the chief feature of the Northern Ireland estate is, therefore, that the larger part of it is not only post-Victorian but post 1969, since when 1,920 places have been provided for adult males at The Maze. Initially emergency provision was made by resort to nissen hut compounds during the internment phase from 1971. Between 1975 and 1978, however, eight permanent single storey, 100 cell blocks were developed adjacent to the compounds. These blocks, known at "H blocks" because of their shape, are self-contained living units for accommodation and administrative purposes sharing jointly certain other facilities, e.g. workshops.

6.45 It follows not surprisingly from this account that we think the accommodation in Northern Ireland, although not without its drawbacks (e.g. the cramped and overlooked site at Armagh), to be relatively the best in the United Kingdom. Even the largest and most crowded prison, Belfast, is well off for internal space in comparison with analogous institutions elsewhere. Northern Ireland seems fortunate too in lacking a Dartmoor or Peterhead.

6.46 One way of looking at Northern Ireland's better performance is, of course, to see it as the result of sheer operational necessity: the government could not have afforded to do anything else. On the other hand, it could be argued the changes in population in England and Wales since 1945 have cumulatively been almost as great. The difference, however, is that the situation at any particular point was less dramatic and urgent. In addition the penal accommodation proved remarkably elastic. Putting things yet another way, it could be said therefore that the penal estate in England and Wales has not received the attention it needed because of its very success in absorbing a vast increase in population. Past actual as opposed to threatened future breakdown or demonstrable incapacity might have been better for its present condition in the long run.

Use of physical resources

6.47 Reviewing the physical condition of the estate does not exhaust the relevant issues because there is still the question of whether the estate is used in the most efficient manner. Accordingly, what follows examines the use of accommodation from three separate points of view: cell-sharing, under-occupation, and the operational practices (including dispersal policy) that spring from classification and allocation procedures.

Cell sharing

6.48 The degree of cell-sharing depends both on absolute capacity and operational choice. Indeed, an equivalence of CNA and actual population does not necessarily lead to no cell-sharing at all. Clearly, at even the most rudimentary operational level, there will be moments when, for example, there is a surplus of inmates at one end of the country and surplus of accommodation at the other. Going beyond geographical accident, there has also to be some specialisation of function between establishments e.g. as to sex and age of inmates, or as to the stage they have reached in the criminal justice process. In addition, although much of the specialisation is required by law, many prison systems have also experimented with elaborate systems of inmate classification and allocation to help, amongst other things, develop special regimes in the hope of greater rehabilitative outcomes.

6.49 In Great Britain cell-sharing is more extensive in England and Wales than in Scotland (c.f. paragraph 3.3 above). This is partly because the disparity between CNA and actual population is greater in the former (11·5 per cent) than in the latter (1 per cent). The main cause, however, beyond that basic disparity and the occasional geographical variations that are bound to arise from time to time in any system, is the decision to confine cell-sharing almost entirely to local prisons, i.e. those that serve the courts direct. The remaining prisons, known as "training" prisons receive sentenced prisoners only and have on the whole been deliberately protected from cell-sharing. The Home Office has defined their role as the containment, treatment and training of sentenced prisoners transferred there after initial assessment in a local prison. It has explained the general practice as follows:

"It is both a matter of policy and, to some extent, of practicability that the training establishments are not, in general, over-crowded. Life could become intolerable if the inmates of training prisons (many serving long sentences) had to live for long periods of time two or even three to a cell. More generally, only in good conditions can a purposeful regime be constructed in terms of work, recreation and amenities. As [another memorandum] records, overcrowding vitiates treatment and training objectives. In any event, in practical terms much of the accommodation in the newer training establishments is not capable of being used in multi-occupation; either dormitories or, more particularly cells, are not of sufficient size to permit over-crowding."

6.50 We are not satisfied by these arguments. In the first place, much of their rationale rests on a belief in those very treatment and training aims which have been called into question and which we have discussed at some length in Chapter 4. Secondly, even if remand prisoners only spent reasonable periods in custody pending their trial, life could still become intolerable after only a few weeks of cell-sharing, especially where there are three to a cell and most of the day is perforce spent locked up in it: that remands in custody to overcrowded local prisons are frequently for months rather than weeks only underlines this point. Thirdly, even on its face, the Home Office explanation does not account for the apparent degree of under-occupation in some of the training prisons, and especially in some of the open prisons.

6.51 It is not therefore surprising that we have received suggestions that the local/training prison dichotomy is unnecessary, wasteful and creates an avoidable diminution of inmate quality of life. Dr King and Mr Morgan made radical proposals:

"We have argued that the normalisation of the prison should involve prisoners being housed in that establishment which is closest to, and will best permit the maintenance of, their community ties. We see no reasons why local prisons, organised so that they are subject to fewer population, escort and other pressures than is currently the case, should not incorporate a sufficient range of health, welfare, educational, recreational, occupational and security facilities such that they can satisfactorily meet the needs of most sentenced prisoners. We reject current Prison Department policy that most sentenced prisoners should be housed in an expanded range of increasingly specialised, and often geographically isolated, training prisons."

They went on to suggest that 21 training prisons should become local prisons thus increasing the latter's number to 45 and spreading the overcrowding more thinly. The Howard League were more cautious: "There would be more flexibility if more prisons were regarded as "local", and prisoners could be kept as near home as possible".

6.52 These are all interesting and challenging points which deserve careful scrutiny. The vigour with which they were pressed by Dr King and Mr Morgan owed a good deal, it seemed to us, to their disbelief in "treatment and training" and their attachment to "humane containment". It follows from the latter that any purposeful aims of imprisonment must be secondary considerations. Accordingly a desire to build and protect associated regimes of some sophistication cannot be dominant. More important is the need to adhere wherever possible to objective, if limited, criteria such as closeness to home and defined cellular cubic capacity per inmate.

6.53 The Home Office's counter-arguments seem to revolve principally about their wish to preserve the training regimes. Work facilities were geared to a certain population and there would be a shortage of employment if that population were exceeded. Further, overcrowding dormitory prisons would exacerbate problems of control, and was often physically imposible in at least the newer training prisons. Local prisons needed different facilities e.g. larger reception units, and better accommodation for legal and family visits. Most training prisons could not be converted to provide them without considerable expenditure. To some extent local and training regimes were inevitably incompatible since the more restricted local prison regimes said to be a consequence of mixed penal functions could not be operated in establishments designed for fully associated regimes. Whilst not opposed to conversion from one type of regime to another—for example the current conversion of Reading into a local prison to relieve Oxford—the Home Office argued there was nothing to be gained by making conditions worse for many throughout the system merely to improve slightly the lot of some prisoners in some local prisons. Although we appreciate this last argument we should stress again that of the average daily population in custody in 1978, no less than 19,512 were held in remand centres and local prisons compared with 11,392 in closed training prisons (Prison Statistics, England and Wales, 1978, Cmnd 7627, Table 1.2.)

6.54 It is apparent to us that these competing approaches turn on competing views about penal objectives rather than different operational preferences. As will be understood from the position we have taken on objectives in Chapter 4, we could not support increased localisation, with the consequent damage to some well-resourced and imaginatively run regimes in the training prisons, unless we could see some substantial counter-balancing advantage. As will appear, we doubt whether localisation even to the extent suggested would remove all overcrowding and we suspect that in addition to the extra capital costs of conversion, increased current expenditure would arise from dispersing the court manning and escorting tasks. We therefore feel that increasing the number of local prisons merely by changing the role of some training prisons is not the answer and that one must find a different solution to the overcrowding and cell-sharing problem of the local prisons.

6.55 Surprisingly perhaps, almost none of our witnesses argued that cell-sharing was of itself abhorrent. There was no evidence that it is injurious to health. It was contended that it was not easy to argue that two men sharing a Victorian local prison cell with a floor space of 13 feet by 8 feet (i.e., the "average" Victorian cell designed to accommodate an inmate *and* his work) are necessarily worse off than an inmate in a modern cell with a floor space of 8 feet by 8 feet. Further, it was said with some force, that many men would prefer to have a companion than be entirely alone, especially in the local prisons where the opportunities for association are severely restricted and where inmates may be locked up for long periods, not infrequently 23 hours a day. In addition, it was pointed out to us that some of the worst effects of overcrowding are not on the cellular accommodation as such but on the services in the establishments such as the drains and kitchens. What did emerge very clearly, however, is that it is the common absence of integral sanitation that makes cell-sharing intolerable and unacceptable. Nor are the disadvantages for inmates alone: it is the officers who have to patrol and control the community housed in such conditions. Although they are in no sense responsible for the conditions, they have nonetheless to absorb the resulting abuse and aggression.

6.56 What then is one to say of cell-sharing itself? The Prison (Scotland) Rules 1952 require each prisoner to have a cell by himself at night unless for medical or other reasons it is necessary for him to be associated, in which case he must have not less than two companions. The Prison Rules 1964 for England and Wales provide that no cell shall be used as sleeping accommodation for more than the maximum number of prisoners specified for that cell in a certificate given under section 14 of the Prison Act 1952

129

without the leave of the Secretary of State. However, the United Kingdom has certain obligations under various international instruments, including the European Convention on Human Rights and the various Standard Minimum Rules. None of these is free from ambiguity and only the Rules deal with the subject directly. In the case of the 1973 European Standard Minimum Rules, the relevant provisions are:

"Accommodation

8. (1) Prisoners shall normally be lodged during the night in individual cells unless circumstances dictate otherwise.

(2) Where dormitories are used, they shall be occupied by prisoners suitable to associate with one other in those conditions. There shall be supervision by night, in keeping with the nature of the institution.

9. All accommodation provided for the use of prisoners and in particular all sleeping accommodation shall meet all requirements of health, due regard being paid to climatic conditions and particularly cubic content of air, minimum floor space, lighting, heating and ventilation.

10. In all places where prisoners are required to live or work,

(a) The windows shall be large enough to enable the prisoners, inter alia, to read or work by natural light, and shall be so constructed that they can allow the entrance of fresh air whether or not there is artificial ventilation. Moreover, the windows shall, with due regard to security requirements, present in their size, location and construction as normal an appearance as possible;

(b) Artificial light shall satisfy the recognised technical standards.

11. The sanitary installations shall be adequate to enable every prisoner to comply with the needs of nature when necessary and in clean and decent conditions.

12. Adequate bathing and shower installations shall be provided so that every prisoner may be enabled and required to have a bath or shower, at a temperature suitable to the climate, as frequently as necessary for general hygiene according to season and geographical region, but at least once a week in a temperate climate.

13. All parts of an institution used by prisoners shall be properly maintained and kept scrupulously clean at all times."

Similarly, the relevant provisions of the UN Rules read:

"Accommodation

9. (1) Where sleeping accommodation is in individual cells or rooms, each prisoner shall occupy by night a cell or room by himself. If for special reasons, such as temporary overcrowding, it becomes necessary for the central prison administration to make an exception to this rule, it is not desirable to have two prisoners in a cell or room.

130

(2) Where dormitories are used, they shall be occupied by prisoners carefully selected as being suitable to associate with one another in those conditions. There shall be regular supervision by night, in keeping with the nature of the institution.

10. All accommodation provided for the use of prisoners and in particular all sleeping accommodation shall meet all requirements of health, due regard being paid to climatic conditions and particularly to cubic content of air, minimum floor space, lighting, heating and ventilation.

11. In all places where prisoners are required to live or work,

(a) The windows shall be large enough to enable the prisoners to read or work by natural light, and shall be so constructed that they can allow the entrance of fresh air whether or not there is artificial ventilation;

(b) Artificial light shall be provided sufficient for the prisoners to read or work without injury to eyesight.

12. The sanitary installations shall be adequate to enable every prisoner to comply with the needs of nature when necessary and in a clean and decent manner.

13. Adequate bathing and shower installations shall be provided so that every prisoner may be enabled and required to have a bath or shower, at a temperature suitable to the climate, as frequently as necessary for general hygiene according to season and geographical region but at least once a week in a temperate climate.

14. All parts of an institutions regularly used by prisoners shall be properly maintained and kept scrupulously clean at all times."

We assume that the thinking behind the Scottish Rule and the U.N. Rule (1) each reflects criminal codes that abhor homosexual conduct in whatever circumstances.

6.57 Although none of these provisions is mandatory and the requirements give the authorities a good deal of latitude, it is difficult to be confident that our more grossly overcrowded accommodation can be defended in the face of what it is evident the Rules are directed towards. Nor is this mere legalism: the Rules have moral force precisely because they are intended and do properly reflect our perception of what conditions in contemporary society it is reasonable to impose. In all these circumstances our opinion is that the Standard Minimum Rules must be interpreted in the UK as requiring at the least in the available accommodation a target of a minimum of no enforced cell-sharing, except in regular dormitories, incorporating continuous ready access to lavatories or integral sanitation as appropriate, depending on the kind of establishment, not only in all new building but also in all redeveloped or substantially refurbished accommodation. We accept that the target may not be achieved for some time, but we think nonetheless it should have high priority. We appreciate that a loss of cell places is involved, and an estimate of the costs is given in paragraph 6.84 below. However, we should make it plain we do not regard these costs as optional: rather, they are simply an unavoidable part of the current price of having prisons at all.

Under-occupation

6.58 We are concerned here not with any trivial degree of under-utilisation that is bound to occur by virtue of the normal turnover of the population and the short lags that will occur between discharge and posting but with prolonged and substantial under-occupation. The point about under-occupation is that it constitutes an inefficient use of resources since capital investment in, for example, training prisons may be lying idle, but be unnecessarily over-pressed in the already overcrowded local prisons from which all the training prison inmates come. Apart from under-occupation caused by inmate riot (e.g. Gartree) or officer industrial action (e.g. Parkhurst), the main problem lies in the open prisons which are consistently running with something like 500 inmates short of their CNA.

6.59 On the face of it, it seems extraordinary that the regimes of the open prisons are not more fully utilised. In conditions of severe overcrowding it would be natural to expect the maximum use to be made of every available training prison place. Many people too will probably regard open prisons as a good thing in themselves and the sort of establishment that should be expanded rather than under-used. The Expenditure Committee went into the question very fully largely from this point of view and, for example, pointed out that the fact that only 10 per cent of males went to open conditions as opposed to 42 per cent females indicated that open prisons could be given a more central place in the prison system. It went on to make recommendations designed to ensure that nothing impeded the pace of allocation of suitable inmates to open conditions and that steps should be taken to diminish their relative isolation from the point of view of convenience of visiting. (Recommendations 25 and 26).

6.60 We are aware of no reasons to disagree with the spirit of these recommendations. We are, however, perhaps a little more hesitant than the Expenditure Committee about the extent to which it is possible actually to expand open prisons and send proportionately more inmates to them. This is because changes in the sentencing practices of the courts over the last decades have made it more likely that those inmates suitable for open regimes will not receive custodial sentences at all. On the other hand, it has to be recognised that the main short-run impediment to sending more inmates to open prisons is the restrictions that exist in every case except Leyhill upon what kind of inmates may be allocated to them. These restrictions derive from specific agreements entered into by the Home Office with the relevant local communities before particular open prisons were inaugurated. Restrictions commonly include prohibitions on the allocation of sex offenders and persons convicted of offences of violence. In the case of

Kirkham Prison a further restriction was imposed on the maximum number of inmates who could be allocated to the prison so that the prison authorities were not free to occupy 200 of the available places even if they could. Our visit to Scandinavia disclosed not only that such restrictions on allocation were rare but that open prisons seemed generally resorted to more frequently.

6.61 We appreciate that the prison authorities tread an uneasy path in relation to open prisons. Whilst many informed observers regard them as inherently a good thing, the local populations upon whose co-operation so much depends tend to be apprehensive about them and suspicious of the allocation procedures. Like the Expenditure Committee we think such fears are misplaced and that, accordingly, the Home Office should actively commence a programme of reaching new local understandings about the nature of offences and where necessary numbers as soon as possible. However, we do not consider it should contemplate increasing the number of open establishments until it has had an opportunity to judge the outcomes of the greater freedom of allocation that re-negotiation gives it.

Categorisation, allocation and the dispersal system

6.62 Whilst most discussion about imprisonment concentrates upon its philosophy, or on how to exclude altogether groups of inmates who may be better dealt with elsewhere in or outside the criminal justice system, managing custody must be the prison services' dominant preoccupation. Custody comprises two fundamental elements.. On the one hand the perimeter of the establishment must not be breached (which includes by absconding in the case of open institutions) and, on the other, the behaviour of the inmates inside establishments must be so regulated that it continues to be orderly and, so far as possible, purposive. These two concerns are usually described as security and control. They are, of course, quite distinct concepts: even complete perimeter security cannot guarantee adequate control within an establishment; proper control depends upon the creation and maintenance of satisfactory relations between all members of a penal community, be they inmates or staff. There is sometimes a tendency to confuse the two concepts and critics, particularly of the present dispersal policy, claim that this is what the Home Office has done. They contend that an exaggerated concern with security may lead to excessively restrictive custody and in consequence to poor control. Some critics contend that this has already happened and point to the disturbances at Hull and Gartree as evidence. The Home Office, however, suggested that poor control in very high security prisons, if it exists, may be the consequence of the relaxed discipline of over-liberal regimes operated to minimise the effects upon inmates of the very severe security. Be that as it may, although security and control are not the same thing, they are obviously related.

6.63 Categorisation is the process whereby inmates are allocated to one of the four security categories recommended by the Mountbatten Report:

133

Category A

Prisoners whose escapes would be highly dangerous to the public or the police or to the security of the State.

Category B

Those for whom the very highest conditions of security are not necessary but for whom escape must be made very difficult.

Category C

Those who cannot be trusted in open conditions, but who do not have the ability or resources to make a determined escape attempt.

Category D

Those who can reasonably be trusted to serve their sentences in open conditions.

6.64 In England and Wales at present about one per cent of all inmates are in Category A, 30 per cent in Category B, 49 per cent in Category C and 20 per cent in Category D.

6.65 Current categorisation procedure depends principally on the completion of standard classification dossiers in observation and classification units in local prisons and regional long term allocation centres. All decisions to place in categories B–D are taken in the field, supervised by regional directors. Inmates are put in category A only following a decision at headquarters by a process which, amongst other things, consults the field on merits and location. Once categorised, inmates are sent to an establishment of the apropriate security: a category B dispersal prison (strictly, there are no category A prisons), an ordinary category B prison (i.e. one of lesser security) and category C, or D (open) prisons. All local prisons should be of category B standard, and there are two species of category C prison depending on the length of sentence. There are in addition some prisons which have specialised regimes e.g. Kingston which takes lifers only.

6.66 As already explained, although the Mountbatten report recommend concentration of the worst security risks into one establishment ("Vectis"), it was decided instead to adopt the counter strategy of dispersal recommended by the Radzinowicz Committee. Discussion about the competing merits of these two strategies has continued ever since e.g. the POA for long criticised dispersal. At their simplest, the arguments at present most commonly advanced in favour of concentration express the preference for putting all the worst risks in one place and thus avoiding, it is alleged, severe breakdowns of control. However, some informed commentators have also raised a variety of cost and regime issues. Although operational questions *per se* are not within our terms of reference, we have felt obliged to examine the continuing controversy because of its potential consequence for resource allocation. If concentration be the right policy, then money may be saved for other parts of the prison system.

6.67 As we see it, there are two principal sets of arguments now put forward against dispersal: the first is concerned with security and the second with control. The security argument maintains that the allocation of both category A and category B prisoners to dispersal prisons means *ex hypothesi* that category B inmates are subjected to a higher degree of security (and resulting regime restrictions) than they need. This has the consequence that unnecessary expenditure is incurred in providing high cost security measures for more prisoners than require it. The answer, it is said, is to put all the category A prisoners together. Because of changed circumstances since the Mountbatten report and the fact that the current allocation policy has probably meant some category B inmates ought to be in category A, resort to concentration would probably throw up more true category A prisoners than could be contained in one Vectis. Nevertheless, that would not undermine a logical argument based upon security grounds: it means only that in 1979 two Vectises are needed rather than one. Even if the security in these has to be higher than in the present seven dispersal prisons, the overall cost of the system will be substantially less. This is because, having thus allocated all the true category A inmates to the two Vectises, the remainder in lower security categories could be allocated to training prisons with adequate security, but not with all the excessive and expensive paraphernalia of dispersal prisons.

6.68 The second and control argument against dispersal derives from the undoubted fact that whatever else dispersal has achieved it has not prevented breakdowns of control and some serious riots. Although some of the original thinking behind dispersal was that it would help to prevent control problems, it was wrong to do so because—accepting that not all category A prisoners give control problems—any categorisation/allocation policy based solely on security criteria is irrelevant to control. In addition to allocating prisoners on security criteria, they should also be assessed both on their likely subversiveness and on their likely response to any subversive influences, that is upon what was described as their "subversive-enforcement quotient". Then within each establishment to which they are allocated, a prisoner would be so located in wings, halls or cells to avoid, so far as possible, allowing the subversive to mix with those most likely to be amenable to subversion. In this way, having first seen to one's security problems, one would then have done what one could to solve one's control problems.

6.69 The Home Office reply to all these arguments accepted that categorisation was not an exact science and that there must always be doubts about its true objectivity. It acknowledged that the criticism that there was a tendency, particularly in the lower security categories, to match inmates less against the training criteria than against the available training prison vacancies, had some validity: "Criteria and instructions are precise and clear but, with the passage of time, their application tends to fall into particular patterns according to the training outlets that are available and thus perhaps cloud the objective aspects of the categorisation and allocation process". They admitted too that they were aware that the process of recategorisation leaves something to be desired, and they have set up an internal working party to review all the relevant procedures. This we think is most desirable. On the other hand we do not think that too much precision should be expected of categorisation procedures. The Home Office then contended that it could not be said that dispersal was more expensive than concentration, partly at least because concentration had not been tried and its real costs identified. Whilst it was true that large sums had been spent on dispersal prisons, not all had been due to the presence of category A prisoners since the prisons would have needed to be improved anyway, and it was doubtful too whether they could necessarily have been kept immune from riot damage costs. On whether dispersal resulted in too many inmates being held in too high a degree of security, they argued that the standards of security in the dispersal prisons were even now not up to the Mountbatten Vectis standard and that, in addition to category A prisoners, many category B inmates needed the standard of security which the dispersal prisons presently provide. As to regime restrictions, dispersal prison inmates were far from under-privileged and repressed: on the contrary, they were well-favoured in comparison with inmates in many other prisons.

6.70 Whilst on the whole we accept the cost arguments and see the force of the regime points, we are not satisfied that the Home Office has struck the right security balance. The number of recent escapes from dispersal prisons show only two in 1973 and three in 1976 when two were recaptured immediately and the third within 24 hours. In 1974, 1975, 1977 and 1978 there were no escapes at all. Without inducing any feelings of complacency, this not only indicates a very high standard of security but it also reinforces the question whether all inmates in dispersal prisons do really need to be there. The issue here is not just one of categorisation (i.e. are the right people in category A), but also whether all the dispersal prison category B inmates are in the right kind of prisons granted that there is a type of category B prison without all the security apparatus of the dispersal prison. We do not think that question has been convincingly answered and we, therefore, recommend it is one to which the working party should give full attention.

6.71 We have found this question of dispersal, and whether it or a system of concentration should prevail, one of the most difficult of the many we have had to consider. Some of us instinctively favoured a policy of concentration, or at least of considerably modified dispersal, on the basis that it seemed better to put all the bad eggs in one basket so that their presence did not adversely affect the regimes that could be offered to other inmates. However, against such considerations we have had to consider the fact that some of the worst control problems arise from category B inmates. Further, it seems unlikely that resolving the dispersal/concentration controversy in favour of one or the other will necessarily abolish control crises, whatever it does for security. The reason for this is that, because of the fundamentally aversive character of prison, there can never be any guarantee that a particular allocation policy will eradicate disturbances.

6.72 In the end we have come to the conclusion that the issue must be determined not by the strength of the arguments in favour of dispersal but of those against concentration. There can be no doubt that the nature of the category A population does pose severe allocation problems. About a third at present have been convicted of terrorist offences and placing them together in one, or even two establishments would pose unprecedented security problems. Again, severe problems of control would also arise since locating them together would encourage them to concert their activities. This has been the experience in Northern Ireland and there are obvious arguments against wittingly running such risks here. It follows that the task of containment on both security and control grounds would seem immeasurably simpler if preventive allocation could be conducted in depth, that is with the prospect of cycling difficult groups of inmates around a system of seven or more establishments. All this is apart from the fact that concentration would pose unknown difficulties about the recruitment and retention of staff. Although such problems might not be insurmountable, the difficulties of selecting staff with the proper motivation and who were prepared to spend at least some reasonable period at a Vectis should not be underestimated. We have therefore concluded that the balance of argument is in favour of continuing with the present dispersal policy. Whatever the arguments in favour of concentration—and we acknowledge some raise important issues which no prison system should ignore—they do not in present operational conditions add up to justifying either a partial or a total reversal of dispersal policy.

A building moratorium

6.73 In recent years it has sometimes been suggested that there should be a halt temporarily or permanently to the building of any new prisons. Such views seem to have had various origins. For example some people have advanced the idea to draw attention to what they regard as excessive use of imprisonment which they consider, in the most extreme case, as an evil in itself. Others have argued for a halt in order to force those concerned to resort to alternatives to custody partly on the basis that, if more prison places are provided, then the courts will in practice use them to the full.

6.74 No-one pressed the case for a moratorium with us. There were, however, some echoes in what a few witnesses put to us. For example, the Governors' Branch drew attention to the fact that prisons could never post "full up" notices and, although they went on to say they did not think such a course practicable, they nonetheless implied that it was at least feasible for government to limit court resort to imprisonment simply by declining to take in offenders above certain maxima. The Howard League more definitely argued that priority should be given to developing alternatives to prison before constructing more prison places. Some other witnesses maintained, as we have already mentioned, that if in England and Wales a large number of training prisons were converted to local prisons, then there would be no case for building more prisons.

6.75 We have already dealt with the arguments about increasing the number of local prisons. The difficulty about limiting the ability of the courts to send offenders to prison on grounds of space insufficiency alone (i.e. posting "full up" signs) is that it would represent a serious interference by government with the independence of the judiciary. It would also be entirely arbitrary and capricious in effect since whether a court could commit to prison would depend not on the nature of the individual and the offence but on whether there was a vacancy as government defined it. As to giving an absolute priority to developing non-custodial disposals, such a course would seem feasible only when custodial disposals were not continuing at a level which imposed serious strains on the fabric of the existing prisons estate.

6.76 We conclude a moratorium is not justifiable for any of these purposes. In current UK conditions a moratorium would have nothing useful to contribute and, indeed, could only be considered at all in total disregard of the relevant factors. However, raising the idea is not wholly worthless if it serves to remind sentencers that their decisions have consequences upon resources which society cannot ignore.

FINANCIAL RESOURCES AND BUILDING PROGRAMMES

(a) *England and Wales*

6.77 Financial provision is, of course, made for the prison service under the same procedures as for other government expenditure. However, it is useful to consider prison costs in relation to others. Taking 1979–80, the total net cost of the law, order and protective services is estimated to be £1,801·9 million or a little over 3 per cent of total public expenditure. Of the total for law and order services, prisons amounted to just under 16 per cent.

	£m		£m
Administration of Justice	54·9	Immigration	18·5
Prisons	232·1	Other protective services	0·4
Probation	72·5	Civil Defence	9·2
Police	1,120·9	Community services	15·8
Fire	262·0	Central and	
		Miscellaneous services	15·6

6.78 The prison service is the only large block of expenditure for which the Home Office is directly and, save for the capital expenditure on prison buildings by PSA, solely responsible. Initially much of the expenditure on the other services is incurred by local authorities supported in a number of cases by specific government grants (e.g. 50 per cent for police and 80 per cent for magistrates' courts and probation services).

6.79 The following table gives the chief categories of estimated prisons expenditure for 1979–90. The expenditure represents the cost of employing 24,000 staff at establishments and about 1,000 at regional and central headquarters, operating 118 existing establishments, providing for 42,000 inmates and commissioning one new establishment. The major commitments of the prison service are shaped by decisions of the courts, and the levels of expenditure are very largely determined by the costs of staff in establishments and headquarters and the scale of the capital works programme.

BREAKDOWN OF SUPPLY ESTIMATES 1979-80: ENGLAND AND WALES

	Printed estimate prices £m
Current Expenditure	
Pay and allowances (outstations staff)	160·8
Other staff expenses (uniforms, training, travelling etc)	8·4
Maintenance, repairs and rentals	10·1
General supplies:	
Victualling	8·2
Other supplies and general operating expenses	21·4
Escort and conveyance of prisoners	3·8
Postal services at prisons	0·3
Other expenses	1·0
Telecommunications services	1·9
Materials and tools for production and training	18·2
Education and training	8·2
Assisted visits to prisoners and other expenditure on welfare	0·7
Prisoners' earnings	2·9
Home Office administration:	
Salaries of Prison Department (including regional offices)	7·1
Professional fees	3·5
General and telecommunications expenses	1·2
	257·7
Less: Appropritaions-in-Aid (proceeds of sales outside the prison service and other receipts)	13·3
Net Total Current Expenditure	244·4
Capital Expenditure (Home Office)	
New buildings, alterations	22·2
Plant, machinery, tools	4·5
TOTAL PRISON SERVICE SUPPLY ESTIMATES 1978–79	271·1
Additional Capital Expenditure (Department of the Environment) Property Services Agency	6·9

6.80 It is of course an important characteristic of this expenditure that a high proportion (75 per cent) is accounted for by predetermined staff and capital costs. Variations in inmate numbers are of limited significance because the direct costs attributable to them (e.g. food and clothing) are proportionately very small. In addition the number of officers employed is governed largely by the type of institution rather than directly by inmate numbers. It follows, therefore, that there is little scope for reallocating current expenditure within a given year unless it be by saving staff costs e.g. by restricting regimes or reducing staff overtime, which has much the same result.

6.81 The next table shows capital and current expenditure on the prison service from 1973–74 to 1978–79 and planned expenditure up to 1982–83. Figure 6.1 displays the material graphically.

EXPENDITURE ON THE PRISON SERVICE— ENGLAND AND WALES

	£ million at 1978 Survey Prices				
1. ACTUAL	1973–74	1974–75	1975–76	1976–77	1977–78
CAPITAL—					
BUILDINGS ETC	29·7(1·7)	28·2(5·2)	35·0(7·7)	27·9(6·9)	25·4(5·5)
VEHICLES, PLANT AND MACHINERY	2·9	3·9	4·0	3·8	2·3
CURRENT	151·5	173·4	185·6	186·9	188·2
TOTAL	184·1	205·5	224·6	218·6	215·9
2. FORECAST	1978–79	1979–80	1980–81	1981–82	1982–83
CAPITAL—					
BUILDINGS ETC	26·6(7·4)	24·4(6·0)	20·5(1·6)	22·0(3·2)	28·2(9.5)
VEHICLES, PLANT AND MACHINERY	3·8	5·0	3·1	4·0	2·8
CURRENT	205·3	202·7	204·9	206·3	205·9
TOTAL	235·7	232·1	228·5	232·3	236·9

Notes

1. The figures in brackets (which are *included* in the totals) represent expenditure by the Property Services Agency of the Department of the Environment on behalf of the Prison Department.

2. The forecast expenditure over the period 1978-79 to 1982-83 takes account of the following major assumptions.

(1) The prison population will increase from an average of 41,970 in 1978–79 to 44,510 by 1982–83.

(2) The number of non-industrial staff of all grades in the prison service will rise to 21,827 by 1980–81 and remain stable thereafter.

(3) Building schemes already in progress will provide a net addition of 3,207 places by the end of 1982–83. Starts will be made on one new prison in 1981–82 and two more in 1982–83.

Under these plans building schemes already in progress were expected to produce a net addition of about 4,700 places by 1981–82, and provision was made to start the construction of one new prison in that year. A further net addition of 3,200 places is expected to be available by 1982–83 and provision will be made to start the construction of two more prisons in that year.

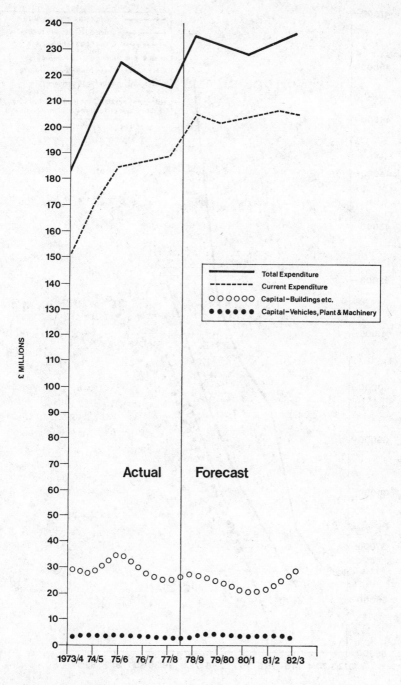

Figure 6.1

**EXPENDITURE ON THE PRISON SERVICE
ENGLAND AND WALES AT 1978 SURVEY PRICES**

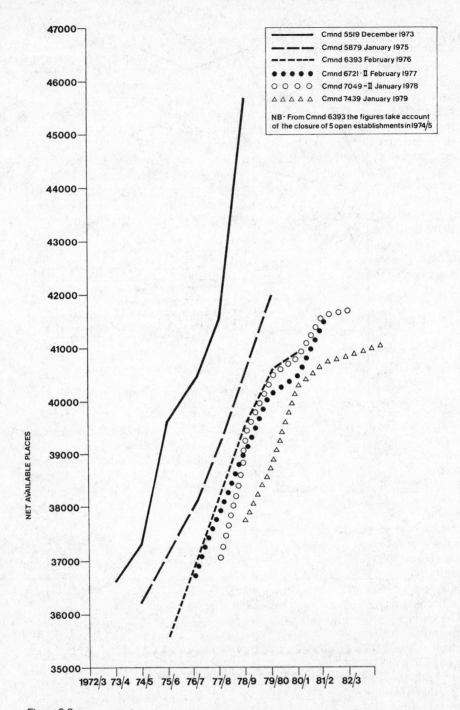

Figure 6.2

**FORECAST AVAILABLE INMATE PLACES AT END FINANCIAL YEAR
ENGLAND AND WALES - From expenditure white papers - 1973-9**

6.82 The building programme has undergone substantial vicissitudes. In 1969–73 prison population projections suggested that planned capacity would be inadequate, even with severe overcrowding, to contain the numbers expected to be committed to custody. A prison construction programme was therefore launched whose aim in 1972 was to provide about 14,000 additional places by 1976–77. When actual numbers in 1972 and 1973 (and the revised projections based upon them) proved to be much lower than feared, the target was adjusted in 1973 to provide 11,000 additional places in the five years to 1977–78. This target was further revised during successive reductions of public expenditure. An illustration of this is provided by Figure 6.2 which shows the effects on plans for the provision of places of successive expenditure White Papers. Whereas, for example, the intention in 1973 had been to provide 41,000 places by 1976–77, that figure was not to be reached, according to the latest expenditure plans published in January 1979, until 1982–83.

6.83 The strategy of the Home Office's building programme has been to make simultaneous progress on three fronts:

(a) the provision of additional inmate places both by the construction of new purpose built institutions and the conversion of former service camps;

(b) improvements and additions to existing establishments, including the provision of staff housing and amenities;

(c) major redevelopment of selected older prisons and establishments based on former war-time camps.

Major building projects are undertaken under an agreed division of responsibility either by the PSA or by the Home Office's Directorate of Works using outside contractors or inmate labour. Basically, the PSA is responsible for the design and construction of entirely new establishments and certain other major works, and the Home Office deals with all inmate labour schemes, most development work, and all maintenance.

6.84 It is obvious that present capital provision is neither intended nor in any way capable of supporting a substantial redevelopment programme. The Home Office has estimated, for example, that the provision of integral sanitation would effectively cost £180 million in replacement of the 5,500 cells lost as part of the modernisation of the Victorian prisons. The 5,500 cells could only be made good by new construction of, say, 12 new prisons. The elimination of cell-sharing at present levels would require the provision of another 8,500 places—a capital investment of £300 million in 20 new prisons. The Home Office also placed considerable emphasis on the requirement for an expanded redevelopment programme for 44 establishments and for both the interim and longer term work which might be needed for 22 others in all costing a further £200 million. £40 million would also be necessary for closing and replacing four establishments providing 1,000 places in all, which are already in poor condition and are not worth retaining for another decade. Such admittedly rough and not we think very reliable estimates amount to about £720 million. All this too is on the assumption that the inmate population is about 42,000 when in fact it is expected to continue to rise. To ensure that the pressures on accommodation get relatively no worse the Home Office considers it should start building at least one new penal establishment a year. Even so investment would be needed to bring prison service accommodation generally up to modern standards. The task could not, it was estimated, be completed in much less than 25 years even if successive governments were prepared to allocate the necessary technical and other resources.

(b) *Scotland*

6.85 Whilst financial arrangements are in principle the same as in England and Wales, there are some differences in practice. First, there is a difference of scale. As the following table shows, the total cost of law, order and protective services is £217·1 million, in fact about 5½ per cent of total public expenditure in Scotland:

	1979–80 (£m at 1978 Survey prices)
Administration of Justice	17·4
Prisons	20·9
Police	119·4
Fire	29·2
Civil Defence	0·9
Central and miscellaneous services	1·6

Prisons therefore represent about 11 per cent of the total as opposed to 16 per cent in England and Wales. Secondly, however, there are differences in the organisation of expenditure in Scotland which make such direct comparisons fallible. For example, the Administration of Justice vote for the Scottish Office includes substantial sums for legal aid in civil proceedings when that expenditure in England and Wales is borne by the Lord Chancellor's Department. On the other hand, the Scottish figures do not include provisions for probation which is done within the generic social work service, and immigration and certain community services are the Home Secretary's responsibility for both countries.

6.86 The estimated cost of the Scottish prison service is as follows:

BREAKDOWN OF SUPPLY ESTIMATES FOR 1979–80

	Printed estimate prices £000
Current Expenditure	
PRISON STAFF	
Pay and allowances	16,111
Other staff expenses	937
MAINTENANCE; REPAIRS; RENTALS	750
GENERAL SUPPLIES AND OPERATING EXPENSES	
Victualling	1,126
Other supplies and general operating expenses	1,918
Escort and conveyance of prisoners	31
Post Office services	132
Incidental expenses	44
PRISON INDUSTRIES	3,167
WELFARE OF PRISONERS	
Prisoners' earnings	342
Education, training and recreation	255
Assisted visits	28
Payments to local authorities (social workers)	326
	25,167

Less:— **APPROPRIATIONS-IN-AID**		
Recoveries in to staff on loan to Northern Ireland	456	
Proceeds of sales, etc.	2,762	
		3,218
Net Total Current Expenditure		21,949
Capital Expenditure		
New buildings, aterations, etc.	1,592	
Plant, machinery, tools and vehicles	413	
		2,005
Total SHHD Prison Service Vote Provision for 1979–80 (Class IX, 8)		23,954

In adition to the above, the following items are provided from other Votes:—

	£000
(a) For HQ Prisons Administration (Class XIII, 22) say	1,000
(b) For new buildings (per Property Services Agency, DoE)	800

6.87 Capital and current expenditure from 1973–74 to 1978–79 and planned expenditure up to 1982–83 is as follows:

EXPENDITURE ON THE PRISON SERVICE—SCOTLAND

£ million at 1978 survey prices

	1973-74	1974-75	1975-76	1976-77	1977-78	1978-79	1979-80	1980-81	1981-82	1982-83
Capital—Buildings, etc.	6·3(0·9)	5·1(0·4)	4·0(1·0)	7·0(4·3)	4·5(2·8)	2·1(0·8)	1·7(0·1)	2·1	2·1	2·1
—Vehicles, Plant and Machinery...	0·3	0·7	0·7	0·3	0·4	0·4	0·3	0·3	0·3	0·3
Current...	15·1	17·3	17·3	16·9	17·6	19·2	18·7	19·1	19·3	19·3
Total Net Expenditure £m	21·7	21·6	22·0	24·2	22·5	21·7	20·7	21·5	21·7	21·7
Daily Average Inmate Population ...	4,800	4,700	5,000	5,000	5,000	5,050	5,100	5,150	5,200	5,200
Total Average Numbers of Non-Industrial Staff	2,016	2,031	2,176	2,384	2,400	2,467	2,489	2,549	2,609	2,609
Total Number of Inmate Places available at end of Financial Year ...	4,300	4,308	4,677	5,186	5,146	5,146	5,146	5,146	5,231	5,285

Note: The figures in brackets (which are included in the totals) represent expenditure by the Property Services Agency of the Department of the Environment on behalf of the Scottish Home and Health Department.

6.88 Although the Scottish building programme has also undergone vicissitudes, their extent, except in one case, has been masked by their occurring within a more modest overall scale of operations. Against the background of rapidly-increasing prison populations in the 1960s, and forecasts which suggested that the population of Scottish penal establishments might rise to about 7,000 by the end of the 1970s, a programme was drawn up for the provision of the following new establishments—

Cornton Vale Institution (Female prison, YOI and borstal)— 220 places
Dungavel Category C prison — 150 places
Glenochil YOI — 500 places
Shotts prison (in 3 phases) —1,060 places
Calais Muir (near Dunfermline) Category C prison — 500 places
Cumbernauld YOI — 500 places

6.89 New building was preceded by the acquisition, in 1969, of hutted accomodation at Low Moss, near Glasgow, which provided 362 places. It was acquired on the understanding that it would be used only for a limited term. Cornton Vale and Dungavel were brought into operation in 1975 and Glenochil in 1976. The first phase of Shotts Prison, which provides only 60 inmate places, was opened in 1978. Restriction on capital expenditure made it impossible to proceed with further phases of Shotts Prison, or with Calais Muir and Cumbernauld.

6.90 In so far as Shotts is concerned, the expenditure cut responsible for its incomplete state has left a truncated monster with all the services, but far too few of the cells, for the inmate population for which it was designed. Thus some future resources were, temporarily perhaps, saved at the cost of wasting investment already made. We think that this decision was a mistaken one and illustrates the irrational effects of certain approaches to cutting public expenditure. There seems no question but that the project should be restored, although the SHHD have told us they would not now press for more than a maximum of 500 inmates on the site, developing Cumbernauld for another 500. They also told us it will take seven years to finish Shotts on this basis, which we found surprising and think should be improved upon: nevertheless, if correct, it demonstrates the further delay and cost which is the penalty of the earlier delay.

(c) *Northern Ireland*

6.91 The situation is again different in some practical respects, although similar overall e.g.. as to the proportion of predetermined current costs. In 1978–79 estimated prisons expenditure was £39 million, of which £28 million represented staffing and inmate costs. Of the remaining £11 million, £6·2 million was for capital works. It will be observed this compares with £2·1 million in Scotland and £26·6 million in England and Wales. Putting this in another way, Northern Ireland's capital spending is almost three times Scotland's with only three-fifths as many inmates, and just under a quarter of England and Wales's capital expenditure with one fourteenth as many inmates. Although the circumstances are different, the comparisons show at least that the money may be found when it is judged desirable.

6.92 Financial provision for future years is as follows:

	1979–80 £m	1980–81 £m	1981–82 £m	1982–83 £m
Staffing and operation costs ...	24·2	24·3	24·8	25·0
Accommodation	14·7	11·7	12·9	9·6
TOTALS	38·9	36·0	37·7	34·6

6.93 Most of the future expenditure on accommodation is in respect of the new permanent prison at Maghaberry and the new cellular buildings at Magilligan prison.

Comparison with other Social Services

6.94 Since we are charged with a requirement to have regard to the availability of resources, we could not offer a judgement on what the prison services require without first seeing how they have fared in comparison with other social services. Indeed, it was pointed out to us that it could not be taken as axiomatic that prisons had done worse. On the contrary, there was evidence to suggest that they had done better proportionately in terms of place provision than schools or hospitals.

6.95 Looking at expenditure in terms of volume there is certainly evidence to support such an interpretation. The next table compares expenditure on prisons since 1968–69 to the end of the current PES period with expenditure on law, order and protective services, education, hospital services and total public expenditure. The table shows that at least in England and Wales prisons' current expenditure has done better than any of the other services including public expenditure as a whole and compares favourably on capital expenditure. Put in another way, current expenditure in England and Wales on the prison service has risen faster than that on selected social services or total expenditure, whilst capital expenditure has fallen less in the prison service than elsewhere. In Scotland, too, current expenditure on prisons has risen faster than that on selected social services as well as more than total public expenditure. Although capital expenditure in Scotland has recently fallen more in the prison service than elsewhere, this is because in a relatively small programme the construction of a single new prison at Shotts, in 1973–78, distorted the figures.

6.96 On the other hand, the volume of figures by themselves do not tell the whole story. For example, volume comparisons can conceal very substantial differences in actual expenditure and the fact that one service has, relatively, done better than another does not mean necessarily that it in in any way approaches the actual level of expenditure enjoyed by the other services.

6.97 In addition, it has been pointed out to us that it is necessary to recognise the fundamental differences between provision for law and order and other social services. The purpose of expenditure on law and order is not to improve the quality of life but to protect it against disruptive forces. The level of protection is determined from what is thought to be necessary. In a period when crime, including terrorism, has been an increasing threat

148

1973-74 = 100

	Prisons		Law Order and Protective Services		Education (i)		Hospital Services (ii)		Total Public Expenditure		Total Public Expenditure in UK	
	current	capital	current	capital	current	capital	current	capital	current	capital	current	capital
ENGLAND AND WALES												
1968-69	68	46	76	50	78	91	95	68	...	...	79	86
1969-70	75	53	82	49	80	85	87	70	...	...	79	83
1970-71	84	46	85	60	84	90	90	74	...	...	81	88
1971-72	95	57	90	67	89	101	93	82	...	...	87	84
1972-73	97	75	97	78	93	107	97	98	...	...	93	88
1973-74	100	100	100	100	100	100	100	100	100	100	100	100
1974-75	114	99	108	101	105	74	103	81	108	117	108	115
1975-76	123	120	115	110	108	69	107	84	111	110	111	108
1976-77	123	97	120	92	108	62	108	80	111	87	111	87
1977-78	124	85	118	74	107	47	111	64	111	56	111	58
1978-79	136	93	123	82	109	42	115	70	117	79	117	80
1979-80	134	90	126	79	111	40	117	68	121	83	120	84
1980-81	135	72	129	80	112	38	119	69	123	77	123	78
1981-82	136	80	131	89	113	38	121	68	124	76	124	78
1982-83	136	95	133	101	113	37	124	68	126	79	126	80
SCOTLAND												
1968-69	74	53	81	53	80	76	83	72	...	...		
1969-70	81	42	83	47	83	83	85	68	...	...		
1970-71	80	39	86	51	86	83	90	69	...	...		
1971-72	92	64	92	61	90	78	93	79	...	...		
1972-73	103	58	96	83	94	94	96	102	...	...		
1973-74	100	100	100	100	100	100	100	100	100	100		
1974-75	105	88	107	81	106	82	101	91	107	93		
1975-76	115	72	115	101	113	74	106	88	111	96		
1976-77	112	111	115	95	109	77	106	73	113	89		
1977-78	117	74	117	82	104	64	109	68	110	82		
1978-79	127	38	121	71	112	55	112	79	114	89		
1979-80	124	30	123	69	113	44	115	78	116	93		
1980-81	127	36	125	71	113	44	116	78	118	94		
1981-82	128	36	127	80	113	43	118	84	119	95		
1982-83	128	36	129	80	113	42	120	93	121	95		

(i) Excludes research councils, libraries and arts.
(ii) Health Service only.
... Figures not readily available.

to society it would have been irresponsible and dangerous not to have increased the level of protection. This threat continues, and the level of current expenditure proposed for the prison service in the next five years is, in the Home Office view, unlikely to meet the demands placed on the service by the courts or the expectations of the public. As to capital expenditure, unless a very large sum is invested in repair, modernisation or replacement of the many neglected Victorian buildings and "temporary" camps in the prison system, it will no longer be possible to house the prison population even in the existing conditions.

6.98 It has been further pointed out that, to assess the adequacy of resources for the prisons programme, regard has to be had to the background of what expenditure was planned for the service, and the changes which then had to be made because of the overriding need for economies across the board of public expenditure. Examination of the 1975 White Paper on Government Expenditure to 1978–79 (Cmnd 5879) shows, for example, that the education programme had reached a peak of over £900 million in 1972–73, reducing to £700 million in 1973–74 (the base year) with planned reduction to £615 million in 1978–79 at 1974 survey prices. Capital expenditure on prisons was, however, planned to increase from £27·6 million in 1973–74 to £29 million in 1974–75 and remain at between £42 million and £44 million a year to the end of the survey period. It is argued that the subsequent severe reductions in capital expenditure suffered by both programmes were much more damaging to the prisons programme than to education, particularly in view of the relative sizes of the two programmes. In other words, the very large prison building programme planned in the early 1970s and agreed by the government of the day never really got off the ground, a point reinforced in Figure 6.2. Against this we appreciate there are other arguments based upon the relative importance to our society of the functions we are comparing. For example, it is not really appropriate to try to compare capital sums consumed by prisons and education because of the much greater importance of the latter. Thus, whereas we may have 50,000 prisoners in penal establishments, 10 million children go to school and looking after their future is an immeasurably more important activity. On that view, therefore, spending over the next five years of £250 million on the education building programme as compared with about £30 million a year on prisons is already out of balance. Although the number of school children is 20 times the number of inmates, the education capital programme is only eight times the prison programme. However, even here we must be careful to compare like with like. As we understand it, the survey of school buildings the DES conducted with the local authorities, and upon which the present capital programme was based, does not imply that the buildings would have to close because of their physical condition. On the other hand, the point about prisons is that some of them will have to close over the next 10 years because they will become uninhabitable on the 24 hour a day 365 days a year basis upon which they must be run. Adding a classroom here and there or refurbishing school premises in other ways is not to be compared with keeping in operation prisons whose occupants may not, at a time of local crisis, merely be sent home.

6.99 We conclude from this examination that, although comparing indices of expenditure is not by itself helpful, it can be illuminating on the way in which expenditure in some areas has moved. More detailed programme by programme comparisons have their limitations if they are not addressed to the merits of the individual programmes themselves. However, the main point remains that none of the evidence we have examined conjures away the problems our community faces about the physical condition of the penal estate.

6.100 We recognise this still leaves the question of availability of resources. As the Treasury have pointed out to us it is not they who decide what money should be spent where, but Ministers who must determine priorities between competing programmes. By the same token we cannot ourselves determine availability since it is beyond our power to do so. We can only draw attention to the facts and recommend the remedies we think appropriate. It will continue to remain for the Government to decide what should be spent.

RECOMMENDATIONS

6.101 So far Chapter 3 and this chapter have established the following principal points:
1. Whilst every effort should continue to be made to reduce the prison populations, for the foreseeable future they can be expected to rise gradually from their present levels.
2. The services have become increasingly staff intensive without there being in all respects adequate control over either the demands for manpower or its deployment. Nevertheless, although there is scope for manpower savings, more staff are needed.
3. With the general exception of Northern Ireland, much of the physical fabric of penal establishments is in very poor condition. The position is worst of all in England and Wales, which has also the worst overcrowding. There are no ways of redistributing the prison populations which would eradicate overcrowding.
4. It should be the stated aim of accommodation policy to abolish overcrowding and establish integral sanitation universally in cellular accommodation.
5. Prison capacity is inadequate as it is: it will become increasingly inadequate under present expenditure plans.

6.102 It follows that there is no alternative but to inject much larger resources into UK prisons than has hitherto been decided. This cannot come as a surprise to anyone who has had more than a passing acquaintance with the services in recent years. The fact is that the community has evaded its responsibilities for too long in the past and that, if we are to continue— as seems likely—to send so many people to prison, then we cannot shrink from providing the resources to ensure that both staff and inmates may be accommodated in premises which are acceptable according to modern standards. It is no good arguing that capital expenditure on prisons should always bear some constant and inferior relationship to capital expenditure on more electorally attractive areas like schools. Bearing in mind that prisons are the institutions of last resort and the ultimate sanction which lies behind all our mechanisms of social control, then we cannot afford to let them collapse on us.

6.103 Because of its relative smallness and apparent unimportance, the prisons capital programme has perhaps suffered more than most from the stop/go policies which have plagued public expenditure for so many years. In addition, the timescale of public financing (i.e. a 5 year forward cast at most) is wholly incommensurate with the timescale in which necessary building operations are conducted. We were told that the difficulties of obtaining suitable sites, especially in urban areas, and planning clearance, the traditional reluctance to use compulsory purchase for land acquisition for penal purposes, the time needed to prepare designs and contracts, the slow pace of actual construction and the problems of commissioning are such that no new establishment is likely to be operational in less than 10 years from conception. Cuts even in the design projects when all the preparatory work has been done do not mean that a programme can automatically be restored instantly on resuscitation because so much of the design work becomes overtaken by fresh developments e.g. the requirements of new safety standards or other fresh procedures. If it is intended to redevelop some of the larger more complex institutions, that redevelopment has to be carefully phased if it is not to result not only in intolerable disruption to the particular institution but also in severe repercussions for the rest of the system. This could mean in respect of some of the older Victorian prisons, a period of 15 years. We do not accept these periods of 10 and 15 years as immutable nor do we think that the Home Office should do so. The need for new or redeveloped buildings is pressing and we urge all concerned to do everything possible to complete all phases of whatever building programmes are decided upon, as quickly as practicable.

6.104 Inevitably, therefore, we find ourselves in the position of recommending a programme of work which is bound to out-last any one government. Bearing in mind the need to avoid inviting governments to bind their successors we have examined as minutely and as scrupulously as we could whether we were in fact obliged to contemplate the commitment of resources over such a long period. It is for this reason amongst others that we reviewed as exhaustively as we did in Chapter 3 the criminal justice context in which the prison populations have to be seen. Again, however, the facts lead to an inevitable conclusion. Above all, our review of the penal estate has established beyond doubt that it has become so run down that, even if future populations were quite a long way below present expectations, there would still be an unaffected need to rebuild and refurbish that estate. In other words, so urgent is the need to recapitalise prisons, that that need will be largely unaffected except by very large population reductions. We should also spell out that, although we urge the very strongest support for the development of non-custodial alternatives, any notion that their development can justify an inadequate allocation of resources to penal establishments is wholly misconceived. In so far as there has been any tendency to starve the services of resources on the grounds that developing alternatives will make those resources unnecessary, then that tendency must be stifled.

152

6.105 We therefore recommend that plans should be drawn up to embark upon a new prison building programme in England and Wales and Scotland designed (apart from completing Shotts in the latter case) progressively to reduce overcrowding to the extent that there shall in no circumstances, except for dormitories or specially enlarged cells, be more than one inmate in any one cell, and either by modernisation or replacement produce integral sanitation and washing facilities progressively throughout the prison system. No capital programme can be regarded as a credible attempt to deal with the current situation if it does not include either the progressive replacement or effective rebuilding of all the older Victorian local prisons, for whose galleried construction there was universal—and we think sound—preference. For such purposes it will in England and Wales be necessary approximately to double present levels of capital expenditure.

6.106 That is by no means the large step it sounds: £50 million a year at current survey prices represents less than 3 per cent of the present law and order vote for England and Wales. That vote in United Kingdom terms is one of the smaller areas by far of government expenditure. In England and Wales for 1979–80, the effect, putting it another way, would be to increase capital expenditure from 9·5 per cent of total prisons expenditure to nearly 17 per cent. In our view these proportions demonstrate yet again how current and capital expenditure have fallen so seriously out of any proper relationship. For similar reasons, therefore, we recommend that the real value of capital expenditure on prisons be maintained and that governments refrain from inflicting upon them the indiscriminate effects of any future general cuts in public expenditure. That way can only lie recurrent, but avoidable, crisis. Indeed, we should go further and indicate that total law and order expenditure has not been kept in proper balance. Successive governments have chosen to respond to public concern about law and order by steering resources towards the police as tangible evidence of their concern. This has both led to the relative neglect of other law and order services, notably prisons, and also increased the pressure upon them as a result of more police activity. Some witnesses commented on the need to consider law and order services more systematically and with such views we heartily concur.

6.107 Successive governments should, of course, review progress and due account should be taken of the actual, as opposed to the merely potential, effect of measures designed to reduce the populations, even though there seems at present no reason to expect changes of a degree which will erode the emphatic existing requirement to repair and replace the main fabric of the estate. Further, the programmes should on no account seek to anticipate increases of population greater than those reasonably forecast. Whilst the fabric should be improved, no-one should think that this will in any way increase the absolute amount of prison accommodation. The fact that the new and refurbished accommodation will ultimately contain much less overcrowdable space may be of greater significance for the management of the criminal justice system that it is possible to foresee: the environment will be changed, therefore, not only for the inmates alone.

6.108 It will no doubt be possible to carry out the new programme in a number of ways. Only rarely, however, would on site redevelopment seem practicable and even then it would be necessary to find accommodation for the displaced populations. One way, for example, of tackling the problem, and at the same time ending the scandal of the conditions in which so many remand prisoners are now accommodated, would be to concentrate in the initial years on a programme of building adult remand accommodation.

6.109 A new building programme will require, amongst other things, the acquisition as well as the redevelopment of urban sites. Judging from the experience of the Home Office over past building programmes, it will be necessary for the government seriously to contemplate resort to their undoubted powers of compulsory purchase if construction times—and costs —are to be kept within reasonable levels. This is not to advocate arbitrary expropriation and brushing aside local objections. On the contrary, we consider it most important that the normal full planning procedures should continue to apply and that compulsory purchase powers be invoked only in the last resort when every reasonable effort has been made to consult and negotiate with the responsible local authorities. Unless this be contemplated, however, there would seem no final way out of the common impasse where everyone agrees in theory with the need for more penal accommodation, but always objects vigorously to any particular site in practice.

6.110 As to manpower, we consider that it is in the long run undesirable for efficient working to be dependent on the excessive amounts of overtime now the case. Depending on the progress of recruitment and developing greater efficiency in deployment, ultimate manpower levels should be such that overtime is substantially reduced and, ideally, removed altogether. This could be done in such a way that the staff might be encouraged by alterations to the structure of their pay (e.g. of the kind mentioned in chapter 8) to co-operate in improved work systems which in turn will throw up the staff savings we think could be made and which could also help improve the staff's quality of life. We fully recognise the sensitivity of staff to some of the possible effects (for example on their earnings) of changes in these areas. Management should therefore display real tact and understanding as well as determination in dealing with them, and it should be a general objective that, consistent with the legitimate interests of controlling public expenditure, the staff's average earnings should not suffer unnecessarily.

6.111 It follows equally that we must be concerned that new building is as economical of staffing requirements as possible. We have already referred to the general preferences for galleried prisons which facilitate both control and economical staffing. Hitherto the objection to building modern galleried prisons has been their greater cost over other forms of construction. We were therefore relieved to hear from the Treasury that they would be prepared to contemplate higher capital costs of construction if such costs would lead to lower long term current expenditure, for example on staff salaries. This seems the only sensible approach to prison building. On any view new establishments must be expected to have a long life and it would seem the very reverse of prudent financing to incur increased long term costs merely to reduce immediate capital costs. This observation applies particularly, of course, to government expenditure which does not distinguish between capital and current funds in the same way as is the practice elsewhere.

6.112 We have not overlooked that our recommendations will have some staffing consequences beyond the prison service grades themselves. They will, for example, necessitate increased professional and technical resources in the Directorate of Works and in the PSA. There can be no alternative to providing these resources if realistic building programmes are to take place. Allocating money to the latter without providing the enabling manpower elsewhere would, of course, be absurd.

6.113 We should add that so concerned have we become about the prison staff that we contemplated recommending that a capital sum should be set aside annually devoted to improving facilities for them. We have decided against doing so not because we wish in any way to resile from the spirit of such a recommendation but because we have come to realise that there are severe practical limits on what building operations may be undertaken tied to such specific aims. Improvements for staff can more economically and sensibly be made as part of properly thought through schemes for establishments as a whole. Nonetheless, we strongly recommend that detailed plans are made for improving staff facilities even if we cannot go so far as to recommend earmarking specific cash sums. We would hope that some of the organisational changes we have recommended would encourage a more positive approach on this point.

6.114 Finally, taking these recommendations as a whole, we stress again that the relatively modest sums involved represent merely the cost of maintaining a vital service in an acceptable condition. They are not extravagant and, indeed, we are above all concerned at the fact that so many members of staff will still have to labour in buildings which have long since passed the limit of their natural life. For their sake too we hope that the government will find it possible to undertake to put right what has for so long been going wrong, quietly but steadily and inexorably.

CHAPTER 7

THE ROLE OF PRISON OFFICER AND GOVERNOR GRADES, THEIR RECRUITMENT AND TRAINING

7.1 In this chapter we shall be examining the recruitment and training of officer and governor grades, and at the same time looking at the role which these grades, and in particular the former, should be playing in the prison services of the 1980s and beyond. Plainly all three of these matters are closely linked. One cannot decide what form of training is required until one knows what role that training is intended to serve, but, at the same time, both the role and the training may depend upon the type of recruit that one is able to attract into the service. On the other hand, the type of recruit that will be persuaded to enter the service will, in some measure, depend on the type of role that he thinks he is likely to perform. Some degree of flexibility will clearly always be required in balancing these various matters against each other. In our view, however, the role which officers and governors should perform is central to the whole issue and we accordingly begin with that.

THE ROLE OF PRISON OFFICERS

7.2 Some elements of a prison officer's role can be clearly defined as essential because of the need for the secure containment of the inmates in penal establishments. This is the purely custodial aspect of an officer's role and involves a responsibility for locking and unlocking, discipline, control, supervision, searching (of persons and places), escorting, and dealing with emergencies. The foregoing are commonly referred to as "discipline duties" and training in such matters is given to all prison officers. In addition there are some officers who possess, and use within the service, certain specialist skills as well. These are, for example, the dog handlers, the works, hospital, and catering officers, and the physical education instructors. Largely because they work closely with inmates it is necessary for them to possess the same knowledge and skills as those officers who undertake discipline duties only. The majority of officers, however, do not work in specialist activities, and in many establishments discipline duties represent the full extent of a prison officer's role. This is often dismissively referred to as being "merely a turnkey". Certainly the discipline duties which we have just described are limited in their character and scope and they clearly do not provide satisfaction for a significant number of officers. Added to the foregoing is the fact that, over the years, more and more specialists such as education officers, welfare officers and psychologists have been introduced into prisons to perform functions which, though specialised and requiring particular skills and knowledge, have appeared to some prison officers to be further restricting the scope of their own employment. This feeling is perhaps nowhere more evident than where a prison officer is called on to escort a prisoner from his cell to an interview with one of these specialists, and then to escort him back to his cell again thereafter. Plainly somebody must undertake such tasks but many officers feel that their role in such circumstances is merely to provide a service to the specialists with the consequence that they become resentful of the presence of the latter within the establishment, and may themselves become progressively more distanced from any kind of involvement with the inmates. During our visits to establishments we received many representations that officers wished to be able to undertake a wider and more fulfilling role though, it is only fair to say, this desire was most frequently expressed in the rather vague and imprecise wish to undertake more "welfare" work. At one end of the spectrum there were those who seemed to wish to drive the probation officers and social workers out of penal establishments altogether and thereafter to take over the whole range of their duties and responsibilities, while at the other end there were those who merely thought that it might be possible to take over some of the functions of the probation officers and social workers; but those falling into this latter category did not seem at all clear about which functions they could in practice take over.

7.3 This desire to enlarge the nature of a prison officer's job is by no means a new phenomenon (see Chapter 2). We are not unsympathetic to this aspiration but before expressing any view on how it might be achieved, we wish to make two things quite clear. In the first place we are quite satisfied that not all prison officers wish this kind of change. We believe that there are many who are quite content with the custodial role which they perform at present, and we can see no reason to take steps which would oblige them against their will to undertake tasks in which they have no interest and for which, perhaps, they have no aptitude. Indeed, we think it is most unlikely that all prison officers would be able to display the aptitude and ability that would be necessary if any widening of their present role was to be contemplated. On the other hand that is no reason for not expanding the basic training of prison officers in the manner which we suggest later in this chapter, so that all may benefit from an increased perception of wider horizons leading to a greater sympathy with increased participation in welfare work, and so that those with the necessary ability may the more readily be identified and encouraged further to expand their interests and their range of duties. There are no doubt many who do have the necessary interest and aptitude and we think that it would be in the interest not only of these officers themselves but also of the criminal justice system as a whole if means were to be found to satisfy these aspirations. In the second place it must be clearly understood that, if there are going to be changes in the present role of prison officers, there must be a commitment to that change at all levels. This will involve, among other things, the introduction of shift systems which will allow far more continuity on the wings. It will also involve a willingness to create new specialities and, above all, a willingness by all concerned to look further than the prison walls to find new ways in which members of the prison service can become involved in a widening range of activities which will be of value not only to themselves but also to society at large.

7.4 One can already find within the prison services some instances of development away from purely custodial functions. For example, prison officers have for many years taken a full part in the therapeutic community life at Grendon; they have been responsible for innovative pre-release courses at Ashwell and Ranby prisons; they take part in an increasing range

157

of welfare activities at neighbourhood borstals; in co-operation with probation officers they are participating at a number of prisons in England in schemes which enable them to become more involved in the welfare of inmates; and in Scotland they have taken part in the experiment of setting up and running the special unit at Barlinnie prison. These examples show what can be done and, above all, show what prison officers are capable of doing.

7.5 We believe that there is scope for extending some of these activities to other establishments. Clearly it is quite unreasonable to suppose that prison officers can take over all of the work which is at present done by probation officers and social workers, particularly when one bears in mind that these specialists are fully trained in aspects of the social sciences of which most prison officers have no knowledge. On the other hand, probation officers and social workers themselves, in evidence to us, have made it quite clear that they are not averse to the introduction of a system whereby, in a spirit of co-operation, prison officers and probation officers could work together on a range of welfare problems relating to inmates. If prison officers could achieve greater continuity of employment in, for example, a particular wing, they would be able to establish relationships with the inmates and would be able to discuss, and perhaps help to solve, problems affecting them. We realise, of course, that this happens at the moment in some instances. We have the impression, however, that, if it happens, it does so by chance rather than by design, and is often frustrated by the fact that in most establishments officers can never be sure that they will remain in a position to maintain a relationship with a prisoner for more than perhaps a day or two at a time. What we have just been describing is a very basic kind of welfare work but we think nonetheless that it should be actively encouraged rather than discouraged. In much the same way we think that there may be scope for co-operation between prison officers and education officers so that prison officers might be able to take part as appropriate in educational programmes within establishments. We have seen some examples of this at the detention centre at Glenochil and we can see no reason why prison officers should not be more widely used in educational programmes, particularly those which are not so much academic as designed to improve an inmate's social skills.

7.6 On a wider plane we recommend that greater consideration than at present should be given to involving prison officers, on secondment, with a range of activities that take place outside penal establishments themselves, for example, pre-release hostels, bail hostels, day centres and day training centres, and all other types of establishment that are presently or may be in the future used in connection with non-custodial measures. Prison officers are already, of course, involved in the running of pre-release hostels where these exist: but we think that the number of officers involved in such activities should be increased wherever possible.

7.7 Furthermore, in addition to prison officers becoming involved in activities outside the prisons, we believe that there is scope for increasing the involvement of local volunteers and community groups outside in appropriate activities within establishments themselves. This already occurs to some extent but we consider that prison officers should be encouraged, in consultation with local governors, to consider ways in which such activities might be expanded. Not only would this be yet another extension of the role of officers, but it would also be a means of introducing a further degree of openness and public awareness into the running of penal establishments. That, as we have observed elsewhere, is something to which we attach importance.

7.8 Such an integration of the prison services into the wider spectrum both of the community and of the criminal justice system would, we believe, be to the advantage of all. On the one hand, it would enlarge the experience and understanding of the officers so as to make them more effective participants in the activities of penal establishments themselves, as well as being likely to give them a much greater satisfaction in the job that they are doing. On the other hand it would introduce into the running of non-custodial establishments a body of men and women with an experience of life inside closed establishments which might well be of assistance and value to the probation and social work services who at present are responsible for the running of these non-custodial alternatives.

7.9 We realise, of course, that any extension of the prison officer's role along the lines that we have discussed is dependent in large measure upon a significant increase in the numbers entering the prison services. We hope, however, that the various measures which we propose in this report will, among other results, tend to increase recruitment figures so that at least a start may be made on the proposals in this part of this chapter. An extension of the prison officer's role is also dependent in equally large measure on prison officers themselves being prepared to consider realistically the best ways in which their existing manpower can be used. This involves not only taking a more flexible approach than has hitherto been demonstrated in respect of manning levels and attendance systems, but also accepting that there is a number of tasks within penal establishments which do not require the skills, experience and training of prison officers for their adequate performance. Later in this chapter we deal with the special problems posed in Scotland and Northern Ireland in relation to clerical and administrative duties. For the moment we should like to deal more generally with those duties where non-prison officer staff may with advantage be employed.

7.10 At present many civilians work in penal establishments. These include clerical and administrative staff in England and Wales, instructors, tradesmen, teachers, probation officers and social workers, doctors and, to a limited extent, nurses. Some prison officers have suggested to us not merely that there should be no further civilianisation, but also that there should be a reduction in the present numbers of civilians. We cannot agree. Many of the civilians who work within establishments possess special skills which are necessary for the effective running of the system and which can rarely be matched by prison officers. In other cases, such as tradesmen and instructors, while some prison officers have the same skills and perform the same duties, there are not nearly enough of them, and it would be folly to attempt to exclude the civilian employees. By contrast there are some duties which are presently regarded as being the sole preserve of prison officers which, in our view, should more properly and economically be performed, in some cases by civilians, and in others by prison auxiliaries. Some such duties are presently performed by prison auxiliaries and night patrols, though the POA have indicated to us that they would like to see these grades phased out and all of their duties taken over by prison officers. We would regard this as a retrograde step, particularly if prison officers are in future to be trained for an extended role which will be at once more fulfilling and more demanding. Indeed, there is current controversy about whether or not the supervision of car parks should become part of a prison auxiliary's duties. We can see no justification for such a task being performed by a trained prison officer and we hope that the POA will speedily come to recognise that this is so. There are also other duties presently performed by prison officers which might with advantage be performed by civilians. We recognise that the extent to which these duties might be civilianised may vary from establishment to establishment and we accordingly say no more about them than to suggest that it is not self-evident that they must in all cases be performed by prison officers. In saying this our object is not to impoverish the prison officer's job. On the contrary it is to release him from the more mundane work so that he may develop and exercise more truly professional skills.

7.11 We have described in Chapter 6 the burden which is placed on the prison services, particularly in England and Wales, by the provision of escorts to court. This is a part of a prison officer's role which, for reasons given in that chapter, is likely to remain for some time to come. We accordingly say no more about it in the context of the present chapter save to repeat that, if means can be found in future to change or at least improve the present system, more officers would be available for the wider range of activities that we have been considering.

Clerical and administrative posts in Scotland and Northern Ireland

7.12 In England and Wales all clerical and administrative work in penal establishments is performed by civilian employees who are general Treasury grade civil servants. In Scotland and Northern Ireland, on the other hand, such work is performed by discipline officers who have voluntarily transferred to this type of work on a permanent basis. Typing and telephonist duties are, however, performed by civilian civil service grades. In Northern Ireland this arrangement has existed since the inception of the prison service, but in Scotland it was introduced after a riot at Barlinnie prison in 1934 in order to provide a permanent reserve of trained discipline officers. Although this role is still advanced on occasions as justifying the retention of discipline officers in administrative and clerical duties, the fact is that such officers have never been called on to perform that function in all the years since 1934. There are some differences between the ways in which th system operates in Scotland and Northern Ireland respectively and, so far as comparative pay scales are concerned, the position in Northern Ireland is particularly distorted because of the payment to discipline grades of the Northern Ireland emergency allowance. On the whole, however, the arrangements in both countries are broadly the same. In what follows we shall, for convenience, be describing the Scottish system, though noting, where appropriate, any significant factors that apply only to Northern Ireland.

7.13 For some time after 1934 the Scottish system attracted a good quality of officer to the clerical and administrative posts. Entrants had to pass an academic test of a reasonably high standard and they then enjoyed the advantages of accelerated promotion to principal clerk officer coupled with the fact that they were not required to do shift work. For a considerable time there was a substantial waiting list of applicants for transfer. The whole arrangement was first called in question in 1972–73 when a review was carried out by the Civil Service Department, the result of which was to demonstrate that the tasks being performed by clerk officers involved, in civil service terms, a range of duties that would elsewhere have been carried out predominantly by clerical officers, in some cases by executive officers, and in the remainder of cases by clerical assistants and/or storemen. At about the same time as this review took place weekend premia were introduced for officers carrying out discipline duties, with the result that these officers became substantially better paid than specialist officers of comparable grade. Consequently, there was an almost immediate decline in the number of officers volunteering for specialist duties, and within a very short period the waiting list for transfer to the clerk officer grade ceased to exist. The result was that a number of clerical posts remained unfilled, and by 1976 the recruitment situation had become so serious that it was decided in Scotland to discontinue the academic tests for entry. This produced a small number of volunteers but it remains very difficult to fill all the vacancies, though this is not apparently the case in Northern Ireland. Certainly, it seems clear that in Scotland the abandonment of the academic tests has brought about a reduction in the standards of office work performed by clerk officers, and it is worth noting that the SPOA, in evidence submitted to us, recommended the reintroduction of an entrance examination.

7.14 The main problem today is that both the Scottish Home and Health Department and the Northern Ireland Office would like to see all clerical and administrative posts in penal establishments turned over to civilian workers, whereas both the POA and the SPOA are totally opposed to this. In favour of retaining the present system it can be said that it has the advantages of widening the range of activities that can be undertaken by prison officers, that it provides a reserve of officers which, notwithstanding the experience of the past, might prove useful in a future emergency, and that it retains within an important part of the organisation of penal establishments a group of employees who are fully aware of security requirements and who are bound by the same discipline code as the majority of those working elsewhere in the establishment. Nevertheless there are several compelling arguments against the retention of the present system. These are:

(a) It is an expensive process to train a prison officer and, if effect is given to the recommendations which we make elsewhere in this report,

161

it will become even more expensive. It is accordingly a complete waste of valuable trained manpower to use it for a purpose that does not require such training, particularly if one accepts that the reserve force theory is in truth no more than just a theory.

(b) The range of tasks performed by clerk officers could perfectly well be carried out by civil servants of appropriate grades at much lower cost. The pay of prison officers has, for some years now, reflected the nature of the duties that are performed by discipline officers and will, we think, reflect that even more accurately if our proposals on pay are implemented. The result of that is that the pay for prison officers has exceeded, and will exceed, that of the civil service grades who would be employed, and are employed in England and Wales, to perform clerical and administrative duties, and that is without taking into account the additional quarters entitlement enjoyed by prison officers. The differentials which will remain under the pay scales that we are proposing can be seen in the following table. The salary scales shown in this table are, in the case of clerk officers, principal clerk officers and chief clerk officers, those which would be appropriate if effect were given to our pay proposals. Two points should be noted in relation to these. Firstly, the salaries for clerk officers begin at the second point on the prison officer's scale. Secondly, the salaries for principal clerk officers in fact straddle the scales for senior and principal officers, rising to the maximum on an eight point scale. In the case of comparable civil service grades the figures are those which will obtain with effect from 1 January 1980. It should also be noted that in the case of the civil service grades we have excluded for comparison purposes those parts of the relevant pay scales which are payable to those under the age of 21, that being the minimum age for entry to the prison service.

Clerk Officer	£3,611–£4,460
Principal Clerk Officer	£4,455–£5,394
Chief Clerk Officer	£6,306–£6,572
Clerical Assistant	£2,600–£3,165
Clerical Officer	£3,123–£4,000
Executive Officer	£4,200–£5,700

(c) Recruitment to fill vacancies might be easier if civilians were to be employed since, in effect, the whole of the civil service would be available for that purpose.

(d) The system of using civilian employees for clerical and administrative duties in penal establishments has always applied in England and Wales, and appears to operate perfectly satisfactorily there.

(e) In both Scotland and Northern Ireland there is a small number of senior administrative posts which are designated as Steward I and Steward II. These are departmental grades equivalent to senior executive officer and higher executive officer respectively, and officers, on gaining promotion to these posts, leave the uniformed service and, in doing so, lose their quarters entitlement. Because of financial disincentives difficulty has ben experienced in filling these posts, and until at least very recently there were three vacancies in Northern Ireland. These disincentives are very substantial on the basis of the pay scales now proposed, as can be seen by comparing the salary range for a chief clerk officer shown in sub-paragraph (b) above, plus 12·6 per cent shift disturbance allowance, with the scales which will be appropriate for SEO and HEO grades with effect from 1 January 1980. The difference is the more marked when one bears in mind the chief clerk officer's quarters entitlement which can be quantified in terms of the maximum rent allowance to which he may be entitled, that is to say £738 per annum. The rates of pay for HEO and SEO grades are as follows:

| HEO | ... | ... | ... | ... | ... | £5,950 to £7,250 |
| SEO | ... | ... | ... | ... | ... | £7,350 to £8,900 |

When one considers that a chief clerk officer would normally be promoted in the first instance to the rank of Steward II (HEO) it is clear from the above figures why there is no great enthusiasm for such a move.

7.15 The SPOA are clearly aware of this problem and in their evidence to us recommended the introduction of a senior clerk officer and the creation of two grades of chief clerk officer, thereby, they say, eliminating the need for stewards, and putting the clerical and administrative grades into the same rank structure as the discipline part of the service. We do not consider that this provides a satisfactory answer to the problem. The introduction of a senior officer rank would merely tend to remove such incentive for transfer as presently exists. Although the principal clerk officer begins his service in that rank at the salary paid to a senior officer, he progresses by stages, and without taking any promotion examination, to the full salary of a principal officer. Under the SPOA recommendation the rank, and pay, of a principal officer would be achieved, presumably, only on further promotion. Furthermore, the proposal does nothing to ease the very substantial financial burden on the service as a whole caused by the fact that officers, paid at discipline rates, are performing tasks that could be carried out at much lower cost by civilian clerical staff.

7.16 In our view the arguments in favour of civilianising the clerical and administrative posts in Scotland and Northern Ireland are overwhelming. These posts illustrate clearly the kind of duties that fall most readily outside the range of duties that we envisage prison officers being trained for and performing in the future, and we accordingly recommend that early action should be taken to bring about a change.

7.17 There will, of course, be difficulties about how a change to civilianisation can be effected. In Northern Ireland special provision will have to be made for the performance of reception duties which are presently carried out by clerk officers. We think that upon any view these duties will still require to be performed by discipline officers rather than by civilians. More generally, however, questions will arise about how the existing clerk officers

163

are to be phased out. Any change will, we believe, have to be a gradual process. Various methods of accomplishing it have been suggested to us but we do not think it would be right for us to state a preference for any particular method since, whichever one is chosen, it will be more likely to succeed if it has been arrived at by discussion and agreement between the interested parties themselves.

7.18 Thus far in this chapter we have endeavoured to describe in some detail those changes which we believe should take place in the role of prison officers involving, in some cases, a shedding of some of the tasks which they presently perform and, in other cases, and more importantly, an assumption of newer, more varied and more demanding responsibilities. This will take time to develop, and the extent to which it does so will vary from establishment to establishment, and it will not be achieved by all officers. At the same time, however, we do not suggest that a new elite of super officers should be created. Rather, what we see as being desirable is some increase and development in the general role of most, if not all, officers, and, beyond that, the prison service as a whole taking on enlarged functions involving more co-operation and flexibility between the prison service itself and specialists both within and outside the service, with the result that there will thereby be an increasing diversity of roles which individual officers can perform according to their individual skills and inclinations.

THE ROLE OF CHIEF OFFICERS

7.19 Although much of what we have already said in this chapter applies equally to all ranks within the uniformed service, there are certain aspects of the role of chief officers to which we wish to draw particular attention. The rank of chief officer is the most senior one within the uniformed grades and in many establishments there will only be one, or at most two, officers holding the rank. It is, however, a rank that is achieved only by those with considerable experience and ability, and it is, in our view, essential that its importance should be fully recognised by junior officers and by senior management alike. From our visits to establishments and from evidence that we have received we have gained the impression that the status and the role of chief officers have declined in recent years. This is, in our view, regrettable and it will be to the advantage of the service, as well as the officers themselves, if steps are taken to improve the situation.

7.20 Part of the problem no doubt stems from a lowering of chief officers' morale that has been brought about by the erosion of pay differentials to which we refer more fully elsewhere. The recommendations which we make on the subject of pay will, we hope, go some way to improving that. We do not think, however, that pay is the only problem. Chief officers are traditionally, and rightly, responsible for the morale and discipline of all the uniformed staff in an establishment and, if that morale and discipline are undermined by forces over which they can exercise no control, then understandably their own morale and status must suffer. We naturally hope that our recommendations as a whole will go some way towards restoring morale throughout the prison services and, to that extent, easing the task of chief officers.

7.21 So far as the positive role to be performed by chief officers is concerned we think that this could be more clearly defined. We have the impression that at the moment chief officers fit somewhat uneasily between staff and management in the sense that, on the one hand, they retain their traditional role, on the military model, as the most senior uniformed officer with a responsibility for the welfare and discipline of the other officers, but, on the other hand, they are increasingly, but not consistently, being involved in the ever-growing complexities of organising and running a modern penal establishment. We are in no doubt that chief officers should be clearly understood to occupy an important role in the management of establishments, and that that role should involve not only acting as adviser to the governor on all matters affecting the running of an establishment, but also exercising personal control over matters such as the detailing of staff under attendance systems. In addition, we consider that chief officers should become increasingly involved in other areas such as personal matters, staff training, local budgetary control, and industrial relations. We are not satisfied that at present chief officers are sufficiently trained in such matters and we therefore recommend that, in the general review of training which we propose later in this chapter, special attention should be given to the particular training needs of chief officers.

7.22 Accepting as we do that chief officers have, by reason of their long experience and the role which they perform within establishments, a special and important contribution to make to the running of the prison services, we think it is unfortunate that at the moment no means exists whereby the relevant Home Departments can obtain their collective wisdom when consultations are taking place regarding developments in the running of these services. Chief officers are, of course, members of the POA but, being so few in number, any views that they may have are likely to be submerged in the general views of that Association. We have no wish to fragment the unity of the POA but we would hope that they, and the Home Departments, would recognise that there may be occasions when the views of the chief officers might have special value, and on many occasions, no doubt, they may coincide with the views of the POA as a whole, thus reinforcing rather than reducing the contentions of that body. Accordingly, we recommend that negotiations should take place between the chief officers, the Home Departments and the POA to find a means whereby the views of chief officers as a body may in future be discovered, where appropriate, in relation to those matters where consultation with other groups of staff is taking place.

THE ROLE OF GOVERNOR GRADES

7.23 We have not been specifically asked to address our minds to the possibility of change or enlargement in the role of governor grades, and we are not aware of any demand for this from governors themselves. This must be a matter for some regret since we, for our part, have no doubt that the role of governors, and the way in which governors themselves perceive that role, must change radically if the prison services are to advance in the future in the way that we think they should. Elsewhere in this report, when dealing with matters such as organisation, regimes and industrial relations

165

we attempt to spell out the new duties and responsibilities, and the new style and approach to management, which we think governors must assume. In the context of this part of this chapter it must be said that the developments which we envisage in the role of the prison officer will also have an effect on the role of governors themselves. If prison officers are going to be trained for, and to take part in, a widening range of activities both within and outside penal establishments it follows that individual governors will have to make themselves aware of the nature and value of these new activities, and will require to have a commitment to their successful implementation. In some instances this may involve governors themselves actually participating in new activities along with prison officers; in others it may mean being prepared to alter regimes and other current practices so that new activities can be accommodated, or so that officers can be made available for training courses and the like; in all cases it will mean keeping a constantly open mind to new ideas, procedures and activities.

RECRUITMENT OF PRISON OFFICERS

7.24 Throughout the United Kingdom there are some variations in the qualifications which a prospective prison officer must possess. These relate mainly to height, upper age limit, and eye sight. In general, however, the common requirement is for a person, male or female, who is at least 21 years of age, who is of or above average height, and who is in good physical health. No formal educational qualifications are required. Candidates are merely required, except in Northern Ireland, to pass a simple test in English, arithmetic, and general knowledge. Advertising for recruits is conducted mainly in the press and to a lesser extent on television, though there is some direct canvassing for potential recruits from the armed forces. If a person shows interest in joining the prison service he or she will be sent a booklet describing the service, and containing an application form. When application forms are submitted they are subjected to a preliminary sift to exclude those who obviously do not comply with the requirements of age, height, nationality, etc, while those who pass through the sift are invited to attend for the educational tests, for interview, and for medical examination. Successful candidates are then selected for the service, subject to successful completion of training and a probationary period of one year.

7.25 In submissions made to the Wynn–Parry Committee some 20 years ago the POA argued that a minimum of three O grade GCE passes should be required for entry to the prison service. These submissions were rejected on the basis that they would present a considerable disincentive to recruitment, and the relatively undemanding educational qualifications referred to in the last paragraph have been all that have been required since that time. Despite that, difficulty has been experienced in finding sufficient recruits wishing to enter the prison services. In part this stems from the fact that the prison services are to some extent likely to find their recruits from the same sources as the other law and order services, and are therefore competing against a wide range of other potential employers. Moreover, there is this added difference, namely that the prison services do not accept recruits below the age of 21 whereas these other services do, with the result that the pool of potential recruits is very much smaller by the time the

166

prison services reach it. With that in mind we have given some thought to the possibility of lowering the minimum age for recruitment and to introducing some form of cadet entry into the service, although we are aware that neither of these has the support of the POA.

7.26 Like others who have considered this problem in the past we have come to the conclusion that the prison services are not at present suitable for any scheme of cadet entry. The basic task of a prison officer is to detain, against their will, men and women of all ages, many of whom are devious and manipulative, and some of whom are on occasions violent. This is a task which, in our view, requires a degree of maturity and experience that is unlikely to be found in anyone much below the age of 21. At the same time there are at present very few tasks involving little or no contact with inmates which would provide suitable alternatives for younger entrants to the service. Consequently we are unable to recommend that further consideration should be given to a system of cadet entry at present. On the other hand, if ways can be found in future to involve the prison services in a range of related activities outside penal establishments themselves, it may be that this subject would then merit such consideration since younger entrants might well be able to gain valuable experience in, for example, hostels or training centres as a preliminary to entering the prison service proper.

7.27 Apart from the question of cadet entry we have also considered whether there should be any reduction in the present minimum age for entry. To an extent any age limit is bound to be arbitrary and to result in the exclusion of at least some who might otherwise possess all the necessary qualities. At the same time any service must clearly indicate the sort of minimum age at which the qualities needed for that service are most likely to be present, and in the case of the prison service we think that 21 is probably about right for the qualities of maturity and experience that we have mentioned above. On the other hand, there may be potential candidates of, say, 20 who have these qualities and who may be lost to the prison services before they reach their 21st birthday. We accordingly recommend that recruitment literature should be reworded to introduce a measure of flexibility by indicating that, while 21 will normally be regarded as the minimum age for entry, consideration will also be given to outstanding applicants who are up to one year younger. Of course, this proposal still involves a measure of arbitrariness, and may not in fact produce many more successful candidates. On the other hand, it should marginally increase the competitiveness of the prison services against the other services already mentioned, and in times of recruiting difficulties it seems to us that any opportunity for improvement is worth taking.

Educational qualifications

7.28 As already observed no formal educational qualifications are required for entry to the prison services, and the educational tests which are given to applicants are of a very elementary character. Like Wynn-Parry we have considered whether there would be advantage in increasing the required standard for entrants to the service but have come to the conclusion that the present standard is sufficient. The raising of the standard might well deter some potential applicants and, in any event, we have no reason to suppose that higher academic standards are necessarily a good indication of a person's potential as a prison officer. On the other hand there must, we think, be some risk that better qualified entrants may be deterred from proceeding with an application to join the prison service if they gain the impression that their qualifications or abilities are not likely to be required and used to the full in the service. We think, therefore, that recruiting literature should be drafted in such a way as to make it clear that there is a place in the prison services for those who are better qualified, particularly if the role of the prison officer is to be expanded in the manner that we have outlined elsewhere in this report. Such wider duties may well provide a challenging avenue for the better qualified to explore, and the existence of such possibilities should be made clear to them at the time when they are contemplating entering the service. Having said that, we should make it clear that we do not see the wider range of prison officers' duties as being reserved solely for those who are better qualified; they will potentially be available to all members of the service. What is important, we think, is that the prison services should be presented as offering opportunities for people of all kinds of abilities.

Previous convictions

7.29 The prison services are expressly exempted from the Rehabilitation of Offenders legislation, and all applicants for entry to the service are required in their application forms to disclose any previous convictions which they might have. In addition to this, we understand, a check is made with the police criminal records office on all applicants who have passed through the preliminary sifting process. There are no fixed rules for determining whether or not an applicant will be rejected because of a previous conviction, but the normal practice appears to be that a previous custodial sentence will be an effective bar to entry. Where a previous conviction has not resulted in a custodial sentence a measure of discretion is exercised depending on the nature and age of the conviction. We have been told that some officers have been permitted to enter the service notwithstanding that they have convictions for, for example, theft or assault but we have received no direct evidence of this. Plainly, a prison officer should be above reproach. However, we have no reason to suppose that the present system of checking is not, on the whole, working satisfactorily and accordingly we do not find it necessary to make any recommendations on this matter.

Minority ethnic groups

7.30 There are today many coloured inmates in penal establishments, particularly in the larger urban areas in England. On the other hand there are very few coloured prison officers, and we think that it would be of advantage to the service if more could be recruited. This view is shared by the Prison Department but they have told us that attempts which they have made to increase the recruitment of coloured officers have met with only very limited success. There can be no easy answer to this problem but it is, we believe, desirable that all efforts should be made to overcome it.

7.31 There are at present three methods of entry to the governor grades. These are: (a) from the prison officer class by limited competition; (b) from open competition for direct entry; (c) by direct promotion from the senior ranks of the prison officer class.

7.32 Under (a) a prison officer is eligible to take a written examination success in which qualifies him or her, after two years' service as a prison officer, to enter for the limited competition (extended interview procedure tests) held in January each year at the Prison Service College under the auspices of the Civil Service Commission. Entry to the governor class is at Assistant Governor II level and recruits from this method of entry largely determine the numbers to be recruited from the open competition.

7.33 Under (b) Assistant Governors II are recruited as a result of an open competition which also takes the form of extended interview procedure tests. Candidates must normally be between the ages of 21 and 35 and, while no specific educational qualifications are required, a degree or diploma is regarded as being desirable. Many of the candidates for entry by this means will already have had experience of work in other, though possibly related, fields.

7.34 Under (c) senior members of the prison officer class—chief officers, senior foremen of works and foremen of works—are considered, along with Assistant Governors II, for promotion to the Assistant Governor I grade at an annual promotion board. The number of such direct promotions from the prison officer class is comparatively small.

7.35 At present about one-half of all governors have entered the grade as a result of passing the limited competition after service as prison officers. The POA, however, is anxious that entry by means of the open competition should cease and that all governors should be recruited from serving prison officers. Like the desire to expand the role of the prison officer this claim has been put forward for many years, and it is one which we can understand. It does, however, present certain difficulties, not least the fact that there are simply not enough prison officers with the necessary abilities to fit them for the role of governors. A Home Office Working Party on the Recruitment of Prison Governors, which reported in 1972, concluded:

> "The predominant conclusion we draw . . . is that there is no large untapped reservoir of potential governors among officers who do not seek promotion or who leave the service."
>
> (Report, paragraph 49)

We have heard no evidence to suggest that the position is any different in 1979, and we therefore recommend that, in the interests of the prison services, the present system should continue. It has in any event the positive advantage that it makes available to the prison services men and women of ability and experience who would otherwise probably continue to follow quite different careers, and not give the benefit of their experience to the service. That is not to say, however, that further efforts should not be made to identify, encourage, and prepare for promotion to the governor grades those serving prison officers who can, with advantage to the service, be given such promotion. The Home Office Working Party proposed that this should be done and we fully endorse that proposal. Furthermore, as indicated in paragraph 7.32 above we understand that the numbers to be recruited each year by means of the open competition are largely determined by the numbers entering through the limited competition. We think that this is a sound approach and recommend that it should continue.

7.36 Those entering the governor grades by the open competition are in any event required, as a result of the implementation of one of the recommendations of the Working Party referred to above, to undertake some service as a prison officer. It is clearly desirable that all entrants to the grades should have had some experience of the work of prison officers but there are two aspects of this requirement on which we wish to comment.

7.37 The first concerns the nature of the work which is undertaken as a prison officer by entrants to the governor grades. We understand at present there is no clear policy of tailoring this period of service to give the potential governor as wide a range of experience as possible. On the contrary, it appears that he is often simply regarded as being an addition to the normal operational strength of an establishment, to be used in whatever task may be dictated by the operational requirements of the establishment. We can understand the desirability of this when establishments are understaffed, but we think that this period of service by future governors could be put to better use if an attempt were made to arrange the period of service to allow the participant to see as much as possible of all aspects of a prison officer's duties. This would include not only service in the wings but also experience in other tasks such as rostering and control room duties.

7.38 Our second comment concerns the length of time to be spent as a prison officer. The present practice is that candidates under the age of 24 spend 12 months as a prison officer whereas those above that age spend only three months. It is no doubt considered that a younger candidate will be more ready than an older one to spend a longer period as a prison officer but we can see no good reason in principle why this distinction should be made. We accordingly recommend that the period of service as a prison officer should be the same for all direct entrants to the governor grades regardless of their age. If this were done, the considerations which have hitherto been seen as justifying the shorter period of service for entrants over the age of 24 might be thought equally to point to a shorter period of common service than 12 months. If, as we have recommended above, the period of service as a prison officer is to be deliberately used to give the entrant as wide an experience as possible, we would have no objection in principle to shortening the length of that service; but we doubt whether any substantial reduction would allow sufficient time for a suitable range of experience to be achieved.

7.39 The subject of training is a very substantial one which we have not, in the time available to us, been able to examine in as much detail as we would have wished. For example, we have received a number of representations concerning detailed matters of specialist training given to works officers and other specialist grades but regretfully we have not been able to reach any conclusions on these matters. Even so far as training in general is concerned we have not found it possible, with a few exceptions, to do more than to make some general observations. Clearly, however, the proper and appropriate training of all grades is of the utmost importance not only as a means of ensuring that the tasks undertaken by the prison service will be carried out as efficiently as possible, but also as a means of giving staff that confidence and self-respect which is an essential element of job satisfaction. Throughout our visits to establishments, and in our examination of the evidence submitted to us, we have reached a clear conclusion that training, at all levels, is neither as effective nor as comprehensive as we think it should be and that it is not given sufficient priority at all levels in the service. We accordingly recommend that, as a matter of urgency, steps should be taken to carry out a searching review of all training facilities and programmes in order to ensure that the best possible provision is being made in this matter. This review should extend not only to the training of discipline officers, but also to that of specialists, such as works and hospital officers, as well. For England and Wales this should be a priority task for the Director of Personnel whose appointment we recommend in Chapter 5. In what follows, accordingly, we do not seek to set out detailed recommendations for change. Instead, we seek to identify at least some of the areas which seem to us to require closer examination and review.

7.40 In England and Wales staff training, except for clerical, administrative, and other non-industrial grades working within the prison service, is the responsibility of P6 Division within the Prison Department. Additionally that Division has a responsibility, as far as governors are concerned, for career planning and development. The Division has financial control over regional and local training, and supervises the operation of the Prison Service College and the two Officer Training Schools, at Wakefield and Leyhill. At regional level regional directors, through regional training units, are responsible for identifying training needs within the region, supporting and monitoring the organisation and standards of local in-service training whilst organising and directing regional training activities and supervising some centrally arranged activities. At local establishment level governors, through staff training committees and training officers, have responsibility for the particular staff training of their establishments. A formal system of communications is maintained between the various tiers over and above the normal range of informal contact or day-to-day consultation. First, there is a Staff Training Advisory Group which meets two or three times a year under the chairmanship of the Assistant Controller, P6 Division, to advise him on training needs for all grades employed in the prison service, and to identify areas of training policy and practice which may require further study with a view to modification or development. Membership includes the Principal of the Prison Service College, senior representatives of regions and members of specialist departments in headquarters. Second, meetings are held four times a year between P6 Division and the regional training units to discuss specific matters of current interest. Third, a liaison committee of senior members of the Prison Service College and Officer Training Schools meets under the chairmanship of the Principal, Prison Service College, to consider possible changes and developments in the content of the Schools programmes. Finally, meetings of local training officers (to which P6 Division sends an observer) are arranged on a regional basis to assist regional training officers in their tasks of monitoring and supporting the organisation and standards of local in-service training.

7.41 In Scotland the training of prison staff is about to become the responsibility of the Personnel Division of prison service headquarters, it having hitherto been under the general oversight of Operations Division. The content and duration of training courses are kept under review by a central committee on staff training, membership of which includes representation of the Prison Governors' (Scotland) Branch of the SCPS, the SPOA, the Principal of the Scottish Prison Service College, and some departmental representation. In addition, at local level at each establishment, there is a local training committee with membership comprising a member of the governor grade, a chief officer (discipline) and the local staff training officer. Prison service training for officers, and to a limited extent for governors, is provided at the Prison Service College near Falkirk, though most of the training for Scottish governors is made available at the English College at Wakefield.

7.42 In Northern Ireland the general arrangements for training are broadly similar to those in Scotland, that is to say that training is organised both at headquarters and at local levels. At headquarters Prison Staffing Branch (1) has general policy responsibility for prison service training, and at establishment level governors have responsibility for training within their establishments through staff training committees and training officers. Northern Ireland has its own officer training school situated within the grounds of Millisle Borstal, and quarterly training meetings are held there under the chairmanship of the Assistant Controller with the Principal of the Officer Training School and training officers from all establishments. An annual meeting is also held at headquarters to consider possible changes in the School programme and to settle training policy for the ensuing year.

7.43 As in so many other things the smaller scale of operations in Scotland and Northern Ireland appears to have the result that the organisation of training functions fairly smoothly. In England and Wales on the other hand there have been complaints that headquarters, and to some extent regional directors, do not show sufficient interest in training, and that they are insensitive to the operational training needs of establishments and staff. There are some features of the organisational arrangements in England and Wales which we think contribute to these complaints and give them some validity.

7.44 In the first place we take the view that training has simply not been accorded its proper importance at headquarters. If effect is given to our recommendation for the creation of a post of Director of Personnel we would expect the holder of that post to assume overall responsibility for the training and career development of all prison service grades, and give these subjects the full and prompt attention which they deserve within the context of related personnel matters.

7.45 In the second place we have been struck by the narrowness of the membership of the Staff Training Advisory Group. We think that the concept of such an advisory body is a sound one but we also think that there is a real risk, as the Group is presently constituted, that it will be out of touch with current requirements in the field and wider developments in education and training elsewhere. We accordingly recommend that its membership should include one or two operational governors, a chief officer, and also representatives of education and training from outside the prison service.

7.46 In the third place, we are, as in other matters, somewhat troubled about the role that is to be performed by regions. The role of regional directors, so far as training is concerned, does not appear to us to be particularly clearly defined. Moreover, there are no regional training establishments, and the financial provision for training at local level which is granted to the regions seems to us to be very small if significant local training programmes are to be initiated and run under regional direction. The most recent annual figures for the financial provision for this purpose are as follows:

						£
North Region	—	—	—	—	—	26,300
South East Region	—	—	—	—	—	24,810
Midland Region	—	—	—	—	—	13,090
South West Region	—	—	—	—	—	22,680

These figures are based on estimates submitted by local establishments and, in the case of, for example, Midland Region, average only a little over £500 per establishment. We think that this low level of financial provision illustrates a degree of ambivalence about precisely what regional directors should be doing so far as training is concerned. If, on the one hand, their role was intended to be merely advisory and supervisory so far as local establishments are concerned there would not appear to be any need for the regions to be given any financial provision at all, apart from that required to sustain their own supervisory and advisory staff. In such a case it would seem that local establishments could obtain their own financial provision direct from headquarters. On the other hand, if regions are to be expected to initiate and operate regional training programmes of any substance then the scale of financial provision would, we think, have to be significantly higher than it is at present. In Chapter 5 we have recommended that for the immediate future the regional training officer should be withdrawn from regional offices. If effect is given to this it would follow that regional directors would cease to have any direct responsibility for training which would then have to be arranged either by the Prisons Department itself or at local establishment level. As we have pointed out in that chapter, however, it may prove necessary within the natural development of the service for certain specialised functions, such as training, to be restored to a regional level at some future date. Were that to happen the present ambivalence to which we have drawn attention should, in our view, be avoided.

7.47 At local establishment level training is normally the designated responsibility of a training officer, who is frequently of principal officer rank. Many of these officers are extremely diligent in attempting to promote the in-service training of members of staff in their establishments, but practically none of them is responsible solely for training, and many of them are so pressed by their normal duties that they have little time to spare to devote to their training responsibilities. Furthermore, even their best efforts are often frustrated by the fact that officers who are due to undertake training cannot be released from other duties for that purpose. These comments apply, so far as we can judge, not merely to England and Wales but throughout the United Kingdom. We doubt whether the present system is the best that could be devised. Not only does it mean that in some cases training is given a low priority within particular establishments; it also means that, because of the rank of the training officer, the training needs of those senior to himself may not receive the attention which we think they should receive. Accordingly, we recommend that local training should be made a shared responsibility between a senior member of the uniformed grades and a member of the governor grades. We appreciate of course that at the moment governors of establishments are in theory responsible for all the training requirements of their establishment, but we think that the identification of one of their number as having a specific responsibility for training would not only give the need for training a higher priority, but would also ensure that such training was considered in the context of all members of staff within the establishment, rather than just those in the uniformed grades. Furthermore, we also recommend that steps be taken to ensure that, so far as possible, these training officers are given the time and the facilities to carry out their duties properly, and that the persons to be trained are made available when required for training purposes.

7.48 The physical resources for training, in the form of the various Officer Training Schools and Prison Service Colleges, can, in our view, best be described as adequate rather than first class. Certainly the accommodation at the Prison Service College at Wakefield is cramped and its location, near to Wakefield prison, is not particularly agreeable. Unfavourable comparisons were frequently drawn between it and the Police College at Bramshill, and, so far as the Officer Training Schools are concerned, some of us have seen for ourselves how they compare with the magnificent facilities provided at the Metropolitan Police Training School at Hendon. Plainly, at a time when substantial capital investment is required for penal establishments themselves (see Chapter 6) it might be argued that training colleges and schools should accept a lower priority for improvement We are not prepared to accept such an argument. The facilities which are provided for training have a significant effect not only on recruitment but also on the morale of those presently within the service and we accordingly recommend that the condition of and provision of facilities in these establishments should be constantly kept under review and that all possible steps should be taken to bring about improvements.

The content of training

(a) Prison officer grades

7.49 The basic training for prison officers consists of a short period of familiarisation at a local establishment followed by a period of training at a training school. The period spent at the training school is eight weeks for officers recruited in England and Wales, six weeks for officers in Scotland, and four weeks for officers in Northern Ireland. While one can understand the short period of training in Northern Ireland because of the need in recent years to train a large number of officers as quickly as possible, there appears to be no other obvious reason why the periods of training should differ so significantly from country to country. We have received no satisfactory explanation for this and we think that the period of basic training for a prison officer should, exceptional circumstances apart, be the same in all parts of the United Kingdom. Indeed, if the content of training is to be expanded in the way that we think it should, it will probably be necessary to extend the period of basic training to something in excess of eight weeks. The training which is given to new prison officers is largely related to the basic range of duties which they will be required to perform after that training is complete. The basic training should be followed after about nine to 12 months' service as a prison officer by a development course of one to two weeks' duration, but sadly the facilities for such training are so strained that many officers have to wait a considerably longer period before such development training is made available to them. The training system in the United Kingdom contrasts sharply with that to be found in certain other countries. In Sweden, for example, basic training lasts for 12 weeks and places considerable emphasis on academic subjects such as the social sciences, psychology, psychiatry, and criminology. This basic training is followed some months later by a continuation course of four weeks' duration which extends the training given in the basic course to matters such as criminal law and trade union affairs. This is an ambitious programme but it suffers from the practical defect that it has not proved possible to make these courses available at the beginning, or even at an early stage, in the careers of prison officers. Indeed, the basic training course is not in general given until an officer has been in service for about two or three years. While we found much to admire in the Swedish system we consider that the United Kingdom approach to basic training is in general preferable, if only because it succeeds in giving an officer, at the beginning of his career, the essential knowledge to enable him to perform his basic tasks properly. On the other hand, there may be problems in restricting training to this alone.

7.50 These problems were highlighted in evidence which we received from some members of the Department of Adult Education at the University of Leeds, all of whom have had considerable experience of and contact with the Prison Service College and Officer Training Schools in England. In the evidence they said:

"During the past ten years prison service training has become increasingly job applied. This has meant that training to do with theories, explanations and ethics about the meaningfulness of roles and functions has not grown in the same way as has job applied training. . . . The present orientation of training seems to be to consolidate existing practice rather than to keep pace with changing perspectives in institutions in other countries and exploring possible applications in Britain, or taking account of what is going on in related services such as probation, social work and the police, in a society which is itself changing . . . . Training which is exclusively job applied fails to offer guidance or a set of ideas in which to operate when job descriptions run out; it leaves the individual in a vacuum in this respect. In this sense, it reduces potential on the job, let alone personal development of staff."

We think that there is considerable force in these views and we accordingly believe that steps must be taken to recognise and respond to them within the framework of all future training programmes. This is particularly so if officers are going to undertake a wider range of duties both within establishments and outside. It will however be necessary to consider carefully how this extra dimension to training is to be supplied.

7.51 We think that the proper course will be to provide it in relatively small measure at the time when an officer receives his basic training, and to provide the bulk of such wider training at a later stage, once an individual officer's own abilities and interests can be more clearly identified. The difficulty, however, is that experience to date tends to indicate that any training after basic training is not very readily achieved. The reason for this is in part that there are simply not enough facilities for it, and in part that staffing deficiencies frequently make it difficult for officers to be relieved of their normal duties in order to take part in such training. If in future training is to cover a wider range of subjects and to be given the higher priority which we believe it should have, it will be necessary to take steps to ensure that the difficulties of the past are overcome and that officers do receive the time, encouragement, and facilities which will be necessary for such training.

7.52 In some instances the range of training that we envisage may involve periods of secondment with related services such as probation, social work and police, as well as appropriate community education services. In others it may involve attendance at courses which are provided by outside agencies or teaching establishments. In yet others it may involve a much greater development than has hitherto been seen in local training programmes designed for individual establishments or groups of establishments. In all cases we think that such training should be seen not merely as a concomitant of promotion but as an ingredient in the career development of all staff.

7.53 So far as teaching staff in the Training Schools are concerned—and this applies equally to the staff in the Prison Service Colleges—it is essential not only that they should be of the highest quality available and properly trained themselves in teaching methods, but also that service in a teaching capacity at these establishments should be regarded throughout the service as a mark of distinction and not, as seems to be thought in some quarters at present, a means of escape for those who are less able to withstand the rigours of service in the field. There seems to be a view which is widely held among governor grades that service in a teaching capacity at the Prison Service College will be detrimental to promotion and advancement in the service. We are not aware of any evidence to support this view but the fact that the view is held at all, and has been expressed to us, is indicative of a failure to present service at the Colleges as being an honour and a valuable stage in a person's career, and we think that urgent steps should be taken to correct this impression. In all respects the Prison Service Colleges and Officer Training Schools should be places of which the members of the prison services can be proud. We do not think that such pride exists at the moment and its absence must be adversely reflected both in the quality and value of the training obtained and also in the morale of those who have anything to do with the training establishments whether as staff or as pupils.

7.54 There is one further feature of prison officers' training on which we wish to comment. This concerns the wearing of uniform during attendance at basic training at the Officer Training Schools. Uniform is worn at the Schools in Scotland and Northern Ireland but is not worn at the Schools in England. The view taken in England has been that it is undesirable to provide uniform universally at this stage since at least some of the officers will ultimately be posted to borstals or detention centres where uniform is not worn. We think that it is important for a new recruit to feel part of the service which he has joined from as early a stage as possible, and we think that one way in which this may be achieved is by the wearing of uniforms during basic training. Certainly we have formed the impression that, at the very least, the wearing of uniform at, for example, the Prison Service College in Scotland and the Metropolitan Police College at Hendon gives the officers concerned a pride in appearance and a sense of identity which we found to be absent both at Wakefield and at Leyhill. We accordingly recommend that the present arrangements in the Training Schools should be changed.

(b) *Governor grades*

7.55 The initial training of entrants to the governor grades must inevitably pose particular problems because of the wide range of backgrounds from which these entrants come. Some will have come after a period of service in the ranks as prison officers, while others, who may cover a wide range of ages, may come either directly from university or college, or after a period of employment which could be of any kind. There must, we think, be sufficient flexibility in training programmes to take account of these variable factors. The present method of training new entrants to the governor grades is to provide a two-year sandwich course during part of which time the entrant works as an AG II in a penal establishment, and for the remainder of the time he either attends the Prison Service College or serves periods of secondment with, for example, the probation service. This arrangement has been criticised on a number of different grounds. Some recent entrants to the grade have criticised it on the ground that they would prefer a continuous course of study rather than one which is broken up by periods of service in a penal establishment. Some of them have also said to us that they have experienced difficulty during the periods of service in establishments either because they felt that they were not being given sufficiently responsible tasks to perform and were being treated by their governors as mere supernumeraries, or because, if they were put ostensibly in charge of a wing, they were in some sense regarded as inferior by the wing principal officer to whom, in theory at least, they were senior. Governors, on the other hand, have criticised the arrangement on the grounds that they are unable to make reasonable and proper use of the assistant governors who are under training because of their frequent departures to college, and some of them have suggested that AG IIs, during their two-year training period, should be formally recognised as being supernumerary with the result that, during the two years, they would be an addition to the strength of the establishment rather than a part of it. We can understand these criticisms but we have come to the conclusion nonetheless that the two year sandwich course is a sensible arrangement. A full-time continuous residential course, lasting perhaps for more than a year, would not, we think, be welcomed by many entrants to the governor grades, and particularly by those who are married, bearing in mind that the Prison Service Colleges do not have facilities for married quarters. Furthermore, we think that a measure of practical experience in an establishment is an essential part of the training process and this would have to take place after the college training if it were continuous and might well be less valuable if performed at that stage.

7.56 We consider, however, that the criticisms which we have received demonstrate at least that there is no uniformity of understanding throughout the service about how the training period should be used, either by the entrants themselves or by their governing governors. We, for our part, believe that it would be wrong to treat AG IIs under training as being merely supernumerary. We think that their training will be best served if, during their periods of service in establishments within the two years, they are given by their governors an increasing range of responsibilities commensurate with their experience and with the training which they have thus far received. This will require a measure of supervision and guidance from their governors which we suspect is not always readily given at present. If, however, this is done in an understanding and intelligent manner, the AG II under training will gradually come to make a more significant contribution to the running of the establishment and will thereby gain in confidence and experience in a way which we think would be unlikely if he were to be regarded throughout the two years as being merely surplus to the normal strength of the establishment. It goes without saying, however, that for this to work in the best way governors must accept that AG IIs under training are, during the two years, in a special category and must be dispensed with during the periods when they are working away from the establishment.

7.57 We have considered how this special category might best be recognised and have come to the conclusion that the answer lies in creating a special rank for the purpose. We recommend that this should be done and that the rank should be designated "Assistant Governor Trainee" or, in short, AG(T). A consequence of this would be that the full rank of AG would be achieved only on successful completion of the two years training course. We believe that the creation of this special rank will have certain advantages. It will indicate quite clearly the special position of the AG during his period of training and it will, we think, tend to concentrate the attention of all concerned—governors and more senior management alike—on the need to make the best possible use of the two year training period. Additionally, it will mean that the Assistant Governors will occupy a full operational rank, a factor which can be reflected not only in the duties assigned to those who hold the rank but also, as we have recommended in Chapter 8, in a suitable differential in salary levels between it and the AG(T) rank.

7.58 In reaching the foregoing conclusion we have also considered whether it should have any further consequences so far as the existing ranks of AG I and AG II are concerned, and indeed whether these ranks should be changed for any other reason. We have come to the conclusion that they should. We consider that any person liable to be placed in charge of an establishment should be seen to be of full governor rank, yet a few smaller establishments are in the charge of an AG I, and in some larger ones an AG I may often have to act up during the temporary absence of the actual holder of the deputy governor post. This problem does not exist in Scotland where there is only a single Assistant Governor rank (presently designated AG II) and those who would be AG I elsewhere in the United Kingdom are designated as Governor IV. In our opinion this practice should be extended to England and Wales and to Northern Ireland. We accordingly recommend that in these countries the rank of AG I should be renamed Governor IV, and, going further than the Scottish practice and therefore extending there also, we recommend that the rank between AG(T) and Governor IV should simply be known as Assistant Governor, since there will, under this recommendation, be no need for any numerical distinction. Apart from, as we believe, improving the status of those acting as governors, the foregoing proposals will in our view give a clearer and more accurate picture of the progression from trainee through to full governor rank.

7.59 So far as the actual content of governors' training is concerned some, though not all, of what we have said in relation to the scope of prison officers' training does not apply since governors' training is in any event more broadly based. On the other hand, much of what we have said elsewhere in this report will have demonstrated our belief that governors—and those responsible for their training—must in future come to terms with the fact that they are occupying responsible management positions which require a wide variety of management skills ranging, for example, from budgetary control to industrial relations, as well as an increased awareness and knowledge of the social services and penal affairs. Furthermore, if at some time in the future the prison service in England and Wales is to be led by someone who has been a governor, it will plainly be necessary for all governors of promise to be given the fullest possible experience of management and administration both in regional offices and at Prison Department Headquarters itself. The training of governors must be alive to all of these factors and must take full account of them from the earliest possible stage.

7.60 At present development courses are given to governors throughout their career, as well as on occasions specialised courses to enable them to acquire particular skills. Apart from one matter to which we shall return shortly we have no quarrel with this arrangement in general. We do understand, however, that a shortage of resources on occasions means that these courses cannot be taken at what would otherwise be the appropriate time. We think that this is regrettable and would hope that means may be found to effect some improvement in future. The main comment that we have about these courses concerns the way in which their content is determined. Our understanding is that the content of such courses is related to the rank which the governor in question holds rather than to the job which he is actually performing at the time in question. This means, for example, that training in industrial relations is given only to those holding the rank of Governor III and above, notwithstanding that many AG Is and AG IIs may be performing the duties of governor or deputy governor in smaller establishments an as such be much in need of some formal training in industrial relations matters. We think that this approach is inappropriate and are pleased to note that it is now in process of being changed.

CHAPTER EIGHT

PAY AND ALLOWANCES

8.1 This chapter explains present arrangements for the pay and superannuation of prison officer and governor grades respectively in the United Kingdom, sets out the claims made, reviews the relevant evidence and recommends certain awards and how remuneration should be uprated in future. We also review certain allowances, including those to both prison service and other grades as well as those paid to the latter only.

8.2 Before turning to the details, we think it necessary to make some general observations. First, whilst we have no doubt whatsoever that members of the prison services are a very important if by no means the largest group of workers in the public sector, it has constantly been borne in on us that they are one of the most isolated. This isolation has at least in the past seemed to be an inevitable concomitant of the work. All prisons, even open ones, are closed institutions in the way in which the term is ordinarily understood. Traditionally the staff have lived very close to the institutions themselves and this, reinforced by the nature of their work, has perhaps led them to mix only amongst themselves. One academic study of officers that we examined demonstrated how far these tendencies existed even at a very large urban prison where the staff were accommodated in somewhat less isolated prison housing estates than we ourselves have sometimes observed. Numbers of officers believe that it is their very occupation itself which inhibits their mixing with the population at large. Whilst we think that this may be a factor and their physical isolation in some cases at the remoter establishments makes any effective mingling virtually impossible, we are not sure that, apart from geographical isolation where it exists, there are generally hostile public attitudes towards prison officers. On the contrary, we think the tendency of members of the service primarily to seek out each others' company is substantially a matter of choice and convenience; it does not necessarily flow from their occupation.

8.3 However, whatever the cause, we have found members of the service (including governors) a somewhat inward-looking group. This has a number of consequences. In particular, they are prone to concentrate on their own terms and conditions of service without a well-informed knowledge of what obtain elsewhere. Further, their beliefs of what applies outside the prison services tend to be unrealistic as well as restricted. Thus, whilst members of the staff during our visits were properly quick to point out to us a number of disadvantages of their work, they did not set against them the value of some of their benefits (for example, free housing and generous superannuation provisions). Further, since the police service is the only other occupational group with whom the prison services have regular contact, it is not surprising as we have shown elsewhere why it is with that group that historically they have tended to compare themselves. In that connection we have, therefore, to record that throughout our inquiry the recent report of the Committee of Inquiry on the Police on pay (the Edmund-Davies Committee, Cmnd 7283, July 1978) has evidently been a powerful stimulant to prison service attitudes.

8.4 Secondly, we have been careful in our approach to remuneration not to regard it in too isolated a sense. Vital though these questions are—in England and Wales pay and pensions amount to about 70 per cent of the net current expenditure on the prison service—we have been anxious to put them in the context of the staff's terms and conditions of service seen as a whole. We have deliberately not, therefore, taken the view that improvements in pay are necessarily the answer to all the difficulties that the staff and management face or the best way of solving them.

8.5 Finally, we should explain that, although many members of staff commonly regard remuneration in terms of their net earnings (ie cash in their pockets after tax, national insurance etc), we have not ourselves been able to approach earnings from that point of view. That is because there is no way in which pay may properly be compared once it has been subject to tax. People's individual circumstances differ so much and are to such an extent a matter of choice that the prospect of achieving an equitable comparison in such circumstances is impossible. It is wrong both to blame the pay system for taxation effects, and also to attempt to allow for them.

8.6 In so far as differentials are concerned, the same kinds of considerations must also apply. Thus, ignoring tax effects, net earnings cannot be the dominant source of comparison between grades if, for example, one grade achieves a certain result only by long overtime working, or by virtue of compensation for a particular condition of service, eg an above average actual night duty commitment.

PAY

Earnings and some comparisons
8.7 Before turning to particular claims and their merits, it is necessary to review the evidence of what prison service grades earn, how their earnings compare with earnings generally as well as with some particular groups with which they are most frequently compared, for instance the police.

8.8 For obvious reasons we thought it important to have a detailed picture before us of the gross average earnings of all staff. Accordingly, a survey was conducted by the Home Departments at our request. The results are at Appendix 7. These were sent to all the appropriate staff associations. In the absence of any comment by them, we have taken it they accept their accuracy. (To avoid a period of earnings distortion, the Scottish survey had to choose a week different from that convenient elsewhere).

8.9 Taking account of the margins of possible error, the main points disclosed by the survey for England and Wales are that
- (a) the average gross pay of some grades exceeded the basic pay of more senior grades eg principal and senior officers earned more on average than chief officers and both grades of Assistant Governor; and Chief Officers I (whose basic pay in any case puts them above Assistant Governors II) earned more on average also than Assistant Governors I.

182

(b) This effect was due in the former case primarily to high average overtime earnings which amounted to about half or more than half of basic pay; in the latter case, long hours gratuity and other emoluments were responsible.

(c) In the case of the prison officers, overtime amounted on average to almost 60 per cent of basic pay, and average gross earnings were in excess of those for Assistant Governors II and only slightly below those for Chief Officers II.

(d) There was on the whole less difference between gross earnings at various kinds of establishment than might theoretically have been expected. For example, although prison officers at local prisons earned most, on average they earned only £8 a week more than officers in open prisons where it might have been expected that there was less staffing pressure. In addition, the officers at open prisons in fact on average earned as much as officers at closed prisons which were not local or dispersal prisons, and closed borstals. We were told that all this may be explained by the fact that the low levels of manning generally require high overtime levels in all institutions, and that the tactical redeployment of staff to help out on detached duty is masked by showing them as still paid at their parent establishments.

(e) Comparing averages for prison service and non-prison service grades, only all grades of Medical Officer, Principal and Senior Psychologists and Chief Pharmacists 4 earned more on average than principal officers, senior officers and officers. Of these civilians, only the Medical Officers and Principal Psychologists were paid more than Chief Officers I.

8.10 The results for Scotland and Northern Ireland vary from the pattern in England and Wales apparently in direct proportion to the amount of overtime worked. Thus, in Northern Ireland the effect of overtime earnings (together with the local emergency allowance which all prison service grades receive) was to increase the pay of the overtime grades above levels in England and Wales. For example, a principal officer in Northern Ireland on average earned more than anyone else in the prison service except a Governor I, a senior officer on average more than anyone below Governor II, and the basic grade officer on average more than a Chief Officer II and slightly more than a Governor III (ie he also earned more than both grades of Assistant Governor).

8.11 In Scotland, however, overtime earnings were such that there was on the whole less inversity between prison officer and governor grades than in Northern Ireland or England and Wales. Thus, for example, although none of the junior ranks on average earned more than Chief Officers II, the latter with principal officers and senior officers on average did earn more than Chief Officers I, of whom there are only a small number in Scotland and whose opportunities for earning long hours gratuity seem much less than in the case of Chief Officers II. All discipline grades except basic grade officers earned more on average than Assistant Governors II but only principal officers and Chief Officers II earned more than Governors IV (ie Assistant Governor Is in England and Wales).

8.12 On the other hand, the Scottish survey showed some unique Scottish features relating to clerk officers. Their overtime earnings were between a sixth and a quarter of their officer counterparts on discipline duties. Nevertheless, and disregarding the value of free uniform, housing and more favourable superannuation, their earnings were somewhat higher than that which their civilian counterparts earned in England and Wales.

Surveyed average annual gross earnings

	£		£
Clerk Officer	3,900·08	Clerical Assistant	2,600
Principal Clerk Officer	4,972·99	Clerical Officer	3,224
Chief Clerk Officer	5,706·03	Executive Officer	4,628

Further, although the civilian Stewards II at £5,814·86 earned more than Chief Clerk Officers, the other benefits enjoyed by the latter would in fact more than close the gap.

8.13 The best source of general comparative earnings is the New Earnings Survey prepared by the Department of Employment who have at our request provided certain additional information. From this it is possible to make some limited sectoral comparisons. The Survey consists of a 1 per cent random sample of the earnings of employees in employment in Great Britain in April each year. A number of factors, however, qualify the use that may be made of the material. For example, although the Survey relates to employees at all levels, because of the limited sample size reliable results in respect of the prison service are available only for officers below principal officer (ie senior officers and basic grade officers). In addition, the fact that different groups of workers have different annual pay settlement dates during the year means that the relative position of any particular group can be affected considerably by exactly when its annual settlement takes place; and the situation observed during a single pay period in April may not represent the year as a whole for some groups subject to demand cycles, weather conditions and so on.

8.14 Table 8.1, derived from the 1979 Survey, compares average earnings of the sample of prison officers below the rank of principal officer with estimated average earnings, first, for the two groups into which the employed population is for convenience customarily split viz manual and non-manual workers, and then for all male employees. The table illustrates amongst other things the relative importance for officers of shift and overtime payments.

8.15 Tables 8.2 and 8.3 bring out the relatively large amount of overtime worked by officers. It was more than three times as much as that worked by all employees and over twice that worked on average by manual workers. In addition although very few employees generally worked on average in excess of 60 hours a week, over one quarter of junior officers did.

8.16 Finally, Table 8.4 looks at the median earnings of junior officers over a run of years to see how they compare with median earnings generally. The table uses the median point (i.e. the figure where 50 per cent of the employees have earnings below the amount and 50 per cent have earnings above it) because

Table 8.1

Make-up of average gross weekly earnings,* April 1979

Full-time men, aged 21 and over, whose pay for the survey pay period was not affected by absence

Occupation	Make-up of average gross weekly earnings				Components as a percentage of total			Percentage of employees who received	
	Total £	Overtime pay £	Shift etc. premium payments £	All† other pay £	Overtime pay %	Shift etc. premium payments %	All other pay %	Overtime pay %	Shift etc. premium payments %
Prison officers below principal officer	129·1	47·8	8·8	72·5	37·0	6·8	56·2	94·3	68·6
All non-manual occupations	113·0	3·9	0·6	108·5	3·5	0·6	96·0	20·3	5·6
All manual occupations	93·0	14·0	2·9	76·1	15·0	3·2	81·8	58·5	23·6
All occupations	101·4	9·8	2·0	89·6	9·7	2·0	88·4	42·6	16·1

*All the estimates in the table are subject to sampling error.
†The term "all other pay" includes incentive pay which for all occupations was £6·4 or 6·3 per cent of gross weekly earnings.

Table 8.2
Average Weekly Hours

Full-time, men aged 21 and over, whose pay was not affected by absence

New earnings survey April of each year	Total hours	Overtime hours (see note)
Prison officers below principal officer		
1973	53·2	13·0
1974	52·5	12·6
1975	54·8	14·6
1976	52·4	12·3
1977	54·1	14·1
1978	55·0	15·1
1979	57·9	18·0
All industries and services manual men		
1973	46·7	6·5
1974	46·5	6·5
1975	45·5	5·6
1976	45·3	5·4
1977	45·7	5·8
1978	46·0	6·1
1979	46·2	6·3
All men		
1973	43·8	4·7
1974	43·7	4·7
1975	43·0	4·0
1976	42·7	3·8
1977	43·0	4·1
1978	43·1	4·3
1979	43·2	4·5

Note: These relate to the actual hours (per week in the pay-period) for which the employees received overtime pay. If, for example, four hours were paid at time-and-a-half the relevant number is four not six.

Table 8.2
Distribution of total weekly hours*

Full-time men aged 21 and over whose pay for the survey pay-period was not affected by absence

	Percentage with total weekly hours in the range:						
	38 or less	40 or less	42 or less	44 or less	48 or less	54 or less	60 or less
Prison officers below principal officer	0	6	7	10	16	36	54
All industries and services manual men	7	38	44	53	70	85	94
All men	29	55	60	67	80	90	96

*Total weekly hours is the sum of normal basic hours and paid overtime hours.

it is generally accepted to be more representative of all observed groups' characteristics than a simple average which can, of course, be distorted by unusually high or low extremes.

Table 8.4
Median Gross Weekly Earnings

Full-time men, aged 21 and over, whose pay was not affected by absence

Median gross weekly earnings	1973	1974*	1975	1976	1977	1978	1979
Including overtime							
(a) Prison officers	44·4	64·8	69·6	86·9	99·4	107·8	136·1
(b) Manual men	36·6	41·8	53·2	62·1	68·2	76·8	88·2
(c) All men	38·4	43·8	55·9	65·8	72·3	82·0	93·9
(d) % age of (a) to (c)	115·6	147·9	124·5	132·0	137·5	131·5	145·0
Excluding overtime							
(a) Prison officer	31·1	44·0	49·0	63·2	72·0	76·4	77·9
(b) Manual men	30·4	35·0	46·1	54·6	59·6	66·5	75·7
(c) All men	33·3	38·1	49·7	59·1	64·7	72·8	82·8
(d) % age of (a) to (c)	93·4	115·5	98·6	106·9	111·3	104·9	94·0

*In 1974 the figures for prison officers are based on what was an unusually small sample and are therefore less reliable than normal.

8.17 Looking at this material as a whole, and bearing in mind all the necessary qualifications, there would seem to be two main conclusions to draw from it. First, the overall picture is one of the junior prison service grades standing well in terms of total earnings—and even better if free housing, uniform and non-contributory superannuation benefits be considered in addition—in comparison with average and median surveyed gross earnings, but working nearly nine hours more per week on average than manual workers to do so. Secondly, the figures do not seem to show that officers' earnings with or without overtime have lost any real ground over the period examined.

8.18 Lastly it will be relevant to set out the current pay scales of the main prison service grades, police and fire services and some civil service grades.

Basic Pay Scales at 1 September 1979

(Annual salaries unless specified otherwise)

	£
Governor I	12,415
Governor II	9,493–10,719
Governor III	7,754– 9,036
Assistant Governor I	6,484– 7,317
Assistant Governor II	4,628– 5,972

187

Chief Officer I	6,086
Chief OfficerII	5,625
Principal Officer	86·14—93·20 per week (4,491—4,859)
Senior Officer	77·15—83·18 per week (4,023—4,337)
Prison Officer	60.54—72.24 per week (3,156—3,767)
Chief Superintendent	12,258—13,110
Superintendent	11,124—11,973
Chief Inspector	8,058— 8,967
Inspector	7,095— 8,058
Sergeant	6,186— 7,095
Constable	4,086— 5,844 (long service increments— 6,186; 6,471)
Assistant Secretary	11,449—13,991
Senior Principal	10,325—12,322
Principal	7,742— 9,951
Senior Executive Officer	6,768— 8,016
Higher Executive Officer	5,520— 6,519
Executive Officer	3,296 (at age 21)—5,272
Clerical Officer	2,902 (at age 21)—3,791
Senior Divisional Officer	8,355— 8,814
Divisional Officer I	7,763— 8,117
Divisional Officer II	7,029— 7,589
Divisional Officer III	6,618— 6,892
Assistant Divisional Officer	6,178— 6,557
Station Officer	5,450— 6,250
Sub-Officer	5,057— 5,252
Leading Fireman	4,935
Fireman	3,624— 4,606 (Long Service Fireman—4,811)

Prison officers' pay

8.19 The number of officers in their various grades is shown in the following table:

	England and Wales			Scotland			Northern Ireland		
	M	F	Total	M	F	Total	M	F	Total
Discipline Grades									
Chief Officer I } Chief Officer II }	159	10	169	30	3	33	19	1	20
Principal Officer	827	28	855	147	17	164	85	4	89
Senior Officer	1,450	15	1,465	207	11	218	87	3	90
Officer	7,865	421	8,286	1,189	107	1,296	1,784	52	1,836
Specialist Grades									
Works Officer (all ranks)	1,237	4	1,241	146	—	146	152	—	152
Hospital Officer (all ranks)	740	2	742	80	4	84			
Instructional Staff (all ranks)	575	2	577	113	7	120			
Dog Handlers (all ranks)	325	1	326						
Catering Officer (all ranks)	310	2	312	46	4	50			
Physical Education Staff (all ranks)	275	6	281						
Prison Service Clerks (all ranks)	—	—	—	118	1	119	80	3	83
Under training	236	40	276						
Prison Auxiliaries	421	58	479						
Temporary Women Officers	—	94	94						
Night Patrol	545	61	606						
Totals	14,965	744	15,709	2,076	154	2,230	2,207	63	2,270
Total UK	20,209								

8.20 The pay of prison officers in England and Wales and Scotland is settled under the Wynn-Parry formula as explained in Chapter 2 after negotiation between CSD and the POA, with the SPOA, the Home Office and the Scottish Office being called in as necessary. As regards relativities with the rest of civil service grades, the formula provides specifically for the POA to make claims for improvements in the level of remuneration in respect of any factors which in their view should be taken into account. The CSD claimed that this was a very important feature which provided the necessary flexibility of approach to keep abreast of changes which may take place both inside or outside the civil service.

8.21 The general effect, therefore, of these arrangements is to give the POA the benefit of civil service pay reviews by a system which allows adjustment of the appropriate points of comparison between prison service and non-industrial civil service grades. The pay of the latter grades themselves is reviewed by a system of job comparison which means that by and large civil service pay is updated in conformity with changes in pay for analogous work in the private sector. This is not a system of indexation (i.e. automatic uprating by reference to an arbitrary point) but the upshot of it is to keep prison officers in step too with the general level of changes outside the civil service.

8.22 There is no separate negotiation for Northern Ireland where pay is determined by the appropriate Northern Ireland authorities. In practice, however, they have followed what has been agreed in respect of Great Britain. On the other hand, there are some different allowances payable in Northern Ireland arising from the special circumstances there, with some of which we deal separately below.

8.23 At present prison officers in the United Kingdom are paid the basic rates set out in paragraph 8.18 for a 40 net hours working week. In addition to the basic rate all officers, including works officers and clerk officers, but excepting those who work in emergency control rooms or as dog handlers (ie in practice in England and Wales only), receive a shift disturbance allowance (SDA) at 12·6 per cent of basic pay. This allowance was first introduced into the civil service in 1971, but first applied (at a rate of 10·1 per cent) to the prison services in 1973: until then prison officers received a night duty allowance for each night actually worked. SDA is designed to reflect amongst other things the relative amount of night duty that occurs in shift working. Because this is greater in the case of emergency control room staff and dog handlers they receive SDA at a higher rate, namely 15 per cent and 20 per cent respectively.

8.24 Prison service grades benefit from the application at the 12·6 per cent level of an "averaged out" SDA. This may be paid when a high proportion of a departmental grade is involved in shift working and it is thought desirable, in order to facilitate movement between different types of shift rosters, or in and out of shift working to pay every grade member (i.e. including day workers) a common rate of SDA. Thus SDA of at least 12·6 per cent is received by all uniformed grades even if they work no nights or shifts at all.

8.25 Overtime at the rate of time and one half is paid for hours worked in excess of a 40 hour week, and unsocial hours premium rates for all hours worked at the weekend and on Bank holidays. These premia mean that for Sunday working, for example, officers are effectively paid at double time. In England and Wales only there is a longstanding agreement that an officer may be required to be on duty, if there is an operational need, for 50 hours in a week, thus committing him to 10 hours compulsory overtime. This includes overtime worked on weekend days. The overtime rate may in no case exceed the maximum plain time hourly rate payable to a principal officer.

8.26 Not all the officer grades receive overtime pay. Under general civil service arrangements, grades whose pay relates to certain national scale maxima (i.e. in the EO, HEO and SEO ranges) receive compensation for extra hours under what are known as long hours gratuity (LHG) arrangements. The effect of these is to substitute a number of alternatives for overtime at time and a half. These range from overtime at plain time to payments based on a percentage of salary provided certain averages of excess hours have been maintained over a stipulated period.

8.27 Apart from the London allowance payable to all grades working in the London area, officers undertaking a variety of special duties receive what are known as responsibility allowances. There are a great number of these allowances paid, for example, to instructor officers in prison industries, hospital officers, caterers, trades officers in the works branch, dog handlers, librarians, physical education instructors and the like. At present the allowances (last reviewed at 1 April 1978) for permanent duties vary from £2·03 for an officer driving motor lorries and undertaking minor repairs to £8·93 for a principal officer trade instructor with a special allowance. Another allowance is inconvenience of locality allowance with which we deal later.

8.28 In addition, other elements of separate remuneration are taken into account either for the purpose of calculating pension or the rate of overtime that may be paid. For example, the fact that free accommodation is in practice an important part of remuneration is acknowledged by the existence of a sum known as the "pensionable value of quarters" (PVQ) which at its maximum married rate at present stands at £8·68 (£9·16 from 1 January 1980) a week and which is aggregated with basic pay for the purpose of establishing the relevant overtime rate. PVQ is also taken into account to establish the rate of appropriate pension when an officer retires. (In Northern Ireland rent allowances are not the same as in Great Britain: they match instead those paid to the RUC).

8.29 It follows from all this that the calculation of officers' pay is a matter of some complexity. Indeed, the multiplicity of allowances and the extent to which they are taxable or pensionable must mean that in a number of cases officers cannot fully understand of what their pay is composed. In addition, the fact that officers in England and Wales have in large numbers declined to have monthly and computerised pay entails a disproportionate degree of clerical effort inefficiently distributed amongst establishments. On visits we have been distressed to observe the degree of clerical effort devoted to working out officers' pay week by week. From what we have seen, the present system cannot survive much longer and we comment elsewhere (paragraph 5.84) on the need to replace it.

8.30 In addition officers may earn not only overtime but also, in certain circumstances, pay at a higher rate if they substitute for an officer in a higher grade. Substitution pay is commonly earned in the prison services because a great many posts must be covered when someone is away for any reason such as leave, or sickness, or any other official duty not connected with the post. In general, it is not possible for work to be shared and, although substitution in each succeeding lower rank is not automatic, operational considerations generally mean that when a principal officer is absent a senior officer acts up in his place and then an officer acts up for that senior officer. Under a national civil service agreement, when an officer substitutes for at least 5 consecutive days, he becomes eligible for substitution pay calculated at the rate he would be paid if he had been promoted to the higher grade. Such pay is paid for each two day period of acting up if a five day period has already been completed on broadly the same work within the previous 12 months. It follows that substantial amounts are earned by many prison officer grades during the year from substitution pay.

191

8.31 The POA evidence was critical of the way in which the Wynn-Parry formula had operated. Although it had not been without advantages, it was totally reliant on pay movement within the non-industrial civil service and was over-reliant on the clerical officer grade because of that group's numerical significance in the working out of the formula. In addition, the fact that the formula could not be applied until the pay of the non-industrial civil service had been settled meant that there were delays in making an award to prison service grades. The POA therefore argued that there was a case for a new approach which would circumvent the disadvantages of the Wynn-Parry formula and yet retain at the same time its advantages, which they recognised lay in its link with objective pay research. In addition since 1958 there had been a number of changes in not only the civil service pay movement but employment conditions generally. As they put it: "The Association accepts that there is no scientific means by which the job content of a prison officer can be accurately measured. For this reason any decision on suitable pay rates for prison officers must be as arbitrary now as it was 20 years ago. Therefore any revised formula for pay determination should take this into account and build in sufficient flexibility to meet changes in future circumstances".

8.32 Starting from the position that pay was the first essential component in the recruitment of staff who had remained for some time in such short supply, the POA put to us an elaborate "Fixed Point Formula" comprising 17 factors. It was designed not only to arrive at an appropriate present level of pay, but also to serve for future uprating in the place of the Wynn-Parry formula. The "Fixed Point Formula" sought amongst other things to balance those features of prison officers' employment which distinguished it from the majority of other non-manual workers (eg stress and environment, shift and nightwork, weekend work, and job mobility) against those aspects of officers' employment which were more favourable (eg free housing, non-contributory pension, and provision of uniform). The proposed formula involved a number of subjective judgments. For example, in respect of stress and environment the POA suggested the proper course was to give officers the same special lead pay that was given to staff serving in special hospitals, ie £633 a year as at 1 April 1978. Some of the other elements involved judgments that had not been actuarily tested eg that the value of the non-contributory pension was such that it justified a reduction of only 3.01 per cent from "the comparator group average pay rates". The upshot of the calculations was to recommend that the basic pay of the basic grade officer should be £122.61 a week.

8.33 Having discussed this formula and its effect with the POA and examined carefully its constituent parts, taking advice where necessary, we have no doubt that it has so many serious weaknesses that we could not recommend its adoption. It is not an objective system of pay calculation since it includes many subjective factors which would provide abundant source for disagreement at every pay review when that was exactly the situation the Wynn-Parry formula was designed to end. In so far as it does depend upon objective data, it represents a claim for pay indexation against the average basic rate earnings as shown in the NES non-manual tables. At the same time, however, the uprating factor relies on the index of rates of wages of manual workers to update NES estimates of earnings of non-manual workers. Even where the formula relies on comparisons with non-manual workers, we think it chooses too large a range of employees. This is because the NES general results for non-manual employees cover employees of all grades and categories in non-manual occupations in businesses and organisations of all kinds and sizes in all industries and services in all parts of Britain. This is a very wide spectrum ranging from junior office and shop staff to the higher paid management in the largest organisations. The POA, however, represents a much narrower range of employees and, in particular, does not represent the higher paid members of the prison service grades. For all these reasons, therefore, we have felt obliged to reject the POA claim.

8.34 Although the "Fixed Point Formula" fails in our eyes in a number of ways, we should make it clear that it fails also for two reasons insofar as it includes a claim for indexation. First, the concept of indexation suffers from a number of serious deficiencies well summarised in paragraphs 29–44 of the first report of the Comparability Commission (Cmnd 7641, August 1979). Secondly we are aware of only two groups in the public sector who have been granted forms of indexation, namely the police and the fire service. There are special circumstances in both cases and neither group are, like the prison services, civil servants. It seems to us that recommending indexation for prison officers could be contemplated only in exceptional circumstances which clearly distinguished them from other civil servants. However, we know of no such circumstances. Nor are we proposing that officers should have withdrawn from them the general statutory protection from the consequences of industrial action given by the Trade Union and Labour Relations Act, 1974, which might arguably lead to them being placed on a par with the police.

Other considerations

8.35 We have not been content with examining pay solely by way of response to POA claims. We have tried also to identify those aspects of the position of prison officers generally that may be said to bear on what they should be paid. We have had to do this, incidentally, without assistance from the CSD and the Home Departments. This was because, on instructions given by the previous government which were not rescinded by its successor, officials gave no evidence on quantum. They did so indirectly for governors but only because governors had already put in a claim for uprating against their colleagues which was under review when we were set up.

8.36 The burden of the earnings evidence is that, whilst since 1958 prison officers do not appear to have slipped behind and they have received through SDA and weekend premia compensation for special features of their working conditions, they have otherwise received no adjustment to the levels of pay throught appropriate in 1958. On the other hand, we judge there are two factors which entitle them to some special consideration.

8.37 The first is that since 1958 they have had to cope and will have to continue to cope with a less favourable penal environment. Putting aside for a moment the poor physical working conditions which we recommend separately should be improved, there is abundant evidence that officers have now to cope with a more sophisticated and more difficult inmate population. This has required them to display more psychological and physical resilience, and to develop handling and managing skills to greater maturity. The measure of the difference can be appreciated when it is remembered that in 1958 there were no dispersal prisons at all, let alone terrorist inmates. Even young offenders were more amenable and tractable than today as well as being many fewer. All the burdens on the services have increased and none of which we are aware decreased. Whilst in large measure these additional burdens have been shouldered by increased staff, an increment of heightened individual stress remains.

8.38 The second consideration is simply the history of recruitment. A payment system that cannot produce sufficient recruits fails the first test of efficacy. The latest figures for the three services are shown in Figure 8.1.

The recommended award

8.39 Having carefully considered all the relevant factors, including the phased increase amounting to about 22 per cent on average following the Civil Service pay award as from 1 April 1979, we recommend the fresh pay scales for officers and ancillary grades set out in Appendix 8a to take effect from 1 January 1980. We recommend further that PVQ be increased from the same date by 5 per cent. The increases are designed to take account of changed circumstances since 1958 and generally increase the attractiveness of the service and thus improve recruitment. The recommended increase is not as high as that claimed by the POA and, indeed, is not much above the Wynn-Parry award following the civil service settlement for 1 April 1979. This is because we do not think that a large improvement in basic pay alone is justified. Although we hope that one effect of the award will be to improve recruitment and therefore to reduce the high amount of overtime working, we have had to have regard to the fact that officers' gross earnings compare well with even average non-manual gross earnings, despite the features to which we have drawn attention. In addition, we do not think it can be said that prison officers are poorly paid in comparison with analogous groups in the public sector, including the police. We have taken careful account of the relationships between prison officers and these groups and consider that the recommended award is reasonable in relation to them.

8.40 We estimate that in England and Wales the full annual cost of the recommended award will be approximately £5 million.

8.41 We should draw attention to the position of chief officers, chief clerk officers in Scotland and the effects for staff who are not in receipt of weekend premium. As regards chief officers we have attempted to do something to improve their position since we think they are the group in the uniform grades whose relative position has suffered unreasonably in comparison with the responsibilities that they possess. We have therefore sought not only to redress the balance but also to introduce a modest incremental scale to recognise and reward their increasing worth after initial promotion. In a similar way we have recommended two long service increments for basic grade officers to reward the greater experience and usefulness of officers who serve substantial periods but who have not been selected for promotion. As regards chief clerk officers, we are aware that our recommendations do nothing to remedy the fact that promotion for them to the civilian grade of Steward II cannot at present be attractive. We do not think the solution to this problem is in paying Stewards II

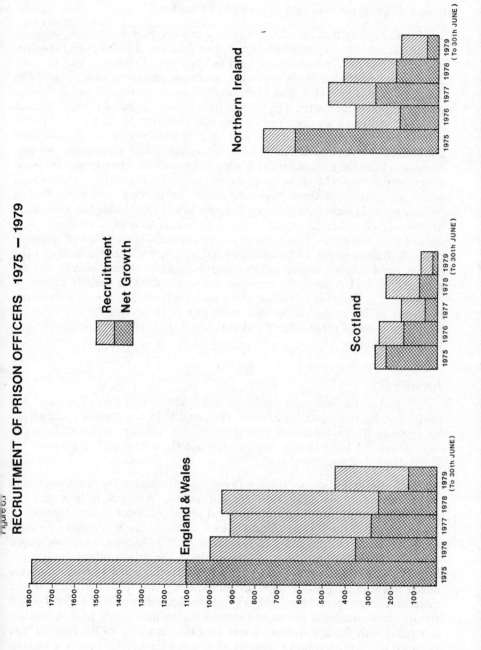

Figure 8.1

RECRUITMENT OF PRISON OFFICERS 1975 – 1979

Recruitment
Net Growth

England & Wales

Scotland

Northern Ireland

more or chief clerk officers less. On the contrary, we think the difficulty at this level is merely a special example of a greater difficulty, namely the retention of clerk officers at all. We seek therefore to deal with this particular problem from a different point of view altogether in Chapter 7.

8.42 As regards those grades not in receipt of weekend premium, we have looked carefully and sympathetically at their position. The effect of the introduction of weekend premium has been to open up, of course, a gap between the earnings of those officers who work weekends and those who do not. The ones chiefly affected apart from clerk officers are trades officers and instructor officers in prison industries. The POA in its evidence suggested that the balance could be redressed by increases in the responsibility allowances for trades officers and instructor officers as part of a general review of responsibility allowances. We have been unable to review responsibility allowances. We are, however, clear that it would be wrong in principle to seek to compensate those who do not work weekends by increasing payments made under some other head where an increase in those payments cannot be justified on merits. This is because it would seem to be as wrong to resort to any "back door" compensation as it would be wrong to extend weekend payments themselves to people who did not work weekends. This is not to say that in the current review of responsibility allowances which we understand is taking place at national level that the relative positions of trades officers and instructor officers should not be changed. In that context, for example, we would think it entirely proper to make changes designed to recruit more trades officers and instructor officers, in so far as it can be shown that more pay is likely to have the effect of recruiting more of those officers and their shortage is not due too significantly to other factors.

Uprating

8.43 Just as we have been unable to accept the "Fixed Point Formula" for initial pay determination, so have we been unable to recommend its adoption for uprating. This is for a number of reasons, only some of which are due to the reservations we have already expressed about the use of such a formula for initial determination.

8.44 In the first place, we think many of the criticisms of the operation of the Wynn-Parry formula since 1958 are ill-founded. Whilst it is true that the departure of the Post Office from the civil service excluded a large number of grades of which the formula formerly took account, the Wynn-Parry formula has nonetheless been adjusted to take account of changed circumstances and in ways which have not been unfavourable to the prison officer grades: for instance, Clerical Assistants have been removed and Higher Executive Officers added to the comparison groups. In addition, it seems to us that many of the dissatisfactions expressed with the Wynn-Parry formula would be better directed towards how successive phases of Government incomes policy have in practice interfered with the application of that formula. In so far as the formula was designed to bring an end to the recurrent negotiating difficulties over the settlement of prison officers' pay (described in Chapter 2), it has been very largely successful. In addition, we are satisfied that it is inherently sufficiently flexible to take account of changed circumstances at any time. Indeed, we specifically draw attention to the recommendations of the Wynn-Parry Committee where at paragraph 98(5) the report laid down that its recommendations "should not prevent the POA from making claims for improved remuneration in respect of any factors which have not been taken into account in any changes in pay which may be made under these recommendations".

Consolidation

8.45 We should record that we have considered very carefully whether there should be a greater measure of consolidation of officers' pay. As we indicated in paragraph 8.29 above, the present construction of their pay is so complicated that there might be thought to be a case for consolidation on those grounds alone. However, this was not pressed upon us by the POA or SPOA and we are satisfied that, at present, there is a substantial difficulty in that it would greatly affect overtime earnings and the weekend premia. Indeed, consolidation in England and Wales at a uniform rate of 12·6 per cent in respect of SDA and an average of 12 hours a week overtime would increase from £5 million to at least £8 million the value of the award we have recommended. None of the evidence before us would justify an award of that order. Nevertheless we recommend that the parties should address their minds to this question of consolidation.

Prison governors' pay

8.46 In England and Wales there are about 560 governors of whom approximately 40 are women. The comparable figures for Scotland and Northern Ireland are (with the numbers of women in brackets) 77 (6), and 40 (1) respectively.

8.47 At present their pay is broadly linked with the pay of certain grades in the administration group of the general civil service. This arrangement follows a recommendation of the Wynn-Parry Committee: "The work of the governor grades is essentially executive, and we recommend that they should be broadly linked with the executive class of the civil service". (Report, paragraph 98). Their current rate of pay (ie as at 1 August 1979) and those of the analogous civil service grades are as follows:—

	£
Governor I	12,415
Governor II	9,493—10,719
Governor III	7,754— 9,036
Assistant Governor I	6,484— 7,317
Assistant Governor II	4,628— 5,972
Assistant Secretary	11,499—13,991
Senior Principal	10,325—12,322
Principal	7,742— 9,951
Senior Executive Officer	6,768— 8,016
Higher Executive Officer	5,520— 6,519
Executive Officer	2,958 (at age of 18)—5,272

197

8.48 Governors belong to the "all hours worked" grades in civil service parlance. This does not mean they work a 24 hour day and a 7 day week, but that their pattern of attendance is sufficiently varied and unpredictable that it is not possible to construct for them weekly conditioned hours within whose limits their attendance would normally fall. Systems of attendance have been drawn up locally to meet the operational needs of establishments, and provide for two rest days in each fortnight to be taken as a complete weekend (Saturday and Sunday together) and two other rest days to be taken as whole week-days.

8.49 Since they have no conditioned hours, members of the governor grades are not eligible to receive overtime or long hours gratuity (LHG), or shift disturbance, on call or stand-by allowances. Similarly, whilst they receive rent and London allowances—ILAs—they may not be compensated for "unsocial" attendances by the payment of night duty allowances (NDA) or weekend and Bank and Public Holiday premia. On the other hand, it is accepted that the remuneration of such grades should properly reflect their average patterns and hours of attendance, taking into account, where appropriate, such factors as "unsocial" hours and availability (similar to on-call) commitments. Governors' "all hours worked" status is to some degree also offset by a more generous annual leave allowance (an immediate 6 weeks) than normal. For example, only staff in grades at Executive Officers (EO) level and above have an ultimate expectation of this leave allowance after varying total lengths of service— 27 years at EO level and 10 years at Assistant Secretary level. An immediate allowance of 6 weeks is otherwise available only to staff graded at Under Secretary level and above.

8.50 At the same time, governor grades have opportunities similar to officer grades to earn substitution pay by acting up, e.g. in the absence of the governor in charge of an establishment. To an extent the more generous leave allowances enhance these opportunities. We understand that acting up is in fact common. One witness told us that he had substituted for his governor on 47 per cent of his working days and received substitution pay for all but 28 per cent of those days. To the extent that the deputy governor is two grades below the governing governor, then acting up is accordingly lucrative.

The Governors' claim

8.51 In Great Britain, governors are represented by the respective national Governors' Branches of the Society of Civil and Public Servants. Northern Ireland governors are members of the Prison Governors' Branch of the Civil Service Professional Officers' Association and are represented by the Northern Ireland Public Service Alliance. In practice, however, there is close communication between the national branches and, with the exception of particular national problems, they each spoke in very similar if not actually identical terms.

8.52 The governors claimed that the recommendations of the Wynn-Parry Committee had been ignored in so far as they related to maintaining differentials within the prison service grades. They argued that although a broad link with the PRU system and the movement of civil service pay in the administration group should be retained, there should be additional measures to consider the special factors applying to the prison service, and specifically to take account of the movement of pay of prison officer grades and its effects on differentials with governors. Accordingly, the annual pay negotiations for governors should be concluded only after the settlement of prison officers' pay. They also wanted a procedure for examining and resolving future claims for changes in internal differentials among prison service departmental grades. They thought the present practice of job evaluating prison governors against the administration group only was inappropriate and unjust.

8.53 We discovered that before our appointment the governors in Great Britain had already submitted a claim on 15 February 1978 under paragraph 28 of the civil service pay agreement to be regraded in comparison with the administration group. The claim was based on three main factors:

(1) there had been an increase in the responsibility of the grades;

(2) there were several factors in the conditions of service of the grades for which their members were not adequately compensated; and

(3) differentials between the governor and prison officer grades had been eroded.

8.54 Since the ensuing job evaluation exercise was already under way when we were appointed, it was agreed that, although the paragraph 28 procedure was effectively suspended by our appointment, we should nonetheless have regard to the report of the job evaluation exercise. Accordingly, we received at the end of April 1979 the report of that exercise carried out by the CSD Staff Inspection and Evaluation Branch. In the ordinary way the report was circulated to the staff association and to the Home Departments concerned. We subsequently received the comments of everyone concerned both in writing and orally.

8.55 The report was carried out by a single staff inspector between September 1978 and March 1979. Its terms of reference were to examine the work of the prison service grades from Assistant Governor II to Governor I and to prepare a report as a basis for negotiating proposals by the SCPS that the pay links of the governor grades with the administration group should be revised as follows (all rates in 1 April 1978 terms):—

£

Governor I	from 10,890 to 11,608
Governor II	from 8,327— 9,403 to 9,827—10,793
Governor III	from 6,802— 7,926 to 8,307— 9,159
Assistant Governor I	from 5,688— 6,418 to 7,003— 7,701
Assistant Governor II	from 4,014— 5,239 to 4,956— 6,388

taking full account of the relative responsibilities of other grades within the institutions, and giving full weight to both the size and nature of the inmate population and the governors' overall responsibility for industrial relations.

8.56 The review was conducted in the normal civil service manner and under a process agreed with the SCPS. The evaluator visited a sample of establishments throughout Great Britain and questionnaires were sent to the holders of governor posts at those establishments. The evaluator conducted interviews in depth, undertook a good deal of background reading in line with recommendations made by governors, and spent time observing governors at work. It was also agreed that he should employ a system of unquantified factor analysis considering the following factors:—

(a) responsibility for the solution of problems;

(b) responsibility for decisions and contribution to the higher level decisions of others;

(c) management responsibility;

(d) representational responsibility;

(e) knowledge, skills and experience necessary to discharge the duties.

8.57 The evaluator found that most of the posts he examined displayed job weights above the middle of their administration group equivalents. He also found a number of posts exceeding grading relativities by up to a whole grade. He noted that the overall spread in job weights was between that appropriate to the upper part of the Executive Officer grade to that appropriate to the upper part of the Assistant Secretary grade range, although he identified only one post at that level. This showed a similar spread to that which existed in the administration group and, with the middle grades at least, to that which currently existed in the governor grades.

8.58 As already explained, the evaluator's report under the paragraph 28 procedure does not make pay recommendations but, rather, forms the basis for a subsequent pay negotiation. In commenting on the report, the Governors made a number of detailed comments which we have considered very carefully. Broadly, they thought the report a bland document which omitted all the unpleasant features of their work and under-rated the exceptional nature of it. As a result, they said, the report reinforced their view that job evaluating governors against administration group civil servants was inappropriate. They stressed the considerations that arose from the operational command and inspection functions undertaken by governors, which imposed peculiar stresses upon them. They thought too that the report paid insufficient regard to all the additional tasks that had recently been imposed upon them, including the time and effort that now had to be spent on industrial relations. Above all they continued to attach great importance to the need for a "mechanism" which would ensure that acceptable differentials with the uniform staff were maintained in future.

8.59 The Governors in England and Wales went on to state not only what they thought were the appropriate grade point comparisons between governor and analogous civil service grades (eg that Governor I should be mid point

Senior Principal scale to top of Assistant Secretary scale) but also what compensation should be added to the resulting scales to take account of other factors. This compensation they assessed as follows:—

"Summary of compensation for other factors

Factor	Proposed compensation	Notes
Weekends	12 per cent	Assessed as double time for Sundays and time and a half for Saturdays
Bank Holidays	1·25 per cent	Assessed as double time for four Bank Holidays
Night, evening duties and early morning	12·6 per cent	Assessed as for Prison Officers
Environment	£300 pa	Assessed as a new rate to reflect the extent Governors have to work in close contact with unpleasant environmental situations
All hours worked	14 per cent	Based on an average of six hours a week paid under long hours gratuity arrangements plus 2 per cent for the benefit to the Service of the flexibility of Governors' hours and rest days
On call	5 per cent	The advantage of a percentage is it reflects the extent of additional restriction on senior Governors
Mobility	3 per cent	To reflect the extent of Governors' greater mobility
Clothing	£110 pa	To reflect the requirement to dress smartly and the wear and tear on clothing through security keys
Pension compensation	5 per cent	Not to be included if two for one claim accepted. Based on buying 10 additional years service to enable 25 years old [entrants] to retire with full pension at 55 because of the stress of prison Governors' work".

8.60 We discussed these points with the governors. They confirmed that what they meant was that, having established the appropriate comparison job weight, 52·85 per cent of that salary plus £410 per annum should be added to it to reflect the special features of governors' work. They added the 52·85 per cent and £410 would be abated in so far as the factors were met in some other way, for example, by their being granted the same superannuation benefits as officer grades.

8.61 The CSD thought that, although the governors had made a large number of detailed observations on the report, they had not in fact challenged the overall validity of its conclusions about job weight. They thought, therefore, that the governors had not shown that the prime determinant of their pay should cease to be fair comparison with that of analogous workers, namely managers and administrators in other fields. They thought such an objective was fully realised through the governors' pay link with the administration group and the facility of periodical reviews of the level of that link under paragraph 28 of the pay agreement. Although they understood the concern of governors with the maintenance of differentials, the governors' experience over differentials was in no way unique. However, current pay arrangements did not rule out the adjustment of vertical pay relativities and were sufficiently flexible to do so. On the other hand, it did not seem appropriate for such arrangements to reflect changes in earnings as opposed to basic pay, as the governors appeared to wish. It did not seem reasonable that an earnings lead should necessarily exist even where considerable overtime working had inflated the pay of subordinate grades. Nonetheless, the CSD thought that governors were probably under-compensated compared with prison officer grades in respect of weekend attendances. They also believed that the requirement to act as duty governor on between two and four nights a month should be taken into account in determining pay.

The award

8.62 We fully appreciate the concern of the governors that they should be properly paid for their unusual duties. We think, however, that there is no practicable alternative, as they themselves saw, to maintaining the system of pay comparison with the administration group recommended by the Wynn-Parry Committee. Having regard to all the circumstances, including the special factors to which the governors themselves drew attention and the phased increases amounting to about 30 per cent on average following the Civil Service pay award as from 1 April 1979, we recommend that governors should be paid at the rates with effect from 1 January 1980 set out in Appendix 8b. We estimate the additional cost of this award over what the grades could have expected normally on 1 January 1980 to be approximately £340,000 in the first year.

8.63 Elsewhere, in Chapter 7, we recommend splitting the AG II grade into a training grade AG(T) and an AG grade into which AG(T)s would move on completion of their probation. When they do so, we recommend their passage to the higher grades should be marked by a special increment. The new grade title of Governor IV we recommend for England and Wales and Northern Ireland should be paid as AG I i.e. the same as the present Governor IV in Scotland.

8.64 As regards uprating, we think the present arrangements under the civil service pay agreement should stand, provided they continue to be operated with the reasonable flexibility recommended by the Wynn-Parry Committee in paragraph 97 of their report. We do not think that there should be special arrangements for determining governors' pay after the settlement for prison officers, nor do we think that when internal prison service grades' relativities are fixed they should be influenced by comparisons of earnings. This is because we regard overtime pay not as a reflection of relative responsibility requiring automatic adjustment in superior grades, but as compensatory for undertaking extra hours of duty. We have nonetheless had regard to what should be the appropriate differentials in the prison service as a whole and our recommendations for governors' pay should be seen alongside those for the officer grades as representing what we think is appropriate in the circumstances. We appreciate why the governors may be attached to preserving past differentials in their favour. However, we consider it would be in principle wrong for us to consider recommending that any particular set of differentials—whether of 1958 or 1979—should be maintained indefinitely. That would be to introduce an unacceptable degree of inflexibility and suggest that circumstances can never change. This just cannot be true and is the reason why we have so explicitly endorsed in paragraph 8.44 what the Wynn-Parry Committee said in paragraph 98(5) of their report about future reviews of officers' pay. Above all we have to point out that inflexibility could work as much against the governors as in their favour. For example, the most recent civil service award has been more beneficial to the upper than to the lower grades. Under a system of fixed differentials as proposed by the governors, they would lose the prospect of such improvements but we see no reason why they should be deprived of those benefits, particularly if a system of wider comparability is to prevail. In this respect therefore, and in this respect only, we differ from paragraph 97 of the Wynn-Parry report in so far as it envisages the indefinite perpetuation of then established differentials.

ALLOWANCES

Inconvenience of locality allowance (ILA)

8.65 With the exception of industrial civil servants, this allowance is paid to all grades (ie prison service and others) working in penal establishments where the location of the establishment satisfies standard criteria. The allowance originated in a decision in 1854 that, in order to reduce the high turnover of staff at Dartmoor, an allowance should be paid to prison service staff in compensation for "the remote and desolate situation of Dartmoor—the privation of all kinds to which officers are there exposed and the severity of the climate". By the time of the Stanhope Committee in 1923, the same allowance was paid in addition at Parkhurst, Camp Hill and Portland, all former convict prisons. Without discussing the merits, the Stanhope Committee recommended (Report, paragraphs 34 and 40) that the allowance be continued, though in respect of Portland it was transmuted into a special borstal allowance to be paid in all borstals. This recommendation was made partly because borstal work in the Committee's view placed greater responsibilities on the individual officer and partly to compensate borstal officers for the fewer opportunities to earn overtime, and sleeping-in and escort duty payments.

8.66 The present allowance dates from a Civil Service Arbitration Award of 1945 when the Arbitration Tribunal had been asked on this issue to rule on the amount of the allowance at Dartmoor, and whether it should be paid at other establishments. The Tribunal found for an increase at Dartmoor and against a claim by the Prison Commissioners that it should be withdrawn from all other establishments then receiving it.

8.67 Payment of the allowance was variously extended subsequently and the present criteria agreed in 1968 are that a prison should be considered to be inconveniently located if (*a*) it is situated more than five miles from a town of 6,000 inhabitants, or (*b*) it is situated more than three miles from a town of 6,000 inhabitants and the nearest access to public transport is more than one mile from the prison. Receiving the allowance at present are 49 prison establishments (as well as 3 farms and 1 quarter area) in England and Wales, 7 penal establishments in Scotland and 2 in Northern Ireland. The rates payable are based, for each establishment, on the local cost of a return trip per week by public transport to the designated town of 6,000 inhabitants plus the cost of a light snack in recognition of both the need for, and the time taken, travelling to the town for weekly shopping. Current rates vary in England and Wales between 62 pence to £2·76 a week. Exceptions to the general arrangement occur in respect of Dartmoor and the Isle of Wight prisons where there is a different basis of calculation. Excepting the impact of pay policy, rates are normally adjusted biennially according to changes in local public transport fares and variations in the relevant retail prices indices in respect of the meal element. Officers at male establishments receive the costs of an accompanied visit; all staff at female establishments receive the cost of an unaccompanied visit.

8.68 We received representations on the allowances from all the relevant staff associations. The Governors wanted them reviewed to update them. The POA suggested that the single rate was anachronistic in respect of married women officers and it was inappropriate, too, that married male officers serving at women's establishments should fail under the existing rules to get the accompanied allowance. In addition, the POA pointed out that the existing rates were now more than four years out of date. Although they had been offered an increase of 10 per cent with effect from 1 April 1978, they had declined that offer on the grounds that it was insultingly inadequate; that the allowances had never in the past been linked to pay movements; and that the allowances were cost related and should remain so. The POA asked for annual upratings and that the allowances should be "grossed up" for tax purposes. The POA in addition asserted that there was a special case in respect of the Isle of Wight prisons.

8.69 The SPOA thought the allowances were inadequate because they covered the officer and his wife, but not the other members of the family. They felt that the allowances should be reviewed in the same way as mileage and subsistence allowances in the civil service. They also suggested that a case could be made for a cost of living allowance for certain areas in Scotland similar to the London Weighting allowance.

8.70 We approached the case for examining these allowances sympathetically since it appeared their intention was to compensate staff for being required to work in unusual locations. However, the more we investigated the position, the more we uncovered their strange history and a difficulty in identifying secure principles which could be fairly applied.

8.71 For example, although the Stanhope Committee made no argued comment, it is plain that the establishments qualifying for ILA in 1923 did so solely because they had in the past been convict prisons. At that time therefore the allowance represented a fossilised vestigial relic of the ancient differential of "convict service" pay. Neither Parkhurst nor Camp Hill could in 1923 have been described as inconvenient locations since both were close to the most substantial town on the Isle of Wight.

8.72 The Wynn-Parry Committee was called upon to decide the Prison Commissioners' claim that the allowance be abolished. Although they recommended the abolition of the borstal allowance, they declined to recommend the abolition of ILA: "If we were asked to recommend the introduction of the inconvenience of locality allowance for the first time, we might well hesitate to make the recommendation: but what we are asked to do is recommend its abolition". (Report, paragraph 85.) Their decision seems also to have been influenced by the 1945 Arbitration decision, although they were careful to point out they were not bound by it. They were evidently reluctant, too, to intervene too climactically in a situation where 27 establishments receive ILA. Further, whereas they felt able to abolish the borstal allowance and reflect it in basic pay, they thought it impossible to do the same for ILAs—no doubt because the new scales were thought incapable of colourably undertaking more than one consolidation.

8.73 As to anomalies, we discovered at Dartmoor, for example, that although a substantial number of staff lived in Plymouth and commuted daily to the prison, they nonetheless received the allowance on the basis that, such is the inconvenience of the Dartmoor situation, then the staff are by that fact alone entitled to compensation. Curiously, the impact of environment becomes reversed when, after a snowfall, the commuters from Plymouth cannot drive through to the prison in which case the prison is deprived of their services. Far from staff seeking to avoid service at Dartmoor, we are told there is a waiting list for vacancies. What once gave only remote and gloomy habitation, now offers secure employment in the middle of one of the most sought after recreation areas in the United Kingdom. We also encountered examples where staff living on the same housing estate were treated differently. Some, because the establishment to which they are attached attracts the allowance, receive it, others do not even though, objectively, their domestic circumstances are indistinguishable. The highest rate of allowance in England and Wales is received by staff at an open borstal in Dorset. There is one case in Northern Ireland where all the staff are in receipt of an allowance although none at all live at the establishment itself. Such anomalies are unavoidable where the allowance attaches to where people work rather than where they live.

8.74 The exclusion of industrial civil servants from the benefit of ILA must now seem inequitable. Historically, they were distinguished from the prison service and non-industrial grades on the basis that, unlike those grades, they were non-mobile and locally recruited. However, nowadays all non-industrial staff below EO are non-mobile and in practice the bulk of the clerical and typing staff are now locally recruited. Whilst it could be argued that the solution to this anomaly is to extend ILA to the industrial grades, such a step would do nothing, of course, about the other anomalies except to reinforce them.

8.75 The CSD and the Home Departments drew attention to the anomalies and claimed that they, with the effect of social changes, amounted to a case for abolishing the allowances. They did not, however, go so far as positively to recommend abolition, contenting themselves with suggesting there should be a root and branch review in conjunction with the staff associations.

8.76 As we have said, we approached this subject with instinctive sympathy for the staff. Had we encountered but a few anomalies, it is doubtful that we would have considered it desirable to disturb the situation if the overall effect was to give reasonable compensation to the overwhelming majority of staff. However, the anomalies are not minor nor are they to be disregarded. In fact they are symptomatic of a fundamentally unsatisfactory situation: the principle of the allowance is insufficient to allow of a sensible rationale in modern conditions for discriminating between establishments. Social and economic changes have not by themselves made the basis of ILA insecure, they have merely drawn attention to its inadequacy. Nor can we foresee any circumstances which will not tend to reinforce the case against ILA, especially since where staff actually live will, as explained in Chapter 11, increasingly become under their own control.

8.77 It follows that we are unable to recommend the review or the extension of these allowances. On the contrary, we recommend they should be phased out by negotiation.

Northern Ireland allowances

8.78 Before we turn to examine the merits of the problems raised in respect of the daily emergency allowance, home to office travel expenses and lodging allowances, we should first make some general points about the Northern Ireland prison service. As will already be evident from the discussion on resources, taking the United Kingdom as a whole the service in Northern Ireland has had to cope with the most severe strains of all: it has faced both the most rapid increase of inmate population and the greatest change in its character. In addition all this has occurred in a province of limited area and relatively small population. It has followed, therefore, that the effect of these changes has not been confined within the institutions themselves but been unavoidably manifest in every way outside. This has created a sense of personal vulnerability not only for officers when off duty, but also for their families.

8.79 No-one visiting penal establishments in Northern Ireland and meeting members of families can fail to be impressed by the remarkable calmness and determination of the men and women undertaking their duties. This is particularly so when it is borne in mind that they are duties which, although vital in any society, are bound to assume a special prominence in one where upholding the rule of law requires such peculiar tenacity. This is a task that the prison service in Northern Ireland shares with the other security forces in Northern Ireland. Notwithstanding that the police and the army are perhaps more obviously in the front line than the prison service, the latter are by no means out of the fray and, indeed, have a task of continuous commitment and containment not undertaken in the same way by the other services.

8.80 We have therefore approached the following Northern Ireland issues very much in the consciousness of the context in which the service operates there. We have no doubt that all the members of the service deserve special sympathy and attention. It was for such reasons, therefore, we were glad to learn the Northern Ireland Office has been properly accommodating in assisting the personal security of staff and their families.

Daily emergency allowance

8.81 The allowance, at present £3·30 a day, is payable to all prison service grades for each day on duty in a penal establishment. It is not payable during absences on annual or sick leave, or rest days, but there is an arrangement that staff may qualify for payment of the allowance whilst attending training courses. The allowance is also payable to certain departmental grades who are employed in prisons and have direct contact with prisoners i.e. medical officers, prison welfare officers, education officers, teachers, and civilian instructors. It is not, however, paid to civilian searchers, responsible for examining inmates' visitors and their belongings.

8.82 The allowance was first paid in 1971. At the beginning it was paid only to those staff serving at detention/internment centres set up that year. It was thereafter extended to staff in all penal establishments. We have been told it was granted to compensate staff for difficult working conditions which took account of the number of truculent and intractable inmates, their segregation into cohesive paramilitary groups, the shortage of cellular accommodation, the problems associated with control and supervision of prisoners in compounds, the exceptional physical discomforts of working in hurriedly constructed temporary prisons, security considerations, long hours of work and verbal and physical abuse by prisoners.

8.83 The POA claimed in November 1977 that the allowance should be increased from £3 to £5 per day. The Northern Ireland Office felt unable to concede that increase and instead offered a 10 per cent increase within the then government's pay guidelines with effect from 1 April 1978. The ensuing dispute resulted in the POA taking industrial action during October and early November 1978. Officers ceased this action and the POA eventually reluctantly accepted the 10 per cent increase on the understanding that their claim for a £2 per day increase would be submitted to the Inquiry. All parties agree that the allowance must be regarded as a temporary one in so far as it is related to the continuing emergency. In addition, however, the Northern Ireland Office contends the allowance was never conceived originally as, and has not subsequently become, a danger money allowance. For their part, the Northern Ireland governors have pressed a case (with which we understand the POA would not disagree) for the allowance to be consolidated and paid on an annual basis. On present values the governors thought the annual sum should be at least £1,000 per annum.

8.84 As we have seen for ourselves, and as assassinations of prison staff have demonstrated, there can be no doubt that staff in Northern Ireland prisons are subject to exceptional stress and strain. We have already recorded our understanding that they feel they are specially vulnerable by virtue of their occupation and that this fact is bound to restrict the lives of themselves and their families.

On the other hand, we note that since 1971 conditions in Northern Ireland prisons have gradually but perceptibly improved and it was in regard to these conditions that the allowance was originally created. The number of special category prisoners has declined. It stood at just over 600 at the end of 1978, 537 on 1 July 1979, and should be below 400 next year.

8.85 The most stressful present custodial work undoubtedly involves the staff responsible for the three H blocks in The Maze prison which house the non-conforming prisoners. As we have seen for ourselves the nature of these inmates' protest is bizarre in the extreme and the filth associated with it abhorrent and degrading. Fortunately, we have been glad to note that this fact has been recognised by the payment of a special allowance of £2 a day in addition to the £3·30 emergency allowance to all staff working full-time in the blocks concerned.

8.86 Further, whilst we would not in any way wish to detract from our appreciation of the way in which Northern Ireland staff carry out their duty in very difficult circumstances, we have to have regard to the fact that the allowance which they are now paid is more than three times the special duty allowance paid to the army (£1 a day) and over one and a half times the enhanced special duty allowance of £500 per annum which the RUC receive. It is also, of course, the case that much larger numbers of soldiers and police officers have been killed as a result of terrorist action. Whilst these factors are recognised by the POA, they have pointed out they are not an armed service like the army and the police, and the dangers they now face are not ones that the bearing of arms in the first place suggest are an integral part of the normal occupational risk.

8.87 As we have said, we are instinctively sympathetic to the prison service. On the other hand, it would be wrong to regard them in isolation. Taking all the considerations together, we have reluctantly felt bound to conclude that there is no sufficient case to justify increasing the daily emergency allowance from £3·30 to £5. Further, in view of the fact that the allowance is at its present rate already considerably in excess of comparable allowances paid to the army and police, there is no case either for increasing it from its present level or changing the manner in which it is paid.

8.88 The POA also asked us to look into the position of female searchers employed to search female visitors to The Maze, Magilligan and Belfast prisons. It was represented that the environmental allowance these searchers received of £1·82 per week was insufficient and that the duties they undertook qualified them to receive the daily emergency allowance of £3·30.

8.89 Whilst we appreciate that these employees undertake an important task and no doubt have to put up with a certain amount of abuse, their position does not seem such that we would be justified in recommending a departure from the principle that the daily emergency allowance is paid solely to those members of the staff in prisons who have direct contact with inmates.

8.90 On the other hand, with the assistance of the Northern Ireland Office, we have considered what, if any, other steps might be taken. Twenty-three staff are involved and at the moment they are paid at the minimum point of the basic grade prison officers' scale plus, of course, the environmental allowance of £1·82 per week.

8.91 The decision to link the pay of these ladies with that of prison officers was taken *ad hoc* in 1972. It is not, perhaps, the most appropriate link since the women are not members of the prison service grades and do not, for example, possess their legal powers. The Northern Ireland Office have proposed that the searchers may be more appropriately compared with the female staff attached to the civilian search unit of the Northern Ireland Police Authority. It has been proposed, therefore, that they should be linked with that grade, retaining their environmental allowance of £1·82 to take account of their special working conditions but be paid in addition a clothing allowance of £112 per annum on the lines of the allowance paid to prison officers required to wear civilian clothing. We think this is a more appropriate link and gives the female searchers more adequate terms and conditions of service and we therefore recommend that it be implemented.

Home to office travel expenses and lodging allowances

8.92 The claim is that these payments at present allowed to staff at The Maze and Magilligan prisons should continue notwithstanding that under ordinary civil service practice they should cease.

8.93 In the United Kingdom Civil Service nationally negotiated rules apply to the payment of all travel and subsistence allowances. Amongst other things, these rules maintain the principle that the cost of travel between an officer's home and his permanent duty station is the responsibility of the officer and in no circumstances that of the employer. On the other hand, where officers are temporarily employed at a place other than their permanent duty station, then the costs of the journey are defrayed by the employer at an appropriate rate. In the same way where in the opinion of the responsible Department it would be unreasonable to expect an officer to make the return journey between home and his temporary duty station because of the distances involved, the officer may be provided with sleeping quarters at the establishment and paid an allowance. These principles seem to us to be sound. To adopt any other, for example, over defraying the cost of the home to permanent duty station journey could lead only to greatly increased public expense since it would be impossible to confine any permanent concession to one part of the civil service.

8.94 Special difficulties have arisen in connection with these allowances in Northern Ireland as a result of the special circumstances in which prison staff had to work during the early years of the emergency. In the first days of their occupation, it was decided to regard The Maze and Magilligan prisons as detached duty stations. The effect of these decisions was to entitle the staff working at the two prisons to mileage and lodging allowances. Belfast prison was in all cases regarded as the notional permanent station for all staff. Applying the usual rules meant officers at The Maze became eligible for paid mileage of up to 40 miles a day and officers at Magilligan for up to a maximum of the daily lodging allowance—at present £7·45 per day. Where officers were provided with sleeping quarters, then the allowance they received was set at one half (i.e. £3·72) of the prescribed daily lodging allowance because accommodation only was provided. (The normal rent allowance continued to be paid to such officers in respect of their homes.) In addition a sleeping-in allowance of £1 per night was introduced in 1972 to compensate for specific defects in the standard of the sleeping accommodation provided.

8.95 We have no doubt that the decision was reasonable in the circumstances prevailing at The Maze and Magilligan prisons at the time. Not only were they both purely temporary establishments but, in addition, the shift system of working meant there was no question of the staff being able to rely on public transport. In any case, staff were frequently called upon to work overtime often with little or no advance notice. No housing was available locally in anything like sufficient quantity to offer quarters adjacent to the establishments, though nor have the staff sought quarters. It followed that daily travel was unavoidable for many officers and sometimes for considerable distances. The possibility of resorting to group transport arranged by the Northern Ireland Office to take officers to the prisons from convenient assembly points was ruled out on grounds of security because of the danger of ambush.

8.96 Since the early days conditions have changed very substantially at both prisons. Both sites have been considerably developed and in neither case could it now be said that they are in any sense temporary stations. Accordingly, the Northern Ireland Office in 1976 sought to negotiate with the POA how the detached duty arrangements at both prisons might be ended or phased out. Following negotiations the standard mileage rate was reduced from 1 April 1977, with a further reduction from 1 April 1978.

8.97 The Northern Ireland Office has contended that it remains unable to regard either The Maze or Magilligan prisons as temporary stations and, accordingly, the continued payment cannot be justified of travelling expenses estimated at £740,000 per annum for 1,220 staff (ie an average of £606) as well as half lodging and sleeping in allowances (estimated to cost £240,000 per annum). It has for some time been artificial to go through a rigmarole of regarding newly recruited staff, in practice posted to either The Maze or Magilligan, as on detached duty from Belfast prison. Increasingly, if not overwhelmingly, the beneficiaries from the payments are not officers who had to put up with initial inconvenience of opening the establishments in the first place but, rather, officers who have rarely worked anywhere else in the Northern Ireland service.

8.98 As to mileage allowance, the POA have pointed out on the other hand that there are no married quarters to house staff and their families in the immediate vicinity of either prison. Officers are obliged to travel within a 40-mile radius to attend for duty at The Maze and within a 30-mile radius to Magilligan. They have to use their own transport because no public transport operates on a direct route to either establishment. Even if public transport were available it would be inadvisable for prison staff to use it because of the security situation. In view of what they see to be the very real difficulties encountered by staff in fulfilling their duty attendances at the two establishments, the POA wish to see the travelling payments retained.

210

8.99 As to the half lodging allowance, the POA have not sought its specific retention: that would presumably follow automatically if the detached duty status of the establishments were retained. They have sought, however, to retain and uprate the £1 a night sleeping-in allowance which has remained unchanged since introduction in 1972. The Northern Ireland Office have maintained to the contrary that it should be abolished. They claim the original accommodation defects have now been remedied and that officers are housed in terrapin buildings each with his own bedroom. Toilet and washing facilities are, however, shared and in the case of The Maze shower units are at present outside the sleeping quarters themselves. Improved accommodation has now been erected at The Maze but the POA has declined to occupy it unless the officers taking advantage of it are also paid the sleeping-in allowance. Although the POA accepts that renovation has been made to the accommodation, they claim that the need for the payment continues. They say it is related to the inconvenience suffered by the staff as well as to the standard of the accommodation. Although money has been spent on staff accommodation, it has been in the main used to provide additional accommodation rather than significantly improving the standard of that already there.

8.100 Although these may not seem the most important issues before us, we have found them difficult ones. It is the emergency and the emergency alone that has led to the establishment of The Maze and Magilligan, the former 3 miles from Lisburn and the latter somewhat off the beaten track. Whilst ordinarily prison officers could expect to live reasonably close to their work, we fully appreciate why they might not wish to do so in Northern Ireland at the present time and that this reluctance cannot reasonably be held against them. The Northern Ireland Office have pointed out that The Maze is not only 3 miles from Lisburn but also only 15 miles from Belfast, and Magilligan is not too remote from a number of towns eg 15 miles from Coleraine, 12 miles from Limavady and 36 miles from Londonderry. These distances, they say, do not warrant, as an alternative to travel allowance, a special allowance for isolation.

8.101 Indeed, if our recommendation in paragraph 8.79 above in regard to inconvenience of locality allowances is accepted, then the case for any fresh special allowance must be further diminished.

8.102 We have concluded that in respect of the mileage allowances our task in effect is to weigh the merits of enforcing a sound general principle against the claims of a particular local situation that a particular concession should be continued. The two positions are not compatible. The weakness of the second is that the POA acknowledges the concession sprang originally from a temporary situation. It has not argued that some fresh arrangement should be substituted nor has it shown, now that The Maze and Magilligan are agreed by everyone to be permanent establishments in fact, why the staff who work there should be treated more favourably than the staff of other Northern Ireland establishments, who may equally travel long distances to work and shoulder identical attendance systems. Whilst it might be argued that the civil service home to office rules were not formulated with the conditions of Northern Ireland in mind, what we think in the end clinches the balance in their favour is that they are more likely than current practice to produce equity between members of the same service.

We therefore recommend that henceforth The Maze and Magilligan be recognised as permanent duty stations and that the current allowances be phased out by negotiation.

8.103 It follows that the half lodging allowances will in principle fall too if this recommendation be followed. However, we think it sensible that those officers at present using the accommodation should be given a period of grace, during which they could continue to receive half lodging allowance and thus be enabled without immediate loss to find closer accommodation for themselves and their families and thus end their reliance on the provided accommodation at the prisons.

8.104 As to the £1 sleeping-in allowance, whilst we can understand the sense of grievance that staff might have if occupying accommodation which they consider does not measure up to an appropriate standard, the issue here is not whether the staff should have the accommodation free but whether they should, in addition, be paid daily compensation. Further, it is relevant to bear in mind that officers using the accommodation continue to receive their full rent allowance without any abatement. In the circumstances we think it in principle wrong that the allowance of £1 a night should continue indefinitely let alone be upgraded. It is true, as we point out in Chapter 11, that some of the bachelor accommodation at The Maze prison is still sub-standard. We recommend there, however, that urgent steps should be taken to improve it, and so far as the remaining accommodation at the prison is concerned, much has already been done to make it of an acceptable standard. That being so there can be no continuing basis upon which the £1 nightly allowance should be paid. On the understanding, therefore, that the Northern Ireland Office will at all times continue to ensure that the overnight accommodation is kept up to a reasonable standard, we recommend that steps be taken to eliminate the £1 a night allowance by negotiation.

Environmental allowances

8.105 These are paid to all members of non-prison service grades working in penal establishments in Great Britain. Approximately 3,000 benefit from the allowances which at present vary from £304 per annum to £95 per annum in four bands whose purpose is to group the non-prison service staff according to the amount of direct contact they have with inmates. The allowances are related to the "lead" paid at various levels to all the staff who work in the four English special hospitals and the one state hospital in Scotland. The lead originated in Broadmoor in 1923 and was gradually applied to the other hospitals thereafter. From 1954 it was extended to grades other than nurses in the special hospitals and is now paid there, in whole or in part, to approximately 2,550 staff. The lead is intended to compensate the special hospital staff for the more onerous duties involved in dealing with inmates of known violent, dangerous or criminal propensities who would not be found in NHS mental hospitals or in prison establishments.

8.106 The environmental allowances originated in two arbitration awards which took effect from 1 May 1960 made by the Civil Service Arbitration Tribunal. These awards originally were made in favour of civilian instructional officers and typing, clerical and executive staff. However, payment of the allowances was extended to other non-industrial general service grades and grades employed on NHS rates of pay and, finally, to industrial civil servants. Since 1962 allowances have been changed following changes in the special hospitals lead according to a formula which has the effect of preserving their relationship with the lead payments. At present, the maximum lead in special hospitals is £633 per annum which is received by all the nursing and occupational staff. The remainder, including the clerical and administrative staff, receive £317 per annum. The four banded environmental allowances are respectively £304, £189, £133 and £95 per annum.

8.107 Environmental allowances are the only allowances in penal establishments paid to members of non-prison service grades which are not paid to the prison service grades too. This is because the pay of the latter includes an element which reflects the environment in which they work whereas the general civil service grades do not have any such component in their pay.

8.108 We have received representations from all the staff associations concerned that the environmental allowances should be increased. The SCPS said that administrative grades in the prison service should be paid the same sum as that paid to administrative grades in special hospitals i.e. £317 per annum as opposed to £95 per annum. The IPCS claimed generally that there should be parity without specifying whether that parity was to be put as the maximum rate of the lead or at the half rate. The IPCS also made two other claims: that psychological assistants should receive the environmental allowance; and that staff at regional offices and headquarters should also receive environmental allowances in those cases where they were involved in visiting penal establishments.

8.109 We have considered whether it is appropriate that the environmental allowances should be continued. Numbers of the staff who receive the allowances at their lower rates have very little, if anything, to do with inmates. In addition, penal establishments are not as coherent in their environment as special hospitals: penal establishments vary from those holding juveniles in open conditions to maximum security prisons, whereas the five special hospitals have inmate populations and security demands which are much more homogenous than those in prisons. Accordingly, it seemed to us that in each allowance band actual working conditions vary a good deal and there would be numbers of staff who endured nothing perceptibly worse in terms of working conditions than their colleagues working in the civil service outside prison establishments.

8.110 On the other hand, we felt obliged to recognise that all members of non-prison service grades could expect to work in a variety of penal establishments and there were therefore arguments of equity in favour of paying equal sums if allowances were to be retained. On the whole we think they should be retained. It is plain in a number of penal establishments that conditions are objectively different from the ones in which general civil services grades could expect to work. Not only is it fair that they should receive some financial recognition of this fact, but it is also desirable that some inducement should exist to ensure that penal establishments are not deprived of their fair share of suitably qualified staff. On the other hand, we do not think it would be right to pay the allowances to anyone merely visiting a penal establishment. In addition, we have not been persuaded that the general relationship of the

213

allowances with the special hospitals lead should be revised, noting that the allowances are due for review under the standard formula. We consider that the review should proceed in the normal way and that, in so far as the allowances are in practice part of ordinary remuneration, it would be desirable that they are in future upgraded simultaneously with changes in pay.

SUPERANNUATION

8.111 Both the officer and the governor grades represented that improvements should be made to their superannuation. The following therefore looks first at the nature of general civil service superannuation benefits, then at their application to prison service grades, and finally examines the claims of each group in turn.

Civil service superannuation benefits

8.112 The Principal Civil Service Pension Scheme (PCSPS) provides for the payment, on retirement at or after the retiring age of 60, of pensions of 1/80th of pensionable pay for each year of reckonable service and for lump sums of 3 times the amount of the pension. Reckonable service, which is counted in years and days, is limited to 40 years at age 60 and to 45 years in total.

8.113 The scheme additionally provides for widows' and children's pensions; ill-health pensions for those who have to be retired prematurely on medical grounds; compensation payments for those who are forced to leave early because of redundancy etc; preserved pensions or transfers of accrued rights to other pension schemes for those who leave voluntarily; and lump sum death benefits in respect of those who die in service. There are special provisions for staff who are injured or killed on duty and there are facilities for the purchase of added years of reckonable service and for the allocation of pension benefits to dependants. If a civil servant is re-employed in the civil service after retiring, his pension is subject to total or partial abatement but, on final retirement, up to 5 years of re-employed service can be taken into account in calculating re-assessed superannuation benefits. These reassessed benefits are based on pensionable pay at the time of first retirement or at the time of final retirement, whichever is the better.

Application to prison officers

8.114 All these benefits and facilities are available to prison officers but in addition prison officers up to the rank of chief officer enjoy the benefit of a retiring age of 55. After 20 years of actual service as a prison officer, further such service reckons at double its length, so that prison officers can be paid full career pensions despite the earlier retirement age. For example, a chief or principal officer retiring at age 55 after 30 or more years in the prison service would receive a pension and lump sum based on 40 years' reckonable service. If he was then immediately re-employed in the basic officer grade, he would retain his lump sum and he would draw a part of his pension in addition to his pay. He could retire finally at age $57\frac{1}{2}$ with a pension based on 45 years' reckonable service and a further lump sum based on his additional, five years' reckonable service. These benefits would be calculated on the pay he was receiving in the higher grade at the time of the earlier retirement, if that was higher than his current pay in the basic grade.

8.115 The earlier retirement age and the faster accrual rate for prison officers were introduced into civil service superannuation arrangements by the Superannuation (Prison Officers) Act 1919. The concessions, which had been recommended by a committee that reported earlier in that year, recognised the abnormal strain and risks which the work of prison officers involves, particularly as they grow older and more vulnerable to outbursts of violence on the part of the people in their charge. It was the committee's view that, while the nature of a prison officer's job did not warrant such an early retirement age as that of a policeman, prison officers should not be expected to serve until age 60. Since at that time the minimum age of recruitment was 25, the double-reckoning of service after 20 years' service ensured that prison officers could retire with a full career pension at any time after age 55.

8.116 Under the arrangements for preserving pension benefits, accrued rights are preserved until age 60 provided that at least 5 years' pensionable service has been completed at the time of leaving. Prison officers have the added advantage, however, that their preserved benefits are calculated on the basis of "uniform accrual" and they receive some benefit of the faster accrual rate even if they resign before completing 20 years' service in the prison service. For example, a prison officer who would have completed 30 years' service if he had remained in the prison service until age 55 but who resigns after nine years' service can now have his superannuation benefits based on 12 years' reckonable service preserved until he reaches age 60.

8.117 As an alternative to preservation of benefits within the PCSPS, all civil servants, including prison officers, may transfer their accrued rights to some other pension scheme and this includes the Armed Forces Pension Scheme. Such transfers are, however, no longer limited to public service pension schemes and a transfer payment can be made to any pension scheme which is approved for the purpose by Inland Revenue and which is willing to accept it. However, because of the contracting-out requirements of the Social Security Pensions Act 1975, the accrued pension rights of civil servants who have more than five years' reckonable service cannot be transferred to schemes which are not contracted-out. The CSD point out this is a relatively minor limitation and, in practice, prison officers who take up other pensionable employment, including those who have less than five years' service in the civil service, can usually take their accrued superannuation rights with them. Since, for those with five or more years' service, the transfer payment is based on a proportion of the benefits that would otherwise be enjoyed under the PCSPS, prison officers who transfer benefit from a calculation on the basis of "uniform accrual". This takes account of the effect of the double counting of years of service in excess of 20 for pension purposes. An officer who would, had he remained in the service until age 55, have completed 30 years service and would have been credited with 40 years' reckonable service for pension purposes, will therefore have his actual reckonable service increased by one-third.

8.118 The scheme provides for the payment of widows' pensions at the rate of one-half of the pension the husband was receiving at the date of his death or, if he dies in service, at the rate of one-half of the pension the husband would have received had he retired on grounds of ill-health on the day that he died. Pensions are also payable in respect of dependent children. No contributions are payable for children's pensions but all male staff, whether they are married or single, are required to contribute at the rate of 1½ per cent of salary towards the cost of the contingent widow's pension. The scheme has been made compulsory because the Social Security legislation requires contracted-out schemes to provide widows' cover for all their male employees and it is clearly preferable for the contributions to be paid during service rather than by deduction from the lump sum retirement benefit or from the death benefit, if the husband dies in service. Those who are unmarried when they finally retire can have their contributions refunded to them, with interest.

Application to governor grades

8.119 Governors benefit solely from the normal PCSPS arrangements applying to civil servants as a whole. None of the special benefits enjoyed by officer grades as a result (ultimately) of the 1919 Act apply in their case, but all the other benefits do.

The POA claim

8.120 The POA represented that, since officers could join before the age of 25, it seemed unfair that they should not be able to retire on full pension after 30 years service even if they had not by then reached the age of 55. In addition, the POA felt that once 30 years had been served the additional accrual up to the statutory limit should be permitted to run immediately rather than only from the age of 55. Thus an officer joining at the age of 22 would qualify for a retirement pension at age 52 and on the maximum permitted under the law at age 54. Elsewhere in their evidence the POA assessed the value of the non-contributory pension as 3·013 per cent of salary in comparison with what they felt were similar, but contributory, schemes for the police, fire service and mental health nurses. In later correspondence, the POA increased the figure of 3·013 per cent to 5·61 per cent in the light of their understanding of figures published by the Government Actuary.

The Government Actuary's calculations

8.121 We looked into this claim carefully with the assistance of the Government Actuary. We wanted to see how prison officers' pensions compared generally, what was the kind of value that should be attached to them, and what was the cost of the improvements claimed. In his calculations the Government Actuary compared the benefits for prison officers with the benefits under the PCSPS to other non-industrial civil servants, with the benefits under certain public sector contributory schemes (ie mental health nurses, policemen and firemen) and also with a representative private sector scheme.

216

8.122 The method of calculation the Government Actuary adopted was that which he had used for the purposes of the civil service pay review and described in detail in his Report on the 1979 review: *Civil Service Pay Research —The 1979 Review of the Adjustment for Differences in Superannuation Benefits*. Most of the assumptions he made about mortality were those contained in his 1979 Report, but appropriate assumptions about average entry and retirement ages of prison officers were made from analyses of the data supplied by the Civil Service Department's computer record. On this basis the value of the benefits of the PCSPS as it applies to prison officers was assessed at 24·9 per cent of salary. Those benefits included family benefits towards which officers paid a contribution of 1½ per cent of salary.

8.123 On the same actuarial basis, the value of the benefits of the PCSPS to other non-industrial civil servants was 17·3 per cent of salary, with employee contributions again of 1½ per cent. In the case of a broadly representative private sector scheme, the value of the benefits would be 13 per cent of salary with employee contributions of 5 per cent.

8.124 The Government Actuary pointed out that the pensions scheme for mental health nurses, policemen and firemen were very similar to those for prison officers but with employee contributions of 6 per cent, 7 per cent and 6¾ per cent of salary respectively. The main difference was that for police and firemen the pension was based on 60ths of pay per year (with power to commute part for a lump sum) whilst for mental health nurses and prison officers the pension was based on 80ths together with a lump sum on retirement of three years pension. On the basis used, the 60ths schemes were the more valuable —the benefits being worth 28·3 per cent of salary. On the other hand, such comparisons were purely between the actuarial value of the pensions schemes and took no account of other factors e.g. that a low retirement age for prison officers was at least partly in compensation for the arduous nature of their job. The POA calculations of value, it was pointed out, were based on misunderstandings about the size of the contributions in the three schemes the POA had in mind, the effects of taxation, and the proper allowance for indexation.

8.125 Pursuing comparative values further, the Government Actuary sought to value the current benefits to prison officers and their pay and pensions package as a whole in comparison with the pay and pensions packages enjoyed by the other groups already mentioned. He showed that if it were desired to equate the value of the pay and pensions package of a prison officer to that of a particular civil servant, policeman etc then the money pay of a prison officer should be 93·8 per cent of the money pay of the civil servant, 96·4 per cent of that of the mental health nurse, 98·3 per cent of that of the policeman, 98·5 per cent of that of the fireman, and 88·2 per cent of that of the private sector employee in a representative private sector scheme.

8.126 As regards the estimated cost of the improvement sought by the POA, it would be about 0·5 per cent of the prison officer payroll in respect of future service, with an additional capital deficiency at the outset of over £3½ million in respect of past service. This was on the basis of data which showed that about one-third of prison officers retired at the earliest opportunity.

CSD observations

8.127 They maintained that the Government Actuary's calculations showed that the special benefits enjoyed by prison officers were expensive concessions and to allow officers to retire on pensions at an age earlier than 55 could only add even more to the costs of the Civil Service Pension Scheme. While it was reasonable that the government, as employer, should be prepared to meet such additional costs if a prison officer were forced to retire because his health broke down or because there was no longer any work for him to do and he had to be compulsorily retired, the extra costs could not be justified in the cases of officers who were fit and able to work and for whom jobs were available. Moreover, the limitation of reckonable service to 40 years at the normal retiring age was applied universally throughout the public services and officers therefore suffered no unfair disadvantage in that respect. For example, civil servants generally could be recruited at age 16 and might be obliged therefore to serve for as long as 44 years before becoming eligible for the payment of super-annuation benefits based on the maximum of 40 years' reckonable service. Similar situations could arise in other public service pension schemes and a reduction in the retiring age for officers would be bound to lead to demands that all public servants should be given the opportunity to retire as soon as they had completed 40 years' reckonable service. The costs were therefore potentially very much greater than those which might arise for the prison service alone.

Conclusions and recommendations on officers

8.128 It is clear the Government Actuary's calculations demonstrate that prison officers enjoy generous pension terms, that the value of the pension represents a substantial addition to their total remuneration, and that further improvements could be secured, of course. only at the cost of substantial additional public expense. The POA offered no evidence to suggest why further improvements were justified except to say that officers joining below the age of 25 would like to have an opportunity to leave on full pension after 30 years. However, although the special arrangements for prison officers are designed to take account of the more arduous nature of their duties, we agree with the CSD that their benefits cannot be seen in isolation from those accorded to the civil service as a whole. In addition, it might be expected that prison officers have shared proportionately in the general increases in the health and longevity of the population at large, possibly even to an extent which might cast doubt on the considerations which moved the relevant committee as long as 60 years ago. We do not, however, think it desirable to pursue this point because, whatever changes may have occurred in absolute standards since 1919, we consider the relative disadvantages endured by officers continue to justify the substantial extra costs their benefits incur. On the other hand, whilst we appreciate an earlier retirement age might be welcome, we have received no evidence to support the view that it is on merits desirable or justified particularly in respect of a non-contributory scheme and we must therefore reject the claim. It follows that the way seems clear for us to recommend only that the pay scales we recommend to take effect from 1 January 1980 should, for pension purposes, be deemed to have applied with effect from 1 April 1979.

The Governors' claim

8.129 Governors requested the same superannuation arrangements as for prison officers. Although acknowledging that the similar claim they made to the Wynn-Parry Committee had been rejected in its report in 1958 (Report, paragraph 70), the governors claimed conditions had changed enormously since 1958. (We note that the Expenditure Committee also considered this claim in its report in 1978 and said: "We do not possess the necessary specialist knowledge of pensions to make a recommendation in this matter, but we think that the governors' case is not overwhelming".—Report, paragraph 139.) The tendency of these changes, the governors maintained, had been to increase the physical, emotional and psychological pressures on staff of all grades and most significantly on governors. Current arrangements were contrasted with the situation in the police and armed forces. It was pointed out, too, that when prison officers were promoted to governor grades then they lost the "two for one" benefit in respect of service over 20 years: this was a disincentive to them to seek promotion. Finally, it was claimed that because governors entered the service later than other civil service grades, they could never hope to earn full pension and so suitable enhancement was justified on those grounds too.

Government Actuary and CSD observations

8.130 According to the Government Actuary's calculations, the cost of granting parity would be about 5·7 per cent of the governor grade payroll in respect of future service, with an additional deficiency of about £3 million in respect of past service. The Government Actuary thought that the improvements sought by the POA, if granted, would have little effect for governor grades since he assumed that relatively few governors would in fact retire at ages where the improvement would have any effect.

8.131 The CSD referred again to the fact that the earlier retirement age and the faster accrual rate for officers had been introduced in 1919 on the recommendations of a committee appointed to inquire into the conditions of service and superannuation of the warder classes. The committee had been impressed by the much higher standard of physical efficiency required of a warder throughout the whole of his career and by the mental strain that continuous and intensive watchfulness imposed upon him. They had suggested that these conditions distinguished the warder class from all other civil servants and justified the concessions they proposed. Whether or not the committee's views were as valid today as they had been in 1919, it was certainly not obvious that the governor grades, who were administrative staff, should be eligible for more generous superannuation terms than other administrative staff, either within or outside the prison service.

Conclusions and recommendations on governors

8.132 We have examined the relevant statistics to see how far they show that governors suffered under more stress than other civil servants. The relevant figures are the two tables following. These record the rates for governors and the non-industrial civil service as a whole for medical retirement and deaths in harness. The figures appear to show that the non-industrial civil service has a premature retirement rate 17·8 per cent higher than governors and a 36·6 per cent higher death rate. As to comparable ages on recruitment, governors are not alone in being unable to earn full pension by age 60. The Civil Service Statistics 1978 show (Table 8) that the average age on entry to the civil service of Executive Officers in the years 1975–77 varied between 24 years 11 months and 23 years 2 months.

Governor grades (England and Wales): Ill-health retirements and deaths in harness 1972–78

	1	2		3	
Year	Total number of Governors in post	Premature retirement on grounds of ill-health		Deaths in harness	
		Numbers	As a % of col 1	Numbers	As a % of col 1
1972	505	2	0·396	4	0·792
1973	510	3	0·588	0	—
1974	499	1	0·200	0	—
1975	524	0	—	0	—
1976	546	0	—	1	0·183
1977	553	1	0·181	3	0·542
1978	559	3	0·537	1	0·179
Average for years 1972–78	528	1·428	0·270	1·286	0·243

Non-industrial civil servants (U.K.-based): Ill-health retirements and deaths in harness 1972–78

	1	2		3	
Year	Total numbers* of non-industrial civil servants in post	Premature retirements* on grounds of ill-health		Deaths in harness*	
		Numbers	As a % of col 1	Numbers	As a % of col 1
1972	504,445	1,039	0·206	1,814	0·360
1973	504,141	1,340	0·266	1,836	0·364
1974	511,326	1,327	0·259	1,662	0·325
1975	517,030	1,672	0·323	1,866	0·361
1976	564,836	1,651	0·292	1,641	0·290
1977	569,852	2,450	0·430	1,807	0·317
1978	567,015	2,397	0·423	1,779	0·314
Average for years 1972–78	534,092·14	1,696·57	0·318	1,772·14	0·332

*From 1975 onwards Foreign and Commonwealth Office is excluded.

8.133 As regards the other arguments, we fully appreciate why governors might wish to have the same pension advantages as are enjoyed by officers. On the other hand, we have to have regard to the reasons why those benefits exist. Whilst it might be said that governors' jobs have become more stressful, the governors themselves acknowledged that this was true of all grades working in penal establishments and not just themselves. Although it is true that governors are not shielded from difficult and stressful situations in respect of inmates, for instance at adjudications and difficult applications, their degree of continuous contact with inmates remains considerably less than that of prison officers. Indeed, in so far as governors increasingly undertake administrative work outside penal establishments, then the degree of contact is lessened. Further, in so far as the determination of their pay recognises the more stressful nature of their duties in comparison with other civil service grades, then the enhancement of their pay is carried through into better pensions; and the evidence of the tables above does not suggest any further improvement is justified. As regards their ability to earn full pensions, their tendency to serve for less than 40 years is not unique. On the other hand, governors may under the PCSPS purchase "additional years" of pension value by means of regular deductions from their pay. The fact that they have in some respects relatively greater pay because of the special nature of their duties and also free housing perhaps puts them in a better position relatively to take advantages of the arrangement than most of the non-industrial civil service. Finally, as to whether the loss of "two for one" is a disincentive to officers seeking promotion to the governor grades, we have —as in the case of the Wynn-Parry Committee—received no evidence.

8.134 Having carefully considered the arguments, we have felt bound to conclude that there is no present case for granting governors parity with prison officers and that their pension entitlement should, therefore, remain as it is. As with officers, however, we recommend that the pay scales recommended to take effect from 1 January 1980 should be deemed, for pension purposes, to have applied with effect from 1 April 1979.

CHAPTER NINE

CONTINUOUS DUTY CREDITS

BACKGROUND

9.1 As we have previously observed, one of the main features that characterised the period of industrial unrest immediately prior to the appointment of this Committee was a series of claims by prison officers for payment of what have become known as "continuous duty credits". We were specifically asked to report upon these claims, and upon the date from which any payment due under them should be made. Since our appointment the POA has put before us a large number of claims, many of which had not previously been put to the Home Office. All of the claims are reproduced in full in Appendix 9 to this report. We considered whether we could properly express views upon claims which had not been presented before our appointment, but we eventually concluded that it would be in the interests of all parties if so far as possible we were to do so, particularly as both the POA and the Home Office were able to deal fully with these claims in their written and oral evidence to us. In doing so, however, we made it clear from an early stage that we were prepared to consider only questions of principle, and that we were not prepared to adjudicate upon any issues involving only individual establishments.

9.2 In the main, CDC claims are claims for payment in respect of meal breaks taken within duty hours, and to understand fully the background to the claims, and the way in which we have approached them, it is necessary to appreciate that prison officers are in general required by national agreement to work net hours, that is to say that they receive payment only for hours actually worked and do not receive payment for any meal breaks which fall within the normal span of their working shift unless that is expressly provided for either by agreement or by a provision in the codes regulating their systems of attendance. In the absence of any such provision the general rule about non-payment for meal breaks must, in our opinion, prevail.

9.3 A great many of the claims put to the Home Office and to us are said to be justified by virtue of the provisions of a Notice to Staff 62/1972, which is also reproduced in Appendix 9. Before proceeding further it is desirable that we should state our understanding of that Notice to Staff.

9.4 The first point to observe about the Notice to Staff is that the provisions it contains are not unique to the prison service. Though it applies only to the prison service and its terms were agreed by the POA, it is based upon a general civil service notice and relates, as its title indicates, to allowances for "on-call" and "stand-by" duties. The provisions of the general civil service notice were not, and were plainly not intended to be, related only to the working circumstances of prison officers. Paragraph 9 of the Notice to Staff, which is the paragraph on which the POA has based many of its claims and which is, we understand, part of the general civil service notice, is in our view a paragraph which contains certain provisions intended to recompense a person who is called out to work for a short period outside normal working hours. It makes no mention of meal breaks and, in general, provides that, where a person is called out for extra duty which occurs more than three hours before the start or after the end of his normal duty, he will receive a minimum overtime credit

222

of three hours, even if the period of extra duty is less than that; in all other cases the period of extra duty will be treated as continuous with the normal period of duty, that is, as if no break had occurred. The paragraph expressly refers to an officer who is "called out to work for a short period outside normal working hours" and we can find nothing in that paragraph, or elsewhere in the Notice to Staff, to support the proposition that a prison officer who is *scheduled* to work extra duty should thereby obtain some special recompense, that is to say payment for a meal break which has to be taken as a consequence of that extra duty. Indeed, paragraph 10a of the Notice to Staff makes it abundantly clear that this was not the intention. That paragraph provides "an officer scheduled to work extra duty either before or after his scheduled shift for the day will reckon only the duty and extra duty actually performed for duty credit, meal breaks being unpaid". Nothing could, in our opinion, be clearer than that. With that introduction we pass now to consider the history of the claims.

9.5 The first claim for payment of CDC occurred early in 1973 and arose in this way. In a number of establishments the system of attendance in operation required main shift staff to start work at 7.45 am. It was assumed that such staff would have taken breakfast before starting work, and the attendance system accordingly made no provision for a breakfast break. In practice it proved necessary to detail a number of such staff to commence work at 7.00 am, and they were assumed not to have had breakfast before starting work. Consequently, they were sent off work for a 45 minute break at about 7.45 am and received no payment for that break. In the result, therefore, the officers concerned were attending their place of work for a longer span than their colleagues who were notionally on the same shift, but were receiving no additional remuneration for doing so.

9.6 This state of affairs came to the attention of the headquarters of the POA and one of their officials, in January 1973, wrote to the Home Office to seek an improvement in the situation. In that letter he said:

"Paragraph 9 of Notice to Staff 62/1972 implies that duty outside normal attendance time will be treated as continuous where it is less than three hours . . .

Accordingly we seek agreement that:

(a) where an officer is normally conditioned to a succession of main shifts entailing the taking of breakfast before duty, any live duty performed before the normal starting time should attract a continuous credit from the actual until normal starting time . . .".

On 17 April 1973 a reply was sent from the Home Office in the following terms:

"Thank you for your letter of 17 January 1973. When an officer who is scheduled to main shifts is required to perform an early morning duty which commences within three hours of his normal starting time for that day the whole attendance should be treated as continuous and any break for breakfast would be paid. This would, however, preclude the officer from having an entitlement to payment for the third meal break taken on that day. We can therefore agree to the points raised in the final paragraph of your letter and confirm that duty performed prior to the scheduled shift should be treated

223

as continuous with that shift and that the main shift itself should not be varied to compensate for that extra duty."

9.7 That letter from the Home Office does not mention the Notice to Staff 62/1972 and does not purport to be setting out an agreed interpretation of its terms. On the other hand, the letter was in reply to one from the POA which did refer to the Notice to Staff, and furthermore a subsequent decision was taken by the Home Office, in circumstances which are obscure, to backdate payments in cases covered by the letter to the date when the Notice to Staff came into effect. These circumstances indicate that the parties concerned regarded what took place as constituting an agreed intepretation of the terms of the Notice to Staff, rather than a new agreement. It is, of course, open to the parties to any document to reach a subsequent agreement as to the interpretation of its terms, and it is not then open to any third party to challenge that interpretation, however mistaken it may appear to be; and we do not seek to do so. Certainly there were compelling reasons of equity for making the concession contained in the Home Office letter and, if the parties concerned chose to express that concession as an interpretation of the Notice to Staff, that must remain a matter for them. We, for our part, have to determine what were the salient features of that concession in order to determine whether or not they establish general principles of wider application which will apply to the various claims which we have to consider. In paragraph 9.9 we shall examine the terms of what we shall for convenience refer to hereafter as "the 1973 interpretation". First it is desirable that we should briefly bring the history of the affair up to date.

9.8 We have already observed that the claim put forward in 1973 arose, in the main, because, in certain establishments, main shifts officers were being detailed to commence work in the morning at a time earlier than that prescribed by the Code of Instructions applicable to the establishments in question. During the ensuing years this practice spread to other establishments and, in at least one case, also involved officers who were scheduled to work a short day shift. It appears, however, that in many, if not most, such cases this arose as a matter of local convenience and not by virtue of any written instruction which could thereafter be referred to as establishing either the fact that such an early start was part of the normal working routine in the establishment in question, or the date at which such an arrangement had been brought into effect. Furthermore, it also appears that no adequate records were kept in establishments to indicate which officers had been involved in early starts, or the frequency of the occasions on which this took place. As a result the Home Office was faced, in the summer of 1978, with a great many claims for breakfast break payments few of which could be established upon the basis of written evidence. That being so, the Home Office and the POA reached an agreement in July of that year that such claims should be considered upon the basis of what came to be referred to as "custom and practice". What that meant in fact was that if officers at a particular establishment could show, by whatever means, that they had been in the habit of starting a shift in the morning at a time earlier than scheduled which necessitated their taking a subsequent breakfast break they should receive payment for that break, notwithstanding that there were no written records to establish any entitlement. Since an individual officer's entitlement could not of course be determined with any accuracy, it was necessary to negotiate for each establishment a sum for payment in respect of each year

224

during which the officer had been subject to such early starts with varying levels of settlement in different establishments. This resulted in the expenditure of some £5·5 million in paying off the claims, most of which were presented during 1978. The situation which gave rise to such a method of settling claims was plainly unsatisfactory and was, at least to some extent, of the Prison Department's own making. Attendance systems are dealt with elsewhere in this report, but we think it right to observe at this stage not only that it is, in our view, a regrettable feature of the existing systems that they, apparently, had to be departed from so often in order to achieve an efficient system of operating within particular establishments, but also that such departures were not recorded in a way that made it possible to identify them in subsequent years.

9.9 Against the foregoing historical background we now turn to express our understanding of the 1973 interpretation and to explain the basis on which we have approached the various claims that have been put to us by the POA. In our view the 1973 interpretation provided quite simply for payment for a meal break in circumstances where an officer is required to start work at a time earlier than that scheduled, and where, as a result, he is required to take a breakfast break which would not otherwise have occurred within his span of duty. We can find nothing in that interpretation to establish any principle of general application and therefore regard it as applying only to breakfast breaks arising in the circumstances described. Since April 1973, it is true, the interpretation has apparently been expanded to apply to officers who are scheduled to a short day shift, whereas the original Home Office latter referred only to those scheduled to main shifts. However, such an expansion merely enlarges the range of officers who can benefit under the concession and does not establish any general principle where none previously existed. So too the description of the nature of the interpretation has undergone some changes over the years. In evidence to us the Home Office expressed it as follows:

"A breakfast break arising from overtime worked in consequence of an earlier starting time than that required of the individual officer on the day in question by the attendance system of the establishment is paid at plain time rates."

We understand that the above description has been used without objection or comment in correspondence between the Home Office and the POA but, although it uses different language from that used in the 1973 letters, we do not regard it as establishing, any more than these earlier letters, any principle of general application.

9.10 Consequently we have approached the claims which have been submitted by the POA upon the basis that they can be granted only if either they fall directly under the terms of the 1973 interpretation or, alternatively, they fall under some other provision of the various rules or Notices to Staff governing the payment of meal breaks, always bearing in mind the general principle set out in paragraph 2 of this chapter, namely that, as net hours grades, prison officers do not receive payment for meal breaks unless some specific entitlement to such payment can be found. We have accordingly proceeded upon a strict basis of entitlement. In some cases we have felt there may be equitable grounds for creating such entitlements, but in all except one of these cases we have taken the view that this must be left as a matter for future negotiation between the parties. We now pass to consider in turn each of the claims which have been submitted.

225

9.11 *Claim 1* This claim relates to unscheduled midday meal breaks which require to be taken during a scheduled shift in circumstances where an early shift is extended to equate with a main shift, where an early shift is extended beyond the termination time of a main shift, and where a late shift is extended by duty in the morning period. Upon one view this claim is analogous to the claims in respect of breakfast breaks which have already been conceded by the Home Office. However, for reasons which have already been given, we do not consider that the 1973 interpretation established any principle which can appropriately be extended by analogy to meal breaks other than breakfast. The present claim is not justified by an interpretation of the Notice to Staff 62/1972 and we accordingly recommend that it should be rejected.

9.12 *Claim 2* This claim relates to the manner in which payments under claim 1 should be made, assuming that claim 1 were to be allowed. Since we have decided that there is no basis of entitlement upon which claim 1 can be granted it follows that we must recommend the rejection of this claim also.

9.13 *Claim 3* This is a claim of limited application for payment in respect of a tea meal break taken by certain officers who work a very long shift from 7.00 am until 9.30 pm. The POA recognise that this is a claim which does not proceed upon any supposed entitlement but is rather a claim for an improvement in the conditions of service of these particular officers. Since many officers at the moment, for example those to whom paragraph 4(*d*) of the Vee Scheme applies, already receive payment for a tea break, we consider that this is a claim for an analogous improvement in conditions of service and this not one on which we can make any recommendation, but is one which might well be a matter for future negotiation.

9.14 *Claims 4 and 5* These claims relate to tea breaks taken before extra duty and either within conditioned hours, or after conditioned hours and prior to the start of the extra duty. In our view they are in the same position as the claim made in respect of midday meal breaks and for the same reasons we recommend their rejection. No entitlement to payment for these breaks arises from the terms of the 1973 interpretation, and likewise we can find nothing either in the Notice to Staff or elsewhere which would provide suitable entitlement.

9.15 *Claim 6* This is another claim which the POA recognises as being a claim for an improvement in conditions of service rather than one which proceeds upon some existing entitlement. Like some of the other claims put forward by the POA it raises fundamental questions about whether prison officers should be regarded as a net hours or a gross hours grade, and it follows that it is not appropriate for us to make any recommendation in this case.

9.16 *Claim 7* This relates to payments for officers who are required to work unscheduled evening duties. We have no alternative but to recommend the rejection of this claim upon the same basis as for claims 1 and 2.

9.17 *Claim 8* This claim concerns those officers, mainly Principal Officers, who work an attendance system known as system IV B of the FGS Code of Instructions. Under that system the officers work a succession of main shifts with two such shifts per week being annotated ^{E}M in the relevant table of the Code. This means that on three days per week they attend having had breakfast before starting duty and on two mornings per week they have, as the Code of Instructions indicates, a liability to attend at 7.00 a.m. On occasions when such officers do in fact start work at 7.00 a.m. they subsequently take a breakfast break for which they receive no payment. The contention of the POA is that these officers are in the same position as those who have had claims paid under the terms of the 1973 interpretation. The Home Office approach to this claim has been that these officers do not have an unscheduled early start. On the contrary, the days when they have such an early start are clearly set out in the Code of Instructions and are therefore predictable. We can see considerable force in the Home Office argument, particularly in the distinction which it draws between, on the one hand, a situation where the incidence of early starts is clearly set out in the Code of Instructions, and, on the other hand, one where the incidence of such starts is entirely indiscriminate. On the other hand, the Code of Instructions for system IV B indicates no more than a liability for early morning duty, and it is not our understanding that such early morning duty invariably takes place. Furthermore, the manner in which the designation ^{E}M is shown in the table, and the pattern within which it falls, suggest that the shift is properly to be regarded as a main shift, that is to say one with an 8.00 am starting time, rather than as one with an earlier starting time. The provisions in the Code of Instructions are not free from ambiguity but, having considered the matter as best we can, we have reached the conclusion that the benefit of any doubt here should be given to the POA. We think that the circumstances of the officers covered by this claim can properly be regarded as falling within the terms of the Home Office letter of 17 April 1973 and that, accordingly, this claim should be granted. It has occurred to us that the subsequent Home Office description of the 1973 interpretation (quoted in paragraph 9.9. above) may seem less favourable to this recommendation in that it refers to the requirements of the attendance system of the establishment whereas the original letter of April 1973 merely referred to "an officer who is scheduled to main shifts". We do not understand, however, that any later description of the agreement by the Home Office was intended in any way to limit its application and we therefore regard it as proper to measure the present claim against the language used in the original letters of 1973 if that language is more favourable to the granting of the claim. If this claim is to be granted, as we recommend, it will follow that payments must be back-dated to the operative date of the 1973 interpretation, the relevant provision of the FGS Code having been in existence since that time. In the light of what occurred in 1978 it may be that difficulty will be encountered in determining the amount at which individual officers' claims are to be settled and a similar approach to that adopted in the latter part of 1978 may have to be employed.

9.18 *Claim 9* This claim relates to those officers who are called in to work on what is scheduled as a rest day and are then required to start work at a time earlier than that scheduled as the starting time of their shift, with the result that they are thereafter required to take a breakfast break. They are thus in precisely the same position as those officers covered by the 1973 interpretation, with this one exception that, under their system of attendance, they are not scheduled to work any shift at all on the day in question, and therefore cannot, upon one

227

view, be said to have any scheduled starting time which can be departed from. It is upon this basis that the Home Office has so far resisted this claim. From an early stage in our deliberations we have had considerable sympathy with this claim but, having taken a strict criterion by which to judge the validity of any claim, we have found it impossible to conclude that the officers in question have established an entitlement to payment. We have already commented on the differences which exist between the basis for entitlement as set out in the Home Office letter of 17 April 1973 and the statement of entitlement given to us by them in evidence. Neither of these, however, supports this claim since the letter refers to "an officer who is *scheduled* to main shifts" and the statement in evidence refers to a break arising "in consequence of an earlier starting time than that required of the individual officer on the day in question *by the attendance system of the establishment*". Neither of the phrases in italics is appropriate to an officer who is called in on a rest day since he is scheduled by the attendance system of the establishment to do no work at all that day, and is not scheduled to work any particular shift. In these circumstances we must recommend rejection of this claim so far as it is based upon an alleged entitlement with, of course, consequential back-dating. On the other hand, we think that the claim has so much to commend it in equity that we accordingly recommend that, with effect from a current date, the breakfast break concession should be extended to include those officers who are working on what is scheduled as a rest day.

9.19 *Claim 10* This claim extends the principle argued for in claim 9 to the extent of maintaining that, where an officer is called in to work on a rest day, all meal breaks should be paid. The POA recognises that there is no basis of entitlement upon which this claim can be met retrospectively, and they accordingly argue that it should be granted as an improvement in conditions of service with effect from a current date. It follows that it is not appropriate for us to make any recommendation in this case.

9.20 *Claims 11 and 12* These claims, although relating to particular circumstances, raise the same question of principle and entitlement as was raised under claim 1. For the reasons given in relation to that claim, we do not consider that claims 11 and 12 can be met, and we recommend accordingly.

9.21 *Claims 13 and 14* These claims are directed only to the date from which payments should be made, and relate to those claims which have already been settled under the 1973 interpretation, and also to those new claims which are said to derive their entitlement from the Notice to Staff 62/1972. The argument is that, since the 1973 interpretation arose from a claim based on the 1972 Notice, and since that Notice was effectively no more than a re-writing of an earlier circular instruction issued in 1965, payments already made and to be made should be backdated to the date of introduction of the 1965 circular instruction, that is to say 17 April 1967. In our view this claim should not be granted. It was not advanced prior to 1973, or at the time when the 1973 interpretation was agreed, and has not been advanced, so far as we know, prior to the setting up of this Inquiry. Indeed, as recently as September 1977, a letter sent by the POA to Branch Secretaries (reproduced in the POA written evidence to us) referred to "improvements which were introduced via Notice to Staff 62/1972". Nothing was said in that letter about any alleged entitlement from an earlier date. Consequently, the entitlement can date only from the date provided for in that agreement and not from any earlier date.

9.22 *Claim 15* This is a comprehensive claim which argues that all un-scheduled meal breaks should be paid as continuous duty. For reasons which we have already elaborated in respect of individual earlier claims we are unable to recommend the granting of this claim.

9.23 *Claim 16* This claim is based upon a construction of certain provisions in the Code of Instructions applicable to establishments which operate the functional group system of attendance. The provisions in question are paragraphs 7k and 9b, which are in the following terms:

"7k The total hours (net) in a scheduled duty shift should not be re-arranged to extend the span of duty by the introduction of an unscheduled midday or tea meal break".

"9b Where an officer is sent off duty prior to the completion of the con-ditioned shift for the day in question, a duty credit will be granted equal to that which would have been granted had the officer remained on duty until the termination of the conditioned shift".

These paragraphs were inserted into the Code of Instructions when it was revised in 1975 for the limited purpose of dealing with particular problems which had arisen in certain establishments, and that this was so was readily accepted by the POA. Having said that, however, if either or both of the para-graphs in question can, as drafted, reasonably bear a wider interpretation, then that interpretation must be given to them. In their written evidence to us the POA has contended that the effect of these paragraphs is to confer a right to payment of all unscheduled midday meal breaks. Before proceeding further we must state that we are unable to accept this as a general proposition. Whatever may be the effect of paragraphs 7k and 9b they can confer no right to payment except in any cases clearly falling under their terms, and to state the claim in the wide terms used by the POA clearly goes well beyond any possible construc-tion of the paragraphs.

9.24 With that general comment we pass to consider the paragraphs themselves. The first point to observe is that paragraph 7k is prohibitive, and confers no explicit entitlement to any payment in the event of a breach. Paragraph 9b, on the other hand, creates an entitlement to a payment, but does not do so in terms which make it clear to all that such payment may be in respect of a breach of paragraph 7k. Furthermore, the construction of paragraph 9b that is contended for by the POA is upon one view in conflict with the general rule that prison officers do not receive payment for meal breaks, and in particular with the pro-visions of paragraph 5c in the Code of Instructions which provides:

"Meal breaks within the scheduled span of duty which permit an officer to be relieved of duty to leave the establishment or his place of duty will not reckon for duty credit."

9.25 We have found this claim very difficult to resolve. The manner in which the relevant paragraphs have been drafted creates an unwelcome ambiguity. On the other hand, if the probihitive paragraph 7k is in fact being breached by management it is at the very least inequitable that that should happen without some suitable recompense being made. Furthermore, in so far as the FGS Code of Instructions is a document which was agreed between the Home Office and the POA, it is plainly undesirable, in the interests of future agreements, whether in the fields of pay, industrial relations, or whatever, that there should be no sanction against the breach of any of its provisions. Consequently, and before considering the claim further, we feel obliged to say that, so long as paragraph 7k remains in the Code, it is management's job to observe its terms and in particular, it is for the Home Office to ensure that this is done. Equally if establishments cannot be run effectively without breaches of the paragraph, then it is management's responsibility either to seek to alter the provision or, to provide unequivocally for the payment of compensation in the event of a breach.

9.26 For the time being we have to make the best decision that we can on the claim as presented and, in an attempt to obtain some guidance, we have sought to relate the relevant paragraphs of the code, and in particular paragraph 7k, to what we understand to be the undisputed facts surrounding this claim. These appear to be that situations were arising whereby an officer scheduled to a "F" or short day shift was being sent on an unscheduled midday meal break in order thereafter to take an inmate on a short escort which terminated within an hour after what would have been the conditioned finishing time of the shift. In such a case the officer's total span of duty was being increased by the amount of the meal break without *prima facie*, any provision being made for recompense. What in fact happened was that the Home Office agreed that a CDC payment should be made in such cases and, additionally, inserted paragraph 7k into the revised code in an attempt to prohibit any recurrence of the situation in question. Whether or not that prohibition has had the desired result in such cases we cannot say. What we do say is that, if it has not, there can be no reason for not making a CDC payment as before to any officer who has his shift extended in the manner described; and it is no answer to say that the extension should not have occurred because it is now prohibited.

9.27 That is not, however, the end of the matter. Thus far we have been speaking of a situation where the termination of an officer's duty is postponed only by the amount of the unscheduled meal break. What the POA are contending in this claim, as we understand it, is that there is equally a breach of paragraph 7k, and consequently an entitlement to payment, in cases where an officer is required to work a number of hours of extra duty and, as a result, is obliged to take an unscheduled midday meal break during the span of his original scheduled shift. Against this contention it can be argued that, where an officer is detailed for extra, and therefore paid, hours of duty, the taking of an unscheduled midday meal break does not involve, in the words of paragraph 7k, a re-arrangement of the total hours (net) of his scheduled duty shift. On the other hand, the interpretation paragraph of the code (paragraph 21) defines "scheduled shifts" as "shifts of agreed length and timing undertaken on conditioned duty days which may include built-in overtime". The effect of that, in our view, is that the scheduled duty shift referred to in paragraph 7k is the shift of the agreed length and timing which the officer in question was scheduled to perform under the particular part of the attendance system applicable to him on the day in question, and that a breach of paragraph 7k will have occurred if, by the introduction of an unscheduled midday break, the total hours of that shift are re-arranged so as to extend the span of duty.

Thus, for example, if an officer who is scheduled to work a 'F' shift with an agreed starting time of 07·30 and an agreed finishing time of 13·30 is required to take an unscheduled midday break, all or part of which falls before 13·30, and thereafter to continue working until, say, 17·30, there will be a breach of paragraph 7k if the termination time of his original scheduled shift, and thus the starting time of his paid extra duty, are postponed by the amount of the meal break occurring before 13·30. For the avoidance of any doubt it must be stressed that this will not be so if, in the example we have given, the meal break is all taken after 13·30, that is after the termination time of the scheduled shift. Nor will it be so in relation to that part of a meal break occurring after 13·30, though it will be so in such a case in relation to that part of the meal break occurring before that time.

9.28 We can see no reason in principle why a breach of paragraph 7k occurring in this way should be treated any differently from a breach occurring in the somewhat simpler circumstances outlined in paragraph 9.26 and, although paragraph 7k itself contains no provision for payment, the fact the payments were agreed and made prior to the introduction of paragraph 7k into the code provides ample justification for making them thereafter. On the whole matter, therefore, we recommend that payment should be made to officers working in FGS establishments for any unscheduled midday or tea meal break, or part thereof, which has occurred within the span of a scheduled duty shift where the introduction of that unscheduled meal break has arisen as a result of a breach of paragraph 7k. It should be noted that paragraph 7k refers to midday and tea meal breaks and consequently, although all of the evidence which we have received in relation to this claim has tended to concentrate on the midday break, our recommendation must extend to all of the breaks that are contemplated in paragraph 7k. Furthermore, it follows from the manner in which we have decided this claim that our recommendation must be retrospective to the date when the revised FGS Code of Instructions came into effect, that is to say 1 June 1975.

9.29 *The Liverpool Claim.* Some time after our appointment industrial action was taken by officers at Liverpool prison in support of a claim for payment for breakfast breaks taken by officers working the short day shift and we were invited by the POA to examine this claim. We made it clear that we could do so only if the claim, upon examination, was shown to involve issues of general principle and application, and that we were not prepared to set ourselves up as arbiters to make decisions upon any disputed issues applicable only to a single establishment. We have been supplied with a substantial amount of information relative to this claim by both the POA and the Home Office and, having examined that evidence, have come to the clear conclusion that no issue of general principle is involved. The issue therefore is one applicable only to Liverpool, namely whether the officers in question have a scheduled starting time of 7·45 am or 7·00am, and therefore we are unable to make any recommendation.

Northern Ireland

9.30 During 1978 there was a number of disputed claims for payment of continuous duty credits put forward by officers serving in Northern Ireland. Since the attendance systems in Northern Ireland are different from those

231

obtaining in England and Wales, the claims put forward were themselves different in character and detail from those now put before us by the POA, and involved different issues of principle. We have been told that all outstanding claims in Northern Ireland have been settled by agreement between the Northern Ireland Office and the Northern Ireland branch of the POA, with the result that there are now no further issues to be resolved there on these matters. We are glad to hear of this and commend the parties concerned for having achieved this result.

Scotland

9.31 In Scotland the attendance systems are different from those operating in England and Wales, and no claims have been put forward by the Scottish POA for payment of any continuous duty credits in respect of meal breaks.

CHAPTER TEN

INDUSTRIAL RELATIONS

Background

10.1 As Chapter 2 has shown, strained relations between staff and management in the prison service are by no means a new phenomenon. From early in the history of the nationalised prison service there were signs, albeit only occasionally gaining expression, of a divergence of interests between managed and managers. There is nothing new in prison staff feeling that those in command of the prison service are more concerned with inmates than with them, or being anxious about pay, allowances and conditions of service. It is, moreover, as we have commented in Chapter 5, a mistake to look back nostalgically to the earlier days of the Prison Commission, and to imagine that in that different organisation, everything was much better than it subsequently became. In fact, the 1950s were an unhappy period for industrial relations in the prison service, a marked contrast to the much happier situation of the 1960s and early 1970s.

10.2 Yet in the last few years industrial action had occurred of a type, and on a scale, never previously witnessed. The first signs of this new trend came in 1973, in the aftermath of a wave of instances of inmate unrest which had occurred the previous year. Although most of the latter were peaceful, violence did occur in a number of establishments in the autumn of 1972, including serious riots at Albany and Gartree. The concern which these incidents themselves caused to staff, and the resulting public interest in issues of prisoners' rights, fuelled the belief that the public were not interested in the dangers and difficulties which officers faced. The reaction of the POA to the Gartree riot was to threaten a national strike unless levels of staff there were increased; later in 1973 the Association instructed all branches, for the period of one month, to work no more overtime than that required under their national agreement with management (then 14 hours per week). This action led to what was to become a familiar pattern of difficulty over the meeting of obligations to the courts and the maintenance of inmate regimes.

10.3 The 1973 concern over manning levels apart, however, the period up to 1975 remained one of relative industrial peace. During the period 1973–75 the annual average number of occasions on which branches took action was only seven, and on all occasions with the support of the National Executive Committee (NEC) of the POA. A new and significant element was introduced into the industrial relations climate in 1975, however, with the decision of the London prisons, whose claim in regard to London weighting allowance was already being dealt with at national level, to take industrial action without official support. The claim ultimately went to arbitration and was upheld. Equally significant was the action of the staff at Cardiff prison, in opposition to certain policies of local management and in support of the transfer of a principal officer, in staging an almost total withdrawal of labour for the best part of a day; this was the first instance of a withdrawal of labour since 1919. September 1975 witnessed the most decisive event of all in the decision of the NEC that "forms of action to be pursued on local issues (including sympathetic actions) are matters within the discretion of the local branches concerned". Armed with this new power, branches entered the next phase of industrial disputes in 1976. The issue was the allocation to each establishment of a "budget" of staff hours, as part of the general restriction on public expenditure in that year. Inevitably, overtime and take-home pay were reduced. How the budget was to be met was to be decided in local consultation between governors and POA branches, and disputes took place at a number of establishments, affecting both services to the courts and inmate regimes. There were some instances of staff withdrawing to the prison gate for brief periods, leaving either only a few officers on duty, or none at all. Although the full rigours of budgetary control were eased the following year, disputes over this issue continued. The NEC, which had originally acknowledged that the prison service could not be exempt from expenditure restraint, nevertheless adopted a formal stance of non-co-operation in manpower controls, instructing branches not to supply information on the use of staff to local management; this has continued until very recently.

10.4 By 1977 disputes were arising over a variety of local issues: for example, over quarters at Dartmoor, weekend working and safe manning levels at Bedford and, in August, over ferry warrants to the mainland for staff at the Isle of Wight prisons. The latter issue continued as far as Albany and Camp Hill were concerned until the 1978 civil service pay settlement, which set the ILA to include the cost of three return car ferry warrants per year; Parkhurst, however, continued industrial action in support of a separate Isle of Wight allowance until after the setting up of the present Inquiry. By the end of May 1978, 26 instances of action by branches had occurred. But during the early part of 1978 a large number of claims had been lodged by individual branches for retrospective CDC payments, as we have described in Chapter 9. Following the POA Conference in May, a vigorous campaign took place, involving widespread industrial action, to secure payments. We described in Chapter 9 the origins of the CDC claim and the basis upon which settlements were made, following a meeting with the Home Office in July 1978, and how it was that local negotiations were still necessary to determine the actual amount payable. Discontent continued because of the local variations which were thus possible and over delays in settlement. At the same time, fresh trouble was brewing over CDC, since a claim had been officially lodged in May for further payments for lunch breaks; a considerable number of branches supported this with individual claims for payment for certain lunch and tea breaks. Matters reached a head in October when an official conference of representatives of some 30 POA branches was held at Pentonville, which resolved upon industrial action from 5 November in support of the meal break claim. It was in the immediate context of that threat that the present Inquiry was established.

10.5 Although resort to industrial action was less in Scotland than in England in the period before the establishment of this Inquiry, there have been signs there, too, of a move away from the earlier belief that industrial action was inconsistent with the demands of a disciplined service. On three occasions, in this period, Scottish officers took industrial action. The first of these was as early as 1972 at the Longriggend remand institution, over alleged delays in the provision of a staff club. Industrial action continued for some six weeks, but except for the first day or two, when there was delay in delivering inmates to court, the work of the Institution was not seriously disrupted. A dispute also occurred the following year at Barlinnie over the allocation of basic staff houses to members of the governor grades, which resulted in a work-to-rule from mid-June until the end of the month. Finally, there was the dispute which spanned the setting up of this Inquiry over the use of the segregation unit at Inverness prison. The use of this unit which began in 1966, was discontinued in 1972 in the face of criticism, mainly from outside the service. It continued to be regarded as available for use, however, and following further publicity in 1978, the SPOA threatened a national work-to-rule unless it were put back into active use. Ministerial assurances that the unit would be used when occasion required, removed the national threat but unofficial action was taken by staff at eight establishments, involving working to rule and a ban on overtime for lengths of time ranging up to three weeks. A delegate conference in January 1979 resolved to suspend action over this issue indefinitely.

10.6 In Northern Ireland the situation has been different again. As Chapter 3 indicates, the prison service there has grown very considerably over less than a decade, and there was no history of industrial trouble among the 300 or so staff employed until the late 1960s. As expansion has taken place, and terrorist incidents, including those directed at prison staff themselves, have increased, there has been a natural growth in concern over working conditions and personal security. The practice has developed of placing a temporary ban on visits, letters and parcels following the assassination of fellow prison officers, but staff have argued that this should be seen as a mark of respect, rather than as industrial action as such. The only specific instances of industrial action have been in support of a claim for an increase in the daily emergency allowance.

10.7 The establishment of this Inquiry, although generally defusing unrest over CDC, has not seen the end of industrial action. In the six months between our being set up and the end of May 1979 industrial action took place on some 31 occasions at 25 different establishments, in addition to the general civil service industrial action over pay which took place in April and which affected regimes at 105 establishments. Action has sometimes continued for only a few days (or even a single day) but on occasions has continued for several months. Some causes of dispute have been purely internal, such as complaints over quarters or objections to particular appointments (especially in regard to civilian staff) or have related to particular cases brought under the discipline code. Some have been protests at the general conditions of an establishment, such as overcrowding or manning levels. Others have related more broadly to conditions of service, such as allowances or the financial provision made for officers injured in the course of escort duties. There have also been two instances during this period of action by members of the non-civil service unions about the civilian craft allowance. In the Scottish service, instances of unrest have occurred more frequently than in the period before we were set up. In Northern Ireland there have, regrettably, been a number of instances of fatal attacks upon prison staff which has led to sympathy action within establishments. The picture in each of the countries suggests that if action on this scale can be contemplated while an independent Inquiry is sitting (which at least provides an argument for postponing action until staff have seen the extent to which its conclusions are likely to meet their particular grievances), then strenuous efforts will be needed to improve the general climate of relations. It is with that issue that the main part of this chapter will be concerned.

10.8 As the preceding description has shown, the forms of industrial action adopted, as well as the reasons for it, have varied considerably. Basically, so far as England and Wales are concerned, action has been of three types. First, action directed at the administration of justice: officers have refused to allow solicitors, police officers or probation officers into establishments to visit inmates; they have prevented the production of inmates at court (resulting, for example, in inmates remaining in custody beyond the remand period set by the court); and they have refused to receive into custody those committed by the courts. The latter has been a growing feature of branch action, especially since the time of the CDC dispute, and when co-ordinated between branches— so that branches not directly involved refuse to accept inmates diverted from the branch in dispute—can have a dramatic and cumulative effect upon the whole operation of the criminal justice system, since the alternative of remanding to police custody must necessarily be a limited expedient. The second type of action relates to prison administration itself: this has included late unlocking; restrictions on the movement of vehicles, staff and supplies; the 'blacking' of particular areas of the establishment or functions within it; and, at the extreme, 'going to the gate'—in other words, temporarily withdrawing labour. Thirdly, there has been action which has directly affected inmates. This has ranged from the complete prevention of classes, exercise, visits or association, and, on occasions, the complete locking up of inmates for 23 hours a day, to minor limitations on regimes, such as stopping the issue of newspapers. Thus, inmates' statutory entitlements, as well as various of the minimum standards prescribed by the United Nations and the Council of Europe Standard Minimum Rules, have been denied.

10.9 It will be seen that the range of action open to prison staff, without the need to resort to the final expedient of all-out strike action, is wide, although not unlimited. Branches have been careful, for example, except in the most extreme cases, to avoid action which would adversely affect the level of overtime and thus take-home pay. Prison officers, moreover, live in close daily contact with inmates and are the first to bear the brunt of any resentment which their action may provoke; if suffering is caused to inmates as the result of industrial action, it is still prison officers who will have the job eventually of re-establishing a working relationship. At the same time, officers are not unaware of general public concern over prison security, and of the damage that would be done to their popular standing if major breaches of security were to result from their actions.

10.10 It is important to note the role of the National Executives of both the POA and the SPOA in these events. The English POA, as we have mentioned, decided in 1975 to devolve to its branches the decision to take industrial action on local issues, but no similar delegation has taken place in Scotland—although it is clear that on a number of occasions the threat of industrial action in Scotland has originated from the branches. The much smaller scale of the Northern Ireland service makes direct comparisons in this area difficult, although it is clear that here too pressures have largely originated from establishment level. More significant even than the fact of industrial action itself, therefore, is this new situation in which the impetus for action has moved in all three countries to branch level, with the elected and paid representatives of the union left attempting to reassert their influence over the course of events. Although it is not for us in this Inquiry to comment upon how the internal affairs of a trade union should be managed, we observe that this development marked a new stage in the changing industrial relations climate of the prison service and the effectiveness of management in responding to it: although we believe the managements of the three services have been scrupulous in dealing with unions only at national level, the new situation (not, of course, peculiar to the prison service) is that there can now be no automatic assumption that agreements reached at national level will be honoured down the line. As our later comments will show, we believe that a strong national executive is not only essential for the future well-being of the prison service but is in the best interests of the staff themselves.

10.11 This is not, however, to imply that national officials have stood idle while authority has passed to the branches. The NEC in England, for example, has made a determined attempt to influence the nature and effects of industrial action through the consultative document on the forms of action which are, or are not, acceptable, which was published in August 1977 and endorsed by the POA conference in the following year. This states that it is contrary to union policy to take action affecting the courts and the rights of inmates to receive legal visits; it also provides that, except in those circumstances, industrial action is a legitimate device when all consultative avenues have failed, and subject to a 'stand-still' period of 10 days. This document was apparently intended as the basis for negotiations with the Home Office, but we understand that although preliminary discussions did take place, further negotiations have been suspended pending the recommendations of the present Inquiry. We gather that on several recent occasions the POA have clearly reaffirmed, in discussions with the Home Office, the views contained in that document on unacceptable forms of industrial action.

10.12 The POA also reiterated to us in oral evidence their belief that industrial action should not interfere with the workings of the courts, pointing out that their policy of crossing picket lines at courts during recent civil service industrial action, indicated their sincerity over this issue. In regard to inmate rights, their position, stated equally firmly to us in oral evidence, is that they remain committed to the basic rights outlined in the Prison Rules and in the Standard Minimum Rules of the United Nations and Council of Europe, but they acknowledge that although their quarrel is never with inmates, inmates are bound to be affected in some degree. The POA stressed to us that staff shortages resulting from a variety of factors (of which industrial action is only one) may lead to the curtailment of inmate regimes, and they argued that, for example, visits had only ever been prevented as an *indirect* result of industrial action. We are encouraged by such statements for we believe that prisoners are among the most defenceless of any group within society affected by industrial action, and whatever the offences that have brought them into prison, the conditions in which their sentences are served should not be made worse as a result of disputes to which they themselves are not a party. Nevertheless, we are aware, from the industrial action that has taken place during our deliberations as well as prior to them, that

237

regimes have been disrupted, inmates have consequently suffered very considerably, and the already grim conditions of certain of the grossly overcrowded local prisons have been made even worse. A major feature of the improved industrial relations climate to which we hope that all sides in the prison service will work, must include not only clear guidelines on acceptable action, but a preparedness on the part of staff to honour them. In this context, we note that the SPOA has not thought it appropriate to offer general guidelines, but that it has offered *ad hoc* advice in the event of industrial disputes; Scottish action has in the main managed to avoid affecting inmates. We note also that the type of action in Northern Ireland, following the killing of a member of the prison service, may have a considerable effect upon inmate regimes, and we were pleased to hear that the decision has now been taken that in the event of further tragic events of this kind, action will be taken over only one day, rather than three. We believe indeed that there are more appropriate ways of demonstrating respect than through such action.

The reasons for current industrial unrest

10.13 Difficult though it is to offer precise or confident diagnoses of the current state of industrial unrest in the prison service, it is important to consider what the factors may have been which have led to this situation. It goes almost without saying that there is no one cause for these developments, but the following are the various factors which have either suggested themselves to us, or have been suggested by others. In the first place, there have been substantial changes in recent years, both in the nature of the job which prison officers are called upon to do and in beliefs about the objectives of the system generally. Previous chapters have referred to the undermining of earlier and confident beliefs in the ability of the system to reform those subjected to it, and the fact that as yet no alternative consensus has emerged over what other positive functions prisons might attempt. This has inevitably meant a period of heart-searching and uncertainty for all within the prison service. At the same time, so it has been represented to us in different ways by both the POA and the governors, the job of prison officers has become more mundane as a result of the increasing introduction of specialist staff into penal establishments and the growing emphasis upon security which has permeated the system since the time of the Mountbatten Report. The way in which the attendance systems have been operated, it has been further suggested, has undermined continuity of contact between individual officers and specific groups of inmates, and this too, has diminished job satisfaction. Being denied intrinsic job satisfaction, the POA argued in oral evidence, officers have been forced to seek compensatory satisfaction in monetary rewards.

10.14 Related to this has been the changing nature of the prison population referred to in Chapter 3. Increasing numbers of difficult and litigious prisoners are now held in prison, leading, it has been alleged, to a further withdrawal of staff from direct inmate contact. Growing feelings of insecurity have inevitably resulted, feelings which have not been helped by the belief that inmates rather than staff have the first call upon management concern and resources. Although, as we have shown, such feelings have existed since at least as early as the Gladstone Committee, this does not minimise the strength with which they are held, nor their contribution to strained industrial relations.

10.15 The increase in inmate numbers has also exacerbated already cramped conditions for staff, and we have seen for ourselves the difficult and unsuitable circumstances in which many work, often without the standard of recreational and canteen facilities enjoyed in other occupations. However soundly-based the civil service rules governing the provision of such facilities (and the department's interpretation of those rules), these factors have further convinced prison officers that management lacks any real interest in them as people and is unconcerned with the betterment of their working environment. We note with interest the suggestion by the Scottish Home and Health Department that one of the reasons why, at least prior to the establishment of this Inquiry, there was less industrial action in Scotland was that the Scottish service has been generally able to do more in regard to the improvement of staff conditions. It is clear that an essential feature of good industrial relations in the prison service is that not only should management be as concerned for staff as inmates, but that it should be seen to be so.

10.16 Two other of the more recent changes in the situation within the service are also significant. The first is that the background and experience of prison officers has also undergone decisive changes. Staff numbers have increased considerably (prison officer numbers in England and Wales, for example, have nearly doubled since 1965), which has meant that the proportion of experienced to comparatively inexperienced staff has significantly declined. So also has the proportion of staff with a service background, although the importance of this as a factor in changed attitudes needs to be considered with caution: we have met some staff recently joined from the services, who have complained that the prison service is less "disciplined" than they had hoped or expected when deciding to enter; on the other hand, we have heard the view in at least one establishment that it was the older ex-service officers who were the more "militant". More immediately, prison staff have not escaped the economic constraints which have affected the country in the last few years. A major cause of concern for prison officers, as the analysis of industrial action has shown, was the introduction in 1976 of the budget of hours, and the serious threat this posed to overtime earnings. Prison officers were made to realise the vulnerability of their relatively comfortable standard of living, depending as it did upon substantial overtime. At the same time, successive rounds of incomes policy prevented the operation of civil service pay research, and thus denied officers the benefit they had previously derived from the Wynn-Parry formula. It may be significant that the introduction of the Wynn-Parry arrangement brought to an end the succession of pay disputes that had immediately preceded it, and that the suspension of that arrangement should have preceded a new wave of industrial unrest.

10.17 Outside the service major changes have also gone on. Recent years have witnessed (or have appeared to witness) a significant shift in the industrial relations climate, in which larger than ever numbers of workers have become unionised and in which unions, both at national and shop floor level, appear to have become tougher in their approach to bargaining. We say "appear" because it is not for us to say whether these supposed changes are real or result more from changes in the political climate and in the reporting policies of the press. What matters is that such beliefs are at large and that they will not have escaped the notice of prison officers. But while external events have demonstrated the rewards of industrial action, officers have remained, as we have commented earlier (Chapter 8), an essentially isolated group. One effect of this is that staff have few yardsticks with which to compare their own pay and conditions of service, and are often insufficiently aware of the substantial additional financial benefits which they enjoy through, for example, the provision of free housing. Given this degree of isolation, and the constant message that industrial action pays substantial dividends, it is perhaps not surprising that officers should have become convinced of the inferiority of their own position and of the fact that only strenuous action can alleviate it. Part of the onus for this situation must be laid at the door of management for its failure properly to keep staff informed on these issues but it is pertinent to note here that despite not infrequent complaints to us by staff of their ignorance of their conditions of service, pension arrangements etc, considerable efforts are made to ensure that new entrants are properly aware of the position and that they know to whom to go for further information and advice throughout their careers. Further steps are obviously needed to keep staff informed of their true relative position, as well as aware of any changes in conditions of service as they occur.

10.18 A further set of factors contributing to the present industrial relations climate is to be found, it has been suggested to us, in the approach and policies of management. We heard many complaints about the position of the prison service as a department of the Home Office, and many maintained that it is this change which lies at the root of all present problems. For reasons discussed elsewhere in this report, we believe that this view, at least crudely stated, depends more upon nostalgia than any objective recollection of the state of industrial relations prior to the dissolution of the Prison Commission, but this is not to say that organisationally all is well. The fact that the Director General of the prison service, particularly in the present industrial climate, has no direct responsibility for personnel matters, is clearly not a desirable situation, and it is also the case that a separate establishment division outside the Prison Department, may contribute, in certain circumstances, to the delay in responding to issues raised by staff to which our attention has so frequently been drawn. More specific criticisms have also been levelled against the management of the Home Office. The POA accuses the Home Office of taking cognisance of industrial relations difficulties only when confrontation actually occurs, and not being able or willing to anticipate trouble and to attempt to head it off. Management is accused of being uncertain in its approach once trouble has actually started, and of leaving it to the POA to take the initiative in seeking a settlement.

10.19 The governors are also critical of the policies which management has pursued in the face of industrial troubles. They contend that they have felt isolated in the face of trouble and bereft of the support from headquarters which they regarded as their due—they complain, in particular that they have been told not to have resort to the Code of Discipline (a point to which we return later). More broadly, they claim to receive inadequate support from headquarters in disciplinary cases, and that recommendations for dismissal are not acted upon. Governors, it is said, have not been told squarely whether they should regard themselves as operating within a disciplined, military-type environment, or in a normal industrial relations situation.

10.20 Various witnesses have also suggested that it is also possible that regardless of the good intentions of those on all sides in the prison service, the machinery itself through which industrial relations are conducted, is inadequate for the demands now being placed upon it. The Home Office, in its official evidence, has acknowledged in general terms that the management task has become increasingly complex, and thus potentially more remote, at a time when as in other areas of national life, staff are demanding increased involvement. Members of the Prison Department Directorate of Psychological Services have suggested that the problem in the prison service is the assumption which underlies the Whitley Council procedure that national negotiating bodies represent their membership and can give undertakings on their behalf. This, they argue, may no longer be the case, which implies that the machinery itself is no longer adequate. More specifically still, a former regional director contended that exchanges at the Prison Department Whitley Council have become formal and stylised, with no honest exchange of views taking place. We shall return to the question of the Whitley Council arrangements, and specifically to the constitution of the Prison Department Whitley Council, later in this chapter.

10.21 There is a further point that we have heard in various guises from prison officers, governors and the Department itself. This is that for whatever reason industrial action has been found to produce results, and that the practice of resorting to such action has developed a momentum of its own. The POA argued that it had been the experience of branches that industrial action produced a response that had not previously been forthcoming, which meant that they would be the more ready to resort to such measures the next time an issue arose. What staff have found, in the opinion of one particular member of the governor grade who submitted written evidence to us, is that not only does action bring results, but that, so far, it has not had any adverse side-effects for the officers concerned; in support of this contention he quoted instances of trades officers having refused work but still being paid at normal rates, and officers called in at overtime rates for escort duty, who had refused the duty but had still been paid although there was no internal task for them to do. The dispute over CDC seems to us to have been not only an outstanding example of action reaping rewards, but the inaugurator of a new phase in industrial relations in the English service. Staff became convinced of a moral entitlement to substantial sums of money which the Home Office, in the event, appeared only to have been prepared to pay in the face of a major threat to the service itself and the administration of justice. The outcome was the conviction, first, that the Home Office was obstructive but fundamentally weak, and secondly, that the National Executive of the POA was incapable of securing the best interests of its members, who must themselves be prepared to take the initiative. It is that twin loss of respect which forms the starting point for the present Inquiry.

The importance of good industrial relations

10.22 The previous paragraphs have described the present features of industrial relations in the prison service and have suggested various factors which may have contributed to this situation. We do not think that any of these is paramount, nor do we believe that any of the parties bears sole responsibility for what has happened. That something has gone wrong with relations between

241

staff and local and central management is undeniable—evidence of distrust, alienation and suspicion occurred too frequently for the reality of that to be seriously in doubt—but for such a situation all must bear some degree of blame. Something must be wrong, for example, with the management style and approach (and approachability) of headquarters, for failing to convince staff that their interests really do matter and to take them fully into account. Local management, too, has an important role to play. Governors must, we believe, accept a positive responsibility for the improvement of day-to-day relations within their establishments, and not assume that it is wholly up to headquarters to tell them how to respond—an approach that we have sometimes detected in what governors have said to us. Finally, it is up to staff, while remaining rightly concerned with their conditions of employment and any legitimate grievances that arise, to recognise (as they have not always done in the past) that there are limitations on management's ability to make concessions in certain major areas, and that there is a need to make full use of negotiating channels before resorting to industrial action. This, we believe, is first and foremost in the interests of prison officers themselves. Whatever immediate advantages may have been won by resort to industrial action, we cannot believe that a situation of continuing industrial relations conflict can be satisfying as a working environment for any but a small handful of those involved. For the job to be truly satisfying, both the symptoms and causes of industrial unrest must be removed. This is even more the case when one considers members of other unions working in prisons such as administrative and clerical staff, civilian workmen and the various specialists. Although we have made little reference to these other groups so far in this chapter (chiefly because they have not been involved in any widespread industrial action), we are aware that their position is often affected to a considerable extent by the action of prison officers. Finally, good industrial relations are essential to enable the Service to discharge its responsibilities both *to* inmates and *for* them. Continuing conflict will mean not only the denial of inmates' basic statutory rights but that the time and effort of senior management will be taken up with these issues to the exclusion of matters more directly concerned with the objectives of the service. It means also the under-utilisation in varying degrees of the substantial resources committed to the prison service. In short, we seek a service properly recompensed and recognised for the important job it does, in which staff have a meaningful and rewarding task to undertake and do it in reasonable surroundings, and in which proper consultation takes place on every issue of concern to staff. It means also having proper procedures for the airing of and settlement of grievances whenever they do occur.

The current machinery for handling industrial relations

10.23 Having thus described both the current state of industrial relations, and the ideal to which we would aim, some description is needed of the current machinery for consultation and negotiation. Prison staff, like all other civil servants, are part of a negotiating and consultative structure comprising Whitley Councils and Committees. The basic principles of Whitleyism, which were adopted in the Civil Service in 1919, are that there should be councils in each industry on which employers and workers are represented, to enable decisions to be reached by agreement between the two sides. As applied to the civil service, the Whitley structure operates at national level (that is, across the whole civil service), departmental level and, where appropriate, at local level (for example, in a penal establishment, an ordinance factory or a social security office). At each level there is an Official Side, representative of management, and a Staff Side, representative of union interests. At national level there is a National Whitley Council for non-industrial staff, comprising Official Side members (mainly Permanent Secretaries of the major Departments), and Staff Side members (mainly the General Secretaries of the major non-industrial trade unions, including the POA). For industrial staff at national level there is a joint Co-ordinating Committee for Government Industrial Establishments. The membership of this Committee includes senior officials of the Civil Service Department, the Department of Employment, the Ministry of Defence and the Department of the Environment; the Staff Side is made up of national officers of the appropriate industrial trade unions.

10.24 At departmental level in the Home Office there are three Whitley Councils to cover the interests of all staff working in the prison service. The Prison Department Whitley Council itself has a Staff Side composed exclusively of the NEC of the POA. The Director General of the prison service is the Chairman of the Council, with the chairman of the POA as Vice-Chairman. The Official Side membership includes the other members of the Prisons Board and senior officers of the Establishment Department. The Council meets twice a year on agenda suggested chiefly by the POA, often on the basis of motions which have been discussed at their Annual Conference. The Council has two standing sub-committees, on uniforms and quarters, and there exist two joint working parties, established under its auspices, on the Role of the Prison Officer and on Prison Officers' Hours of Duty. The interests of all other non-industrial staff in the prison service are covered by the Home Office Whitley Council chaired by the Permanent Under-Secretary of State, with the chairman of the Home Office Staff Side as Vice Chairman. The members of the Staff Side include representatives of the unions (except the POA) representing non-industrial civil servants within the Home Office, including the prison service. The Council normally meets once a year, on a formal basis, when it takes note of the decisions and actions of the year. There are three standing sub-committees, on Training, Staff Suggestions and Personnel Management. Finally, for industrial staff employed throughout the Home Office, including the Prison Service, there is the Departmental Joint Industrial Council. This is chaired by an assistant secretary in the Establishment Department, the Vice-Chairman being the chairman of the trade union side. Members of the latter include national officers of the appropriate industrial trade unions. The Council meets twice a year and conducts its business broadly on the same lines as the Prison Department Whitley Council.

10.25 Below the departmental level, there exist in a number of prison establishments local Whitley committees, with the governor as chairman. These discuss matters affecting the local working conditions of staff, such as accommodation, welfare, overtime attendance and leave arrangements. At some establishments there are separate committees for non-industrial and industrial staff; in others there is simply a joint committee.

10.26 The level at which business takes place, and the procedure which applies, depend upon the nature of the subject under review. For non-industrial civil servants, agreements on pay and conditions of service are made at national level, between the Civil Service Department and either the National Staff Side or the union(s) concerned. In this regard, the position of departmental grades, that is, those grades peculiar to only one department, has come into line with that of other civil servants since 1972: prior to that it had been the department itself, subject to strict guidelines and continuing surveillance by the Civil Service Department, which conducted negotiations with its union. The rationale for this change was that it would avoid duplication of effort and enable unions to have direct access to those with whom decisions rested. Among the issues classified as "conditions of service", negotiated nationally and applying to the generality of civil servants (including prison officers), are leave entitlements; payment for overtime; weekend and public holiday working; shift disturbance and night duty allowance; travel and subsistence; transfer terms; superannuation; compensation for loss of personal property; disciplinary matters; and such questions of civil service practice and propriety as the rules governing parliamentary candidature. The application in departments of national agreements is decided at either departmental or local level. For example, within the framework of a grade's nationally-negotiated conditioned hours, the arrangement of the working week or the need for overtime, can only be determined by departmental or local management in the light of work requirements. Such discusssions, however, remain subject to the terms of the national relevant agreement, which cannot be varied departmentally without specific authority from the Civil Service Department.

10.27 As well as three levels for the conduct of business between management and unions, three broad types of business can be identified: consultation, negotiation on arbitrable matters, and negotiation on other matters. The definitions are not watertight, however, nor perhaps universally recognised—a possible further reason for some of the recent troubles in the prison service. Consultation relates to those matters on which management will attempt to gain the consent of staff and to take account of their views, but over which it regards itself as being free to take the final decision. This right, it has been argued to us, is particularly important in an operational service like the prison service, where those in charge must be able to take decisions and act on them, often at short notice. The Whitley machinery at all three levels may be used for consultative purposes. Arbitrable matters are defined by the Civil Service Arbitration Agreement: broadly, these are matters of pay and pay-related conditions of service; manpower matters are not negotiable. Negotiation on such matters take place between the Civil Service Department and a union or consortium of unions. If there is a dispute the union(s) can go unilaterally to the Civil Service Arbitration Tribunal unless the government feels that there are overriding reasons of policy why it cannot permit a third party to intervene. Negotiations on non-arbitrable matters cover two areas: national or departmental procedural agreements, and local or departmental negotiations on the interpretation of agreements on such matters as allocation of overtime or local attendance arrangements. If there is a disagreement the issue can be referred up for advice; if there is no higher level it is open for renegotiation or, finally, management may take administrative action and the union may consider some form of industrial action.

10.28 It has recently been agreed within the National Whitley Council that in view of the substantial changes that have taken place latterly, both in attitudes to industrial relations and in industrial relations legislation, the time has come for a general review both of the Whitley system and of the way it is used. This review will be conducted at the departmental level, and be concerned with such questions as the effectiveness and representativeness of the current Whitley strucure. Departmental councils will also be encouraged to consider issuing guidelines to local Whitleys to encourage them into more wide-ranging subjects than tend normally to be considered, possible issues being the allocation of local resources; organisational proposals; all aspects of the immediate work environment; and those parts of the employment relationship which are not subject to determination elsewhere, such as arrangements for flexible working hours and the distribution of overtime. It has been emphasised to us that these reviews need not inhibit any proposals we might make in regard to the Whitley organisation within the Home Office.

10.29 The previous paragraphs have described the current Whitley arrangements as they apply in England and Wales. The principles which they describe are the same in Scotland and Northern Ireland, but the structures differ in some respects. The common feature, as far as Scotland is concerned, is that the only staff association represented on the Scottish Prison Service Whitley Council is the SPOA. The historical reasons for this are plainer in Scotland than in England, since until comparatively recently the SPOA enjoyed a virtual monopoly of staff representation in the service; the governors tended to see themselves as part of management, the Governors' Committee which represented them acting as a consultative body rather than a staff organisation. The position has changed since the mid 1960s with the gradual introduction of civilian instructors and professional and technical officer grades and the assimilation into the Administration Group, and membership of the Society of Civil and Public Servants, of the prison stewards who had formerly been members of the SPOA. These other grades are represented on the Scottish Office Whitley Council, but have been pressing, over the last few years, for admission to the Prison Service Whitley Council. We understand that despite some hesitation on the part of both the SPOA and the Scottish Office Staff Side, an arrangement was reached for the admission of other prison service grades to the Prison Service Whitley, in return for admission of the SPOA to the Scottish Office Whitley Council. Regrettably, the break-up of the Scottish Office Staff Side, which occurred during our deliberations as a result of the disagreements between the various unions during the negotiation of the 1979 civil service pay settlement, means that there is temporarily no Scottish Office Whitley for the SPOA to join. Not unnaturally, the latter has declined to offer hospitality until such time as this can be reciprocated.

10.30 In Northern Ireland there is no departmental Whitley machinery. The POA (a branch of the national POA, rather than a separate body as in Scotland) has a seat on the Staff Side of the Northern Ireland Central Whitley Council, although matters affecting prison officers are normally resolved departmentally, that is as a result of direct discussions with the prison divisions of the Northern Ireland Office. The governor grades form a sub-branch of a branch of the Civil Service Professional Officers' Association, itself a constituent body of the Northern Ireland Public Service Alliance; other non-industrial staff in prisons are represented directly by the Northern Ireland Public Service Alliance. Most industrial staff are members of the Northern Ireland Civil Service Association. Both the Alliance and the Association are represented on the Staff Side of the Northern Ireland Central Whitley Council. We understand that an attempt is currently being made by the Northern Ireland Public Service Alliance to persuade the Northern Ireland Office to creat a departmental Whitley Council.

10.31 It should be noted that the pay of prison officers in all three services is negotiated centrally by the POA, the Home Office and the Civil Service Department, the first two consulting as necessary with their opposite numbers in Scotland and Northern Ireland, on whose behalf they act.

Improving the climate of industrial relations

10.32 In what follows, we suggest various changes which we believe will contribute to an improved industrial relations climate in the prison service. What is important is to tackle the causes and not just the symptoms of industrial unrest. We do not believe, however, that either together or separately, these proposals will have the desired effect, unless the right frame of mind is also present. Industrial relations are not a complex or esoteric science, but they do depend upon good management practices and attitudes on the one side, and an appropriate spirit of understanding and co-operation on the other. Without a commitment on both sides to improving the operation of the prison service (one effect of which, if genuine, will be improved industrial relations), nothing we recommend in terms of organisation or procedural agreements will have any effect. All that our proposals can do is to create a framework for a new approach. Thus, transferring the establishments function to the Prison Department will not of itself be a panacea—the staff currently employed in that division of the Home Office appeared to us to be no less involved in, and informed about, prison issues than their colleagues in the Prison Department—but it will provide the setting necessary for senior prison management to demonstrate to the service the care and concern which we believe to be essential. What we seek is the process of persuading prison staff away from the cast of mind into which they appear to be settling, whereby resort to industrial action is seen as the immediate response to any problem, and a determination on the part of management to ensure both that the industrial relations climate will improve and to convince staff that things will get better. One further point needs to be made right at the outset. It is important, in considering the state of industrial relations in the prison service, not to ignore the substantial harmony and sense of duty that does still exist. We have all, particularly those of us with experience of industry, been impressed by the response of staff, in the course of industrial disputes, to the declaration by the governor of a state of emergency. When, in the opinion of the governor, the establishment has reached a serious state of crisis, staff have not hesitated to resume their normal duties. Nothing must be allowed to jeopardise the underlying loyalty which that implies.

The importance of resolving conflicts locally, wherever possible

10.33 As we have indicated, complaints about the remoteness of central management and the length of time taken to produce replies, have figured frequently in both the official evidence put to us by the associations and in conversations with staff in establishments. In taking note of these views, we had of course to remind ourselves that belief in management as remote and uncaring is not unusual in a large organisation. Equally, we recognised that some complaints derive from the fact, not that management is slow or remote, but that it has on occasions to say no. Nevertheless, the Home Office itself acknowledges that the long lines of communication and limited resources which characterise the present situation, can cause delay and accentuate the impression of remoteness. Under present arrangements a staffing matter referred through the official chain may, depending on the issue in question, go through governor, to region, to P6 Division of the Prison Department and then to the Establishment Department (who, if appropriate, consult with the union concerned). We note that in Scotland and Northern Ireland, the smaller size of the prison services, the absence of regions and the lack of any split between the establishment function and prison management make these problems less severe. In Northern Ireland, for example, all matters affecting pay and conditions of service of discipline and governor grades are dealt with in a single headquarters section, and the lines of communication could not be shorter. Nevertheless, even in these two countries, prison officers' representatives had some complaints; in Northern Ireland it was over delays in implementing what they regarded as reasonable proposals emanating from their monthly area meetings, and Scottish officers resented the fact that the settlement of certain issues at national level meant that they were done in England, and thus at a further remove from Scottish influence. In the light of these comments, and bearing in mind the difficulties about the resolution of many issues at local level which we shall come on to consider, we conclude that a major element in the re-establishment of a positive industrial relations climate in the prison service must be the breaking down of barriers between managers and managed. What this means in practice is that in the industrial relations field all must seek to settle disputes at the local level so far as possible.

10.34 From this basic belief, we sought to explore with the Home Departments the extent to which they were committed to the local resolution of disputes. It became clear that although they were not resistant to the principle—the Northern Ireland Office, in particular, stated specifically their belief that "local issues should so far as possible be settled in consultation with the governor"— they had substantial practical reservations on the feasibility of this happening more widely than at present. In the first place, many of the most important issues for staff, pay and conditions of service, are ones which must be considered nationally, with no room for local negotiation. This we are bound to accept; even to return to the earlier situation of direct negotiation between the Home Office and the Civil Service Department would enable only a marginal increase in flexibility for the managers of the prison service, and do nothing for the local tier. We are clear also, that there can be no question of national agreements being interpreted by any other than those who made them originally —to determine otherwise would be a prescription for industrial anarchy. A more difficult area, however, is that of the *application* of national agreements to the local situation. In the straightforward case where the agreement provides that it is to apply in a given set of circumstances, there should be no problem about local management and staff considering together whether those circumstances apply—a situation which might occur, for example, if significant numbers of staff take advantage of the new provisions on living out of quarters, and local decisions are needed on the size of housing stock to be maintained (see Chapter 11 below). There are, however, two problems, which were drawn to our attention by the Home Office. In the first place, there may be cases where it is difficult to determine whether what is in dispute truly involves only a question of the local application of a national agreement, or goes beyond that into questions of interpretation. Such an issue can only be resolved nationally. (A good example of this is in questions over the local operation of duty systems). In the second place, even disputes which are strictly concerned with questions of local application may have to be taken, at least in part, out of the realm of local negotiation. The Department's fear is of decisions at one establishment having repercussions for other parts of the prison service or, indeed, for the civil service at large, since even a decision to apply an agreement in a particular way can lead to claims for similar treatment elsewhere. However soundly-based those claims, it may simply be beyond the overall resources of the system to concede them generally. Manning levels exemplify such difficulties. On the one hand, there must be room for taking account of and, where appropriate, acting upon local views about manning levels. On the other hand, manpower is the prison service's most important and expensive resource, and no responsible and accountable central management could contemplate delegating the power of decision entirely to the local level.

10.35 We do not doubt the sincerity of the Home Department's concern with uniformity and with avoiding pressures for equality of treatment—indeed, we had some sympathy with one Home Office official who complained that he had experienced "nothing but knock on [the term currently used to describe this phenomenon] over the last year". Yet despite this concern on the part of prison management, that is precisely the situation with which they are continually faced, coupled with strained industrial relations. We suspect, indeed, that it may be the lack of an effective local negotiating tier which has, on occasions, stimulated claims and encouraged the emergence of unofficial staff representative groups.

10.36 It is this latter reflection which convinces us, despite the difficulties, that we are right to put such emphasis upon the local dimension. In the first place, we believe that more purely "local" matters could be settled locally than actually are. Although it is not easy to decide between the claim of many governors that their freedom of action has been curtailed in recent years, and the Department's assertion that governors often do not use the powers they do possess, we think that there is scope, without any increased delegation of powers, for greater exercise of local initiative. Equally important is a style of management in establishments in which staff are regularly involved in day-to-day decision-making and in which adequate channels exist for talking out problems as they arise. We recall one establishment, in particular, where a previously poor industrial relations climate has been strikingly transformed by precisely these means. We would encourage the Home Office to remind governors of the full extent of their powers, and governors to make the fullest use of them. A resolve to consult and involve staff wherever possible is clearly also a first essential.

10.37 We considered whether we should go further and recommend the delegation of fresh responsibilities to local management, but have concluded, albeit reluctantly, that we cannot at present identify any further areas over which central management can relinquish ultimate responsibility. Nor, as the system currently operates, would there be any incentive for the responsible discharge of even a measure of increased delegation to governors—for example, there would be no reason for a governor, authorised, say, to negotiate manning levels, to imperil the harmony of his establishment by not conceding what is asked. Changes designed to improve industrial relations must in any case be made gradually. This is not to rule out the possibility, however, that fresh areas might emerge during the course of union/management negotiations. We believe, moreover, that the experiment in devolved financial responsibility which we have suggested in Chapter 5 will, if successful, lead ultimately to a situation in which governors become more responsible for, and conscious of, the broader implications of their actions. In that setting, and the new atmosphere which we believe it will create in prisons, increased delegation to the local level may be more feasible. There is, however, an important corollary to this for staff, and it applies in the present situation also. This is that if there is to be more local resolution of difficulties and more staff involvement in decision-making, (the two are linked in that disputes are less likely to arise if full and effective consultation takes place at an early stage) staff must accept the resolution of issues on their merits, within the particular situation of the establishment, and not by reference to apparently similar concessions gained elsewhere.

10.38 There are two more specific points in regard to local industrial relations practice which we would make. Some kind of joint meeting point is clearly needed at which local management can engage in a genuine process of consultation with staff, and at which the latter can negotiate corporately on matters of joint interest. Any committee or group created for this purpose would necessarily reflect the numerical dominance of the POA, but it would not preclude either the POA or other unions from discussing separately issues peculiar to their own members. Such bodies would not be essentially different from the current local Whitley Council arrangements, and we were encouraged at the extent of support for the latter's introduction in every establishment. We are aware that local Whitleys, where they exist, are not always regarded with much enthusiasm by the staff concerned; sometimes they have been greeted with high expectations but have been found subsequently to be 'talking-shops' with little effectiveness, power or influence. The scope of local Whitley Councils is necessarily limited to matters within the managerial competence of the governor and it is the limitation on his authority, actual or supposed, which has no doubt led to this disillusionment. If the new preparedness to resolve issues locally becomes a reality, the local forum will have the potential to take on increased significance. We believe it essential, in this new climate, that such points of contact should exist—whether still called Whitley Councils or given a new name—both to establish a forum for negotiation and to ensure that the interests of the minority groups working in prisons are not ignored. If there are staff in some establishments, as we have heard there are, who have been hesitant over participating in such local meetings, we would urge them most strongly to think again. We consider later in this chapter the general question of Whitley arrangements in the prison service, and the sort of procedural agreement which might govern the process of negotiation at all levels, including the local.

10.39 The second point relates to the desirability of designating someone within the establishment, below the level of the governor, responsible for personnel matters, as happens at some establishments we have visited. Such a person, who would best be an assistant or deputy governor, would have line responsibility for personnel to the governor and would act as a channel for complaints and a trouble-shooter in the event of disputes occurring. He would ensure that local agreements and practices were properly recorded, and would intervene if agreements were being broken. Under the procedure which we later suggest for the handling of disputes, such a person might appropriately take the chair at the initial domestic stage. The Governors' Branch would wish to go a stage further and create a personnel management department in all large establishments. We do not believe, however, that a 'department' as opposed to an individual, is desirable since it would imply that the management of staff is a specialist function rather than being the responsibility, as we think, of all concerned in the management of the prison service. For the same reason, we do not agree with the Governors' Branch that an objective should be to "remove much of the routine work of dealing with the staff associations from the governing governor". The whole tenor of our proposals is that the governor should become more, not less, concerned with the management of staff than he is at present. We are concerned to assist managers in the management task, not to distance them from it.

The national level

10.40 As we have indicated, there is a range of issues, often the most important so far as staff are concerned, which can only be considered nationally. No service wholly dependent upon central government funding can escape the central regulation of its financial and manpower resources. The problem of recent years has been that although this distinction between local and national issues is clearly understood by the NEC of the POA (who stressed it again to us), that understanding has become less clear at branch level. Just as we have called for a new determination to resolve locally throughout the service, so we believe that staff must accept this distinction and acknowledge that industrial action within individual establishments is inappropriate until the issue in question is taken up as union policy for negotiation through the normal channels. One element in the procedural agreement discussed below would be the clear statement of this principle.

10.41 We have considered, nevertheless, whether there might be advantage in returning to a situation in which more issues are negotiated directly between the Home Office and the POA, albeit under the close control of the Civil Service Department—in effect, to the situation in regard to pay and pay related matters, prior to 1972. The argument for such a change is that it would give to the head of the prison service (however described) a central role in negotiations on matters which most directly concern his staff. A major criticism of the present Home Office structure is that the Director General has no responsibility either for pay or personnel; a change on the lines being considered here would be the equivalent to what we recommend elsewhere in regard to the location of the Establishment Divisions. The counter argument is that as CSD has the final say, such a change would merely be adding to the bureaucracy. We have not felt qualified to make a recommendation on this issue, but the thought is offered to the Departments concerned in the context of the general approach to industrial relations which we are outlining. But what we do feel it imperative to emphasise is that prison management cannot begin to take effective control of the system unless it is kept closely involved in the settlement of issues of so much concern to its staff.

10.42 Re-emphasising the issues which are appropriately for resolution only at national level is likely to have an impact upon the national organisations of the unions concerned. As has been shown, the delegation of certain authority to branch level in 1975, and the events of subsequent years, have challenged the standing and influence of the National Executive Committee of the POA. We gather that, although there has been no similar delegation in Scotland, the situation there is not without parallels. Because we believe that strong union authority is important both for the presentation of claims and for the resolution of difficulties, we welcome any development which adds to the role and standing of the national executive. We also suggest that in the existing complex industrial relations environment of the prison service the present permanent staff of the POA and SPOA appears remarkably small—and in Northern Ireland, non-existent. We are aware of the sterling work done by the elected members of the NEC in taking responsibility for groups of establishments, but we are conscious of the strains which this must place upon serving officers and that a full-time official would inevitably be better placed in terms of contacts and information. The POA, we gather, are currently considering an increase in their full-time staff and we commend to them the thought that the cost involved may well be a small price to pay for the benefits it will bring. Whether such additional staff might be organised regionally in England and Wales to provide support on a geographical basis, will doubtless be a further issue for the POA, regardless of what we say below about a regional personnel tier.

The regional level

10.43 We also reflected whether there might be a place for an intermediate negotiating stage in the regions. The idea had the support of the Governors' Branch who argued strongly for a formal link between the staff associations and regional management, one of their suggestions being the establishment of some form of regional Whitley Council. The Home Office response was similar to our own view on the involvement of regions in casework: that there is no "regional" personnel policy as such, and that it is impossible to conceive issues which are not either local or (if questions of uniformity are raised) necessarily national. This means that if issues were raised regionally, reference would still have to be made to headquarters before any ruling could be given. Another factor was the additional staffing demands which would be made by creating a regional tier. We also gather that only the very largest government departments have introduced a regional disputes tier, and that doing so has not only slowed the resolution of issues, but tended to discourage resolution at the local level. The POA took a similar line. They too argued that there were no specifically regional issues, any issues of general application within one region being likely to apply to all regions, and they stressed also the staffing implications.

10.44 These arguments seem to us decisive. We do not, however, rule out any involvement at all by the regional offices in industrial relations issues.

We believe there must be many occasions where a local issue proves incapable of resolution, not because it is not purely local, but because the parties simply cannot agree. In such cases, we believe that the situation is not necessarily best resolved by proceeding straight to the national level, in the form of direct discussions between the union headquarters and the establishment division. Far better, we believe, would be reference to the less physically remote and more informal environment of the regional office at which, possibly under the chairmanship of the regional director, the issues could be considered afresh. The POA discounted even this role on the grounds that the governor would always have checked his position with the regional director before taking it up in negotiation, and that therefore the regional office would not be a genuine avenue of appeal. This is to misunderstand the nature of the suggestion. We envisage the regional director essentially as an "honest broker", providing comparatively neutral ground for the reconsideration by both parties of the positions they have taken up. The fact that the regional director and his staff had no formal personnel function would itself be an advantage. We believe that this would fit quite naturally into the regional directors' enhanced operational role, and need not, despite what was said to us by the Home Office and one of the present regional directors, entail the provision of additional staff to support him. We believe, indeed, that a good deal of informal resolving of disputes already goes on from the regional offices. All that we are proposing is to take this a stage further by incorporating into any procedural agreement a requirement to refer to the regional office before a local dispute is brought up nationally. The Governors' Branch invited us to go a stage further by endorsing the idea of a regional conciliation and arbitration service. There is a danger that that would over-formalise the proposal, at least initially, but we commend the idea to the Department, if experience of the increased involvement of the regions subsequently suggests something more is needed. Finally, we stress, what should be abundantly clear from what is said above, that the existence of the regional tier must never be allowed to diminish efforts to resolve at establishment level first.

A procedural agreement for the prison service

10.45 One of the features of the present system is that except in regard to the arrangements for taking arbitrable matters to the Civil Service Arbitration Tribunal, no guidelines exist for dealing with grievances and other matters which either staff or management would like to pursue. The Home Office, when we raised this issue with them, were not in principle opposed to the idea of agreements, but they were cautious about anything which might interfere with the current arbitration arrangements. Similarly, they were doubtful about procedures for handling non-negotiable matters, on the grounds, broadly, that staff would assume a final say in matters which were ultimately for management to determine. They made the point also that procedures were only of value if they were honoured, instancing some of the industrial action which has been taken since the publication of the POA's draft guidelines, often in direct opposition to the spirit of that document.

10.46 It is clear, from what both the Home Office and the POA have said, that current arrangements for handling arbitrable matters work well, and are acceptable to both sides: in regard to them a procedural agreement would simply enshrine present practices. On the other hand, we find difficult to accept the objection that procedures in regard to those issues over which management must take the final decision, would delay that final decision still further. The Home Office indicated to us the range of issues which it regards as falling within this category, and it is very wide indeed, including some which seem to us to come within the definition of "conditions of service" which we had supposed *were* negotiable matters. The problem is that whatever management's view of its own rights in such matters, staff will not be inhibited thereby from taking industrial action where they feel sufficiently strongly—action which may, incidentally, add further to the delay. We see (for example, from Dr Henry Parris's study of *Staff Relations in the Civil Service*, 1973) that conflict between the proposition that certain issues lie solely within the competence of management, and the ability of unions to challenge that assumption by industrial action, is one that has developed generally within the civil service in recent years; to ignore the fact that such issues do lead to disputes is no prescription for improved relations. We therefore conclude that a procedural agreement is essential, even in regard to issues on which, on any reckoning, management can do no more than consult staff, to ensure that each issue is properly considered, that all avenues for agreement have been explored, and that both sides will have had proper time for reflection and preparation. It goes almost without saying that a key test of determination on both sides to create a new spirit in the prison service, will be the extent to which the provisions of such an argeement are scrupulously honoured.

10.47 The details of such an agreement must be a matter for negotiation between the parties—as we gather is currently happening in Scotland between the SHHD and the SPOA—though it is our view that there should, first and foremost, be a national procedural agreement, albeit one containing provision for local variations on local domestic stages. The parties will need to consider whether purely consultative issues will require a separate procedure; the position of unions not directly involved in the dispute; the question of a conciliation stage; and the possibility of arbitration (by ACAS or some other body) on issues that are currently non-arbitrable. What is essential for inclusion, however, is a clear statement of what issues are reserved for national resolution, the nature of negotiations at establishment level, the time to be allowed for each stage, the form in which the regional office will be involved, how the headquarters organisations on each side will operate, what forms of conciliation and arbitration are appropriate (if it is decided to include them), and the nature of un-acceptable industrial action.

Industrial action: statutory protection

10.48 A question which we have been forced to examine and which has implications for the final stage of any procedural agreement, is whether prison officers should be subject to any limitations or restrictions in respect of industrial action on their part. There are two main reasons why this might be considered. One is the peculiarly helpless position of inmates to which we have already referred; the other the crucial importance to the maintenance of the criminal justice system (and thus the very fabric of society) of the prison service, in regard both to its services to the courts and its discharge of the sentence of the court. The Governors' Branch, in particular, invited us to consider this issue, pointing out additionally the effects of industrial action on them as managers and on the position of officers in their relationship with inmates. Despite these considerations, however, we could not escape the practical problems of such a development. A major problem is that of definition. Merely to ban strike action as such would, as our description of recent industrial action has shown, have had no effect at all upon the pattern of unrest. But to go further and prohibit particular actions short of an all-out strike, raises the immediate problem of deciding where lines should be drawn and the machinery needed to determine whether particular actions fall within the guidelines. Such a development, moreover, would represent a substantial change in the conditions of service of prison officers who, like most other employees, enjoy the general statutory protection from the consequences of industrial action given by the Trades Union and Labour Relations Act 1974. The price for such a change, if it could be agreed, would have to be considerable, and would raise immediately the position of other staff employed within the prison service, including those at headquarters. It is difficult to contemplate members of other unions remaining entitled to their statutory protection while prison officers were not; equally, they could not be expected to renounce their right without similar compensation. 'Buying-out' prison officers would have considerable implications for the civil service at large, and although we do not believe, in the last resort, that such considerations should be overriding, they add powerfully to the other practical difficulties. Finally, and decisively, is the problem of enforcement, since the difficulties of imposing criminal sanctions, in the event of a mass walk-out by prison officers, are too obvious to need stating. During the course of our deliberations we learned of the strike in April 1979 by New York State prison officers and of the substantial fines (under the Taylor Law of 1967) which were imposed both on individuals and the union itself before the return to work, some 16 days later. It is difficult to determine whether return to work resulted more from the penalties imposed or from the significantly improved pay contract negotiated during the course of the action. What is clear is that the State was hesitant about applying the full rigour of the law to the striking officers, and took steps to soften the effects of the financial penalties, once the action was over. This implied recognition that sanctions may have only a limited role in the resolution of industrial relations problems seems to us significant, particularly when the events are seen in the broader context of American industrial relations, in which the tradition of free collective bargaining in the public service is far less developed than it is here.

10.49 We have thus concluded that there is no scope for a change in the *status quo*, even if such a change were desirable. Even on the latter point we are uncertain, since we believe that whatever favourable terms were negotiated for the abandonment of the right, the inability to take action could, without an improvement in the general industrial relations climate, lead eventually to resentment and frustration. It is far more important to create a situation in which all within the prison service recognise the need to work at improved industrial relations, knowing the results if they do not. This is not, on the other hand, to rule out the possibility that agreements on abstention from industrial action might on occasions be written into a specific agreement such as a pay settlement, to last for the period of the agreement. It is also essential, as we have indicated, that procedural agreements should define the forms of industrial action which both sides agree to be illegitimate. We state again our conviction that actions which cause inmates suffering or delay appearances in court are, regardless of the nature of the dispute, not only unjustified but positively immoral. From all that it has said, we do not believe the POA dissents from that proposition.

10.50 In this context, we considered the legal position under both domestic legislation, and in regard to the United Kingdom's international commitments. In particular, we were concerned to know who was liable in law in the event of an inmate's statutory rights being denied. The position is that the Prison Rules confer on prisoners a range of entitlements, but that these are not legally enforceable rights, and an action against either a governor or the Department for infringement of an entitlement would probably fail, whether the failure to observe the Rules stemmed from an industrial action or not. Similarly, the Standard Minimum Rules of both the Council of Europe and the United Nations are advisory only. On the other hand, the European Convention on Human Rights does confer individual rights on prisoners and impose international obligations enforceable through the international machinery established under the Convention, even though the actions or omissions resulted from industrial action. Beyond the immediate field of the conditions in which inmates are held, it is possible that industrial action which, for example, prevented the production of prisoners in court might amount to contempt of court or even a criminal conspiracy to pervert the course of justice. Action which prevented the release of a prisoner might constitute false imprisonment. Action which, deliberately or negligently, allowed a prisoner to escape might be actionable under the common law offence of escape. The present position in regard to productions at court, is that responsibility rests with the governor, and it has been suggested to us that this obligation might be broadened by addressing warrants to 'each and every' member of staff. This would re-emphasise the shared responsibility of the whole establishment and encourage staff to think harder about the implications of this particular form of action—as well as placing them in contempt of court if the inmate is not produced. We recommend that the necessary amending legislation be introduced to bring about this change.

10.51 We have also considered the relationship between industrial action by prison officers and the Code of Discipline. The Code contains no exemptions to cover the situation of industrial action, and an officer refusing particular duties in furtherance of such action is technically in breach of the Code. The current position is that management regards the Code as binding in regard to purely disciplinary matters, but does not believe it an appropriate tool with which to respond to an industrial situation. It has rarely been employed in that context and it is the general advice of the Departments that it should not be. Staff and management are in no doubt of the bitterness that would be caused if any such attempt were made. We believe that the approach which has been worked out reflects well on the industrial good sense of the two sides, but we do not believe the position to be satisfactory in the longer term. We recommend redrafting the Code to exempt action taken in furtherance of a dispute and in accordance with the procedural agreement.

The Prison Department Whitley Council

10.52 A feature of the current staff relations structure of the English and Scottish prison services is, as indicated, that their respective prison Whitley Councils provide seats on the Staff Side only for representatives of prison officers. The reason for this is now lost in history, although the justification in Scotland, as mentioned, was, until comparatively recently, easier to sustain than in the English service. As we have indicated, links between the two departmental Whitley Councils in Scotland have been agreed and will go forward as soon as other Staff Side disagreements have been resolved. Our attention has been drawn to the English position, however, as we have been conscious on occasions of an underlying suspicion and mutual antagonism between the various groups working in prisons, which has both fuelled, and been fuelled by, recent industrial unrest. The number of other grades working in the English system is now so considerable as to call in question the validity of a Prison Department Whitley Council on which they are not represented. The Home Office argued for the inclusion of all non-industrial staff on the Prison Department Whitley Council. They are, moreover, prepared to go further and to explore the possibility of those industrial staff not covered by the joint consultative machinery being represented by the Whitley Staff Side, and whether local authority staff on secondment to prisons (as education and probation officers) might also have a part to play in the civil service consultative machinery, commensurate with their different employment status. The Department emphasised that *ad hoc* meetings with individual unions on matters of sole interest to them would not be affected by any such arrangement, and the POA would continue to enjoy the direct access to management that it has always had in the past.

10.53 The POA, when we explored the position with them, were adamant that the present arrangements should remain unchanged, instancing the value both of the regular meetings of the Council, and their informal contacts, under its auspices, with the Department. An enlarged Whitley Council, they claimed, would become bureaucratic and inhibit consideration of the sort of issues which it had in the past enabled them to consider, such as inmate/officer relations. All other groups of prison staff (except for governors) might find work in a variety of areas of government, a distinction which they claimed entitled them to a separate forum; governors were part of management and thus, in a sense, participated anyway on the Official Side.

10.54 None of these arguments seem to us to have any validity. What the POA had to say about the effectiveness of the machinery seemed oddly at variance with what they had previously told us of the poor state of industrial relations in the prison service. Nor do we accept that the presence of other associations would inhibit discussion of some of the issues of most direct concern to prison officers. The Home Office has provided us with a list of subjects discussed at recent Prison Department Whitley Council meetings which, they suggest, would have been of interest to unions other than the POA; as this includes such issues as annual leave for attendance at TUC training courses, regional office responsibility for female establishments, pay arrangements at Bank Holiday periods and consultation with staff on plans for new establishments, we conclude that significant areas of present business not only could be discussed in a broader context, but ought to be. Nor do we follow the argument that being a departmental grade of itself qualifies for separate treatment, especially when, as in the case of governors, there is a further departmental grade which is not treated in that way. To suggest, moreover, that membership of the Official Side is the same as participation on the Staff Side, seems to us to betray a considerable misunderstanding of the basis of the Whitley system. Nor do we believe that it is to advantage of the POA to remain cut off from the development of general civil service union thinking and approaches. If, on the Scottish model, the POA were to join the Home Office Staff Side, in return for Staff Side seats on the Prison Department Whitley, the POA would have access to debate on a broader range of relevant topics. The Home Office has also provided us with a list of topics from recent Home Office Whitley Council agenda, in which, it is suggested, the POA might well have had an interest. These include such matters as the control of public expenditure, open reporting, facilities for union representatives and staff welfare services. We conclude that the arguments point decisively to the establishment of a truly representative Prison Department Whitley Council on which all grades working in the prison service should be represented. With appropriate safeguards for individual unions' rights of direct access, no-one should suffer thereby. If prison officers are serious in their desire for a greater sense of unity and identity in the prison service, a unity which our organisational changes are designed to enhance, we believe they will accept the logic of not denying that unity at the central negotiating and consultative stage. We hope the Department will explore further its own suggestions in regard to industrial staff and employees of the local authorities.

Industrial relations training

10.55 We received frequent calls for improved industrial relations training. The preparedness to express dissatisfaction in overt action which so distinguishes the present situation from that which obtained even in the working memory of most of the present governing governors, means that local management cannot avoid involvement in an often highly complex industrial relations situation. We are thus heartened to discover that the Departments accept the need to instruct managers in the skills and insights that are available. There is a distinction to be made between training in the specific handling of disputes and broader management skills, but we were pleased to hear that they regard the former as only one element within the latter: what is essential in our view is skill in preventing fires—in the sense of a management approach that prevents the root causes of industrial unrest from developing—as well as extinguishing them when they do occur. A management element is currently provided in the induction course for Assistant Governors II; in the development training for administration officers; and during the post-promotion courses of senior officers, principal officers, chief officers, Assistant Governors I and Governors III. The induction course for assistant governors is long enough for this to be substantial, and although it does not yet include specific training in the handling of disputes, it does provide the foundation on which that aspect can be developed. Disputes training has now been provided for all governing governors and regional directors, and the intention is to expand such training to all holders of deputy governor posts. Inevitably, there still remain gaps to be filled and it is arguable that all the governor grades should be versed in the theory and practice of industrial relations, as early as possible in their career. (The general question of the training needed for the governor grades, and at what stage in their career, has already been considered in Chapter 7.) A specific point put to us by both the Home Office Staff Side and the Governors' Branch, was that training in this area was also needed for headquarters staff and union representatives. Certain efforts in the direction of headquarters staff training are, we gather, already made by the Central Training Branch of the Home Office (and doubtless by the equivalent bodies in Scotland and Northern Ireland) and we are aware that recruits to the administrative grades through the administration trainee scheme all receive a measure of management training as part of their general training at the Civil Service College. We have not explored the nature of the instruction thus available to headquarters staff, but we do believe that skill in these areas may prove as vital for administrators in the years to come as for local management. We welcome the Home Office's own suggestion that outside expertise may be helpful. We are pleased, also, to hear from the Home Office that prison governors are instructing staff in the use of local machinery and procedures, to the profit of both sides. The Scottish Prison Service is considering making available the facilities of their training school at Polmont to SPOA branch representatives, to enable them to sit in on seminars on how the Whitley machinery is intended to work. All of these are hopeful signs of what we would regard as the right approach to these issues, and we trust that they will be developed further.

The Code of Discipline

10.56 The POA put to us a number of detailed points in regard to the Code of Discipline and the general disciplinary system in prisons. These relate in the first instance to the procedures for adjudicating on disciplinary charges, how statements of the charge should be handled, whether fresh evidence should be admissible after the initial charge has been laid, and the form in which governors should refer more serious cases to higher authority. Other issues of concern to the POA's membership which were put to us include the present practice of requiring a written explanation of an officer's conduct, the availability to the police of statements and other documents assembled in the course of an internal investigation, and the current rules governing remuneration during suspension from duty. We took evidence at some considerable length on all these issues from the POA and from the Home and Central Departments and in doing so became increasingly aware of the complexity of the issues involved. At the end of the day, we became convinced that it was not for an outside body to prescribe the detailed changes that might be made. To do so might create a situation, albeit unwittingly, less satisfactory than that which currently obtains, or which falls short of the best arrangement that might be found—and might imply, by commenting on only certain aspects of the Code, that all is well with the rest of it. What appears to us far more desirable is that the two sides should consider together what changes might be introduced and how the Code and other disciplinary practices might be made more appropriate to current conditions. We gather that the Home Office fully accepts the need to consider revision of the Code, which has been in its present form since 1963, and that only the pressure of other business has so far prevented this from being undertaken. We were encouraged in our suggestion of a joint approach by the knowledge that the Scottish Home and Health Department and the SPOA have recently had a joint working party on these lines which has produced a revised Code; we gather that the working party looked in great detail at the sort of issues which have been troubling the POA, and we believe that a similar study in England would be the best way forward.

10.57 We would, however, offer some general reflections to assist in such a study. We gather that the origins of the detailed provisions governing the handling of charges lie in the recognition of the particular vulnerability of prison officers to inmate allegations, and also to potentially rough and arbitrary justice from some governors. We are confident that the latter no longer applies, but we are conscious of the extent to which complaints by inmates have increased in recent years. Prison officers are rightly concerned with the protection of their position and with procedures which ensure a speedy and correct decision. Management must take due account of that concern. At the same time, however, sections of the public have become increasingly concerned about what is done in prison, and are naturally suspicious of anything which hints at secretiveness or a desire to prevent the proper investigation of complaints. In their own interests the POA must beware of any policy in regard to police investigations which suggests that they are anxious to create for themselves a privileged position, or to prevent the proper discovery of the truth.

10.58 One further point was put to us in regard to disciplinary matters which relates not so much to the Code of Discipline as to the consequences of action under it. This is that officers who are suspended from duty during the investigation of allegations should receive averaged earnings calculated on the basis of the pay, allowances and overtime which they might have been expected to receive. The current civil service procedures, which apply to prison officers, are that suspended staff may have their remuneration stopped wholly or in part; will receive no payments in respect of the overtime which might have been worked; and, on termination of the period of suspension, may either be required to forfeit monies received during the period of suspension, or have restored to them the equivalent of full pay (not including overtime). The practice in the prison service is, in fact, to suspend on full pay (basic salary plus allowances, except that the shift disturbance allowance ceases after 30 days). In suspending on full pay, the Department is apparently going further than the general practice elsewhere in the Home Office and the civil service at large; this is in recognition of the particular vulnerability of prison officers to inmate allegations, and of the significant contribution made by overtime to regular earnings (which means that suspension on, say, half pay would be that much more serious for prison officers than other grades). Prison officers are not in fact required to forfeit remuneration paid to them during a period of suspension. The general position in the civil service is that there is no contractual obligation on the part of management to provide overtime, and that it can therefore only be paid when it has actually been worked. There is only one exception to this rule that we are aware of, and that is that prison officers forced to take sick leave as a result of assaults by inmates in the establishment do receive a notional overtime payment. We gather that the POA are currently pursuing a claim for similar payments in the case of officers injured during the course of escort duties, and their case in regard to suspension is, in effect, that an officer accused, but subsequently vindicated, can be regarded as having lost money as a result of a verbal assault as opposed to a physical one.

10.59 The Home Office appears not unsympathetic to the POA's contention, in the few cases when an officer is reinstated having been found not guilty of the allegations, but there are strong arguments against the concession because of the effect it would have in other situations in the civil service where suspension or any loss of overtime without blame attached (such as attending a training course) takes place. Once again, it would be wrong for us to pronounce on a negotiable issue, especially one which could have bearings upon the claim in regard to escorts which is currently the subject of negotiation. Our only comment is to reiterate the point above in regard to inmate allegations, and to suggest that there is room here for further negotiation and that other members of the National Staff Side might be prepared to regard prison officers as a special case, provided any concession were limited strictly to suspensions of the type we have described.

CHAPTER ELEVEN

WORKING CONDITIONS, QUARTERS AND OTHER CONDITIONS OF SERVICE MATTERS

11.1 Throughout this report we have dealt, where appropriate, with matters concerning the conditions of service of those who work in penal establishments. Our purpose in this Chapter is to comment on, and make recommendations about, a number of conditions of service matters which have not been considered in detail elsewhere. The fact that these matters have been included in what is the last main Chapter of this report should not be taken as indicating that we regard them as being of lesser importance than what has gone before. Indeed, as we observed in the very first paragraph of this report, the underlying causes of industrial unrest are invariably to be found below what appears on the surface, and that applies equally to what follows in this Chapter as it does to what has gone before. As may be imagined we received, during our visits to establishments, many complaints upon a wide variety of issues related to conditions of service. Some of these only involved individual officers or individual establishments and we are not able to deal with them here. What we are concerned to do in this Chapter is to concentrate on those matters which affect most, if not all, establishments, and which seem to us to be most in need of comment.

WORKING CONDITIONS AND FACILITIES FOR STAFF

11.2 Among the most vocal complaints made to us during our visits was the one which asserted that the facilities provided for staff are very poor indeed when compared with those provided for inmates. As one POA branch representative put it: "All that we want is parity with prisoners". Our own observations have in many cases confirmed the validity of this complaint. We have ourselves seen officers crowded into tiny muster rooms with no adequate locker or other facilities, staff toilets which were a disgrace, and office staff working in Portakabins with barely enough space to install a typewriter. Although inmate toilet facilities are in many instances no better than the staff facilities which we have described, we have also seen many cases where they are far superior. Furthermore, we have seen many instances of extensive and expensive recreational and sporting facilities being provided for inmates without any commensurate improvements having been made in the facilities for staff. We accordingly recommend that urgent attention should be paid to improving the working conditions and facilities for all staff in penal establishments. In this connection we would draw attention particularly to the need for adequate toilet facilities, office accommodation, and rest rooms. Additionally, bearing in mind that prison officers, and in particular dog handlers, may have to spend a large part of their working day outside in inclement weather, we recommend that suitable facilities should be provided wherever possible for showers and for drying clothes.

11.3 One other aspect of working facilities which was drawn to our attention concerned the provision of messes and clubs. We have seen some officers' messes which are very bright, spacious and attractive. By contrast, we have seen others which are dingy and cramped. We realise, of course, that the constrictions of space, particularly in older urban establishments, may prevent the enlargement of some of these messes. At the same time we consider that all efforts should be made to have messes which are as bright and agreeable as possible. This must be primarily the responsibility of individual governors and we accordingly recommend that they should all review their messing arrangements as a matter of urgency in order to see what improvements are necessary and can be effected. The provision of clubs presents rather different problems. Official policy is to make provision for clubs at establishments which do not have readily available other local facilities for recreation. This means that in some areas there are no officers' clubs, and we have received representations that clubs should be provided at least in some of these places. One factor which has prompted the current official policy is the desire to persuade prison staff to integrate as fully as possible into a local community rather than being isolated and inward-looking. We think that this is an important consideration and one which may gain in importance if, in the next few years, an increasing number of staff choose to live out of quarters. On the other hand the existence of private club facilities is valuable for the morale of any organisation, and an official policy which has the effect of reducing that morale is less likely to gain the support of staff in relation to other matters. We accordingly conclude that a more liberal policy in this regard would be appropriate and we recommend that any application for a club at a particular establishment should henceforth be looked at as favourably as possible.

QUARTERS

11.4 One of the most valuable elements in the remuneration of prison service grades is the provision of free housing. Moreover in an era of rising housing costs this item is perhaps even more significant than it has been in the past, and consequently should not be undervalued. Despite that, among the most frequent complaints that we have heard during our visits to establishments, apart from those relating to pay, have been those concerning the subject of quarters. These complaints have been put to us by members of staff of all ranks, and also by their wives, and have related to many matters, though principally to the rules governing the circumstances in which a person may live out of quarters, and to the condition of the quarters themselves. Before considering these complaints in detail it may be helpful to describe the present provision of quarters and the way in which that provision has come about.

11.5 Quarters have been provided for some categories of staff from the early days of the prison service and for many years the unions have regarded quarters as a substantial benefit for their members and have pressed for the maximum possible provision. On the whole the management has not resisted this pressure since quarters have offered a number of advantages: they have in the past helped to meet the operational and security needs of individual establishments; they have assisted mobility; and they have made a substantial contribution towards the recruitment and retention of suitable staff for the service. As a result the relevant departments have, except in Northern Ireland, a very large

stock of quarters, varying considerably in age, condition and location. At the
end of 1978 the provision in each country was as follows:

	Number of Married Quarters	Number of Single Quarters	Number of Entitled Staff
England and Wales	11,009	1,184	15,007
Scotland	1,662	96	2,294
Northern Ireland	58	885	2,200

The very low number of married quarters in Northern Ireland is explained by
the need, in recent years, to provide within a short space of time a very large
amount of single accommodation for the staff who have been employed to
man Maze and Magilligan prisons, both of which are establishments that were
built on sites not previously used by the prison service.

11.6 The prison service staff who have an entitlement to a free quarter are
the governor grades, full-time chaplains, and all prison officer grades. Under
the relevant Prison Rules staff may be required to occupy quarters assigned to
them and the practice has been that they will only receive a rent allowance
towards the cost of private accommodation if no suitable quarter is available.
Quarters for married staff, and for staff who qualify for a married quarter by
virtue of their rank or personal circumstances, are provided unfurnished except
for a cooker. Occupants have no liability for internal or external maintenance
and decoration, and do not pay rates. Some other prison service staff, such as
farm managers and agricultural workers have an entitlement to a quarter on
payment of an appropriate rent. Quarters vary in size and standard according
to grade of staff or family size. In general governor grades and officers of chief
officer rank are entitled to what is known as a major quarter which is provided
without regard to marital status or size of family. The corollary of this provision is that such quarters are treated as designated quarters, that is to say
that the occupants concerned are obliged to live in them whether they like it
or not. For the remaining prison officer grades quarters of a lesser quality,
known as minor quarters, are provided, and are allocated generally on the
basis of family size though some such quarters are reserved for particular
classes of officer such as engineers, dog handlers etc. Single officers are entitled
to a single quarter which generally consists of a furnished bedroom with
shared use of lounge, bathroom, kitchen and other facilities.

11.7 The location of quarters varies from establishment to establishment
but most commonly, in both old and new establishments, they are to be found
in large clusters at or near the prison wall. The condition of quarters also
varies from establishment to establishment and, although in general the poorer
conditions are to be found in older quarters, our experience when visiting
establishments indicated that this is not always the case.

Living out of quarters

(*a*) Officer grades

11.8 We have already indicated that one of the principal complaints made to
us concerned the rules governing the circumstances in which a person may
live out of quarters. That complaint was expressed in a number of ways.

Reference was frequently made to the growing tendency for home ownership in society at large and to the fact that prison staff are precluded from taking part in this tendency, at least with the assistance of a rent allowance, except in circumtances where no suitable quarters are available for them. Reference was often made in this context to the number of officers who are presently living out of quarters and seeking to purchase their own homes even without the benefit of rent allowance as indicating the size of this desire. There are apparently about 350 such cases, which represent less than $2\frac{1}{2}$ per cent of the total: on the other hand, the fact that any officers at all are prepared to do this is indicative of some desire. Additionally, many members of staff drew our attention to the difficulties which they would face upon retirement if they were unable to purchase their own homes during the course of their service. Further complaints on this point concerned the rule about designated quarters which could result in a member of staff having to occupy a quarter which was much larger than he required with all the resulting expense on heating, cleaning etc. Yet another complaint was that the standard of maintenance, decoration, and provision of facilities such as cental heating, was inadequate in quarters and could only be put right if members of staff were permitted to own their own homes and to make their own provision for such matters. A further and more general criticism of the need to occupy quarters was made by those living in quarters of the kind which we have described in paragraph 11.7, that is to say those arranged in clusters at or near the establishment itself. The point here was that, although there were certain advantages in relation to the time taken to travel to work, these were far outweighed by the disadvantage of living constantly in close proximity to other prison staff and their families. This was said to give rise to feelings of tension and of isolation from the community at large which were of no benefit either to the individuals concerned or to the image of the prison service within society. We consider that there is a great deal of weight in many of these criticisms and we have heard with pleasure that negotiations which have continued since our appointment have now reached a satisfactory conclusion whereby much more flexibility has been introduced into the rules governing entitlement to live out of quarters.

11.9 An agreed Notice to Staff issued by the Home Office contains two main features. The first is that permission to live out of quarters and the grant of a rent allowance will no longer be linked with the availability of quarters; and the second is that chief officers and senior works grades should no longer have an entitlement to a major quarter unless one is available. We consider that these provisions will go a long way towards meeting many of the complaints that were put to us. We think it is unlikely that there will be a sudden vast exodus from quarters: rather, we would anticipate a gradual increase in the numbers moving out with, in any event, a sizeable number still choosing to remain in quarters. For that reason we would expect that there will always be enough officers wishing to live in quarters beside an establishment to provide the immediate operational cover which, despite communications which are now, of course, much better than in the 19th century, some establishments still require. On the other hand, all officers will be given a certain freedom of choice that has hitherto been denied to them, and we regard that as an important advance. Chief officers and related grades will, of course, lose their entitlement to major quarters. That is the inevitable consequence of, on the one hand, giving them freedom to live out and, on the other hand, envisaging a situation where they may, if they wish, occupy a smaller quarter which is more suitable for their requirements. This consequence was recognised by the POA in its policy on quarters and, in general, we would expect this provision to be beneficial.

(b) Governor grades

11.10 During the period of our appointment discussions were taking place between the Home Office and the Governors' Branch of the Society of Civil and Public Servants to see whether a similar scheme could be introduced in relation to governors' quarters. Just before completion of this report we were advised that these discussions had reached a satisfactory conclusion, the effect of which is substantially the same as the proposals applicable to prison officer grades. Once again we welcome this development.

Condition, repair and maintenance of quarters

11.11 Observations which we made during our visits to establishments indicate that there are considerable local variations, as well as variations within individual establishments, in the condition, character, and state of repair and maintenance of quarters. We, of course, have seen quarters in only about one-third of all establishments in the United Kingdom, and we are therefore unable to say whether our experience is typical of all quarters. We would be somewhat surprised, however, if what we have seen is not broadly representative of the whole. Such variations as we have seen have been the subject of substantial criticism from officers and their wives who, on some occasions, have drawn our attention to quite significant differences in the quality of the quarters within the same establishment and, on other occasions, have looked back regretfully at apparently superior quarters which they have previously occupied at other establishments. On yet other occasions, it must in fairness be added, officers and their wives have conceded quite properly that their quarters were at least as good as the best accommodation available from local authorities. We can well understand these criticisms, particularly since some of the quarters which we have seen were in very poor condition indeed. On the other hand, some variation in condition and quality must be inevitable in a service which has been providing quarters for its officers for more than a century. Since 1972 all new minor quarters have had to comply with the minimum standard recommended for public sector housing in 1961 by the Parker Morris Committee, and since then an attempt has been made to bring some older properties up to the same standard. We were told, however, by representatives of the Home Office that, at least so far as England and Wales are concerned, there is no clear official policy about this. No doubt, like many local authorities, the Home Office has found that the upgrading of older property to Parker Morris standards can be enormously expensive, and on occasions quite impossible because of differences in design, room sizes etc. In our view, however, these are not reasons for having no policy at all. Bearing in mind that, over a period, more and more quarters should become vacant as a result of the new proposals for allowing permission to live out, we recommend that official policy should be clearly directed to disposing of sub-standard quarters which are not capable of reasonable improvement, to retaining those which can most effectively and economically be improved, and to formulating a staged programme for the carrying out of such improvements.

265

11.12 In considering this programme the Home Departments should also, in our opinion, be prepared to review existing regulations concerning what may, or may not, be done in the matter of improvements. We have been told, for example, that external porches may be added to a house only if it is in an exposed position at a coastal establishment, notwithstanding that the weather may be just as inclement inland as it is on the coast. If this is provided for by existing regulations, then it is a clear example of what we have in mind. If it is not, then we consider that it should be made clear to all staff that no such local variations will apply.

11.13 The repair and maintenance of quarters have traditionally been the responsibility of the Works Branch of the prison service, but increasingly that Branch has become understaffed so that in some instances essential maintenance and repair work has either been delayed or even not done at all, and in others such work has been contracted out to an outside agency such as a private contractor or a housing association, as in the case of, for example, Barlinnie. This latter course has, we are told, proved to be a mixed blessing. It, of course, relieves the works officers of their responsibility for quarters and enables them to apply their scarce resources to the upkeep of the establishment itself. On the other hand, householders feel that they are treated more impersonally by outside agencies, and have complained to us that there is also a tendency for these to put off attending to repairs or maintenance work until such time as they have accumulated a number of jobs which can all be attended to in the course of a single visit. We have no doubt that, for obvious reasons of efficiency, a Foreman of Works would often adopt the same approach, but we have nonetheless been particularly struck by the volume of evidence to the effect that delays on the part of outside contractors are greater than would be the case if the work was not contracted out. Any kind of delay is bound to cause annoyance to a house-holder and we recommend that in all establishments ways should be looked for to reduce these to a minimum.

11.14 Although most of the complaints which we have received are under-standable, we think that many of them are the inevitable consequence of a system of provided housing and might well, though we have not been able in the time available to us to carry out any comparative studies, be echoed in other comparable systems. At the same time prison staff see the provision of quarters as forming part of their total emoluments, and that this is a fair way to view the provision appears to be confirmed by the fact that a notional allowance is made to an officer's pay in respect of the pensionable value of quarters (PVQ). With regard to this part of their emoluments staff expect that there will be a reasonable quality of provision and also a measure of uniformity. That is plainly not the case at the moment and we have considered whether we can offer any suggestions as to how it might best be achieved. It is clear that it can only be achieved in a physical sense by a very substantial capital expenditure which, even if funds could be made available, would not be justified in all cases, particularly if the total number of quarters is going to be diminished as a result of current moves towards greater freedom to live out. Consequently, any more acceptable arrangement is likely to take a different form.

11.15 One possibility would be to consolidate rent allowance into basic pay, and thereafter to charge a rent for quarters. Depending on the system of fixing rents that was selected, this might enable differences in quality and condition to be reflected in the rent charged. One consequence of such a course would be to remove PVQ as a notional element in pay. At the moment PVQ is, in our view, somewhat anomalous since it is designed to add to an officer's ultimate pension an element in respect of his housing emolument, but at the same time it is also taken into account for calculating rates of overtime, though not rates of basic pay. There is no obvious logic in this, and there seems much to be said for any course that would result in the disappearance of PVQ in its present form.

11.16 A second possibility would be to allow members of staff to purchase the quarters which they presently occupy. This would allow them the freedom to carry out improvements and repairs at their own expense, and in accordance with their own wishes. On the other hand, there might be a risk, as has been asserted in cases where local authorities have contemplated similar schemes, that only the best houses would be purchased, and the prison departments would be left with all the poorer ones. This is clearly a real risk, and it is, of course, essential that at all times the departments should retain a sufficient number of good quarters for incoming tenants. On the other hand, the prison departments are perhaps in a somewhat better position than local authorities to be highly selective about the sale of quarters to tenants and to exercise a substantial measure of control over the manner and extent of such an operation. Accordingly, we do not think that this suggestion should be excluded from all consideration since it should be possible for the prison departments to consider offering for sale only quarters in particular localities, or particular streets, or even, in some cases, individual specified houses.

11.17 A third possibility that might be considered is the one which we understand to be presently under consideration by the armed forces whereby serving officers and other ranks may be offered an opportunity of half buying and half renting their quarters. Under this scheme a half share in the equity of the property would be purchased with the aid of a building society loan, and this would be transferable from quarter to quarter as the person concerned moved around in the course of his service. At the end of the person's service the quarter finally occupied would be purchased back by the armed service involved and the occupier would receive a considerable amount of capital for investment in the ordinary housing market.

11.18 In the time available to us we have not been able to examine any of these proposals in detail, and indeed there may well be others which have not come to our attention. We are accordingly unable to make any recommendation about which, if any, ought to be pursued. We think, however, that the present arrangements regarding quarters might well benefit from some radical change and we recommend that they should be reviewed. We accordingly offer the above suggestions to the interested parties as appearing worthy of further examination in the course of that review.

11.19 Even if any of the foregoing suggestions finds favour it will plainly take some considerable time to bring it into effect. We have accordingly considered whether there are any useful proposals that we can make which may help to bring about some improvements in the short term. Many of the complaints that we have encountered concern matters such as the delays in carrying out maintenance work, and the intervals which elapse between occasions when quarters are redecorated. As we have said, many of these matters are inevitable consequences of a provided quarters system. At the same time we have the impression that a significant number of members of staff would be prepared and able, to undertake some of these tasks themselves, particularly redecoration, even at their own expense. There are obvious difficulties about permitting this kind of "do-it-yourself" work on an unrestricted basis, but without relieving the Home Departments of their responsibilities, we recommend that it should be allowed wherever possible.

11.20 One question which would, no doubt, arise in this connection would be whether or not any such work should be financed either wholly or partly at public expense. While there will be some instances where such a claim could never be justified, there may, in our view, be others where the claims cannot be dismissed so readily. For example, the interval between the dates for redecoration at public expense is quite substantial and we think that, in some instances, a case could be made for at least providing partial financial assistance to a tenant who was willing to undertake some redecorating himself. More obviously, there would be a case for some public funding where a tenant was prepared to carry out an improvement that would be to the long-term benefit of the property, as, for example, by engaging a contractor to install central heating. We believe that there is scope for development here, but the details of any scheme would have to be worked out in consultation between the Home Departments and the other interested parties, including the trades unions concerned. We accordingly recommend that the Home Departments should express a commitment to examine this proposal thoroughly, and to take early steps to set up the necessary discussions.

Rent allowance

11.21 If certain of the proposals which we have made in paragraphs 11.14 to 11.18 were to be implemented there would be no need to give further consideration to the problems of rent allowances. However, these proposals, even if adopted, may take some time to bring into effect and it is accordingly desirable that we should say a few words on this subject. The present system for determining rent allowances is based upon a national scale which, apart from a London supplement which is payable in certain cases, contains no local variations. The scale runs from a minimum to a maximum figure and the amount to which any member of staff will be entitled is determined having regard to a number of matters such as the interest which he pays on a building society mortgage, the purchase price of his house, and other items such as rates and insurance costs. The allowances, which were last fixed on 1 August 1978, vary between, for prison officer grades, a minimum of 33p per week and a maximum of £738 per annum, and, for governor grades, a minimum of £52 per annum and a maximum of £998 per annum. The basis for calculating allowances was determined in 1957, and increases since that date have been linked to the housing cost item in the index of retail prices. In recent years house prices have risen more steeply than this item in the index, and most staff now purchasing accommodation find that they qualify automatically for the maximum allowance.

In 1976 the Home Office put a proposal to the Civil Service Department for the renegotiation of the basis for rent allowances, but were advised that the pay policy then in force precluded a review of the existing agreement. At the end of 1978 5,294 allowances were paid to prison officer grades (37 per cent of all such staff in post), and of these allowances 65 per cent were at the maximum rate.

11.22 We have received a number of cricisms of the present system. First, it has been said that the basis of calculation produces figures which are too low when compared with the actual cost of housing and with allowances paid elsewhere, for example to the police. Secondly, it has been said that the system is unsatisfactory in that it involves an undesirable disclosure of one's private affairs in order to qualify for the allowance, and it has been represented to us that it would be much more satisfactory to have a system like that presently operated in the police whereby rent allowances are fixed at different levels around the country as a result, in brief, of valuations for typical houses fixed by the district valuer. We consider that there may be some justification for the present dissatisfaction with the system of fixing rent allowances, particularly if it is producing figures which are, on any view, lower than is fair and reasonable. If rent allowances are to continue, we recommend that further consideration should be given to reviewing the system and we would hope that the Civil Service Department would find it possible to take part in such a reappraisal. We have not been able to examine the police system in detail in the time available to us. At first sight it appears to have certain advantages, though these may well arise more readily in a system of separate police forces than in a single unified service. It may also have certain disadvantages, though we are not at present aware of these. All we can say at the moment is that, if there is to be a reappraisal of the system of calculating rent allowances, it would appear sensible to examine the police system in detail in the course of that exercise.

11.23 Before leaving the subject of rent allowances we wish to say a few words about the rent allowances which are paid to single officers, and those paid to married officers whose spouses are themselves members of the prison service. In the former case the maximum allowance is one half of the married rate and for officers up to the rank of principal officer at present amounts to £5·55 per week. Many single officers have made the point to us that, although they are entitled to draw the rent allowance at will, it is quite inadequate to pay for any reasonable accommodation at current market prices. For that reason the POA has suggested that the rate should be increased to two-thirds of the married rate. Our own experience of current prices tends to suggest that there is force in this proposal and we recommend that effect should be given to it. In the case of officers whose spouses are themselves members of the service the present position is that both are entitled to rent allowance but only one gets the full married rate while the other gets a single person's rate. This is somewhat illogical if the entitlement to quarters is regarded purely as a part of every serving officer's emoluments. It is, of course, an illogicality which would disappear under any system which provided for a rent being paid in respect of quarters. For the present, however, much of the rationale for the provision of quarters springs from a wish to provide family accommodation rather than an extra emolument, and on that basis the present arrangements make reasonable sense. We do not propose any change on this point.

269

Bachelor quarters

11.24 Much of what we have said so far relates mainly to married quarters, and there are certain problems which apply only to bachelor quarters which we should mention. These concern the standard of and facilities provided in such quarters. The problem is that, with two notable exceptions that we have encountered, bachelor quarters appear generally to be of a poor standard, and are consequently subjected to much adverse criticism from those who live in them. The exceptions are at Holloway, where, as part of the rebuilding programme, new blocks of flats have been built for all the members of staff, including those who live alone, and at Cornton Vale where similar flats were constructed as part of the original design. The bachelor quarters in these establishments consist mainly of self-contained two-person or three-person flats where each occupant has either a large bedroom or bed-sitting room to herself, and in the former case a shared use of a lounge, and in both cases a shared use of kitchen and bathroom facilities. We visited some of these flats and were impressed by their quality. Furthermore, most members of staff to whom we spoke seemed satisfied with the accommodation provided. By contrast a great deal of the male bachelor accommodation which we have seen left a lot to be desired and the department's awareness of this is no doubt reflected in the fact that single male officers are presently entitled to draw rent allowance rather than live in quarters, even when such quarters are empty and available. Much male bachelor accommodation appears to consist of very small rooms in a prefabricated building with a common living room which is shared by all of the occupants of the building. We all found this type of accommodation to be very depressing and consider that it is unsatisfactory to expect single officers to live, perhaps for years on end, in such conditions. This kind of criticism is particularly appropriate in Northern Ireland, where as we have already observed, there is a very large number of bachelor quarters. We appreciate that most of these were built within a very short space of time to meet a sudden emergency need, and we also accept that a significant amount of money has been spent in recent times in attempting to improve the condition of some of these quarters. It is also true that when we visited some of the bachelor quarters at The Maze prison which have not so far been improved we did so on a day when the weather conditions were particularly adverse, with the result that the wind and rain were almost as noticeable from within the quarters as they were outside. Nonetheless, we consider that improvements could and should be made both in Northern Ireland and on the mainland for the benefit of those who, for whatever reason, live alone, and we accordingly recommend that steps to this end should be taken as soon as possible.

Future use of vacated quarters

11.25 If the current policy to allow greater freedom to live out of quarters is carried into effect the result will be, over a period of years, that an increasing number of quarters will become surplus to requirements, and will have to be disposed of in some way or another. At present there are statutory rules governing the disposal of such property, and these have been criticised by the POA as making it difficult, if not impossible, to demolish unwanted property, and by the works branch of the POA as involving lengthy periods of time when empty quarters have to be maintained and protected from vandalism. We think that these rules might bear re-examination if their effect is to require the departments to retain unsatisfactory quarters upon the argument that, by reason of their proximity to an establishment, they would pose a security risk if made available to the general public. On the other hand, we recommend that careful thought should be given to the alternative uses to which such property might be put by the departments themselves, such as the provision of extra accommodation for administrative and other ancillary staff, who are in many cases at present obliged to use very cramped accommodation within establishment precincts, or, alternatively, the provision of pre-release or other hostel accommodation which might well ultimately be staffed and supervised by prison officers. This would involve an extension of their present role of the kind which we have discussed elsewhere in this report.

Security of quarters in Northern Ireland

11.26 During our visit to Northern Ireland we visited a number of married quarters in Belfast, some of which had in recent times been subjected to terrorist attacks. Some of the wives who we met were obviously, and very understandably, in a highly nervous condition. We can fully understand why this should be so and we should like to record publicly our admiration for the way in which they have nonetheless managed to retain a considerable cheerfulness in the face of such adversity. Clearly there can be no total amelioration of their present situation until the present troubles in Northern Ireland are resolved. In the meantime, however, the Northern Ireland Office has supplied us with details of certain measures that are now being taken which, it is hoped, will provide some additional security in these quarters. The measures which are being taken have, we understand, the approval of the POA. For obvious reasons we do not propose to disclose in this report the details of these measures. We are satisfied that the Northern Ireland Office is fully aware of the problem and is doing all that it reasonably can to bring about some improvement.

OTHER CONDITIONS OF SERVICE MATTERS
Transport for prisoners

11.27 One aspect of staff conditions which has been brought to our attention is the transport which is used to convey prisoners to and from courts. In many instances this transport is hired from local firms, and it has been subjected to criticism on the grounds of reliability and security. We have ourselves travelled in such transport during our visits to establishments and sadly have had occasion to confirm the accuracy of the complaints concerning reliability. On the other hand, it has been represented to us by the Home Office that the reason for using hired transport is one of cost, it being considerably cheaper than would be the case if the prison services were to supply their own vehicles in all cases. Plainly the cost of providing transport must be a significant factor in determining the form which such transport should take. We note, however, that in his report of his inquiry into security at Leicester Prison, following the Hughes escape, the Chief Inspector of the prison service recommended:

"The arrangements for the use of hired vehicles should continue to be kept under review. The use of such vehicles will always be necessary. To meet the requirements of individual establishments, the suitability of the service to be provided must always override considerations of cost, and the list of tenders should be widened."

271

We fully endorse what is said there and would merely add that the reliability of the service, as well as its security, is a factor which should be subject to the same considerations.

11.28 A further feature relating to hired transport which has been of concern to the POA concerns the insurance cover available to prison officers while being conveyed in such transport, and the circumstances in which departmental aid will be available to them in the event of their being involved in a traffic accident. We have seen a copy of a letter which was sent from the Home Office to the POA on 1 May 1979 which deals very fully with this problem. The situation which it presents appears to us to be a satisfactory one and we do not think that it is necessary for us to describe that situation or to comment further on this matter.

Conditions in Crown Courts

11.29 In its written evidence submitted to this Inquiry the POA drew attention to the poor and at times insecure conditions which are to be found in Crown Courts where prison officers undertaking escort duties are required to spend a large proportion of their working time. In all, 75 Crown Courts in England and Wales were listed as having defects of one kind or another. This list had been submitted to the Home Office in April 1978 and, not surprisingly in view of its length, it took some considerable time before all of the complaints could be examined and reported on. Ultimately, however, the investigations were concluded and a letter, of which we have seen a copy, was sent to the POA in March 1979. From that letter, and from other evidence submitted to us, we are satisfied that the Home Office is well aware of the deficiencies in question, and of the need to do something about them. There are, however, certain difficulties, not least that the responsibility for Crown Courts rests, not with the Home Office, but with the Lord Chancellor's Department, and that, in some cases, expenditure on certain Crown Courts cannot be justified because the buildings in question are due for replacement in the course of the next few years. Such problems apart, we recommend that the Home Office should continue to keep a close watch on the facilities provided in Crown Courts, and that they should maintain such pressure as may be necessary on the Lord Chancellor's Department to have as many deficiencies as possible put right.

Safety at work, and public health legislation

11.30 We have received some criticism from the POA and others concerning the fact that the Crown, and thus penal establishments, are exempt from the provisions of legislation relating to health and safety at work and public health. The response from the relevant departments has been that, notwithstanding the exemption, they nevertheless seek to comply with all of the statutory obligations which are imposed on other users of premises. We have no doubt that this attempt is genuinely made but we nonetheless think that the absence of inspection by the relevant public inspectors, who are of course able to compare standards with those obtaining elsewhere, may result not only in some shortcomings being overlooked but may also create the impression that the departments are concealing something from the public gaze. As we have said elsewhere in this report we think that the running of penal establishments should be more open to public scrutiny, and one way in which this might be achieved would be by making such establishments open to inspection by those persons and bodies who are charged with the maintenance of proper standards elsewhere in public and private life. We accordingly recommend that prison establishments should be open to inspection by HM Factory Inspectors, Public Health Inspectors and similar officials to the same extent as any private establishment. Constitutionally the criminal sanctions contained in the relevant legislation for breaches of its provisions cannot apply to the Crown, and thus cannot apply to prisons. Nevertheless we have no doubt that, subject to questions of security, any recommendation by a safety, health or welfare inspector would be acted upon by a governor when brought to his notice. Failing this, a report to the regional director, to the appropriate Director at headquarters or ultimately to HM Inspector of Prisons would, if justified, no doubt achieve the desired result.

Mobility and postings policy

11.31 The prison services are required to provide and to staff penal establishments in all parts of the United Kingdom, and that factor alone makes it essential that prison staff should accept an obligation of mobility, that is to say an obligation to be transferred from one establishment to another whether they wish it or not. Were it not so the result, in England, would be that popular establishments in the north east and south west would be overstaffed whereas those elsewhere, and particularly in London, would have far fewer staff than they require. During our vistis to establishments, and in oral evidence, we heard many grumbles about the mobility obligation, but we are entirely satisfied that they cannot in general be entertained. Indeed, as we shall see, some of the detailed complaints which we received were without foundation. On the other hand, where there is an obligation on staff to be mobile there is a corresponding obligation on those who order the moves not only to adopt a sympathetic approach to those who are affected by them but also to keep under constant review all the rules and regulations concerning postings to ensure that they do not give rise to any unnecessary transfers, with all of the resultant ill-feeling that such incidents are bound to create.

11.32 In relation to mobility governor grades are in a somewhat different position from uniformed grades in that fairly regular moves to different types of establishment are seen as an essential part of career development and broadening of experience. We regard this as being an inevitable feature of a governor's life and would not propose that it should be changed. On the other hand, we have heard from some governors of a large number of transfers having taken place within relatively few years. This inevitably has a disruptive effect on matters like children's schooling and we would therefore venture the view that a degree of continuity in one place may be just as important for career development as a frequent gaining of experience in new establishments.

11.33 So far as officer grades are concerned it has frequently been asserted to us that transfers against an officer's wishes are a regular feature of work in the service. We have received from the Home Office statistics for 1978, applying to England and Wales, which show quite clearly that this is not so. Of course, and inevitably so, initial postings from the Officer Training School may not always coincide with a particular officer's wishes, but we understand that even this is so in only about 10 per cent of cases. So far as established officers are concerned there were, in 1978, 1,062 transfers of which only 24 were made for operational and management reasons: the remainder were made on promotion (325), at the officer's own request (393), or on applications by officers for advertised posts or specialised duties (320).

11.34 Transfers on promotion do present special problems. Many officers feel that more consideration should be given to making such promotions *in situ*, and we, for our part, do not consider that there should be any objection in principle to such a practice. On the other hand, there may be no suitable vacancy in the officer's own establishment and, even if there is, there may be a waiting list of more senior officers anxious to transfer to that establishment; and it seems reasonable that they should be given priority. Consequently, we consider that a substantial number of transfers on promotion will always be necessary. Having said that, however, we must add that, in our view, attempts should always be made, if this is desired, to transfer such officers to another establishment in the same locality rather than to one at the opposite end of the country. The Home Office claims that it is its policy to do this whenever possible. We recommend that this should not only continue to be official policy but also that all steps should be taken to make that policy as effective as possible.

Promotion examination results

11.35 Reference to postings on promotion leads us to mention briefly the many complaints which we have received from uniformed officers concerning the very long periods that are said to elapse between the sitting of promotion examinations and the receipt of the results. This is clearly a matter of vital interest to the officers concerned and we recommend that every effort should be made to intimate these results as soon as possible.

Transfers at public expense

11.36 At present when a member of staff is transferred from one establishment to another he or she will receive payment of removal expenses at public expense if the transfer has occurred on promotion, as a result of an application by the officer concerned for an advertised or specialist post, or where the transfer is occasioned for operational or management reasons. In general transfers are not made at public expense where they take place at the officer's own request. There is one exception to this. Under rules which have existed since before the Second World War officers serving at certain inconvenient stations have been entitled to a transfer at public expense after seven years' service at these establishments. This concession has gradually been extended to all establishments which presently attract the inconvenience of locality allowance and, in 1942, the qualifying period was reduced to five years for staff serving at Dartmoor. Elsewhere in this report we have recommended that payment of ILA should cease. We have consequently had to consider whether the right to transfer at public expense which arises from the designation of inconvenient stations should continue, and with this we have also had to consider representations that the concession should be extended to other establishments, such as dispersal prisons, where it is said that staff are subjected to particularly stressful conditions. We have considered this matter with care and have reached the conclusion that the reasons which compelled us to recommend the termination of ILAs are equally cogent in relation to transfers at public expense. Furthermore, we are unable to accept any alternative basis upon which such transfers might be authorised. Although staff serving in dispersal prisons undoubtedly have a difficult and responsible task to perform, we do not consider that any resultant stress is significantly different from that sustained by staff who work in, for example, a large and busy remand prison. Consequently, our recommendation must be not only that the right to transfer at public expense should not be extended, but also that the existing concession relative to inconvenient establishments should cease.

SUMMARY OF PRINCIPAL CONCLUSIONS
AND RECOMMENDATIONS

Chapter One: Introduction

Although the Inquiry was set up as a result of some particular pay and allowance disputes, the real causes of deteriorating industrial relations over a long period were more fundamental. They included dissatisfaction with the way the services were run, the state of the buildings, and the physical conditions for staff and inmates. (1.1)

The terms of reference have been interpreted as necessitating an examination of the criminal justice background to imprisonment in order to make worthwhile recommendations on resources. For similar reasons, the report spells out what it is thought modern penal objectives should be. (1.6)

The pace of work has made some omissions unavoidable and detailed recommendations have not been offered in every case except where appropriate. (1.6–1.7)

The recommendations should be seen and treated as a whole. (1.18–1.19)

The fact that an Inquiry has been necessary into what has gone wrong should not be taken to mean that nothing is right. The UK is fortunate in the men and women it has secured to run its penal establishments. They deserve all necessary support from the public. If we turn our backs on our prisons, we turn our backs on our society and our values. (1.20–1.21)

Chapter Three: The Prison Populations

Current populations

All the prison populations have risen since the War. Apart from the special circumstances in Northern Ireland, the main cause of the increase has been the rise in crime. Until recently, in England and Wales, this has been matched by the tendency of the courts to send proportionately fewer offenders to prison. (3.1–3.13)

Overcrowding is worst in England and Wales, and is least in Scotland. (3.3)

The inmates have generally become more criminally sophisticated and represent greater problems of control. (3.15–3.18)

All inmate population forecasts show upward trends. (3.19–3.25)

Successful attempts to reduce inmate populations in Holland and Sweden suggest that UK practices, especially sentencing policy, require re-examination. (3.26–3.30)

The scope for reduction

Every effort should continue to be made to reduce the inmate populations. (3.30–3.34)

It is wrong both in principle and in practice to imprison mentally disordered offenders and the DHSS should take urgent steps to ensure that the NHS lives up to its proper responsibilities in respect of them. (3.35–3.44)

Prison should be avoided wherever possible for fine and maintenance defaulters as well as for drunkenness. More determination should be shown in dealing with alcoholism, and local voluntary schemes should be encouraged, where appropriate, with government grants, both to start and maintain them. (3.45)

Petty persistent offenders represent a series of intractable problems which require continuing effort to find solutions, not only to keep such people out of prison but also to keep them out of the criminal justice system as a whole. (3.46–3.49)

Non-custodial disposals should continue to be developed wherever possible, though there seem to be difficulties in the way of expanding some of them. (3.50–3.55)

Executive intervention through remission schemes and parole should be kept under consideration. (3.56–3.60)

The Interim Report of the Advisory Council on the Penal System, *The Length of Prison Sentences*, should be acted upon. (3.65)

There should be continuing vigilance over the number and length of remands in custody. Alternatives to custodial remand should be encouraged and defendants remanded in custody should be brought to trial as soon as possible. (3.66–3.68)

However, in general none of these possible developments singly or together will absolve society from the need to support for the foreseeable future a substantial penal population. (3.72)

Chapter Four: Objectives and Regimes

Objectives

Whilst the first objective must be secure custody, that alone is not enough. (4.2)

There is a need for restating modern objectives because the language, if not all the practical content, of Rule 1 has become overtaken by various developments. (4.8–4.20)

Little systematic or precise evidence on objectives was received. Although "humane containment" seems to enjoy some support, both it and "treatment and training" should be rejected as sole objectives in favour of a new Rule 1 centred on "positive custody". (4.26)

Regimes

Regimes should continue to be based on useful work but greater efforts should be made to establish a full working week and improve managerial performance. (4.31–4.39)

Rigorous education of all kinds should be expanded where possible, including on a full-time basis. Rule 47(17) should be extended to include education if necessary. (4.39–4.43)

The facilities for remand prisoners should be improved. (4.44)

Positive custody

"Positive custody" should become the guiding aim and penal establishments should therefore be as hopeful and purposive communities as possible. (4.46)

Amongst other things "positive custody" means that the management of penal establishments should be consistently characterised by an openness of approach and mind not only to the staff but to all public requirements as well as to the interests of the inmates. (4.48)

Chapter Five: Organisation

Headquarters

There is no evidence suggesting the need for substantial change in the organisation of the prison services in Scotland and Northern Ireland. (5.2–5.3)

A senior Cabinet Minister, who should be the Home Secretary, should remain accountable to Parliament for the running of the prison service in England and Wales. (5.7)

Central administration ought to have shown itself more responsive to growing feelings of dissatisfaction with the organisation and management of the service as a whole, especially in the field of personnel management. (5.9)

Establishment Division 3 should be absorbed within the Prison Department. (5.12)

The Prison Department should have a reliable view of comparative unit costs of its operation and be capable of developing financial controls which enhance efficiency and managerial performance. (5.34)

Governors must be capable of having proper regard to the efficiency and economic use of public resources. (5.39)

Steps should be taken at the earliest possible opportunity to develop selective accounting improvements within the Prison Department to increase the quality and detail of the financial information available to headquarters, as managers of the whole service, and to each governor, as manager of his or her establishment. This should be one of the first tasks of the relevant division in the Directorate of Finance and Administration. (5.40)

The prison service should be reorganised with a view, first, to create within it a greater degree of unity and identity than presently exists; secondly, to give the Prison Department more standing within the Home Office; thirdly, to identify those areas of its administration and work which should be the concern and responsibility of the most senior management. (5.42)

The affairs of Her Majesty's Prison Service in England and Wales should continue to be directed by a Prisons Board. (5.44)

The Prisons Board should be headed by a Chairman, who would be the accounting officer for the prison service, with direct access to the Secretary of State, and who should be of Second Permanent Secretary rank. (5.45)

There should continue to be only one Principal Establishment Officer for the whole of the Home Office including the Prison Department. (5.45)

The Chairman should either be a career civil servant, an ex-governor, or someone from outside the civil service. He should remain in post for at least five, and preferably seven, years. (5.46)

The Prisons Board should include a further six members of whom four should originate either from the general civil service or the governor grades, the first being an ex-governor and having a rank between that of Deputy and Assistant Under Secretary of State, but the others having the latter rank. Their titles should be:—

(a) *Deputy Chairman and Director of Operations*

(b) *Director of Personnel*

(c) *Director of Regimes*

(d) *Director of Finance and Administration*

In addition the Prisons Board should include two entirely independent non-executive members, appointed by the Home Secretary. (5.47)

Casework at present dealt with both at headquarters in London and in the regions should all be dealt with at headquarters. (5.47)

The new prison service should have its own Finance Division and it should be considered whether it should also have its own Principal Finance Officer. (5.47)

The Director of Prison Medical Services and HM Chief Inspector of Prisons should no longer be members of the Prisons Board. (5.48)

The DPMS should automatically be invited to join a meeting of the Prisons Board when its agenda includes medical questions. (5.49)

An urgent review should be initiated of what should be done to encourage more and better qualified doctors to join the Prison Medical Service. (5.49)

Inspection

There should be a system of inspection of the prison service distanced as far as may be practicable from the Prison Department. (5.61)

In-depth inspections of particular establishments should in future be carried out by the regional directors. (5.62)

There should be constituted within the Home Office an independent department to be called the "Prison Inspectorate", headed either by someone independent of the civil service or by a senior ex-governor, with the same rank as that to be held by the Deputy Chairman and Director of Operations. (5.62)

Except where security considerations dictate otherwise, the reports of HM Chief Inspector of Prisons should be published and laid before Parliament, and each year his Department should make a general report on the whole prison service, for inclusion in that year's Report of the work of the Prison Department. (5.62)

Regions and establishments

Regional directors should be given the widest possible operational powers, and for the immediate future their role should be principally in the field of operations. All the regional specialists should be dispensed with or withdrawn to headquarters. (5.75)

Regional directors should encourage individualism and indeed experiment by governors within their own establishments. (5.82)

Governors should be given as wide powers as possible to deal with personnel and industrial relations problems within their particular establishment. (5.82)

Discussions should start between the Home Office and the Governors' Branch to identify those large and complicated establishments, to which a Deputy Governor only one rank below that of the governing governor might be appointed (5.83)

Up to date business machines should be allocated to penal establishments. (5.84)

There should be a commitment to a new management style which unambiguously reasserts leadership from the centre. (5.89)

A house journal should be produced for circulation among establishments. (5.89)

Boards of Visitors and Visiting Committees

Boards of Visitors should continue, as at present, to exercise both an adjudicatory and an inspectorial function. (5.103)

Boards of Visitors should have an obligation to concern themselves not only for inmates but also for the welfare of prison staff and their families. They should consider the desirability of making themselves readily available at their establishments at specific and advertised times to talk to staff or inmates wishing to see them. Boards should also be encouraged to do more to involve their prison and its community, staff and inmates, in the local community. (5.104)

Immediate steps should be taken to secure the necessary statutory authority to regularise the position of Visiting Committees for adult establishments in Scotland. (5.105–5.106)

Immediate steps should be taken to secure that proper and adequate training, instruction and information are made available to the members of all Visiting Committees in Scotland. (5.106)

Chapter Six: Resources

Manpower

Prison service manpower has almost doubled in Great Britain in the last 15 years. This was partly in response to new commitments (e.g. increased inmate populations) and partly a result of improved conditions of service and improvements for inmates. (6.1–6.5)

Court escort and dock manning duties, especially in England and Wales, consume a large part of prison service manpower. Although there is no case for a separate escort service (6.14), the Lord Chancellor's Department should be required by the Home Office to pay for these services on an agency basis with a view to encouraging both Departments to search for manpower economies. (6.18–6.20)

The former refusal of the POA in England and Wales to participate in the monitoring of overtime was an unnecessary impediment to the efficient allocation of public money. (6.22)

280

Average earnings are very dependent on overtime. Average overtime at 12 hours a week in England and Wales is good neither for the service nor for the officers and their families. (6.23)

The extraordinary persistence of high levels of overtime earnings raises the question of whether manpower is being used efficiently. (6.25)

The present system for determining complementing in England and Wales is unsatisfactory and new and improved arrangements for staff inspection should be set up as soon as possible. (6.26–6.30)

There should in England and Wales be a single attendance system for prison officers which should conform to certain specified criteria. The change should occur as part of a thorough review of working methods including conditions of service. (6.31–6.36)

Physical resources

Looking at the penal estate as a whole, the worst prisons are very bad indeed, but the worst are not necessarily always Victorian prisons. Dartmoor prison should be closed and Peterhead prison should be substantially redeveloped. (6.41–6.42)

The Northern Ireland accommodation is probably the best of all. England and Wales on the other hand seems to have suffered because of its very success in absorbing a vast increase in population but without its needs at any one point being as demonstrably dramatic or urgent. (6.46)

In England and Wales there is no case for largescale localisation i.e. converting training prisons into local prisons. (6.54)

Acceptable modern standards—for the staff as for inmates—require that the European and the United Nations Standard Minimum rules should be interpreted in the UK as requiring a minimum target of eliminating enforced cell sharing and incorporating integral sanitation not only in all new prison buildings but in all redeveloped or substantially improved accommodation. Such a minimum target should be given high priority: the costs are not optional but simply an unavoidable part of the current price of having prisons at all. (6.57)

The Home Office should actively commence a programme of reaching new understandings with local communities about the restrictions which have been imposed on the numbers of the inmates who may be sent to open prisons and the nature of their offences. (6.61)

The Home Office working party on categorisation and allocation should review with particular care whether all those category B inmates at present in dispersal prisons need to be sent there. (6.70)

A review of the arguments in favour of concentrating rather than dispersing category A prisoners does not show that a partial or total reversal of dispersal policy would be justified. (6.72)

There is no case for a moratorium on building new prisons, but the idea is not wholly groundless if it serves to remind sentencers that their decisions have resource consequences which society cannot ignore. (6.76)

Present capital provision is neither intended nor in any way capable of supporting a substantial redevelopment programme either in England and Wales (6.84) or in Scotland (6.90).

Although expenditure on prisons in England and Wales has not invariably compared unfavourably with selected social services and total public expenditure, expenditure on prisons because of its small volume has suffered disproportionately from successive cuts in expenditure plans. (6.94–6.98)

The penal estate has become so run down that rebuilding and refurbishing is inevitable, and the necessary work is bound to stretch beyond the life of one government. Although there should be the strongest support for developing non-custodial alternatives, action there should not result in starving prisons of resources. (6.104)

Plans should be drawn up for new prison building programmes in England and Wales and in Scotland aimed at both eliminating cell sharing other than in dormitories or specially enlarged cells and at producing integral sanitation and washing facilities progressively throughout prison establishments. No programme can be credible which does not deal with the Victorian local prisons. In England and Wales this will entail approximately doubling present capital expenditure. (6.105)

Progress of the programme should be reviewed in the light of the actual, as opposed to the merely potential, effect of measures to reduce the inmate populations, and should not seek to anticipate increases of population beyond those forecast. (6.107)

The fact that the new programme may require accommodation to be found for populations displaced would argue for concentrating its initial effort on adult remand accommodation and ending the scandal of the conditions in which so many remand prisoners are held. (6.108)

The government should seriously contemplate resorting to compulsory purchase powers to keep construction times and costs within reasonable limits, but this should not be done except in the last resort and normal planning procedures should be observed. (6.109)

A dependence on excessive overtime is undesirable; it should be substantially reduced and ideally eliminated. Reduction should be handled sensitively and with due regard to the staff's average earnings. (6.110)

New building should be as economical of staff as possible. (6.111)

Sufficient technical and professional resources should be made available to support the building programme. (6.112)

Detailed plans should be made for improving staff facilities. (6.113)

Chapter Seven: Role of Officer and Governor Grades, their Recruitment and Training

Role

The desire expressed by prison officers to extend their role and to undertake a wider range of duties should be encouraged. (7.3)

Existing experiments in which prison officers undertake wider duties should be extended to other establishments. (7.5)

Greater consideration should be given to involving prison officers, on secondment, with a range of activities outside penal establishments. (7.6)

Greater involvement of local volunteers and community groups outside should be encouraged in appropriate activities within establishments. (7.7)

Prison officers should take a more flexible approach than hitherto to manning levels and attendance systems, and should accept that there is a number of tasks within penal establishments which do not require the skills, experience and training of prison officers. (7.9)

The present number of civilian and ancillary employees in penal establishments should not be reduced. (7.10)

Clerical and administrative posts in Scotland and Northern Ireland should be civilianised. (7.12–7.16)

It is essential that the importance of the rank of chief officer should be fully recognised by junior officers and by senior management alike. (7.19–7.22)

In so far as there are changes in the role of prison officers there must also be changes in the role and commitment of governors. (7.23)

Recruitment

The prison services are not at present suitable for any scheme of cadet entry. (7.26)

The minimum age for recruitment to the prison services should remain at 21, but consideration should be given to outstanding applicants who are up to one year younger. (7.27)

The present educational requirements should not be altered, but recruiting literature should make it clear that a widening range of duties being performed by prison officers offer opportunities for people of all kinds of abilities and provide a challenging avenue for the better qualified to explore. (7.28)

All efforts should be made to recruit more coloured prison officers. (7.30)

The present system of recruitment to the governor grades should continue, but further efforts should be made to identify, encourage and prepare serving prison officers for promotion to the governor grades. (7.35)

The period of service as a prison officer undertaken by direct entrants to the governor grades should be of the same length for all and arranged to allow the participant to see as much as possible of a prison officer's duties. (7.37–7.38)

Training

Training is neither as effective nor as comprehensive as it should be, and at all levels it is not given sufficient priority. (7.39)

As a matter of urgency, steps should be taken to carry out a searching review of all training facilities and programmes not only for discipline officers but also for specialists. In England and Wales this should be a priority task for the Director of Personnel. (7.39)

The Staff Training Advisory Group for England and Wales should be expanded to include one or two operational governors, a chief officer, and representatives of education and training from outside the prison service. (7.45)

If regions are to play a part in training, their role should be clearly defined, and they should be adequately funded. (7.46)

Local training should be made a shared responsibility between a senior member of the uniformed grades and a member of the governor grades. (7.47)

The condition of the Prison Service College and Officer Training Schools, and the facilities provided in them, should be constantly kept under review, and all possible steps should be taken to bring about improvements. (7.48)

The period of basic training for a prison officer should, exceptional circumstances apart, be the same in all parts of the United Kingdom. (7.49)

Basic training should be expanded to prepare officers for a wider range of duties and in-service training be seen not merely as a concomitant of promotion but as an ingredient in the career development of all staff. (7.50–7.52)

Teaching staff in the Prison Service Colleges and Officer Training Schools should be of the highest quality available and should be properly trained in teaching methods. (7.53)

Uniform should be worn by recruits at Officer Training Schools in England and Wales. (7.54)

The two-year sandwich course for the training of new entrants to the governor grades should remain. (7.55)

Periods of service within establishments during the two years should be used to give trainees an increasing range of responsibilities. (7.56)

The existing rank of Assistant Governor II should be replaced with a new rank of Assistant Governor Trainee, AG(T), for recruits during the two-year training period and a new single rank, Assistant Governor, for all who have successfully completed the two-year training period. (7.57–7.58)

The existing rank of Assistant Governor I in England and Wales and Northern Ireland should be redesignated Governor IV. (7.58)

The training of governors must be fully alive and responsive to changes in the role and duties of governors which are recommended throughout this report. (7.59)

Chapter Eight: Pay, Allowances and Superannuation

Pay

Prison service grades are to some extent an isolated and inward looking group who may not always appreciate the true value of their pay and other benefits e.g. housing and superannuation. (8.3)

Questions of remuneration are best considered in the context of the staff's terms and conditions of service seen as a whole. (8.4)

An earnings survey showed that differentials, especially in England and Wales and above all in Northern Ireland, were often disturbed because of high overtime earnings. (8.7–8.12)

Comparison with earnings generally showed that junior prison service grades stood well—and even better if free housing, free uniform and non-contributory pension were considered in addition—in comparison with average gross earnings but worked longer than average hours to do so. There was no evidence to show that they had lost any real ground recently. (8.13–8.17)

The fixed point formula proposed by the POA for present and future determination of prison officers' pay is not an objective system of pay calculation, and its adoption is not recommended. (8.34)

Since officers' gross earnings compare well a large increase in basic pay is not justified, but pay should be increased to newly recommended levels over those originally agreed with effect from 1.1.80 to reflect the more difficult control problems since 1958 and the need to recruit more officers. (8.39)

The increases include some special enhancement and the introduction of a modest incremental scale for chief officers, as well as two long service increments for basic grade officers. (8.41)

Increases in the responsibility allowances for officer instructors and trades officers to improve their relative positions should not be ruled out but can be justified on recruitment grounds only. (8.42)

The Wynn-Parry formula should continue to be applied to the uprating of prison officers' pay subject to its continuing to be operated with the flexibility recommended in paragraph 98(5) of the Wynn-Parry Report. (8.44)

Whilst the consolidation of certain allowances into basic pay could not now be justified, the parties should address their minds to the question of consolidation. (8.45)

The system of pay comparison with the Administration Group recommended by the Wynn-Parry Committee should continue to be applied to the determination of governors' pay and new pay scales taking into consideration the report of the CSD review are recommended to take effect from 1 January 1980. (8.62–8.63)

The existing arrangements for uprating governors' pay should be maintained, subject to their continuing to be operated with the flexibility recommended in paragraph 97 of the Wynn-Parry Committee Report. Internal prison service relativities should continue to be fixed by reference to basic pay rather than earnings; these differentials should not be fixed indefinitely but should remain flexible to meet changing circumstances. (8.64)

Allowances

Inconvenience of locality allowances should be phased out by negotiation. (8.77)

There are no sufficient grounds for increasing the Northern Ireland daily emergency allowance or altering the present basis of eligibility, much as the position of the prison service in Northern Ireland deserves special consideration. (8.88)

Although female searchers in Northern Ireland prisons should not qualify for the daily emergency allowance, they should retain their present environmental allowance and be linked for pay purposes with the female staff attached to the civilian search unit of the Northern Ireland Police Authority at the same time receiving an additional clothing allowance of £112 per annum. (8.91)

As to home to office travel expenses and lodging allowances in Northern Ireland, the principles of the United Kingdom civil service rules should prevail. The Maze and Magilligan prisons should be recognised as permanent duty stations and the current reduced rate travel allowances should be phased out by negotiation. The payment of half-rate lodging allowance should continue for a period of grace from the negotiated end of the allowances. On the understanding that the Northern Ireland Office will ensure that all overnight accommodation provided is kept up to a reasonable standard, it is recommended that steps be taken to eliminate the £1 per night sleeping-in allowance by negotiation. (8.92–8.104)

Environmental allowances and their relationship with the special hospitals lead should be retained. Whilst they should not be extended to staff not permanently stationed at penal establishments, it is desirable that in future the allowances be upgraded simultaneously with changes in pay. (8.110)

Superannuation

Prison officers enjoy generous pension terms the value of which represents a substantial addition to their total remuneration, and further improvements could only be secured at substantial additional public expense. The officers' pay scales recommended to take effect from 1 January 1980 should, for pension purposes, be deemed to have applied with effect from 1 April 1979. (8.114–8.128)

In so far as governors' duties are more stressful than those of other civil service grades, this is reflected in the determination of their pay, and in turn in an enhanced pension. There is no evidence to justify parity with officers' pensions. The pension entitlement of governors should therefore remain unchanged but the governors' pay scales recommended to take effect from 1 January 1980 should, for pension purposes, be deemed to have applied with effect from 1 April 1979. (8.133–8.134)

Chapter Nine: Continuous Duty Credits

No recommendations are made on claims 3 (9.13), 6 (9.15), 10 (9.19) and 17(9.29). Claim 8 should be granted with backdating to 1 October 1971 (9.1) and claim 9 should be granted with effect from a current date (9.18). Claim 16 should be granted in certain specified circumstances with payments backdated to 1 June 1975. All other claims should be rejected for the reasons explained.

Chapter Ten: Industrial Relations

Despite the substantial fund of loyalty and sense of duty that still exists in the prison services, willingness to resort to industrial action has increased in recent years, and still continues. (10.1–10.7)

Action taken has affected the administration of justice, prison administration and the welfare of inmates and has, on occasions, run counter to the stated position of the POA on the limits of acceptable action. (10.8–10.12)

Reasons suggested for current unrest include loss of confidence in treatment objectives, the distancing of staff and inmates as a result of the changing nature of the prison population, increased emphasis on security and growing numbers of specialists in prisons (10.13–10.14); poor working environments (10.15); changes in staff backgrounds and experience (10.16); the effects of incomes policy (10.16); apparent changes in the general industrial relations climate and the effects of this on the comparatively isolated position of prison officers (10.17); the failure of management to take the initiative in responding to industrial unrest, and to support governors faced with disputes (10.18–10.19); the inadequacy, for present purposes, of the Whitley Council machinery (10.20); and experience that industrial action produces results (10.21).

For the current situation, staff and management at all levels must share some degree of responsibility. (10.22) Improved relations will result only partially from organisational changes; more important is that staff and management recognise their joint responsibility for improving the operation of the prison service. (10.32)

A key factor will be the resolve of governors to consult staff and to resolve disputes locally, wherever possible. Governors could generally make more use that at present of existing powers. It has not been possible to identify any new responsibilities which could at present be delegated to governors, but this may eventually be possible in the climate of increased local financial accountability which may follow from other proposals, or arise out of negotiations. A corollary of increased local resolution of disputes is the acceptance by staff that issues must be decided on merit, not by reference to practice elsewhere. (10.33–10.37)

There should be a joint meeting point in each establishment at which local management can consult staff, and at which the latter can negotiate corporately on matters of joint interest. (10.38)

An assistant or deputy governor should be designated at each establishment as a channel for complaints and a troubleshooter in the event of disputes occurring. This would not mean the governor being less concerned in the management of staff than he is at present. (10.39)

Staff must acknowledge that there are certain issues which can never be settled locally, and must be for national negotiation. (10.40)

The Home Office and the CSD should give consideration to a return to the situation in which matters of pay and conditions of service are negotiated directly between the Home Office and the POA. (10.41)

The POA and the SPOA should consider the advantages which might accrue from increasing the size of their full-time staff. (10.24)

Whilst no personnel function should be established now in the regional offices, the regional directors' role as "honest brokers" in local disputes should be developed. (10.43–10.44)

Current arrangements for handling arbitrable issues are acceptable to both parties, but a national procedural agreement is needed for dealing with other negotiable and consultative matters. The details of a procedural agreement are for negotiation but must include a clear definition of national and local issues, the nature of negotiations at each level, the time allowed, the form of any conciliation and arbitration stage, and the nature of unacceptable industrial action. All unresolved issues, whether national or local in origin, should be taken through procedure. (10.45–10.47)

Despite the very special role played by the prison service, it is not feasible to deprive them of the statutory protection currently enjoyed under the Trades Union and Labour Relations Act 1974—although there may be occasions when, by mutual agreement, abstention for a limited period from particular forms of action might be written into specific agreements. (10.48–10.49)

The necessary amending legislation should be introduced to enable warrants for the production of inmates at court to be addressed to all members of the prison staff. (10.50)

The Code of Discipline should be amended to make clear that its provisions do not apply to industrial action taken in accordance with any procedural agreement. (10.51)

It is wrong for the POA to remain the sole staff side representative on the Prison Department Whitley Council. Access to the Council should be allowed to other grades working in the prison service, while preserving individual unions' rights of individual access to management on matters of sole concern to their members. (10.52–10.54)

Current moves to extend the scope and coverage of training in management and in the handling of disputes should continue. (10.59)

Consideration should be given to the renegotiation of the Code of Discipline. An underlying consideration should be the particular vulnerability of prison officers to malicious allegations, and the need to avoid any suspicion of over-sensitiveness on the part of staff to external investigation. (10.56–10.57)

The claim for averaged overtime payments during suspension from duty must also be a matter for negotiation between the parties. It is an area where the other staff associations might agree, in view of the vulnerability of prison officers previously noted, to regard the latter as a special case. (10.58–10.59)

Chapter Eleven: Working Conditions, Quarters and Other Conditions of Service Matters

Working conditions for staff

Urgent attention should be paid to improving the working conditions and facilities for all staff in penal establishments, including in particular adequate toilet facilities, office accommodation, rest rooms, showers, and facilities for drying clothes. (11.2)

Governors should review their messing arrangements as a matter of urgency in order to see what improvements are necessary and can be effected. (11.3)

Any application for a club at a particular establishment should be looked at as favourably as possible. (11.3)

Quarters

Current proposals to allow prison officer and governor grades greater freedom to live out of quarters are welcomed. (11.8–11.10)

Official policy should be clearly directed at disposing of sub-standard quarters which are not capable of reasonable improvement, to retaining those which can most effectively and economically be improved, and to formulating a staged programme for carrying out of such improvements. (11.11)

In all establishments ways should be looked for to reduce to a minimum delays in carrying out the repair and maintenance of quarters. (11.13)

The arrangements under which quarters are provided for staff should be reviewed. (11.18)

The carrying out of decorating and similar work by the tenants of quarters should be encouraged wherever possible. (11.19–11.20)

Further consideration should be given to reviewing the system of calculating rent allowances. (11.22)

The rent allowance payable to single officers should be increased to two-thirds of the married rate but there should be no other changes. (11.23)

Steps should be taken to improve the condition of bachelor quarters throughout the United Kingdom. (11.24)

Careful thought should be given to the alternative uses to which vacated quarters might be put. (11.25)

Other matters

The security and reliability of hired transport are factors which should override considerations of cost. (11.27)

The Home Office should keep a close watch on the facilities provided for prison officers in Crown Courts, and should maintain such pressure as may be necessary on the Lord Chancellor's Department to have as many deficiencies as possible put right. (11.29)

Prison establishments should be open to inspection by HM Factory Inspectors, Public Health Inspectors and similar officials to the same extent as any private establishment. (11.30)

While mobility among officer grades and particularly governor grades is an inevitable feature of life in the prison services, the rules and regulations relating to postings should be kept under constant review to ensure that they do not give rise to any unnecessary transfers. (11.31–11.32)

There should be no objection in principle to promotions *in situ*. (11.34)

Where a transfer is made on an officer's promotion attempts should always be made, if this is desired, to transfer him or her to another establishment in the same locality. (11.34)

Every effort should be made to initiate promotion examination results as soon as possible.

The concession which permits an officer to transfer from an inconvenient station at public expense after having served there for a specified number of years should cease. (11.36)

J D MAY (Chairman)

DOREEN BELLERBY

M BETT

L F EDMONDSON

J A GARDINER

RACHEL GIBBS

NICHOLAS HINTON

MYLES HUMPHREYS

C G B NICHOLSON

JOHN NIGHTINGALE

R M MORRIS (Secretary)

ALAN HARDING (Assistant Secretary)

ALAN FRASER (Assistant Secretary)

1. Recess, Birmingham Prison.
   Washing and toilet facilities for the inmates of a landing.

2. Inmate accommodation, Birmingham Prison.
    The sort of conditions in which remand prisoners may be confined in the older local
    prisons.

3. Staff muster room, Peterhead Prison. Many prisons lack such a facility, even of this standard.

4. The joinery shop, Peterhead Prison. Inmate working conditions in a Victorian prison.

5. New workshops, Glenochil   Modern purpose-built workshops in a Young Offenders' Institution.

6. Kitchen, Wakefield Prison.   Cooking facilities for a prison accommodating up to 800 inmates.

7. Central kitchen, Cornton Vale. Main cooking facilities for a modern prison with a population of under 200.

8. The centre, Birmingham Prison. ... All parts are both visible and accessible, reducing control problems.

9. Corridor in modern purpose-built living accommodation, Portland Borstal.
A relatively small section of accommodation is visible from any one point; this has
implications for manning levels and control.

10. Birmingham Prison.
   Exterior view of a typical Victorian local prison, completed in 1845.

11. The Verne. An example of a redeveloped Victorian military site.

APPENDIX 1

List of Organisations which submitted Written Evidence

Central Government

Home Office
Scottish Home and Health Department
Northern Ireland Office
HM Treasury
Civil Service Department
Lord Chancellor's Department
Department of Health and Social Security
Government Actuary's Department
Crown Office

Other Organisations

Apex Trust
Association of Chief Police Officers of England, Wales and Northern Ireland
Association of County Councils
Association of Directors of Social Services
Association of First Division Civil Servants (Home Office Branch)
Association of Metropolitan Authorities
Association of Teachers in Penal Establishments
Association for the Psychiatric Study of Adolescents
Barrow and Geraldine S Cadbury Trust
British Association of Prison Governors
British Medical Association
British Psychological Society
Central Council of Probation and After-Care Committees
Cheshire Education Committee
Chief Officers' Conference
Church of England Board for Social Responsibility
Church Army
Civil Service Union
Civil and Public Services Association
Community Service Volunteers
Conference of Chief Probation Officers
Criminon
Diocese of Armagh
Diocese of Coventry, Bishop's Council for Social Responsibility
Exeter Diocesan Council for Social Aid
Family Service Units
Haldane Society of Socialist Lawyers
Home Office Branch of the Society of Civil and Public Servants
Home Office Departmental Joint Industrial Council
Home Office Departmental Whitley Council, Staff Side
Howard League for Penal Reform
Inner London Education Authority
Institution of Professional Civil Servants
Justices' Clerks' Society
Leicester Anchor Association Ltd
Liberal Party
Library Association
Magistrates' Association
National Association for the Care and Resettlement of Offenders

National Association of Prison Visitors
National Association of Probation Officers
National Council for Civil Liberties
National Institute of Adult Education (England and Wales)
National Prisoners' Movement (PROP)
Northern Ireland Probation and After-Care Service
Northern Ireland Public Service Alliance
Nottinghamshire Probation and After-Care Service
Parole Board
Parole Board for Scotland
Police Superintendent's Association of England and Wales
Portia Trust
Presbyterian Church in Ireland
Prison Officers' Association
Prison Officers' Association (Northern Ireland Branch)
Prison Officers' Association (Works Branch)
Prison Department Outstations Branch of the Society of Civil and Public
    Servants
Prison and Borstal Governors (England and Wales) Branch of the Society of
    Civil and Public Servants
Prison and Borstal Governors (Scotland) Branch of the Society of Civil and
    Public Servants
Prison and Borstal Governors (Northern Ireland) Branch of the Society of Civil
    and Public Servants
Radical Alternatives to Prison
Royal College of Psychiatrists
Salvation Army
Scottish Association for the Care and Resettlement of Offenders
Scottish Council for Civil Liberties
Scottish Council of Fabian Societies
Scottish Liberal Party
Scottish Prison Officers' Association
Social Welfare Commission of the Roman Catholic Bishops of England and
    Wales
Society of Conservative Lawyers
Society of Friends
Society of Friends, Littlehampton Meeting
South East Thames Regional Health Authority
South West Herts Community Health Council
Southwark Diocesan Synod
Strathclyde Group of the Howard League for Penal Reform in Scotland
St Anne's Shelter and Housing Action Ltd
West Yorkshire Probation and After-Care Service

APPENDIX 2
List of Names of Persons who gave Oral Evidence

Central Government
Home Office

Sir Robert Armstrong KCB CVO
Mr N F Cairncross CB
Mr D J Trevelyan
Mr M S Gale MC
Mr A W Glanville
Mr A D Gordon-Brown
Mr M J Moriarty
Mr K J Neale OBE
Mr D A Peach
Mr T G Weiler
Mr G W Fowler
Mr P Beedle
Mr J F D Buttery
Miss E M Chadwell
Mr D W Fisher
Mr K Gibson
Mr M D Macleod
Mr S G Norris
Mr A R Rawsthorne
Mr C H Taylor
Mr E A Towndrow
Mr L J F Wheeler
Mr R J Pearce
Mr J R Troop
Mr K J Bradley
Mr E W A Fryer
Mr E A Grant
Miss S M Fairhead

(Prison Medical Service)

Dr J H Orr
Dr W Oldham
Dr G Pollitt
Dr W Stephen
Dr D O Topp
Dr B D Cooper
Dr P A Trafford
Dr R A Washbrook

Scottish Home and Health Department

Mr A L Rennie
Mr D J Cowperthwaite
Mr J Scrimgeour
Mr J Keeley
Mr A M Thomson
Mr P A Glynn
Dr R A Ratcliff
Dr J A Morton

Scottish Office

Mr A H M Mitchell

Northern Ireland Office

Mr J F Irvine
Mr E N Barry
Mr S C Jackson
Mr W G Robinson
Mr R Gibson
Mr B Storey

Treasury	Miss J M Forsyth
	Mr D Butler
	Miss M King
Civil Service Department	Mr P F Clifton
	Mr G T Morgan
	Mr W E Wightman
	Mr G H Wollen
	Mr A S Halford
	Mr B Hennah
	Mr A Burton
	Miss S L Scales
Central Policy Review Staff	Mrs J Bridgeman
Department of Health and Social Security	Dr E Shore
	Mr N M Hale
	Mr P J Wormald
	Dr M J MacCulloch
	Mr C Emerson
	Miss S P C Wright-Warren
	Mr C Lake

Staff Associations

Prison Officers' Association	Mr P Waugh
	Mr K Daniel
	Mr D Evans
	Mr P Rushworth
Prison Officers' Association (Works Branch)	Mr T A Cadman
	Mr W Quirie
	Mr D Simons
	Mr S Twine
	Mr R Ward
Prison Officers' Association (Northern Ireland Branch)	Mr J McGookin
	Mr A Campbell
Scottish Prison Officers' Association	Mr J B Renton
	Mr A S Crichton
	Mr D McCallum
Chief Officers	Mr D Branch
	Mr L H R Claxton
	Mr H A Godfroy
	Mr M Russ
	Mr F Stevens
Society of Civil and Public Servants Prison and Borstal Governors' Branch England and Wales	Mr F B O'Friel
	Mr W J Abbott
	Mr J Blakey
	Mr R Clarke
	Mr A Fitzpatrick
	Mr A M E de Frisching
	Major P L James
	Mr G E Morris

Scotland	Mr E Campbell
	Mr A G Coyle
	Mr C W Hills
	Mr M J Milne
Northern Ireland	Mr W Kerr
	Mr W McConnell
Prison Department Outstations Branch	Mr S J Archer
	Mr J Cain
	Mr G G Gilbert
	Mr D Heywood
	Mr A Lewis
	Mr K E Shirley
Association of First Division Civil Servants	Mrs B M Fair
	Mr W N Hyde
	Mr S G Norris
Association of Teachers in Penal Establishments	Mr D M McCarthy
	Mr P R Shore
Civil and Public Services Association	Mr M Chipchase
	Mr R F Gilbert
	Mr A A Parker
	Mr P Thomason
	Mrs B Thompson
Civil Service Union	Mr M Barke
	Mr T Dickinson
	Mr K Oram
	Mr T Talbot
Home Office Departmental Whitley Council (Staff Side)	Mr R C Morris
	Mr W S Burton
	Mr R Gunn
	Mr L V A Heasman
	Mr D J Merrick
	Mr K S Perera
Home Office Joint Industrial Council	Mr F W Cottam
	Mr P Adams
Institution of Professional Civil Servants	Mr M Creamer
	Mr D Ebdon
	Miss W Harrison
	Mr J Hunt
	Mr B Weir
Northern Ireland Public Service Alliance	Mr J Cooper

Other Organisations

Association of County Councils	Mr I Benson
	Mr P J Coles
	Mr W Done
Association of Directors of Social Services	Mr W B Harbert
	Mr A W Hunt
	Mr W H Laming
	Mr W J Rea-Price
	Mr N Stacey

Association of Metropolitan Authorities	Mr M Neale
	Mr P T Sloman
Barrow and Geraldine S Cadbury Trust	Mr A E Wilson
Howard League for Penal Reform	Mr L J Blom-Cooper
	Mr M Wright
Inner London Education Authority	Mr P Clyne
	Mr S Heaven
	Mr P Lincoln
National Association for the Care and Resettlement of Offenders	Mr I Crow
	Mr G Wilkins
National Association of Probation Officers	Mr M C L Bruggen
	Mr D Finch
	Mr D MacLauchlan
	Mrs G Thornton
National Council for Civil Liberties	Mr W Birtles
	Mr J McVicar
	Mr C Soley MP
National Prisoners' Movement (PROP)	Mr G Coggan
	Mr R Pooley
	Mrs E Pooley

Other Witnesses

Rt Hon Merlyn Rees MP
Lord Harris of Greenwich
Rt Hon The Earl of Longford KG
Mr Robert Kilroy-Silk MP
Sir Arthur Peterson KCB MVO (formerly Permanent Under Secretary of State at the Home Office)
Mr E D Wright CB (formerly Director General of the Prison Service)
Brigadier M S K Maunsell CBE DSO (formerly Inspector-General of the Prison Service)
Dr R D King
Dr S D M McConville
Mr R Morgan
Dr J E Thomas
Mr J E Hall Williams

APPENDIX 3

Visits

Establishments Visited in England and Wales

Prisons

Albany
Aylesbury
Birmingham
Bristol
Brixton
Cardiff
Coldingley
Dartmoor
Exeter
Ford
Gartree
Grendon
Holloway
Leyhill
Liverpool
Long Lartin
Manchester
Parkhurst
The Verne
Wakefield
Wandsworth
Wormwood Scrubs
Wymott

Borstals

Portland
Rochester
Prescoed

Remand Centres

Ashford
Pucklechurch

Detention Centre

Usk

Training Establishments

Prison Service College, Wakefield
Officer Training School, Leyhill
Officer Training School, Wakefield

Other Establishments

South East Regional Office
South West Regional Office
North Regional Office
Midland Regional Office
Offices of Prison Department Headquarters

297

ESTABLISHMENTS VISITED IN SCOTLAND

Prisons

Barlinnie
Special Unit, Barlinnie
Cornton Vale
Inverness
Peterhead

Other Establishments

Glenochil Young Offenders' Institution and Detention Centre
Polmont Borstal
Scottish Prison Service College, Polmont
Prisons Division, Scottish Home and Health Department

ESTABLISHMENTS VISITED IN NORTHERN IRELAND

Prisons

Armagh
Belfast
The Maze

ESTABLISHMENTS VISITED ABROAD

France

Fleury-Mérogis Prison
La Santé Prison
Ministry of Justice, Paris

Denmark

Herstedvester Prison
Horserød Prison
Vridsløselille Prison
Department of Prison and Probation, Copenhagen

Sweden

Kumla Prison
Tillberga Prison
National Prison and Probation Administration, Norrköping

OTHER ESTABLISHMENTS VISITED

Metropolitan Police Training School, Hendon
Broadmoor Special Hospital

APPENDIX 4

Visit to France, 1–4 April 1979

1. The Inquiry spent three working days in France, visiting the Ministry of Justice, Fleury-Mérogis Prison—which comprises male and female *maisons d'arrêt* (local prisons), the National Officer Training School and a *Centre de Jeunes Détenus*—and La Santé high security prison.

2. The French prison population, which has increased rapidly in recent years, is currently just under 37,000 (not including juveniles)*. The female population, now around 1,100, has risen particularly sharply both in size and seriousness of offence. Appropriate mental hospital conditions still exist in France for mentally abnormal offenders, but there are two establishments for psychopaths. The French believe that the overall population will continue to increase and that there is little scope for influencing this trend by the sort of measures adopted, for example, in the Netherlands. There are currently some 180 penal establishments, varying considerably in size from the very large institutions like Fleury-Mérogis, which had 4,000 inmates when visited, down to small prisons run by senior uniformed staff, some of which have as few as 30 inmates. The building programme aims to provide three additional prisons a year for some time ahead. 149 of the 180 establishments are *maisons d'arrêt*, fulfilling local prison functions as understood in Britain; the rest act as regional holding facilities for longer term prisoners. There are no open prisons.

3. There is little in the way of organised penal pressure groups in France and public opinion appears generally hostile to liberal developments. The central administration enjoys the status and respect which attaches generally to the public service and increasing prosperity has preserved moderate attitudes among the public sector unions: these factors have contributed to a confident and determined style of penal management. The present Directeur is drawn from the corps of *Prefets* (i.e. from the most senior category of officials) and has come from outside the Ministry of Justice. It is technically possible, but most unlikely, that a former governor might hold the position. The other main headquarters posts are occupied by *Magistrats* who similarly move in and out of prison administration. The same applies to the Inspector who undertakes a regular inspection programme as well as special inspections at Ministerial request.

4. France is divided into nine penal regions under the direction of ex-governors who exercise an operational oversight, particularly in regard to the smaller establishments. An important additional feature of the French system are the 211 *juges d'application*, members of the *Magistrats* corps and attached to courts, with responsibilities in regard to remission, punishment, parole and home leave. Governors' disciplinary powers, for example, are restricted to segregating prisoners, more severe penalties being up to the *juges* to authorise, albeit often on the governor's advice. The relationship between the juge and the governor may thus be a delicate one. The juges are also responsible for handling most types of inmate complaint—in a sense, a system of internalised judicial oversight. The *mediateur* (ombudsman), the administrative courts and members of Parliament appear to play a less significant role. French inmates enjoy full rights of litigation but, like all French citizens, have no individual access to the European Commission of Human Rights. Each establishment has a *Commission des Surveillances*, chaired by the local *Prefets*, with general oversight functions roughly analogous to certain of the powers of Boards of Visitors.

5. There are currently some 13,000 prison officers, about 3,000 short of the manpower target of 1 officer to 2·5 inmates. Recruitment is proceeding reasonably well, despite the entry standards and quite intensive psychological tests, but the needs of

---

*The population of France in 1975 was 52·7 million.

299

new establishments take up much of each year's increase. Officers undergo an initial eight-weeks' training and there is some degree of continuation training thereafter. There is little opportunity for officer specialisation in France. There are no works officers, for example, the works function being performed by the Ministry's own Works Department, and the bulk of prison clerical work is civilianised. There are opportunities for officers to enter the administrative, social worker and governor grades but few officers appear to make use of them—although officers do frequently take charge of small establishments. Desire on the part of officers for involvement in treatment and training does not seem to be an issue in France. External entrants to the governor grades have all been graduates since 1975, the degree requirement including a diploma in political studies. As indicated, governors enjoy fewer powers than their British counterparts and appear to have less control over their regimes.

6. The pay of French prison officers appears broadly in line with that in Britain. It is, however, tied more directly to civil service scales (which include teachers and the police), the scales being organised in a way that involves a high degree of wage indexation but more rigidly preserves differentials between different groups. Overtime working appears to be less than in Britain, although there are similar pressures for it and, more generally, for increased manning levels. There is no general provision of free housing, although some quarters are available at each establishment to provide a reserve of officers for emergencies. French prison officers are prohibited from industrial action and the union approach is generally moderate and management-orientated. A particular feature of labour relations in the public sector is the *commission paritaire*, on which staff and management are represented equally, whose function is not only consultative but has decision-making powers in certain personnel management areas.

7. The allocation of longer-term prisoners is managed centrally in the French system, and although there is no formal system of classification, a form of dispersal policy applies to the most serious security risks. Apart from exercise and work, there is little opportunity for association in French prisons, an aspect mitigated by the fact that a high proportion of establishments have integral sanitation. The fact that instances of suicide occur more frequently than in Britain may not, however, be unconnected. The current working week for prison industries is something over 30 hours (40 being the target) and inmates can earn the national minimum wage—with appropriate deductions for keep and some compulsory savings. One reason for high wages may be the heavy reliance which prison industries place upon work from private firms. There is, however, a high degree of penal unemployment, no more than half the population—possibly less—currently being employed.

APPENDIX 5

Visit to Scandinavia, 22–27 April 1979

1. The Inquiry spent five working days in Scandinavia, two in Denmark and three in Sweden. In Denmark it visited the Department of Prison and Probation in Copenhagen, Horserød open prison, Vridsløselille closed prison and Herstedvester psychiatric prison. In Sweden members visited the National Prison and Probation Administration at Norrköping, Kumla closed prison and Tillberga industrial prison.

Denmark

2. The pattern of recorded crime in Denmark was one of a sharp increase during the 1960s, followed by a slower rate of growth in the 1970s and an actual fall in two years in the middle of the decade. The easing in the rate of increase in recorded crime during the 1970s, plus the fact that violent and sexual offences play a very small part in the total, and the position of the Director General as a well-known public figure (the present incumbent has been in post since 1971), all contributed to a generally tolerant public attitude towards the penological developments of the period. These developments were initiated by a three-fold programme of legislative reform in 1973. The first element was the amalgamation of the prison and probation services (the latter having previously been privately organised although with substantial central government funding). This was essential if resources were to be transferred from custodial to community projects. The second step, in line with general disillusionment with treatment-orientated approaches, was the phasing out, almost entirely, of the indeterminate sentences previously available to the courts. Finally, there had been moves, by reducing sentence maxima and directing the prosecutors accordingly (in Denmark public prosecutors may recommend particular sentences), to reduce the length of prison sentences. The effect of these various changes had been to reduce the average daily population from about 3,500 in 1970 to something just under 3,000 in 1978*.

3. Parallel with these developments had been changes affecting the numbers and organisation of prison staff. The total staff running Danish prisons (some 2,925, including the central administration) is roughly equal to the number of inmates and had been reduced by the equivalent of some 200–300 since 1971, during a period when working hours had been reduced and a new establishment opened. Despite the prevailing belief that the Danish service was under-staffed, it had been possible to carry through this reduction with the agreement of the unions—although they had insisted on cuts being made uniformly across the service, rather than selectively as had been hoped.

4. The style of management within institutions has also changed. More "democratic" structures have been introduced which have tended to undermine the intermediate management tiers so that officer hierarchies have been flattened. This is particularly the case where, as at Horserød prison, the establishment has been divided into a series of self-governing units. The governors grades attend the monthly meetings of such units only as observers, natural leaders being allowed to emerge—one result of which has been that there is now little obvious role for the subordinate officer ranks, the only purpose of, say, the senior officer rank being to reward long service. At the recently opened Ringe prison, which the Inquiry did not visit, changes in staff role have been taken a stage further by dispensing altogether with the services of specialist staff; discipline officers with skills in carpentry were appointed (about two thirds of officer recruits are skilled workers), who live and work in close proximity to the inmates and are allowed to decide their own duty rosters. Although it is said that the changed environment in most Danish prisons has now been largely accepted by staff,

---

*The Danish population in 1978 was 5·1 million.

301

it was acknowledged that uncertainty over roles and objectives may be contributing to what is one of the major current problems in the Danish system, very high levels of absenteeism due to sickness.

5. Danish prison officers are members of an ordinary civil service union, their pay being negotiated centrally with the Ministry of Finance without the involvement of the prisons administration. In practice, however, the main pay negotiations usually include a small additional increment within the discretion of the Director General, following further direct negotiations with staff. It was apparent, also, that the Director General had been able to acquire some part of the savings resulting from the manpower reductions for the augmentation of the pay of more responsible posts. The public service in Denmark does not enjoy any formal linkages as in the United Kingdom with comparable outside employment; prison officers are less well paid than the police.

6. Prison governors are nearly all lawyers who are well paid at the level of judges and police chiefs. Although direct recruitment at deputy governor level is possible, the preferred practice now is for recruited lawyers to spend a few years in the central administration first, before moving out to establishments. Experience of, and sympathy with, the problems and procedures of the central administration is thought to be important for the governor grades. As far as officers are concerned, the present practice of recruiting around the ages of 23–24 is believed to be right, although lower entry ages are permitted, rather than recruiting staff immediately upon completion of their education.

7. Of the 3,000 inmates currently comprising the Danish prison population, about 800 are on remand and 500 in the special Danish category of "lenient" imprisonment—most of which are drunken drivers doing short sentences of from seven days to a maximum of two months. The ordinary sentenced population is thus around 1,700, of whom more than half serve from the outset in open conditions. There are no limitations in the Danish system on the types of offender that can be sent to open prisons, and there is apparently a considerable degree of public tolerance of the high level of absconding that is the inevitable result. There was less public acceptance of escapes from closed institutions, of which over 70 took place in 1978—although it is held in the Danish system that a certain level of escapes is not only tolerable but to be welcomed as a sign that the degrees of security and control imposed are not unduly repressive. The current plan is to set acceptable escape targets for each establishment. Denmark experiences similar problems to those of Britain in regard to mentally abnormal offenders, following a reduction in the number of closed mental institutions. At present, Herstedvester acts as a final refuge for difficult and disturbed inmates from other parts of the system (and some psychiatric hospitals), and there is pressure on the mental hospitals to accept greater responsibility for such offenders.

Sweden

8. The National Prison and Probation Administration (NPPA) was moved from Stockholm to Norrköping some three years ago, a move which resulted in a very substantial change-over in staff. There are regular contacts with the Ministry of Justice in Stockholm and central government is closely involved in the policy of the administration through the compilation of the annual budget. The NPPA itself is under the control of a board, chaired by the Director General (with a casting vote) and consisting of members of Parliament and representatives of the employers and trade union organisations and the Health and Welfare and Labour Market Boards. The total staff of the Administration is around 6,000, of whom 3–400 work at Norrköping and a further 850 are professional probation staff. Together they are responsible for some 70 prisons, 20 remand centres and 60 probation offices.

302

9. Four basic principles for the correctional system had been enunciated in 1974 as part of a general reorganisation. These were that probation should be the main instrument in correctional policy; that there should be close co-operation between the prison and probation services throughout the sentence; that sentences should be served as near as possible to home areas; and that co-operation should be developed between the correctional system and the social services of society at large. The prison system is accordingly divided into national and regional institutions. There are some 21 national institutions for long-term prisoners (that is, those serving sentences of more than one year). Fifteen of these are closed (with a capacity of 1,400) and six are open (with a capacity of 575). The remaining 50 establishments, some of which are very small, are divided into 13 regions and can accommodate a total of 2,000 inmates. Their job is to hold short-termers near to their home areas and to provide a bridge back into the home community for long-termers towards the end of their sentence. The total prison population is now a little over 4,000, having risen slightly in the last year or so as a result of an increase in the proportion of those serving sentences of two years or more. The probation service, whose permanent staff are assisted by some 10,000 volunteers, is also organised regionally (although covering smaller geographical areas than the prison regions) and currently provides for a total caseload of some 16,500.*

10. The main qualitative changes that have taken place in the Swedish prison population in recent years have been the growth in numbers of, on the one hand, illiterate prisoners and, on the other, of educated and articulate prisoners; of prisoners sentenced for drug related offences; and of mentally disordered offenders for whom insufficient places can be found in closed mental institutions. Parole/remission is granted in Sweden, subject to the decision of local supervisory boards (and a central Supervisory Board in the case of those serving sentences of more than one year), normally at the two-thirds point in sentence. Powers do exist however to parole at the half-way stage. The parole decision is based almost entirely upon predicted future behaviour (employment plans etc), rather than upon previous behaviour or behaviour in prison. Within establishments the system of sanctions is mild, the maximum award of loss of remission being ten days, and home leave being forfeited only if a previous leave has been abused, not for indiscipline in the establishment.

11. Recruitment of prison officers is carried out locally at each establishment, by a process in which a representative of the officers' union participates. Governors have authority to appoint temporary staff, the grade through which most potential officers enter the service, but powers of permanent appointment are reserved to the NPPA. The importance of the local selection procedures has, however, been increased with recent developments in labour legislation which has increased the difficulty of dismissing temporary staff. The majority of officers remain at their initial establishment. The training programme currently consists of an initial fortnight introductory course at the establishment followed, after some 2–3 years, by an extended course at Norrköping, designed to bring officers up to pre-university standards in the behavioural and social sciences. The fact that this long delay between recruitment and training apparently causes few problems within establishments, suggests that its main purpose is the improvement of the professional status of prison officers. There is a further continuation course, roughly six months after this course, but there is no on-going training thereafter.

12. Recent industrial relations legislation has re-emphasised the similarity of position between workers in the public and private sectors. Prison staff thus have full rights of industrial action during the negotiation of a collective agreement, but are restricted, like everyone else, while the agreement itself is in force: an example

---

*The Swedish population in 1979 was 8·2 million.

of how this applied in principle was provided by the recent instance in which the Stockholm Labour Court had ordered back to work and fined the staff of a community hostel who had started taking industrial action. There is in fact no recollection of recent industrial action in the prison service. The other side of recent developments in trade union legislation is the need to consult staff (although they have no right of veto) on every significant management initiative, a provision which places a considerable burden upon the staff of the NPPA. Pay negotiations are conducted both centrally within the civil service, and by the NPPA, the division of functions being that the allocation of sums to particular grades is a central responsibility, with the NPPA negotiating directly on the particular civil service pay grading appropriate to particular grades of prison officer. The restriction upon the NPPA is the fact that it has to keep within its budget; since the same unions represent staff in a variety of agencies and ministries, this is a further limitation upon the amount of variation which in practice takes place. Overall, management/staff relations appeared comparatively harmonious although complaints were to be heard (perhaps surprisingly in a small organisation which could concentrate directly upon operational issues, rather than being distracted by the need to provide advice for ministers) about the remoteness of headquarters, its delay in responding and its failure to be properly attuned to operational needs.

APPENDIX 6

Accommodation in Use in Great Britain on 31 October 1978

List A indicates the size, age and primary use of each establishment in England and Wales with some assessment of its present physical condition. Similar information for Scotland is at List B.

List A includes sites where a work force of prisoners was held in temporary quarters in order to construct permanent accommodation. It does *not* include new establishments under construction or approved for early construction on virgin sites. The third column of the Annex indicates the certified normal accommodation (CNA) i.e. the uncrowded capacity of all the available units of accommodating cells, cubicles or dormitories. The fourth column (Age) adopts 1930 as the dividing line between the new purpose-built prisons, which are expected to have a life at least to the end of the century, and older buildings. Establishments used exclusively for female inmates are denoted (F). The following terms have been used in the final column to describe work in progress or planned:—

"New prison" —A temporary camp housing direct labour to build one or two new permanent prisons. The camp will be closed on completion of the building work.

"Improvement" —Usually a prison of substantial construction now in need of modernisation but retaining existing living accommodation.

"Replacement" —Usually a prison where sub-standard accommodation is being slowly replaced while the prison continues to operate.

In the same column, if there is no work in progress or planned but the need for such work is foreseen before the end of the century an assessment of the development potential is given as follows:—

"Excellent" —Location, site, and services would allow modernisation/redevelopment for a variety of purposes.

"Moderate" —Scope for modernisation/redevelopment but constraints on alternative uses and on operational value.

"Poor" —Poor location and/or inadequate site or services for modern penal establishment.

Abbreviations are as follows:

D.C.	Detention centre, Junior (Jun) or Senior (Sen)
Disp.	Dispersal prison
RC	Remand centre
Tng.	Training prison
Y.P.	Young Prisoner establishment

LIST A

Establishment	Primary use	CNA	Age	Physical condition	Future potential
Acklington	Closed Training	327	Camp	Poor	New prisons
Albany	Closed Tng. Disp.	294	Post-1930	Good	—
Aldington	Senior D.C.	116	Camp	Fair	Poor
Appleton Thorn	Open Training	319	Camp	Poor	Excellent
Ashford	Remand Centre	400	Pre-1930	Poor	Excellent
Ashwell	Open Training	400	Camp	Fair	Replacement
(F) Askham Grange	Open Training	120	Pre-1930	Fair	Improvement
Aylesbury	Closed Tng. Y.P.	295	Pre-1930	Fair	Improvement
Bedford	Local Prison	169	Pre-1930	Fair	Poor
Birmingham	Local Prison	603	Pre-1930	Fair	Improvement
Blantyre House	Senior D.C.	122	Pre-1930	Fair	Poor
Blundeston	Closed Training	418	Post-1930	Good	—
Bristol	Local Prison	579	Pre-1930	Fair	Improvement
Brixton	Local Prison	654	Pre-1930	Fair	Improvement
Brockhill	Remand Centre	177	Post-1930	Good	—
Buckley Hall	Senior D.C.	139	Pre-1930	Fair	Excellent
(F) Bullwood Hall	Closed Borstal	137	Post-1930	Good	Improvement
Camp Hill	Closed Training	487	Pre-1930	Good	—
Campsfield House	Junior D.C.	70	Post-1930	Good	Moderate
Canterbury	Local Prison	246	Pre-1930	Fair	Poor
Cardiff	Local Prison	340	Pre-1930	Fair	Moderate
Channings Wood	Closed Training	260	Camp	Poor	New prison
*Chelmsford	Closed Training	—	Pre-1930	Fair	Improvement
Coldingley	Closed Training	296	Post-1930	Good	—
(F) Cookham Wood	Closed Training	56	Post-1930	Good	—
Dartmoor	Closed Training	550	Pre-1930	Fair	Improvement
Deerbolt	Closed Borstal	285	Camp	Poor	Replacement
Dorchester	Local Prison	155	Pre-1930	Good	Improvement
Dover	Closed Borstal	246	Pre-1930	Fair	Moderate
(F) Drake Hall	Open Training	150	Camp	Poor	Moderate
Durham	Local Prison	708	Pre-1930	Fair	Improvement
(F) East Sutton Park	Open Borstal	65	Pre-1930	Fair	Poor
Eastwood Park	Junior D.C.	146	Post-1930	Good	—
Erlestoke	Closed Tng. Y.P.	205	Camp	Fair	Replacement
Everthorpe	Closed Borstal	304	Post-1930	Good	—
Exeter	Local Prison	372	Pre-1930	Fair	Improvement
Featherstone	Closed Training	484	Post-1930	Good	—
Feltham	Closed Borstal	270	Pre-1930	Poor	Replacement/ Improvement
Finnamore Wood	Open Borstal	79	Camp	Good	Poor
Ford	Open Training	534	Camp	Fair	Improvement
Foston Hall	Junior D.C.	65	Pre-1930	Fair	Poor
†Gartree	Closed Tng. Disp.	391	Post-1930	Good	—
Gaynes Hall	Open Borstal	161	Camp	Poor	Moderate
Glen Parva	Closed Borstal	300	Post-1930	Good	—
Gloucester	Local Prison	196	Pre-1930	Fair	Poor
Grendon	Closed Training	325	Post-1930	Good	—
Gringley	Open Borstal	72	Post-1930	Good	—
Guys Marsh	Open Borstal	265	Camp	Poor	Replacement
Haslar	Senior D.C.	100	Camp	Fair	Poor
Hatfield	Open Borstal	180	Camp	Poor	Replacement
Haverigg	Closed Training	520	Camp	Poor	Poor

Establishment	Primary use	CNA	Age	Physical condition	Future potential
Hewell Grange	Open Borstal	136	Pre-1930	Fair	Excellent
Highpoint	Closed Training	301	Camp	Fair	New prisons
Hindley	Closed Borstal	312	Post-1930	Good	—
Hollesley Bay	Open Borstal	487	Post-1930	Fair	Replacement/ Improvement
(F) Holloway	Local Prison	221	Post-1930	Good	Replacement
Hull	Closed Tng. Disp.	318	Pre-1930	Good	—
Huntercombe	Closed Borstal	141	Camp	Poor	Replacement/ Improvement
Kingston	Closed Training	140	Pre-1930	Good	—
Kirkham	Open Training	608	Camp	Poor	Excellent
Kirklevington	Junior D.C.	150	Post-1930	Fair	Poor
Lancaster	Closed Training	153	Pre-1930	Poor	Poor
Latchmere House	Remand Centre	128	Post-1930	Fair	Improvement
Leeds	Local Prison	592	Pre-1930	Fair	Poor
Leicester	Local Prison	229	Pre-1930	Fair	Poor
Lewes	Local Prison	319	Pre-1930	Good	Improvement
Leyhill	Open Training	331	Camp	Poor	Replacement
Lincoln	Local Prison	354	Pre-1930	Fair	Improvement
Liverpool	Local Prison	1,016	Pre-1930	Poor	Improvement
Long Lartin	Closed Tng. Disp.	350	Post-1930	Good	—
Lowdham Grange	Open Borstal	304	Post-1930	Fair	Excellent
Low Newton	Remand Centre	181	Post-1930	Good	—
Maidstone	Closed Training	530	Pre-1930	Fair	Poor
Manchester	Local Prison	1,087	Pre-1930	Fair	Moderate
Medomsley	Senior D.C.	117	Pre-1930	Fair	Poor
(F) Moor Court	Open Training	76	Pre-1930	Fair	Poor
New Hall	Senior D.C.	104	Camp	Fair	Poor
Northallerton	Closed Training	143	Pre-1930	Fair	Poor
Northeye	Closed Training	345	Camp	Good	Improvement
North Sea Camp	Open Senior D.C.	166	Camp	Poor	Poor
Norwich	Local Prison	391	Pre-1930	Fair	Improvement
Nottingham	Closed Training	207	Pre-1930	Fair	Excellent
Onley	Closed Tng. Y.P.	420	Post-1930	Good	—
Oxford	Local Prison	143	Pre-1930	Poor	Poor
Parkhurst	Closed Tng. Disp.	480	Pre-1930	Poor	Improvement
Pentonville	Local Prison	910	Pre-1930	Poor	Moderate
Portland	Closed Borstal	519	Pre-1930	Good	Improvement
Preston	Closed Training	427	Pre-1930	Fair	Moderate
Pucklechurch	Remand Centre	171	Post-1930	Good	—
Ranby	Closed Training	488	Camp	Poor	Replacement
Reading	Closed Training	160	Pre-1930	Good	Improvement
Risley	Remand Centre	644	Post-1930	Fair	Moderate
Rochester	Closed Borstal	376	Pre-1930	Fair	Moderate
Rudgate	Open Training	378	Camp	Fair	Excellent
Send	Junior D.C.	118	Post-1930	Fair	Moderate
Shepton Mallet	Closed Training	162	Pre-1930	Good	Improvement
Shrewsbury	Local Prison	170	Pre-1930	Fair	Poor
Spring Hill	Open Training	200	Camp	Poor	Moderate
Stafford	Closed Training	536	Pre-1930	Fair	Improvement
Standford Hill	Open Training	551	Camp	Poor	Improvement
Stoke Heath	Closed Borstal	360	Post-1930	Good	—
(F) Styal	Closed Training	196	Pre-1930	Fair	Excellent
Sudbury	Open Training	384	Camp	Poor	Replacement
Swansea	Local Prison	229	Pre-1930	Fair	Poor

307

Establishment	Primary use	CNA	Age	Physical condition	Future potential
Swinfen Hall	Closed Tng. Y.P.	182	Post-1930	Good	—
Thorp Arch RC	Remand Centre	101	Post-1930	Good	—
Usk (Main)	Senior D.C.	105	Pre-1930	Good	Poor
Usk (Prescoed)	Open Borstal	104	Camp	Poor	Replacement
Verne	Closed Training	618	Post-1930	Good	Improvement
Wakefield	Closed Tng. Disp.	790	Pre-1930	Fair	Improvement
Wandsworth	Local Prison	1,247	Pre-1930	Fair	Improvement
Wellingborough	Closed Borstal	344	Post-1930	Good	—
Werrington	Senior D.C.	110	Pre-1930	Good	Poor
Wetherby	Open Borstal	240	Camp	Poor	Replacement
Whatton	Sen./Jun. D.C.	215	Post-1930	Good	—
Winchester	Local Prison	484	Pre-1930	Fair	Poor
Wormwood Scrubs	Local Prison	1,229	Pre-1930	Fair	Improvement

Notes:

*Chelmsford—temporarily closed after fire.
†Gartree—condition good after riot damage repair.

	Type	Design capacity	First used for offenders	Classification		
Aberdeen	Prison	177	1903	A	11	Y
Barlinnie	Prison	898	1880–86	A	11	Y
Castle Huntly	Borstal	114	1947	C	1	W
Cornton Vale	Prison (Female)	124	1975	C	1	W
	YOI (Female)	42	1975	C	1	W
	Borstal (Female)	53	1975	C	1	W
Dumfries	Prison	27	1883	A	1	Y
	YOI	115	1965	A	1	Y
Dungavel	Prison	151	1975	C	1	W
Edinburgh	Prison	371	1919–25	A	11	X
	YOI	153	1965	C	1	X
Friarton	YOI	63	1963	A	11	Z
Glenochil	YOI	498	1976	C	1	W
	DC	180	1966	C	1	W
Greenock	Prison	185*	1910	A	11	W
Inverness	Prison	78	1902	A	11	Y
Longriggend	Remand Institution	197	1963	C	1	W
Low Moss	Prison	383	1969	B	111	Z
Noranside	Borstal	106	1963	A	11	X
Penninghame	Open Prison	68	1954	A	11	X
Perth	Prison	466	1842	A	111	Z
Peterhead	Prison	359	1888	A	111	X
Polmont	Borstal	419	1912	A/C	11	W
Shotts	Prison	60	1978	C	1	W
		5,287				

Classification Codes

1. Category (even though redevelopment/modernisation may have started):
   A. Pre-1930 old buildings.
   B. Camps and similar sub-standard construction.
   C. Post-1930 permanent construction.

2. Condition of buildings:
   1 Good.
   11 Fair
   111 Bad.

3. Redevelopment/modernisation:
   W. Already in progress, substantial capital funds spent or committed.
   X. Excellent potential.
   Y. Moderate potential.
   Z. Poor potential.

*Reduced to about 30 places during period of reconstruction.

APPENDIX 7

EXTRACTS FROM EARNINGS SURVEYS IN UNITED KINGDOM*

RESULTS

Main components of gross pay

1. Table 1 shows for each of the most important Departmental grades of particular relevance to the Inquiry the average figures for England and Wales for gross pay and for the main components of gross pay. To facilitate comparisons amongst the grades, average pay is given in weekly terms; corresponding figures in monthly terms are given in Table 2.

2. Grades are shown (with one exception) in descending order of basic pay but, as can be seen from the table, certain grades have average gross pay above that of grades with a higher basic rate. This is because the contribution to gross pay of components other than basic pay varies widely between the grades. For the Governor grades, for instance, basic pay represents almost all of the gross pay whereas for Senior Officers and Prison Officers basic pay accounts for only about half of the total. The contribution that overtime or long hours gratuity payments make to the total pay varies widely between different grades: for Principal Officers, Senior Officers and Prison Officers overtime payments accounted for between a quarter and a third of the gross pay, for other non-Governor grades overtime and long hours gratuity accounted for between 10% and 20% of gross pay and Governor grades received no such payments.

3. It is estimated that addition of the pensionable value of quarters to average gross pay of the various grades would increase the average remuneration by the following amounts:

Grade	Estimated addition to average gross pay	
	Weekly	Monthly
	Weekly	Monthly
Governor I, II and III	£9	£37
Assistant Governor I and II	£8	£35
Chief Officer I and II	£7	£31
Principal Officer		
Matron	£5	£21
Senior Officer		
Prison Officer		

Variations in gross pay between different types of establishment

4. Table 3 shows the average gross pay for Senior Officers and Prison Officers for different types of establishment. Results for other weekly paid staff are not given because when sub-divided by type of establishments the numbers of officers in these grades in the sample were too small for estimates to be reliable. Information for the monthly paid grades is not given because the numbers in the sample of establishments were so small that the information might permit the identification of individuals. The main point arising from this table is the relatively small variation in estimated average gross pay of prison officers working in different types of establishment; the average ranges only from £117 to £125 per week. Average gross pay for Senior

---

*Full text of survey for England and Wales will be published by the Home Departments with their other evidence.

310

Officers shows substantial variation, ranging from £130 to £157 per week. However, it needs to be remembered that the sample included only four establishments of each type and the lower and upper bounds of the estimates have to be taken into account.

Pay of women officers

5. Table 4 gives the average gross pay of female officers at three female establishments selected in order to provide an indication of the spread of earnings throughout the women's service, not to provide estimates of overall average pay. The figures for staff in the open prison and the open borstal were based on all female officers employed in these establishments. Results are not quoted for more senior grades as the numbers employed were so small that individuals might be identified. Comparison of results in Tables 1 and 4 shows that,

(a) there were some differences in basic pay arising from the sample, male and female officers being on different points on the pay scales;

(b) Prison Officers of the basic grade in all these three establishments received lower gross pay than the estimated average for officers in male establishments, mainly because the female officers received less overtime payments;

(c) female temporary officers in the closed prison and the open prison received higher gross pay than the average estimate for auxiliary officers in male establishments; in the closed prison this was accounted for mainly by London Weighting and in the open prison by higher overtime payments.

6. Table 5 shows the value of maximum rates of rent allowance and of the pensionable value of quarters for both governor and officer grades.

Reliability of results

7. It should be borne in mind that results quoted in this report are estimates and therefore subject to error. There are two main sources of error:

(a) for both monthly and weekly paid staff, data could be analysed only for one pay period; every effort was made to select a "typical" month and week but results could be different (to an extent which it has not been possible to quantify) if another pay period were examined;

(b) for weekly paid staff, there was time to analyse the pay of only a sample of staff and the estimate of average gross pay is therefore subject to sampling error. In Table 1, the possible error of an estimate is shown as lower and upper bounds outside which the true value is unlikely (1 in 10 chance) to lie. Given the importance of overtime pay, the representativeness of the sample depends critically upon whether the selected establishments were representative in terms of the amount of overtime worked, but no assessment of this has been possible.

8. Tables 6 and 7 set out the main results derived from similar exercises undertaken in Scotland and Northern Ireland respectively.

311

Table 1

Main components of average weekly gross pay by grade, England and Wales

£'s

Grade	Basic	Substitution	Over-time	Long hours gratuity	Pensionable emoluments	Non-pensionable emoluments	Average gross pay*	Lower bound	Upper bound
Monthly paid staff in all establishments									
Governor I	209	—	—	—	5	}5	214†		
Governor II	176	—	—	—	2	}2	178†		
Governor III	149	2	—	—	3	}3	155†		
Assistant Governor I	119	6	—	—	2	}2	127†		
Assistant Governor II	97	2	—	—	2	}2	100†		
Chief Officer I	102	—	18§	16	18	18	138†		
Chief Officer II	95	—	—	14	16	16	126†		
Weekly paid staff in male establishments									
Principal Officer	81	(a)	40	—	22	10	153‡	147	159
Matron	81	(a)	—	—	20	5	105‡	101	109
Senior Officer	72	(a)	40	—	24	8	145‡	140	150
Prison Officer	60	(a)	35	—	19	8	122‡	118	126
Night Patrol	57	(a)	15	—	12	7	91‡	80	102
Auxiliary/Temporary Officers	54	(a)	14	—	11	2	82‡	73	91

*Components may not sum exactly to average gross pay because of rounding.

†Monthly pay converted to weekly basis. All staff included but only one pay period covered.

‡Sample estimates for one pay period; the true value of average gross pay is unlikely to lie (1 chance in 10) outside the range defined by the lower and upper bounds.

§Special payment in November only.

(a) Staff receiving substitution pay were excluded from the sample.

312

Table 2

Main components of average monthly gross pay by grade, England and Wales

£'s

Grade	Components of pay*						Average gross pay*	Lower bound	Upper bound
	Basic	Substitution	Over-time	Long hours gratuity	Pensionable emoluments	Non-pensionable emoluments			
Monthly paid staff in all establishments									
Governor I	908	—	—	—		23	930†		
Governor II	764	—	—	—		10	774†		
Governor III	649	10	—	—		14	674†		
Assistant Governor I	519	25	1	—		10	553†		
Assistant Governor II	423	9	5	—		11	434†		
Chief Officer I	445	—	1	71		80	601†		
Chief Officer II	411	1	—	62		72	547†		
Weekly paid staff in male establishments									
Principal Officer	352	(a)	174	—	96	44	666‡	639	692
Matron	352	(a)	—	—	87	22	457‡	439	474
Senior Officer	313	(a)	174	—	104	35	631‡	609	653
Prison Officer	261	(a)	152	—	83	35	531‡	513	584
Night Patrol	248	(a)	—	—	52	30	396‡	348	444
Auxiliary/Temporary Officers	235	(a)	61	—	48	9	357‡	318	396

*Components may not sum exactly to average gross pay because of rounding.
†All staff included but only 1 pay period covered.
‡Sample estimates for one pay period; the true value of average gross pay is unlikely to lie (1 chance in 10) outside the range defined by the lower and upper bounds.
(a) Staff receiving substitution pay were excluded from the sample.

313

Table 3

Estimates* of average weekly gross pay in male establishments by grade and type of male establishment, England and Wales

	Grade					
	Senior officer			Prison officer		
	Average gross pay	Lower bound	Upper bound	Average gross pay	Lower bound	Upper bound
Local prisons	150	140	160	125	116	134
Dispersal prisons	141	126	156	123	116	130
Other closed prisons	142	131	153	117	108	126
Open prisons	135	125	145	117	109	125
Remand centres	157	146	168	124	111	137
Closed borstals	130	122	138	117	113	121
Open borstals	138	124	152	122	118	126
Detention centres	148	126	170	122	119	125
All establishments	145	140	150	122	118	126

*Sample estimates for one pay period; the true value of average gross pay is unlikely to lie (1 chance in 10) outside the range defined by the lower and upper bounds.

314

Table 4

Female officers in female establishments: components of average weekly gross pay by grade, England and Wales

Grade	Type of establishment	Components of pay*						Average gross pay†	Lower bound	Upper bound
		Basic	Substi-tution	Overtime	Long hours gratuity	Pension-able emolument	Non-pension-able emolument			
Prison Officer	Closed prison	55	—	22	—	19	3	99†	95	103
	Open prison	56	—	20	—	13	7	96‡		
	Open borstal	56	—	4	—	12	5	78‡		
Night Patrol	Closed prison	59	—	4	—	15	4	82†	79	85
	Open prison§									
	Open borstal§									
Temporary Officer	Closed prison	57	—	14	—	18	2	91†	86	96
	Open prison	55	—	27	—	12	6	100‡		
	Open borstal§									

*Components may not sum exactly to average gross pay because of rounding
†Sample estimates for one pay period; the true value of average gross pay is unlikely to lie (1 chance in 10) outside the range defined by the lower and upper bounds.
‡All officers included but only one pay period covered.
§Not given because the number employed were so small that individuals might be identified.

Table 5

Rent allowance and pensionable value of quarters, England and Wales

Grade	Maximum rent allowance		Pensionable value of quarters
	November 1978 (as paid at time of survey)	February 1979 (retrospective to August 1978)	
Governor I	£973 per year (£18·64 per week)	£998 per year (£19·12 per week)	£574 per year (£11·00 per week)
Governor II			£562 per year (£10·77 per week)
Governor III			
Assistant Governor I	£720 per year (£13·79 per week)	£738 per year (£14·14 per week)	£468 per year (£8·97 per week)
Assistant Governor II			
Chief Officer I	£720 per year (£13·79 per week)	£738 per year (£14·14 per week)	£476 per year (£9·12 per week)
Chief Officer II			
Principal Officer*			
Matron	£10·80 per week	£11·10 per week	£7·52 per week
Senior Officer*			
Officer*			

*Married rates: single rates are half married rates.

At the date of the survey rent allowances were payable to:—

    21 per cent of all Governors I, II and III.

     9 per cent of all Assistant Governors I and II.

    22 per cent of all Chief Officers I and II.

    37 per cent of all other Prison Officer grades.

316

Table 6

Gross Earnings Survey—Scotland

Average gross earnings by grade for week ended 20 October and month ended 31 October 1978

Table I—Weekly Paid Staff

	Number of staff	Basic pay	Taxable allowances	Overtime payments	Sunday premium	Saturday premium	Gross pay	
					(Included in overtime amounts)		Weekly	Annually
		£	£	£	£	£	£	£
Officer	1,303	69·10	3·93	32·54	6·91	3·62	105·57	5,504·15
Senior Officer	249	80·27	3·14	35·29	7·79	4·35	118·70	6,189·55
Principal Officer	170	90·64	2·77	33·94	8·28	4·09	127·35	6,640·83
Clerk Officer	31	66·93	2·69	5·18	—	0·27	74·80	3,900·08
Principal Clerk Officer	66	85·10	2·85	7·42	0·27	0·32	95·37	4,972·99
Engineer Officer II	11	87·17	2·20	14·08	1·49	2·20	104·17	5,431·76
Engineer Officer I	13	93·18	0·77	17·20	4·17	1·01	111·15	5,796·00
Free Workmen	45	59·75	2·97	7·10	—	—	69·82	3,640·64
Electrician	4	57·05	4·11	—	—	—	61·16	3,189·05
Typist	33	50·29	4·11	—	—	—	54·40	2,836·62

317

Table II—Monthly Paid Staff

	Number of staff	Basic pay	Taxable allowances	Overtime payments	Sunday premium	Saturday premium	Gross pay	
					(Included in overtime amounts)		Monthly	Annually
		£	£	£	£	£	£	£
Chief Officer II	24	458·29	5·50	100·46	—	—	564·25	6,762·62
Chief Officer I	6	509·56	0·12	—	—	—	509·68	6,116·26
Chief Clerk Officer	17	465·05	7·46	2·99	—	—	475·50	5,706·03
Steward II	5	476·50	8·07	—	—	—	484·57	5,814·86
Steward I	2	586·00	7·92	—	—	—	593·92	7,127·04
Assistant Governor II	34	446·87	11·84	—	—	—	458·71	5,504·52
Governor IV	11	520·42	5·04	—	—	—	525·46	6,305·61
Governor III	17	673·82	1·78	—	—	—	675·60	8,107·17
Governor II	3	757·79	—	—	—	—	757·79	9,093·48
Governor I	4	907·50	47·59*	—	—	—	955·09	11,461·05

*Includes £6·86 non-taxable allowances.

Table 7

Gross Earnings Survey—Northern Ireland Prison Service

Average gross earnings by grade for week ending 20 October 1978 and month ending 31 October 1978

| | Weekly earnings | | | Monthly earnings | | | | | | |
	Officers	Senior Officers	Principal Officers	Chief Officer II	Chief Officer I	Assistant Governor II	Assistant Governor I	Governor III	Governor II	Governor I
	£	£	£	£	£	£	£	£	£	£
Basic pay	56·30	69·81	79·51	411·17	444·92	408·62	493·75	583·38	707·75	907·50
Shift disturbance allowance	10·14	12·22	12·82	54·46	62·37	—	—		—	
Pensionable allowances	5·61	6·10	5·98	25·06	26·99	22·64	12·78	24·86	33·33	16·66
Non-pensionable allowances	2·53	4·24	3·96	19·15	15·45	18·40	13·45	22·67	28·36	19·09
Overtime	50·50	57·94	94·71	186·24	—	—	—			
Sunday premium	11·11	12·18	13·47	—	—	—				
Saturday premium	6·02	7·47	6·77	—	—	—				
Emergency allowance	18·95	18·74	18·05	65·15	75·67	54·83	60·43	69·20	62·00	54·00
Standby allowance	0·02	—	—	2·53	—	—	—		—	
Total	161·18	188·70	192·14	672·23	811·64	504·49	580·41	700·11	831·44	997·25
Total expressed as annual rate	8,404·38	9,839·37	10,018·73	8,066·76	9,739·68	6,053·88	6,964·92	8,401·32	9,977·28	11,967·00

319

APPENDIX 8a

Prison Officer Class—Recommended Basic Pay Scales from 1 January 1980

	£ per annum
Chief Officer I	6,838
	6,972
	7,105
Chief Officer II	6,306
	6,439
	6,572
Senior Foreman of Works	6,682
Foreman of Works	6,444

	£ per week
Engineer I	100.75
	102.88
	104.48
	105.97
Engineer II	93.17
	95.30
	97.29
	98.31
Principal Officer/House Matron	95.53
	98.18
	100.75
	103.46
Senior Officer	85.45
	87.65
	89.93
	92.21
Prison Officer	66.81
	69.26
	71.78
	74.41
	77.13
	79.94
	82.74 (after 12 years' service)
	85.54 (after 15 years' service)
Prison Auxiliary/Temporary Officer	65.61
	66.81
	67.93
	69.18
	70.23
	71.50
Night Patrol	69.97
	71.08
	72.21
	73.46
	74.78
	76.03

Examples of approximate gross weekly earnings of discipline officers from 1 January, 1980, if the pay scales recommended by the Inquiry are implemented

Grade	Point on scale	1 Basic pay	2 Basic pay, SDA and weekend premium	3 Pay as at 2, expressed in £ per annum	4 Basic pay, SDA and weekend premium and 12 hours' overtime per week*	5 Pay as at 4, expressed in £ per annum
		£	£	£	£	£
Prison Officer	Minimum	66·81	83·83	4,371	118·22	6,164
	After 5 years' service	79·94	100·09	5,219	140·39	7,320
	After 15 years' service	85·54	107·03	5,581	149·85	7,813
Senior Officer	Minimum	85·45	106·92	5,575	149·70	7,805
	Maximum (after 3 years' service)	92·21	115·29	6,011	161·11	8,400
Principal Officer	Minimum	95·53	119·40	6,226	166·02	8,656
	Maximum (after 3 years' service)	103·46	129·22	6,738	175·84	9,168

*12 hours' overtime has been selected because it is the average weekly overtime for all overtime officer grades. In practice some will earn less and some will earn more.

321

APPENDIX 8b

Prison Governor Class—Recommended Basic Pay Scales from 1 January 1980

	£ per annum
Governor I	15,750
Governor II	11,750–13,750
Governor III	9,550–11,250
Assistant Governor I (Governor IV in Scotland)	7,250–8,200
Assistant Governor II	5,700–6,850

APPENDIX 9

Continuous Duty Credits

(A) EXTRACT FROM THE POA WRITTEN EVIDENCE.

2 CLAIMS RELATED TO UNSCHEDULED MEAL BREAKS

CLAIMS 1 AND 2

Unscheduled Mid-Day Breaks

30. These occur in the following circumstances:

    (i) when an early shift is extended to equate with a main shift;

    (ii) when an early shift is extended beyond the termination time of a main shift;

    (iii) when a late shift is extended by duty in the morning period.

31. The Association recognises that no prison officer has the choice of working overtime unless management is willing to allow the overtime to be worked. For this reason all extra duty is an intrusion into an officer's free time.

32. Where extra duty necessitates a meal break being taken this effectively extends the span of duty before overtime can be earned. An example of this is where an officer is conditioned to an early shift from 7 am to 1.45 pm.

33. Where such an officer is required to work extra duty to 5 pm or beyond it is usual for him to take an unscheduled mid-day meal break of 60 minutes. This is usually taken in full by the termination time of his conditioned shift (1.45 pm).

34. However the 60 minutes is deducted from the net duty. The consequence of this is that the officer must work until 2.45 pm in order to complete his quota of net hours. From that point on he is earning overtime. If, for example, he worked to 5.00 pm this would accumulate a duty credit of $2\frac{1}{4}$ hours at the appropriate overtime rate.

35. On the other hand if the same officer was sent off duty at 3.45 pm he would qualify for a continuous duty credit payment from 1.45 pm. Likewise, if he returned at 1.45 pm after taking a 60 minute meal break and was informed he was not required the break would be treated as duty.

36. The Association realises that these are rare examples but they do pinpoint the inequity of credit arrangements involving extra duty and unpaid meal breaks. For this reason the POA believes that its claim is the only fair corrective. This claim falls in two parts.

37. The first, and main, part is that any part of any unscheduled mid-day meal break taken within the conditioned span of a shift should be treated as duty. This means that in the example quoted any part of a mid-day break taken before 1.45 pm should not be deducted from the shift and should be paid since management decides when overtime is to be worked and when the meal break is to be taken. By the same principle it follows that where a late shift starts at 12.30 pm and is extended by extra duty in the morning we contend that any part of an unscheduled mid-day break taken after 12.30 pm should be similarly treated as duty since it is taken at managerial behest.

38. The second part of this claim relates to the manner in which the extra duty part is credited. Obviously there is a legitimate CDC claim where this extra duty starts within three hours of the conditioned starting time or ends within three hours of the conditioned finishing time. Such cases are rare. In the vast majority of instances the extension, either early or late, is outside the three hour limit for CDC.

39. Notice to Staff 62/1972 makes provision for a minimum duty credit of three hours in such cases.

40. It is the view of the Association that this minimum credit should apply in all cases of extension of duty not covered by CDC terms. In cases connected to unscheduled mid-day meal breaks this would only occur normally with early shifts extended to the termination time of the main shift. The additional credit involved would be limited but is justified nevertheless.

41. In accepting the right of management to decide if overtime is to be worked the Association recognises that arbitrary and sudden cancellation of extra duty is possible. For this reason the Home Office has refused to accept that there should be minimum spells of extra duty where extra duty is required and has retained to itself the authority to decide. In these circumstances overtime is strictly a managerial instrument applied for managerial convenience and, therefore, confers no right at all on an individual officer except the right to refuse to attend where the upper limit of 10 hours (net) extra duty in a week has been exceeded.

42. The second part of this claim is clearly linked to Notice to Staff 62/1972 and it is the view of the Association that the minimum three hours credit provision should be made retrospective to 1 October 1971.

43. That part of the claim dealing with the credit for the unscheduled mid-day meal break is less easy to decide for purposes of retrospection. However the Association believes there is justification in applying 1 October 1971 as the proper effective date.

44. Notice to Staff 62/1972 is a distilled version of a civil service agreement dealing with payment for "On-Call and Standby" arrangements. Since most non-industrial civil servants work gross hours with meal breaks paid it has been constructed with this assumption. Unfortunately prison officers work net hours. This has led to anomalies and the serious disputes referred to. It has also led to circumstances in which nobody is really certain of how its terms can be applied fairly, given that its terms have been permitted to apply in the first place.

45. It is the view of the Association that in accepting custom and practice to decide CDC entitlement, the Home Office has, morally, conceded a case for retrospection on this particular claim to the operative date of Notice to Staff 62/1972.

46. This is 1 October 1971. Throughout the period involved the meal breaks now attracting CDC payment were treated as being unpaid. It was not until it came to light that officers were being detailed to commence duty locally at *either* 7 am *or* 7.45 pm in an unpredictable and inconsistent manner that it was realised payment would have to be made on the presumption that 7.45 pm was the *conditioned starting time* and that earlier duty requirement was a matter of managerial convenience.

47. Taken to its logical conclusion it must be presumed that any late shift has an established conditioned starting time which a meal break should not be allowed to alter since it is taken at managerial convenience to facilitate extra duty. Equally an early shift should not be seen to be extended by the introduction of an unscheduled meal break.

48. In other words the principle of not letting an unscheduled meal break interfere with what can be recognised as the conditioned and pre-determined shift span is identical. The only difference is that, by its nature, the break comes within the three hour CDC limit whereas other extensions attached to mid-day meal breaks do not. For this reason the Association believes there is justification in seeking retrospective payment on the grounds of equity, custom and practice and by analogy with the principles involving payment of the breakfast breaks referred to.

324

49. Furthermore it is the view of the Association that the use of the term "normal" in relation to starting and finishing times recognises the spans of duty undertaken by "gross hours" workers whose meal breaks are paid and is not intended to deal with circumstances involving deduction from the hours credited within the "normal" starting and finishing times which would include full credit for meal breaks taken as part of basic hours.

Tea Meal Breaks

50. There are four varieties of tea meal break which the Association wishes to submit claims for. These are:

(i) tea meal breaks in certain long shifts which have three unpaid meal breaks within their conditioned span. These are pre-scheduled breaks;

(ii) tea meal breaks taken between the end of a main shift and the commencement of extra duty;

(iii) tea meal breaks taken in conditioned hours to necessitate extra duty during the evening;

(iv) tea meal breaks taken exclusively in extra duty time.

CLAIM 3

Tea Meals—Long Shifts

51. As the result of a motion unanimously adopted at the 1978 Annual Conference of the POA it is now Association policy that tea meal breaks in certain long shifts should be reckoned as duty. This is a long overdue improvement.

52. The vast majority of long shifts have a breakfast before duty starting time (7.45 am) which attract CDC payment in the event of the officer being brought on duty at an earlier time. However, a very small minority of prison officers are conditioned to attendance systems which require them to start work at about 7 am and finish at about 9.30 pm. These officers usually work in reception and gate areas.

53. Those conditioned to such shift patterns are the only officers not compensated for taking a third meal break on duty in a single day. To this extent they are unfairly and unfavourably treated.

54. The Association does not believe it reasonable in this day and age that the circumstances described above should be allowed to continue. However, having said that, it recognises that any alteration to the status quo on this particular matter will need to be from a current date.

CLAIM 4

Tea Meal Before Extra Duty

55. This claim relates almost exclusively to trades officers. These are uniformed prison officers who work as tradesmen and have regular main shifts which end at 5 pm. They may be required to work overtime during the evening up to 8 pm. Some are required to work later.

56. It is customary for trades officers to take a tea meal break from 5 pm to 5.30 pm. This does not reckon for duty credit purposes.

57. Having looked at the matter the Association believes that there is no moral difference between this and the CDC arrangement for early attendance which is already paid. Both tend to fall within the three hour limitation on CDC and both form part of the general fabric of the duty requirements of their grades. The only real difference is that the extra duty is undertaken at the opposite end of the respective shifts. This, if

325

anything, reinforces the present claim since it is unarguable that a three hour extension into an evening is socially, physically and domestically more intrusive than a 45 minute extension into an early morning.

58. Accordingly the Association claims that any extension of duty during the evening which finished within three hours of the conditioned finishing time for the day should attract continuous duty credit payment, retrospective to 1 October 1971.

59. In circumstances where the extra duty concludes more than three hours after the conditioned finishing time a minimum credit of three hours should apply in accordance with paragraph 9 of Notice to Staff 62/1972. The effective date in this case would be 1 October 1971.

60. The Association believes the above to be wholly consistent with its claim regarding unscheduled mid-day meal breaks in that it differentiates between properly described continuous duty credit and the minimum three hour duty credit.

Claim 5

Tea Meals Within Conditioned Hours

61. In some circumstances officers are required to take unscheduled tea meal breaks in order to work extra duty. This is exclusive to those working main shifts with an overtime detail during the evening.

62. For continuity purposes and in order to comply with the staffing and regime needs of the establishment at which they are employed they are compelled to take a tea meal break in conditioned hours. There is no choice in this matter since they are required to commence extra duty at the time when they would normally be going home.

63. Since no tea meal break is more than 30 minutes in duration they must undertake duty for up to half an hour of what would, in other circumstances, have been their free time before they are deemed to have completed their conditioned duty for the day. From that point on they are earning overtime.

64. Here, once again, are circumstances in which managerially determined extra duty creates the need for a meal break which is deducted from net hours and which, in turn, alters the finishing time. This is analogous with the situation created by breakfast breaks in certain establishments earlier this year but does not fall within the purest definition of continuous duty credit.

65. Indeed the Notice to Staff 62/1972 credit arrangements make no provision for this type of circumstance which simply re-inforces the persistently held view of the Association that its terms were devised specifically for "gross hours" workers whose meal breaks would be treated as duty in the circumstances described.

66. For this reason the Association believes it is justified in suggesting that such tea meal breaks should be treated as duty consistent with the view it has already expressed on unscheduled meal breaks taken in duty time and that retrospection should be granted from 1 October 1971 and the grounds of custom, practice and equity.

Claim 6

Third Meal Break Taken in Extra Duty

67. Even with the advantage of continuous duty credit prison officers are entitled to payment of one meal break per day as a maximum. Until entitlement to CDC was conceded in 1973 this had to be a third meal break and payment was limited to 30 minutes. This rule still applies to double shift working.

326

68. Many prison officers work rotating early, long and late shifts. When they are conditioned to a late shift their *scheduled* and unpaid meal break is 30 minutes and on early shifts their *scheduled* meal break is 45 minutes.

69. Such officers may be required to work a double shift. This means that they may be given extra duty before a conditioned late shift *or* be given extra duty after concluding an early shift. Neither shift has facility for a mid-day meal break and this matter has been dealt with separately.

70. It is the view of the Association that any third meal break should be treated as duty regardless of credit arrangements for mid-day breaks and that any third meal break taken in extra duty time should qualify. Thus an officer working an early shift extended to the late evening should be credited with that part of the unscheduled mid-day meal break taken before 1.45 pm as well as the tea meal break of 30 minutes. For the officer conditioned to a late shift the mid-day break should be credited insofar as it intrudes beyond the starting time of the late shift with the breakfast period of 45 minutes being paid on the basis that it is the third meal break of the day, taken in extra duty time.

71. The Association is not wholly satisfied that there is justification for retrospection on this claim. This is contingent upon the attitude of the inquiry towards the unscheduled mid-day meal break claim.

72. In 1973 the Home Office accepted entitlement to CDC for prison officers on condition that any such payment replaced the third paid meal break. This effectively changed the nature of a paid third meal from the standard 30 minute tea break taken in duty time to the break created by extra duty. However, this was in the context of only one meal break being credited in any day. The various claims now being submitted seek radical change in this arrangement and for this reason the Association tends to the view that its claim in this regard is more appropriate to a current date for application.

Claim 7

Unscheduled Evening Duties

73. These are almost exclusively undertaken by discipline officers but are, occasionally, worked by instructors.

74. Invariably an officer required to work an unscheduled evening duty is conditioned to a main shift with an evening extension. The main shift may have a conditioned finishing time between 5 pm and 5.30 pm and the extension may be to any time from 8 pm to 9.30 pm. This depends on the system of attendance involved. In these circumstances an unscheduled evening duty can have a span which falls either side of the three hour limitation for continuous duty credit entitlement.

75. This being so the Association submits that any unscheduled evening duty which terminates within three hours of the conditioned main shift finishing time should attract a continuous duty credit payment and that unscheduled evening duties with a termination time more than three hours after the conditioned main shift should attract a minimum duty credit of three hours. Both claims are seen by the Association as being retrospective to 1 October, 1971, in accordance with Notice to Staff 62/1972.

Claim 8

Early Main Shifts

76. This claim is related exclusively to an attendance pattern known as System IV.B. of the Functional Group Working System (FGS) Code of Instructions................

77. As a general rule only principal officers are attached to this system. They work a succession of main shifts with two such shifts per week being annoted ^{E}M. This means that on three days per week they attend having had breakfast before starting duty and on two mornings per week they have a *liability* to attend at 7 am. The note in Appendix A to the FGS Code makes it clear that an ^{E}M shift indicates liability for early morning duty.

78. Principal officers conditioned to System IV.B. attendance are paired with their next subordinate grade (senior officers) to provide the necessary supervisory cover at certain penal establishments. Their liability to work either during the evening or early morning is subject to institutional requirements. It is the view of the Association that any ^{E}M early attendance is a legitimate continuous duty and should be credited as such back to 1 October, 1971.

79. The attention of the inquiry has already been drawn to the substantial payments made in respect of early morning attendance in establishments working Scheme Vee. The practical effect of this is that Scheme Vee shifts are all now presumed to have a starting time of 7.45 am.

80. Principal officers in Scheme Vee establishments are conditioned to main shift attendances by Rule 22(a) of the Scheme Vee Code of Instructions which reads as follows:

22. *Surplus Evening Duty Availability*

(a) This will normally only occur in the case of Principal Officers where the incidence of the "pairing" of subdivisions, only some of which include a Principal Officer, produces more than are needed in the evening to fill evening duty Principal officer posts. Therefore, a Principal Officer allocated to a subdivision will normally be regarded as on a main shift on those days when the subdivision is scheduled for an evening duty or short day shift. Where there is a requirement for one principal officer to be on duty in the evening and two are allocated to the evening duty subdivisions the one of the two higher up the Principal Officers evening duty roster will do the duty (and be scheduled to a short day next day) and the other work a main shift on both days.

81. It can, therefore, be seen that principal officers in Scheme Vee work a succession of main shifts with a liability to work during the evening and early morning. In this they do not differ from their colleagues working System IV.B. The only real difference is that System IV.B is a refined version of the duty format described in Rule 22(a) of the Scheme Vee Code.

82. The Association cannot accept that Home Office refusal to treat ^{E}M shift early attendance as continuous duty credit is anything other than unwarranted and unjust. However it does pinpoint the incongruity of working arrangements which compensate employees differently for undertaking the same duties. In these circumstances it is little wonder that confusion is rife throughout the Prison Service about what may or may not be permitted on certain duty credit payments and that anger and frustration are now so prevalent.

3 CLAIMS RELATED TO SCHEDULED MEAL BREAKS

Introduction

83. Part 2 of this document covered claims related to unscheduled meal breaks. These are meal breaks, not originally intended, which occur as a direct consequence of managerial requirement for extra duty.

328

84. Prison officers are conditioned to five day week attendances but are often required to work on one, or both, of their rest days in a week. In Scheme Vee places they are required to work built-in overtime on certain duty shifts during their alternate "weekends on" which form part of their five day week requirement.

85. In such circumstances it is necessary for prison officers to take meal breaks and the attention of the Inquiry is directed to the inequity in permitting these to continue unpaid as at present.

CLAIMS 9 AND 10

Rest Day Call-In Attendances

86. Every penal establishment has a daily detail of duties to be undertaken by prison officers. These are referred to as essential tasks and the daily staffing needs are dictated by the essential task list (ETL) together with variable external commitments.

87. The available staff are matched against the ETL and have their duties extended to cover shortages. Where this is inadequate to meet the daily needs additional staff are called-in from their rest days. It follows, in consequence, that rest day call-in is governed by two factors outside an individual officer's control. These are:

(i) staff availability against staffing requirements; and

(ii) whether an officer is liable for call-in duty in his rostered turn.

88. Officers may be called in from their rest day to undertake early, late or main shifts. The rules prohibit call-in for long shifts and work in the afternoon only or evening only.

89. Due to their task related nature, rest day call-in duties normally cover conventional shifts contained in the system of attendance being worked. For this reason meal breaks are taken at a time dictated by the local regime since the call-in duty simply covers the conditioned shift of an absent officer.

90. Shifts vary in length and timing. And so do the unpaid meal breaks within their span. This produces a situation where the intrusion into an officer's rest day is not matched by the pay he receives. Fairly typical examples are listed below:

Shift	Gross Span	Overtime
Early	$6\frac{3}{4}$ hours	6 hours
Early	6 hours (no break)	6 hours
Late	9 hours	$8\frac{1}{2}$ hours
Main	$9\frac{1}{4}$ hours	$8\frac{3}{4}$ hours
Main	$10\frac{1}{2}$ hours	$8\frac{3}{4}$ hours

91. In the last example, above, the span of duty is extended by bringing the officer on duty early which means an unpaid meal break must be taken. This has already been challenged by the Association to no avail.

92. It is the policy of the Home Office that such breakfast breaks cannot be paid because—

(i) prison officers work net hours; and

(ii) no prison officer has a scheduled requirement to attend on a rest day.

Whilst this is factually correct it is nonsense in the practical context, particularly since 11 July this year. Since that time Scheme Vee main shifts have been deemed to have a 7.45 am starting time with early attendance compensated with CDC payment and with the breakfast break treated as duty.

93. What this means is that an officer can work four days and have his breakfast treated as duty but on the fifth day have an unpaid breakfast even though his span of duty, place of duty and breakfast time is identical with the four preceding days. Once again this exposes a fundamental weakness in duty credit arrangements. Also it demonstrates how the Home Office is getting away with "free" early morning cover by providing the same pay for an officer attending at 7 am as one attending at 7.45 am on a rest day. The same rule applies to officers covering the two varieties of early shift listed above.

94. It is the view of the Association that where prison officers attend on rest day to cover unfilled conditioned shifts with breakfast before duty starting times the early morning attendance should be treated as analogous with a continuous duty credit attendance and made retrospective to 1 October 1971.

95. The Association believes that all meal breaks taken on rest days should be paid. They represent an intrusion into an officer's free time for reasons of managerial convenience. This alone is sufficient cause to the POA for payment.

96. It is recognised that prison officers are conditioned to net hours and that meal breaks within a conditioned span of duty are unpaid. However extension of this principle to free time encroachment is something which warrants serious questioning.

97. In presenting this view the Association believes that meal breaks taken on rest day cannot be treated as free time, or in fact, something about which an individual officer has any choice.

98. It has already been established that no prison officer has a prescriptive right to be called-in from a rest day. This being so the attendance, its timing and length are managerially determined. So, too, are the duties any officer will undertake. These are factors which determine when (and even if) a meal break must be taken.

99. Shifts are arranged in such a manner that meal breaks are taken to fit the regime requirements of the establishment. For this reason they are a necessary part of a call-in duty and should, in the opinion of the Association, be treated as such.

100. In presenting this claim the Association recognises it is seeking a change in the status quo and foresees a current date of application as being reasonable and fair.

CLAIMS 11 AND 12

Built-in Overtime

101. Certain shifts, particularly at the weekend in Scheme Vee have extensions during the afternoon which comprise exclusively of built-in overtime. These shifts are broken by an unpaid meal break which is part of a pre-scheduled requirement.

102. This was originally intended to protect minimum earnings on transition to five day week working which, at the same time, abolished the hour per week-day compulsory overtime introduced in 1940 to assist the war effort and which had continued for 26 years!

103. The fact that this formed part of an agreed attendance pattern gave rise to the belief that officers conditioned to these shifts had a prescriptive right to work the built-in overtime attached thereto. This belief was never tested until early 1977.

104. In April, 1976 there had been a cut of about a million hours from the Prison Service manpower budget. A case was submitted from the remand centre at Low Newton to the effect that officers were not being allowed to work the built-in overtime attached to certain weekend shifts. The branch was supported by POA/HQ. This culminated in the expression of Home Office policy contained in the opening paragraph of the following letter:

ETG 101/3/7

Home Office
31 May 1977

Dear Mr Rushworth,

Low Newton Remand Centre—Shift Extensions

Thank you for your letter of 18 May 1977.

The answer to this whole problem is contained in the third paragraph of my letter of 11 May. That is to say that there can be no automatic extension of *any* shift for any length of time, but only for so long as there is an operational need.

The fact that on Sunday an "E" shift is designated to follow the Saturday "DED" whereas an "A" shift on Saturday follows a Friday "MED" demonstrate the inconsistencies which exist, giving rise to so much confusion. It would be more logical in my view if it was an "A" shift on both occasions, and this is an issue I hope we will be able to discuss when we are revising the code of instructions.

Yours sincerely,

J W MARCH

105. The above reply makes it plain that the term "built-in overtime" is really a misnomer and that it is no more than a prenotified liability to work *if required by management*. No other construction can be put on the words used by the Home Office.

106. This, in turn, seriously questions the manner in which these shifts have been devised. Particular attention is directed to the "B", "C" and "E" shifts in Scheme Vee.

107. These are identical shifts which commence in the morning (weekends only) and have five conditioned hours with $2\frac{3}{4}$ hours "built-in overtime". An unpaid meal break is taken from noon until 1 pm and this is followed by 45 minutes of conditioned duty before overtime commences.

108. As the shifts concerned have only five conditioned hours it is the contention of the Association that they are de-facto early shifts and as such should have no facility for a meal break at mid-day. For this reason they should have a duty span from 7.45 am to 12.45 pm and, if extended by extra duty, be compensated in like manner to that of our claim on unscheduled mid-day meal breaks. It follows, in consequence, that we believe extensions during the afternoon period following such shifts should be treated as continuous duty credit or should attract the minimum three-hour credit depending on the termination time of the extra duty.

109. Whilst we seek identical treatment on this matter as with unscheduled meal breaks we do not seek identical retrospection. Until receipt of the Home Office letter of 31 May 1977 the Association had accepted, in good faith, the right of an officer to work "built-in overtime". The fact that this question had not been previously tested tends to prove the Home Office honoured this presumption even though the "right" involved was more apparent than real. Accordingly the Association seeks retrospection on this claim to 31 May 1977, the date of the letter from the Home Office asserting managerial discretion to disregard "built-in overtime".

4 MISCELLANEOUS AND SUPPLEMENTARY CLAIMS

110. Paragraphs 30 to 109 inclusive cover the claims being submitted by the Association for payment of certain meal breaks. However the POA would be failing in its duty if it did not draw the attention of the inquiry to two specific supplementary claims which have the active support of half our membership serving at penal outstations together with a miscellaneous claim submitted by the Association.

111. The miscellaneous claim in this section relates to the effective date for payment of CDC and matters related thereto. Notice to Staff 62/1972 has an effective date of 1 October 1971. However NTS 62/1972 is an updated version of Circular Instruction 66/1965. Minimum and continuous credit payments are the same now as then.

112. When Scheme Vee was introduced in April 1967 a minimum overtime credit of three hours for rest day call-in was written into the Code and has remained. This, most certainly, links five-day week working to the duty credit arrangements provided by CI 66/1965.

113. On 17 April 1973 the Home Office conceded a claim submitted by the Association the effect of which was to treat all early attendance on main shifts with a breakfast before starting time as continuous duty. This covers all payments already made under Notice to Staff 62/1972 and all claims related to that Notice.

114. Until recently the Association believed that six years was the maximum retrospective period which could be made by law. However recent information has prompted the view that the six-year limit applies from the date that entitlement was first established. This, in turn, produces the conclusion that CDC and minimum three-hour credit payments are applicable from 17 April 1967 and not just 1 October 1971. Accordingly the Association invites the inquiry to consider the following:

    (i) Making 17 April 1967 the effective date for all CDC and minimum duty credits already paid; and

    (ii) making 17 April 1967 the effective date for all current outstanding claims linked directly or related to 1 October 1971.

115. The central core of Association policy is that in all cases not already covered by the exchanges of correspondence reproduced in Appendix B to this document there is a need to first establish the principles involved and then address arguments to the appropriate date for payment. This has already been done in Parts 2 and 3.

116. However, a substantial part of the membership serving in penal establishments (49·66 per cent as established by card vote) believe there is no principle to establish at all and that entitlement already exists. These are sub-divided into two main groups.

CLAIM 15

117. The first group believe that all unscheduled meal breaks justify payment as continuous duty with retrospection to 1 October 1971. Therefore the Inquiry is invited to give consideration to this assertion.

CLAIM 16

118. The second group is concentrated in FGS places and believes that paragraphs 7k and 9b of the FGS Code confer a right to payment of all unscheduled mid-day meal breaks as from the promulgation date of the revised Code (1 June 1975). Paragraphs 7k and 9b read as follows:—

    7k "The total hours (net) in a scheduled duty shift should not be re-arranged to extend the span of duty by the introduction of an unscheduled mid-day or tea meal break."

    9b "Where an officer is sent off duty prior to the completion of the conditioned shift for the day in question, a duty credit will be granted equal to that which would have been granted had the officer remained on duty until the termination of the conditioned shift."

119. Those who support this particular view suggest that these two paragraphs, when read in conjunction, produce an entitlement to credit any unscheduled mid-day meal break as duty. This construction can be put on the two paragraphs in question even though this was not intended when they were originally drafted.

120. However it is fact that nothing appears in the Code which prohibits payment of unscheduled mid-day meal breaks and that the Code of Instruction is a joint collective agreement which is binding in honour on both parties to it.

121. Whilst the above extracts are from the FGS Code they both involve principles of general application which are agreed and recognised as such by both the POA and Home Office. Indeed work is currently under way to consolidate the Codes for both Scheme Vee and the FGS in a single document applicable to all attendance systems. Paragraphs 7k and 9b of the FGS Code are being thus incorporated and are intended for universal application. This being so the Association contends that any favourable consideration of the "7k/9b" argument should apply equally to all prison officers regardless of their attendance system.

122. In recognising that paragraphs 7k and 9b of the FGS were drafted for purposes other than those contended in this claim, the Association has considerable sympathy with the interpretation being applied. The reasons are as follows:

123. Paragraph 7k was inserted in the final stages of drafting the revised FGS Code in order to prevent an abuse brought to light at Leyhill Prison. This is mentioned in the claim of 15 May 1978 regarding unscheduled mid-day meal breaks. The very nature of paragraph 7k then gave rise to arguments about the treatment of unscheduled mid-day meal breaks and periods of duty attached thereto.

124. These could not be resolved and, in order to clear the Code in time for the 1975 Annual Conference of the POA, it became necessary to leave this matter out-standing to be dealt with separately. From that time hence the Association has been seeking recognition of the status of unscheduled meal breaks and the claim of 15 May 1978 is no more than a progression from arguments left in abeyance when paragraph 7k of the FGS Code was agreed.

(B) HOME OFFICE NOTICE TO STAFF 62/1972

NOTICE TO STAFF 62/1972
ALLOWANCES FOR "ON-CALL" AND "STAND-BY"
("SLEEPING-IN") DUTIES

Call-out bonus

1. It has been agreed with the National Staff side that the above allowances shall be increased as follows with effect from 1.10.71, and these rates shall supersede those quoted in Addendum No. 1 to Circular Instruction No. 66/1965 from that date:—

	Existing rate	Revised rate from 1.10.71
(a) "ON-CALL" ALLOWANCE		
Periods of more than 12 hours	40p	75p
24 hour period at weekends, public and privilege holidays	75p	£1·50
(b) "STAND-BY" ("SLEEPING-IN" ALLOWANCE)		
Weekdays	83p	£1·50
24 hour periods at weekends, public and privilege holidays	£1·55	£3

Call-Out Bonus

2. It has also been agreed that with effect from 1.10.71 where staff are unexpectedly called out in an emergency (whether or not they are in receipt of an on-call allowance) and the work performed exceeds 2 hours, a bonus of 1 hour at the appropriate overtime rate, or a credit of 1 hour towards long hours gratuity payment, will be allowed as a more favourable alternative to the existing arrangements for paying a minimum overtime credit. Thus if an officer is unexpectedly called-out for an emergency and works for $2\frac{1}{2}$ hours he will be credited with $3\frac{1}{2}$ hours; and for 3 hours he will be credited with 4 hours. This concession applies only to unexpected call-out in an emergency. Where the attendance outside normal hours begins within 3 hours of normal starting time or ends within 3 hours of normal finishing time the attendance should be treated as if it were continuous with normal duty; two or more call-outs during a spell of on-call duty would similarly not entitle an officer to greater duty or overtime credit than if the attendance had been continuous.

3. Arrears should be paid as soon as possible.

4. The opportunity has been taken to consolidate and bring up to date the terms of Circular Instruction No. 66/1965 and Addenda Nos. 1 and 2 to Circular Instruction No. 66/1965, all of which are now superseded. Current regulations on allowances and duty credits for "on-call" and "stand-by" duties are given below.

Eligibility

5. "On-call" and "Stand-by" allowances in the Civil Service are limited in scope to those in non-industrial overtime grades, and non-overtime grades who are eligible for long-hours gratuities, whose scales of pay do not include an element for liability to perform "on-call" or "stand-by" duties. Members of professional classes of Civil Servants are not eligible to receive the allowances.

Payment

6. "Stand-by" allowance (for sleeping-in duties) is paid on the same basis as overtime and night duty allowance. Payment should therefore be made no later than the second pay day after the end of the charted period in which the stand-by duty was performed (ie at the same time as payment for any overtime which may have been worked during that charted period). This change will necessitate some amendments to the Record of Sleeping-in Duty (Book No. 1162) and a copy of the appropriate amendments is attached as an appendix to this Notice. In future each double page of Book No. 1162 will be used for only one charted period, and the appropriate dates should be entered under the deleted figures. The amendments should be made in manuscript. There are no other changes in the use of Book No. 1162. A revised record of stand-by duty will be produced in due course as part of the proposed new overtime recording procedure.

"On-call" Allowances

7. These allowances may be paid to those officers who have a specific roster commitment to be continuously and immediately available at their homes, outside the normal duty hours of their grade, for periods of more than 12 hours between spells of duty (75 pence a night) and full 24 hour periods at weekends and public and privilege holidays (£1·50) or proportionately to the period of duty. To be eligible to claim the allowances, staff must be *required* to remain at home for the whole of the rostered "on-call" period. Staff who are allowed to leave their homes during the "on-call" period provided they leave word where they can be found, or staff who are under no compulsion to remain at home but who have a liability to attend for duty if an emergency arises and they can be contacted, are not eligible to receive the allowance for "on-call" commitments.

8. In prison department establishments, such "on-call" liabilities as exist for staff within the scope of the scheme normally fall within the categories described in the final sentence of the previous paragraph. This Notice should not, therefore, occasion the payment of "on-call" allowances to any staff at prison department establishments. If, however, any Governor (or Warden) considers that "on-call" duties, qualifying under the terms of the previous paragraph for payment of the allowance, have been performed the facts and full details of the duties performed should be reported to Establishment Division 3 and approval obtained before any payment of an allowance is made.

Duty Credits—"On-Call" Duty

9. An officer of a grade within the scope of the scheme who is called out to work for a short period outside normal working hours, whether or not he is eligible to receive an "on-call" allowance, may be given an overtime credit for the hours actually worked, subject to a minimum overtime credit of 3 hours notwithstanding that the work which he was called upon to perform when called out may have taken him less than 3 hours. The 3 hours minimum credit does not apply, however, if the attendance outside normal hours begin within 3 hours of the normal starting time or ends within 3 hours of the normal finishing time. In these cases, the attendance should be treated as if it were continuous with normal duty, ie as if no break had occurred. In no circumstances will any 2 or more call-outs during a spell of "on-call" duty carry a title to greater duty or overtime credit than if attendance had been continuous. When the period of "on-call" duty exceeds 2 hours the provisions of this paragraph will not apply if the officer had been unexpectedly called out in an emergency and a call-out bonus will be given as described in paragraph 2 above.

10. For overtime grades of the prison officer class, in order to make the position clear in the various circumstances which more frequently arise, some within the scope of the previous paragraph and others outside it, the following guidance is given.

(a) an officer scheduled to work extra duty either before or after his scheduled shift for the day will reckon only the duty and extra duty actually performed for duty credit, meal breaks being unpaid.

(b) an officer who works extra duty voluntarily, on the understanding that he may opt for payment in cash because the interval between completion of normal duty and the start of the extra duty (or vice versa) is more than a reasonable meal break, will reckon only the period of extra duty actually performed for overtime payment.

(c) an officer, having gone off duty for the day with no specific detail to return to duty before the start of his scheduled duty on the next day, who is unexpectedly called back to duty to meet an unforeseen emergency, will be credited with extra duty as follows:

(i) if the period of emergency duty actually performed exceeds 2 hours, he will be credited with the actual period of time spent on the emergency duty, plus the one hour bonus as defined in paragraph 2, and subject to the conditions stated in that paragraph.

(ii) if the period of emergency duty actually performed does not exceed 2 hours, he will be credited with 3 hours of extra duty subject to the conditions in paragraph 2.

(iii) if the finishing time of the emergency duty in (i) and (ii) above is within 3 hours of the finishing time of duty or extra duty performed on that day or the starting time of the emergency duty is within 3 hours of the starting time of the next period of scheduled duty or extra duty, the duty credit will be as if there had been no break between scheduled duty (or extra duty) and the emergency duty (or vice versa), notwithstanding that the officer may have taken a meal or been off duty for part of the period so reckoning for duty credit.

(d) an officer who has gone off duty for the day, but has been warned that he will be required to work for a short period outside normal working hours (and more than 3 hours after the end of his duty shift), and does in fact perform this duty, will be given a minimum overtime credit of 3 hours, or an overtime credit for the hours actually worked if they exceed 3. He will *not* be eligible for "call-out" bonus, because this is not unexpected call-out. Such cases will mainly affect works staff and hospital officers.

(e) an officer who is "called-in" to perform duty on a rest day, ie a day on which no conditioned hours of duty are scheduled to be performed, will reckon at the appropriate "call-in" overtime rate the hours actually performed subject to a minimum credit of 3 hours duty to which the multiple rate will then be applied (even though the work he was actually called upon to perform may have taken less than 3 hours) unless the period of duty performed is soon after scheduled duty (or extra duty) on the previous day and therefore falls within the terms of (c) (iii) above. This minimum credit of 3 hours will *not* apply to duty immediately preceding, during, or immediately following a "sleeping-in" duty which bridges a duty day and a rest day; only the actual duty performed on the rest day will reckon as multiple overtime rates (paragraphs 13 and 14 are relevant). Officers "sleeping-in" should be from those who are scheduled for normal duty on both the days spanned by the "sleep-in"; only in emergency should an officer be detailed for a "sleep-in" which uses a duty day and a rest day.

"Stand-By" Allowance

11. Officers within the scope of the scheme (see paragraph 5 of this Notice) who do not normally live at their place of work but who have a specific roster commitment to remain at their place of work overnight after a full day's duty may be paid a "stand-by" allowance, for each such rostered attendance. The allowances are £1.50 a night to cover the period between the closing of an office in the evening to its opening the following morning and £3 for each full 24-hour period on Saturdays, Sundays and public and privilege holidays. The allowances are payable only to staff who are required to remain at their place of duty for the whole of their rostered periods in order that they may, if needed, be immediately available. Staff who are allowed to leave their place of work during "stand-by" duty provided they leave word where they can be found and staff whose scales of pay include an element for liability to "stand-by" at their place of work outside normal duty hours are not eligible to receive "stand-by" allowance.

12. The requirements for the overnight "stand-by" allowance to be paid are satisfied by prison officers "sleeping-in" in prison department establishments. The records of "sleeping-in" duty (B.1162) should be maintained as in paragraph 6 above and Statement of Variable Allowances (Form No. 961) should continue to be used for recording the allowance.

Duty Credits—"Stand-By" Duty

13. Staff in overtime grades receiving "stand-by" allowances, if called upon to perform any work during their "stand-by" period, should be paid overtime for the hours actually worked.

14. The arrangements for duty necessarily performed during the period of stand-by ("sleep-in") are not altered by the above paragraph. Duty credit will continue to be

given for a single disturbance of a half-hour or more, or for a number of shorter disturbances which accumulate to half-hour or more, odd minutes in the total credit for the "night" being rounded to the nearest 15 minutes.

15. This notice to Staff has been agreed with the Prison Officers' Association.

Enquiries

16. Any queries should be addressed to Pay Section, Establishment Division 3, Portland House (telephone 01-828 9848 extension 109).

JHJ BECK
ETG/69 5/34/1
Establishment Division 3
Home Office
6 April, 1972

Printed in England for Her Majesty's Stationery Office by Oyez Press Limited
Dd 161909   K56   10/79